A
THOUSAND
LEAGUES
OF BLUE

A
THOUSAND
LEAGUES
OF BLUE

THE SIERRA CLUB

BOOK OF THE PACIFIC

A LITERARY VOYAGE

EDITED BY JOHN A. MURRAY

SIERRA CLUB BOOKS

SAN FRANCISCO

Copyright © 1993 by John A. Murray
Pages 425 and 426 constitute an extension of this copyright page.

Library of Congress Cataloging-in-Publication Data

A Thousand leagues of blue : the Sierra Club book of the Pacific : a
    literary voyage / edited and with an introduction by John A. Murray.
       p.   cm.
     Includes bibliographical references.
     ISBN 0-87156-452-1 : $15.00
      1. Pacific Ocean—Literary collections.   2. Voyages and travels—
    Literary collections.   3. Oceania—Literary collections.
    4. American prose literature.   5. English prose literature.
    I. Murray, John A., 1954– .   II. Sierra Club.
    PS648.P27T58   1994   93-23196
    810.8'0321823—dc20   CIP

Production by Robin Rockey
Cover design by Christine Taylor
Book design by Christine Taylor
Composition by Wilsted & Taylor
Printed in the United States of America
10 9 8 7 6 5 4 3 2 1

To my son

whose birth taught me more about nature

than all those years in the wilderness

When gliding by the Bashee isles we emerged at last upon the great South Sea . . . now the long supplication of my youth was answered; that serene ocean rolled eastwards from me a thousand leagues of blue. There is, one knows not what sweet mystery about this sea, whose gently awful stirrings seem to speak of some hidden soul beneath; like those fabled undulations of the Ephesian sod over the buried Evangelist St. John. And meet it is, that over these sea-pastures, wide-rolling watery prairies and Potters' Fields of all four continents, the waves should rise and fall, and ebb and flow unceasingly; for here, millions of mixed shades and shadows, drowned dreams, somnambulisms, reveries; all that we call lives and souls, lie dreaming, dreaming, still; tossing like slumberers in their beds; the ever-rolling waves but made so by their restlessness. To any meditative Magian rover, this serene Pacific, once beheld, must ever be the sea of his adoption. It rolls the midmost waters of the world, the Indian ocean and Atlantic being but its arms. The same waves wash the moles of the new-built California towns, but yesterday planted by the recentest race of men and lave the faded but still gorgeous skirts of Asiatic lands, older than Abraham; while all between float milky-ways of coral isles, and low-lying, endless, unknown Archipelagoes, and impenetrable Japans. Thus this mysterious, divine Pacific zones the world's whole bulk about; makes all coasts one bay to it; seems the tide-beating heart of earth. Lifted by those eternal swells, you needs must own the seductive god, bowing your head to Pan.

Herman Melville, *Moby Dick*

CONTENTS

PREFACE

*Behold the much-desired ocean! Behold! all ye men, who have
shared such efforts, behold the country of which the sons of Comogre
and other natives have told us such wonders!*
    Vasco Nuñez de Balboa
    September 25, 1513

Toward the rear of the mammal collection at the University of
Alaska museum, in one of those corridors where visitors never go
and even curators become lost, is the skull of a Pacific sperm whale.
Some native children discovered the treasure on an isolated beach
near their village after it had lain on the sand all winter, picked clean
by the wolves and eagles, washed by the waves, purified by the sun.
What storm deposited the relic, and what fate befell the rest of the
leviathan, are secrets known only to the tides. The lower jaw was
never found, nor any of the massive scrimshaw teeth, each five
inches in diameter, which enable a sperm whale to consume a great
white shark as easily as a grizzly devours a salmon. The skull, more
than eleven feet in length, was shaped like a fishing boat, with the
braincase, like a pilot's cabin, in the rear, and the greatly elongated
facial bones, like flat open decks, extending toward the frontal blow-

hole. When I rubbed the chalk-colored occipital shield with my fingers it gave off the brine scent of the sea, and I thought of the warm blue tropical lagoon where the whale had been born, of the black depths one mile down where he and his harem had hunted giant squid, of the typhoons that had scattered proud fleets and flattened coastal cities while the solitary old male had cruised beneath the turbulence undisturbed.

Each of the essays in this anthology, like that skull, have been brought back from the Pacific. They are artifacts of the mind, their edges worn smooth not by waves but by literary craft; and, in a sense, this collection is like a museum, in which you find galleries and exhibits, from Barry Lopez's meditation on what Charles Darwin's Galápagos Islands mean to a late-twentieth-century thinker, to the traditional folklore of the Melanesians, stories that provide a distinctly different view of nature than that found in Western civilization. I have organized the selections geographically, roughly dividing the Pacific region into the northern and southern hemispheres. This seemed a rational way of presenting such a large and complex portion of the globe, which ranges from the Arctic to the Antarctic, from Asia to the Americas, and also includes extensive parts of Australia. I have also weighted the book more toward contemporary writings, restricting earlier pieces to those by Captain Cook, Jack London, Herman Melville, Charles Darwin, Mark Twain, and John Murray. About half the book's selections are presented in their original length; wherever possible, entire essays or chapters have been included to provide maximum exposure to the various authors and subjects.

Certainly no single collection can thoroughly survey an area of this magnitude. I have tried, though, to cover as many of the major biogeographic regions of the Pacific as possible. Readers can experience the wilds of New Guinea along with Edward O. Wilson and climb the volcanoes of Hawaii with Rick Bass. They can travel to James Michener's beloved Samoa in the company of Andrew Mitchell and explore the backcountry of Borneo with Alfred Russel Wallace. Dave Wallace transports readers to the nature sanctuaries of Japan, a temperate world of *torii* gates and *kami* spirits, and David Campbell reveals the miracle of life on and around the Antarctic Peninsula. *A Thousand Leagues of Blue* was a challenging anthology to assemble, if only because of the size of its subject and the scope of the available resources; for each author represented, there are ten more equally worthy of inclusion. As a result, many Kierkegaardian choices had to be made. Hopefully, the selection process has been successful and will provide readers with a geographically and stylistically diverse sampler.

The study of the oceanic islands, archipelagoes, and littorals has become more urgent in recent years as more and more wild places—from Yellowstone to the Serengeti—have become *de facto* islands, separated from the genetic and physical communities that once replenished them. In this sense, the Pacific provides a timely focus, and these readings are instructive. Few regions have been so ravaged by post-industrial civilization as the Pacific, whether we look at the effects of the first European rat plagues or the consequences of Franco-American fission and fusion bomb testing. Even the decline of sperm whales from overhunting has had an insidious effect, as the giant squids, no longer checked by predation, have fed without restraint upon the krill, thus depleting the Pacific krill fishery. More recently, the chlorofluorocarbons in your home refrigerator, aerosal spray cans, and automobile air-conditioners have eroded the ozone layer over Antarctica, resulting in an epidemic of malignant melanomas in South Pacific marine mammals. Similarly, coastal communities hard-pressed for cash have courted logging companies, only to find that clear-cutting soon destroys the bedding streams of the salmon industry that has long sustained them. "As soon as we take one thing by itself," wrote California nature writer John Muir, "we find it hitched to everything in the universe."

In the end, the Pacific is more than a series of environmental case studies, an ethics lesson, an historical admonition, the inspiration for Brian Wilson's love ballads, or the Hollywood backdrop for Clark Gable as Fletcher Christian in *Mutiny on the Bounty*. Thoreau understood these deeper implications when he wrote in *Walden*: "What was the meaning of that South Sea expedition . . . but an indirect recognition of the fact that there are continents and seas in the moral world, to which every man is an isthmus or an inlet, yet unexplored by him." Exactly. Look for "whole new continents and worlds within you." Explore the "Pacific Ocean of one's being." Search "your own higher latitudes." If these readings do nothing else, they should stimulate us to strive for just that, to engage in self-exploration as much as geographic travel. Nurture the tropical splendor of Charles Darwin's Tahiti within yourself and you will find the lost imaginative paradise, the fertile child's world, of Post-Impressionist painter Paul Gauguin. Follow Pam Frierson down into the dark lava tubes of Hilina Pali in Hawaii and reexperience the preternatural comfort of the womb and all the metaphoric mysteries of Plato's cave. Dive with Edward Abbey on the Great Barrier Reef and witness the morning splendor of creation. You will also detect there—in the way, for example, angelfish violently settle territorial disputes—what Konrad Lorenz observed, that aggression is a pervasive and dark truth of nature, empowering evolution and making possible the changeless, ever-changing flux of energy and matter we call, for lack of a better word, life.

J. A. M.

ACKNOWLEDGMENTS

I would like to thank David Spinner and Jon Beckmann at Sierra Club Books, who immediately saw the value of this collection and gave it their enthusiastic support. No anthology can be assembled without the eager assistance of authors and their agents and publishers, and I thank them all for their cooperation. I would like to express my gratitude to my colleagues for the past six years here at the University of Alaska, Fairbanks, especially John Morgan, Eric Heyne, Jim Ruppert, Dave Stark, Mark Box, Mike Schuldiner, Joe Dupras, Roy Bird, Joan Worley, and Lillian Corti. As always, I thank my parents for years of love and encouragement. And, finally, a very special thanks to Fen, for sacrifices and kindnesses too numerous to list.

INTRODUCTION

And if there had been more of the world,
  They would have reached it.
    Luis Vaz de Camoens, *The Lusiads*, VII, 14

On January 12, 1836, Charles Darwin sailed toward Sydney, Australia. From the sun-bleached wooden deck of the HMS *Beagle* the dark-haired, twenty-seven-year-old geologist noted "a straight line of yellowish cliff" that reminded him of Patagonia. A prominent lighthouse, positioned on an outcrop of stratified sandstone, indicated to Darwin the ship was nearing a "great and populous city," the first European-size city the travelers had encountered since departing South America. Sydney appeared initially to be "a magnificent testimony to the power of the British nation," capable of putting the Spanish and Portuguese ports of the New World to shame. On closer inspection, however, Sydney disappointed the homesick Britons. For one thing, the colony was relatively young compared to those in the Americas, and in its earlier years attracted all sorts of unusual people, a *milieu* similar to the American Far West of Francis Parkman and Josiah Gregg. There were, for example, the infamous "iron gangs" comprised of convicts assigned to guarded

1

work details, such as building roads. For another, the physical land-scape of New South Wales was nothing like Britain. Darwin found Australia to be dry and barren, afflicted with "the curse of sterility." The open-canopied eucalyptus groves he compared unfavorably with the lush green hardwood forests of Britain, and expressed pity for "the inhabitants of this hemisphere, and of the intertropical re-gions" who "lose perhaps one of the most glorious . . . spectacles of the world—the first bursting into full foliage of the leafless tree."

Four days later, traveling inland about 120 miles to Bathurst, in the center of a burgeoning cattle region, Darwin saw his first "black aborigines" carrying spears beside the road: "It is very curious thus to see, in the midst of a civilized people, a set of harmless savages wandering about without knowing where they shall sleep at night and gaining their livelihood by hunting in the woods." Darwin re-called that the native Australians were "rapidly decreasing" in num-ber and blamed their demise on the preemption of their homelands by European immigrants, together with the spread of alcohol by unscrupulous traders, European diseases for which they had no immunity, and the extinction of wild animals. In an often-cited pas-sage, Darwin then observed that "Wherever the European has trod, death seems to pursue the aboriginal. We may look to the wide ex-tent of the Americas, Polynesia, the Cape of Good Hope, and Aus-tralia and we find the same result." With this statement, and others in the book, the emergence of the modern, ironic perspective on na-ture and culture can be seen. This point of view still pervades the genre of nature writing that Darwin helped to create and is certainly evident in many of the contemporary selections gathered in this vol-ume. Part of Darwin's legacy, then, was to wed the dry, Lockean em-piricism of Cook and the other Enlightenment explorers with the passionate moral indignation of the Romantics with whom Darwin

◆—◆—◆—◆—◆

was familiar from Cambridge (particularly Cambridge alumni Wordsworth, Byron, and Shelley).

The Pacific, as Darwin well knew from his two years on the ocean, is a realm of superlatives. Fully one-third of the Earth's surface is occupied by the Pacific and its associated seas, such as John Steinbeck's Gulf of California, the Russian Sea of Okhotsk, and the legendary South China Sea. The Pacific is nearly twice the size of the Atlantic and larger than the Atlantic, Mediterranean, and Indian oceans combined. More than 25,000 islands are found in the Pacific. That is five times the number of stars visible on a clear summer night at sea level. Three of the islands—New Guinea, New Zealand, and the main island of Japan—are so substantial they are referred to as "continental islands." New Guinea is twice the size of California. Many of the world's great rivers ultimately discharge their waters into the Pacific. These include the Colorado, Fraser, Columbia, Amur, Yellow, Yangtze, and Mekong. And there are vast rivers of salt water in the Pacific, such as the powerful Japanese and Australian currents, that by comparison make the freshwater rivers seem like spring-fed brooks. The tallest mountains in the world are found not in China, Nepal, or Tibet, but in the middle of the Pacific; Hawaii's Mauna Loa (13,680 feet) begins not at sea level, but on the floor of the ocean 20,000 feet below the waves. The deepest canyons on the planet are also found in the Pacific. The Marianas Trench east of the Philippines is 35,480 feet deep. If you could sink a jumbo jet to the floor of the Marianas and somehow see all the way down to it, the silhouette would appear as tiny as that of a plane flying six-and-one-half miles overhead. Everything in the Pacific is on a large scale. One would have to travel to Mars to find larger volcanoes and visit the moons of the gas planets to find more impressive canyons.

Despite popular images of sun-washed tropical beaches and

quiet lagoons, moonlit "Some Enchanted Evening" seas, and gently swaying coconut palms, the Pacific is often the scene of nature's most violent displays of power. On August 26, 1883, the Krakatoa volcano in central Indonesia exploded as if hit by a submarine full of ICBMs. The blast was heard 1500 miles away in Australia. Within an hour, fifty cubic miles of mountain had been extruded and 35,000 Javanese and Sumatrans were dead from the superheated shock wave, lava and pumice bombardment, and giant tidal waves. Had this volcano been located in a more populated area, as with Fuji in Japan or Vesuvius in Italy, the death toll would have been in the millions. On April 1, 1946, a prodigious tidal wave, generated by seismic activity in the North Pacific, struck the Aleutian Islands and completely swept a U.S. Coast Guard lighthouse out to sea. The reinforced concrete structure had been located on a rocky point *ten* stories above the high-tide mark. Five hours later the same tsunami struck Hawaii, killing 159 and causing $25 million in damage. It then sped south over the equator to slam into Chile, rebounded back, and hit the other side of Hawaii, causing more damage. In 1958 a colossal sea wave climbed nearly 2000 feet up the side of Spur Island in Alaska, stripping the old-growth forest to the bedrock. It is estimated that the annual number of earthquakes in the Pacific Basin exceeds one million. For the most part, these are minor tremors, but some are not. The Japanese earthquake of 1703 left 200,000 dead, and the Tokyo earthquake of 1923 killed 100,000.

Other perils are posed by animals. Each year unwary swimmers in Australia and New Guinea disappear into the cavernous bellies of saltwater crocodiles, and great white sharks regularly kill or maim surfers and swimmers in Australia and California. In the summer of 1993 two swimmers were killed by sharks in separate incidents near Sydney, Australia. Far to the north, in the Russian Far East, Alaska, and the Canadian Pacific, the primary danger consists of brown

◆━◆━◆━◆━◆

bears. Fatal attacks and severe maulings occur on a yearly basis in all three areas. On May 4, 1993, for example, a man walking in the forest near Soldotna, Alaska, was attacked by a brown bear guarding a moose carcass. The victim underwent ten hours of reconstructive surgery on his head and face and survived only because he carried a .44 magnum revolver and was able to shoot the bear to death as it mauled him. Other dangerous animals are much smaller—the insidious bacteria and parasites of the tropics—and cause the strange fevers and sudden deaths that sometimes afflict residents and travelers.

On a different note, the Pacific offers some of the finest examples of nature's beauty on Earth. Chief among those are the coral reefs, which occur in a zone thirty degrees north and south of the equator from Panama and the Galápagos west through the South Pacific to Australia, the Philippines, Indonesia, Malaysia, and the Asian coast. The Indo-Pacific reefs were originally studied in the last century by Charles Darwin, Alfred Russel Wallace, and John Murray, each of whom advanced theories to explain atoll reef, fringing reef, and barrier reef formation. Divers from around the globe flock to the clear, warm waters of the South Pacific, where it is still possible to find 250-pound groupers, seven-foot Napoleon wrasses, and the solitude of isolated reefs. One of the most interesting places for diving in Micronesia is Truk Lagoon, where on February 17 and 18, 1944, a major naval engagement took place. A total of sixty-four ships now rest on the bottom of the lagoon and have formed a network of artificial reefs that attract schooling fish, predators such as sharks and barracudas, and large assemblages of manta rays. The Palau Islands at the farthest edge of Micronesia offer the famous "blue holes," a series of 100-foot vertical shafts that offer tremendous views of coral formations and of the large schooling fish that live in association with plankton concentrations. In the Tuamotu Archipelago in

◆━◆━◆━◆

French Polynesia, divers are attracted to the two passes on Rangiroa Atoll where up to 1600 gray sharks can be seen at one time, aligned face forward into the current that carries food outward from the lagoon into the open sea.

Another far-famed diving spot is the Great Barrier Reef of Australia's Pacific coast, which is visited in this book by Edward "Cactus Ed" Abbey, normally known for his writings on the deserts of the American Southwest. Abbey was sent to the Land Down Under in 1971 to write an article for *National Geographic* magazine and, as part of his research, snorkeled on the reef, which has occupied much of its present location for more than a million years (making it the oldest living community on Earth). Abbey explains a controversial theory accounting for the crown of thorns starfish plague, which has devastated large portions of the reef: "The starfish is multiplying because one of its natural enemies, the shellfish called giant triton (*Charonia tritonis*), has been drastically reduced in number as a result of commercial and amateur shell collecting." If true, this cause-and-effect relationship demonstrates the fragility of complex ecosystems in the tropics.

Similarly, marine biologist John Culliney explains in his essay how the once-pristine waters of Kaneohe Bay in Hawaii have been devastated by water pollution, primarily from sewage discharge. The effluent has clouded the waters, killed the corals, and resulted in lethal plankton blooms. Culliney sadly concludes that "In a more environmentally sensitive time and society than plantation-era Oahu, Kaneohe Bay might have become a national Park . . . Today, the bay's fate should prompt the citizens of Hawaii and the United States to safeguard what remains of the bay's natural heritage and warn against further avoidable destruction . . ." An even more serious, and widespread, problem afflicting coral reefs in the Pacific is that of coral bleaching, the loss of the symbiotic algae that color cor-

◆—◆—◆—◆—◆

als. In 1982 up to 90 percent of the corals in Panama, Costa Rica, and the Galápagos were killed as a result of coral bleaching. In 1983 up to 90 percent of the coral were bleached on the Society Islands, the Great Barrier Reef, the Thousand Islands of the Java Sea, and elsewhere in the western Pacific. The cause of this catastrophe is not yet known with certainty, but the weight of the evidence points to global warming, which increases water temperature beyond the narrow band in which coral can survive.

The mountains of the Pacific have inspired the human race since the days of marsupial lions and giant cave bears. Probably the most revered, if not most photographed, mountain in the region is Mount Fuji, a 12,385-foot volcano located about fifty miles west of Tokyo in central Japan. The name Fuji comes from the idiom *fu-ni* (not two), which means the mountain has no equal, is without peers, and derives at a greater distance from the ancient Ainu word *hu-chi*, meaning fire god. Fuji, which last erupted in 1707 and is still considered an active volcano, figured in heavily with Japanese Shintoism, a national religion involving the worship of nature. The woodcut prints of Hokusai (1760–1849) in *One Hundred Views of Mt. Fuji* (1834) made the distinctive snowcapped peak a part of world culture and influenced Western art during the 1860s, helping to liberate American and European painters from stale conventions. Mount Fuji is part of the Klyuchevskaya Complex, which runs from Kamchatka through Japan and includes more than seventy active cones. Several of the volcanoes in Kamchatka exceed 15,000 feet in height and can be seen eighty miles away.

There are more than 400 volcanoes in the "ring of fire" encircling the Pacific, and many remain active. During the summer of 1992, Mount Spur, just west of Anchorage, Alaska, exploded violently in a scene of lightning and black ash like something out of Dante's *Inferno*. A jumbo jet flying on the edge of the debris cloud lost power in

◆━◆━◆━◆━◆

all four engines and, after restarting one engine, made an emergency landing at Anchorage. In the South Pacific are the weirdly castellated towers and spires of 13,500-foot Mount Kinabalu in Borneo, a mountain with more than seventy-two genera of orchid, a phenomenal profusion not uncommon in that part of the world. Ayers Rock—a smoothly curved monolith of red sandstone on a vast desert plain—forms the center of the mythic Dreamtime so important to the culture of Australian aborigines. Equally important to native religion are the Alps of New Zealand; the Maori believe these peaks are the abode of their dead ancestors. Across the Pacific in Chile, many climbers and nature writers, including Bruce Chatwin and Paul Theroux, have expressed the opinion that the soaring granite spires of the Torres del Paine (Towers of Paine) in the southern Andes may be the most beautiful mountains in the world.

Covering the mountains and valleys of the Pacific are some of the most complex forests and valuable hardwood timber stands known. One of the reasons the forests are so lush is the rainfall. At Waialeale in Kauai, Hawaii, for example, about forty feet of rain falls each year. In 1948, the record year, the total reached 624.1 inches, which is more than one foot every week. As a result, in parts of Hawaii and elsewhere, there is a tremendous profusion of life. Indonesia supports more than 10,000 tree species and 20,000 plant species. Critics might say these dark, virgin forests of Joseph Conrad and Norman Mailer novels are very nice, but why save them when the countries are so desperate for the cash their timber represents? One reason is that the jungles are nature's own pharmacopoeia. Tropical plants are constantly evolving toxic chemicals to protect their roots, bark, leaves, buds, flowers, fruits, and seeds from myriad hungry animals. Scientists can use some of these potent natural poisons to fight human disease. The value of the Pacific forests in this respect was underscored in 1991, when researchers isolated a compound from a rare gum tree in Sarawak, Malaysia, that was 100 percent effective in killing the virus that causes AIDS in laboratory experiments. Unfortunately, when the team returned to Sarawak—in a twist like something out of an Old Testament parable—the tree had been cut down by loggers. Because trees in the tropics do not grow in pure stands, but are found dispersed throughout a region, it is essential that substantial tracts of forest be preserved.

The Indonesian island of Sumatra, near Sarawak, is losing its forests faster than any other island in the region, partly because of a 3.3 percent annual population growth (which means the population will nearly double in the next twenty years), but also because of the rapacious Japanese timber industry. The Philippines presents a particularly sad story. At the time of the Spanish-American War, forests covered virtually all of the archipelago. This was down to 66 percent by 1945. Currently forests cover only about 20 percent of the islands, and only 1600 square miles of forest are held in reserve in the entire country. Vietnam, one of the poorest Pacific Rim countries, is another depressing case, having lost about 8500 square miles—an area the size of Massachusetts—to U.S. defoliants in the 1963–1975 war years. Vietnamese foresters are trying to replant mangrove and hardwood species under artificial canopies of quicker-growing species such as eucalyptus and acacia. On a positive note, Vietnam has a good record with regard to national parks, such as Muong National Park, which harbors an incredible profusion of plant and animal life and somehow survived half a century of more or less continual war. Throughout the Pacific, many more national parks are needed, because it is only in such parks that timber-cutting is prohibited. In sanctuaries such as Olympic National Park (United States), Lamington National Park (Australia), Mount Cook National Park (New Zealand), O Le Pupu-Pu'e National Park (Western Samoa), Minami Alps National Park (Japan), Kinabalu

◆━◆━◆━◆━◆

National Park (Malaysia), Mindanao Mount Apo National Park (Philippines), and Udjung Kulon National Park (Indonesia) there is guarded hope for the future.

The Pacific fauna are as beautiful and fascinating as can be found. In the far northeastern corner of Asia lives the Siberian tiger, the largest cat in the world (up to 840 pounds), which roams the birch forests along the Amur River. Even in recent years, the big cats have been spotted on the outskirts of the Russian port of Vladivostock. On the Russian border with North Korea and China a small relict population of Asiatic leopards clings to an island of habitat within a few miles of the sea. Japan's Hokkaido Island supports both the brown bear and the rare snow monkey. Across the Pacific, the world's biggest bears (up to 1500 pounds) lord over the Kodiak and Admiralty Island groups in Alaska, and in this book readers can share in Charles Sheldon's hunt. If nothing else, Sheldon's bloody account shows how far naturalists have come in one century, from hunting bears—even sows and cubs—to passively observing, photographing, and writing about them. Farther south, the number of mammal species increases dramatically, from about forty at the latitude of Alaska to 400 in the Indonesian Archipelago straddling the equator. Of particular interest in the tropics are the primates: the proboscis monkey, the Kloss's gibbon, the pig-tailed langur, the Mentawai leaf monkey, and the ever-elusive orangutan. In this volume, the excerpt from Alfred Russel Wallace's work chronicles a hunt for specimens of orangutan. Just how far science has advanced in a relatively short period of time—its major evolution in consciousness—is strikingly evident when comparing Wallace's hunting piece with that written by Edward O. Wilson on the Emperor of Germany bird of paradise in New Guinea. "The outer qualities of [this bird], its plumes, dance, and daily life, are functional traits open to a deeper understanding through the exact description of their constituent parts. They can . . . alter our perception and emotion in surprising and pleasant ways."

Unfortunately, many animals in the Pacific are endangered, particularly on the islands: the wooly rhinoceros of Java and Sumatra, the monkey-eating eagle of the Philippines, the mouse deer of Borneo, the black tree kangaroo of New Guinea, the Tasmanian wolf (a marsupial carnivore), the clouded leopard of New Guinea, and the Asian elephant of Sumatra. Others are gone forever, such as the Japanese tiger, the Javan tiger, the Bali tiger, the Stellar's sea cow, the New Zealand moas, the Korean humpback whale, and the California grizzly. One of the most pressing problems facing the region, again on the islands, are the many introduced species, such as the South American canebrake toad (which is poisoning predator birds with its toxic skin) in Australia; the wild boar, chamois, red deer, trout, and goat in New Zealand; and the mongoose in Hawaii. Only time will tell if we can save habitat and control alien species to the extent that indigenous animals have a chance in their Pacific homelands.

The people of the Pacific are as diverse as the islands. The earliest evidence of human occupation in East Asia was found in Java and dates to about 1.3 million years ago. Human in this instance refers to *Homo erectus*, a precursor of *Homo sapiens*, and the site yielded both stone tools and charcoal, indicating the use of fire. The first modern humans—people who could walk through downtown Singapore or Seattle with you or me and not draw any stares—were present in Borneo by about 120,000 years ago. Considerable migration occurred between 40,000 and 30,000 years ago, when glaciers covered the higher latitudes and the seas were much lower, and travel from the Asian mainland south into Australia was much easier. Sometime in this period the people of the Pacific—in locations from Korea to Australia—began to switch from nomadic hunting lifestyles

◆━◆━◆━◆━◆

to sedentary agricultural ways of life, which led to the growth of small villages, trading centers, city-states, provincial countries, and consolidated states. A considerable amount of archaeological evidence—excavated houses and buildings, pottery, rice storage buildings, artifacts, artwork, and burial locations—attests to this long period of development and is found from the Aleutian Islands south to Australia.

The settlement of Polynesia is one of the great epic stories of the human race. It occurred in two distinct phases. The first, mentioned above, incorporated western Melanesia into the domain of the immigrants. The second included New Guinea, Polynesia, and Micronesia and was completed by about A.D. 1000, by which time the seafaring Polynesians had visited almost all the islands in an enormous triangle from New Zealand to Hawaii to Easter Island. New Zealand was the last to be settled and is a story of particular interest in this discussion because the Polynesians hunted moas—huge, wingless birds—to extinction not long, from an historical perspective, after they arrived. Too often, debate on the subject of human-induced extinction has dwelled only on the sins of Western, developed societies. It is important to remember that all organized human groups are capable of destroying the environment, if they possess the technology to accomplish that fact. New Zealand's Maori, who were studied intensively by pioneering anthropologist Margaret Mead earlier in this century, are also unique in that they are one of the few human societies that switched from agriculture back to hunting and gathering.

To the north, the people of New Guinea are distinctive in that they speak more than 1000 dialects and languages. In contrast to the Maori, many of the New Guinea tribes have for generations practiced sustained-yield land management and have protected various animals and forests through rituals and taboos. Up to 80 percent of

◆ ◆ ◆ ◆ ◆

the original forest is still intact on New Guinea, and, if the Japanese timber industry can be controlled, there is hope that this important refugium can be preserved through the next century. Peter Matthiessen's selection in this book provides valuable insights into a remote corner of the island, where the people still live much as they did before Western contact. The Baliem Valley was seen from the air for the first time in 1938, was not visited until 1954, and had never been studied before Matthiessen's 1961 expedition, during which David Rockefeller, son of former Vice-president Nelson Rockefeller, was killed.

What is happening to the Pacific Basin environmentally is happening everywhere: unbridled human population growth (more than 200 milion people in Indonesia, the world's fifth-largest country), loss of critical wildlife habitat (coastal areas, riparian ecosystems, and old-growth forests), resource development (oil in parts of Indonesia and timber clear-cutting on Borneo), disappearing predators (the Pacific coast jaguar of Mexico), and increased air and water pollution (Osaka, Japan, and Taipei, Taiwan). Especially troublesome since World War II have been the nuclear testing programs of France and the United States in the South Pacific. Between 1975 and 1992 the French conducted nearly 200 atmospheric and underground tests at their facilities in French Polynesia. Similarly, the United States has conducted extensive nuclear testing on the Marshall Islands at Bikini and Enewetak atolls. A smaller program detonated nuclear weapons on Amchitka Island in the Aleutians. As a result, vast areas of formerly pristine nature are now contaminated with deadly radiation. In some cases, hot spots will exist for thousands of years. One can only question the wisdom of further testing, even underground testing, when the weapons have been shown in hundreds of cases to operate as designed. Another distressing problem has been clear-cutting in Malaysia, Indonesia, the northwest-

◆—◆—◆—◆—◆

ern United States, and British Columbia. It is particularly egregious in the case of the United States because of the strong stand taken by several administrations on the need to preserve tropical rain forests. The hypocrisy of denouncing the actions of Japan with respect to Southeast Asian forests, while selling U.S. Pacific rain forests at a substantial loss to the same agent, is clear. Other problems are more insidious: geothermal development in Hawaii (which threatens geological stability and native religious practices), tropical fish collecting (especially in the Philippines), and drift-net fishing (in which dolphins and other marine mammals are killed as well as the fish being sought). The Pacific will endure. We can be sure of that. But much of its diversity will be preserved for posterity only if conservationists pool their resources and work aggressively now.

Since Darwin's time, nature writing as a genre has changed in five significant ways: it has shed much of the taxonomizing of the post-Linnaean period; it has moved from homocentrism to biocentrism; it has become increasingly political; it has assumed more of a personal voice and included more autobiographical information; and it has become more "literary" in the sense of narrative craft. All of these characteristics are present to varying degrees in the contemporary essays included in this anthology. One of the most representative in this respect is Edward Abbey's "The Reef," which skillfully blends factual reportage, scientific writing, personal observation, political commentary, and lyric description. On the one hand, the author's self-deprecating humor and ironic self-perspective come right out of Mark Twain, as we see in the latter's visit to the Hawaiian volcanoes. On the other, Abbey is as meticulously concerned with getting his biology right on the controversy concerning the crown of thorns and the giant triton as Charles Darwin was in differentiating between the finches of the Galápagos based on bill type and ecological niche. The three ubiquitous themes found in con-

◆ ◆ ◆ ◆ ◆

temporary nature writing—liberation, communion, and renewal—are also present in the Abbey piece, as he wrestles with the larger questions of freedom and responsibility, community and individual action, and self and nature. At the current time, nature writing is arguably the most important prose genre in English, and the essays included here—by practitioners as diverse as Barry Lopez, Annie Dillard, Peter Matthiessen, Edward O. Wilson, and David Rains Wallace, among others—would certainly seem to bear out that statement. The Pacific is as enriched by these writers' words as it is by the brilliant red-freckled orchids of northern Borneo, the electric blue and pollen yellow Queen Alexandra's butterfly of New Guinea (the world's largest butterfly), and the zebra-banded green emperor angelfish of Ponape's Kwajalein Atoll reef.

The natural history literature of the Pacific region is worth studying for several reasons. First, the Pacific is a microcosm of the world. What has happened ecologically in the Pacific since the voyage of Magellan—habitat and species loss as a result of human population growth and Western technology—has occurred across the planet. The islands of the Pacific have the highest extinction rates on Earth, and to study them—the patterns and shapes of species' decline—is to gain insights that can be helpful elsewhere. Second, because nature writing has become one of the most important literary forms of the late twentieth century, any study of the genre—particularly in the comparative context—is helpful to understanding both literature and culture. Third, because the history of the Pacific is intertwined with the history of the United States and Western Europe, there can be no full accounting of Western culture and its relationship to nature without a study of the Pacific. Fourth, insofar as many scholars believe that the next century will be the "Pacific Century," with economic and political power shifting away from North America and Western Europe to the Pacific Rim countries, it would seem prudent to focus attention on the region. Fifth, the natural history literature of the Pacific is important finally for its own sake, representing the highest expression of the residents of and travelers to this magnificent region of the planet.

About ten years after the atomic bomb was dropped on Hiroshima, a little girl named Sadako Sasaki, who had been two at the time of the explosion, began to develop the unmistakable symptoms of radiation sickness. While she was staying at the Hiroshima Red Cross Hospital someone told her, in keeping with an old Japanese tradition, that if she folded a thousand paper cranes (the white crane is sacred to the Japanese) she would be cured of her illness. Despite a neat pile of paper cranes on her bed each day, the disease steadily worsened. Word of her condition soon spread throughout Japan and the world, and donations for Sadako's treatment flooded into the hospital. She died on October 20, 1955. Three years later, on May 5, 1958, a statue was dedicated to her at the Hiroshima Peace Memorial Park. If you visit the park today, you can see the statue, standing on a twenty-foot pedestal in the garden. It depicts a young girl, her hands outstretched upward as if imploring mercy, the fingers releasing golden cranes into the heavens. All Sadako wanted was to lead a normal life, to have children of her own, and to watch her children grow up and raise families of their own. Her dying so young, like that of so many innocents in that war and others, was a great injustice. That the first, and hopefully last, use of atomic weapons occurred in the Pacific, with the word deriving from the Latin *pacem*, meaning peace, is a tragic irony worthy of the novels of Yukio Mishima or the films of Zhang Yimou.

Let us resolve to keep the Pacific peaceful, to treat human beings and nature with respect, and to channel our naturally competitive spirits into the realms of art, as we see in the essays gathered here,

◆◆◆◆

and science, where we can battle the darkness of our ignorance until the sun goes supernova. Who knows but that the cure for the HIV retrovirus plague may reside in the jungles of Samoa or Malaysia (potential cures have been extracted from trees in both), or that the great nature book in English will be written by someone living in the Pacific region (Thoreau always looked west and, had he lived longer, would have joined Whitman, Emerson, Muir, and others in San Francisco). The Pacific was there when our ancestors were mudskippers in tidal mangrove swamps, crawling up barnacled roots on outstretched pectoral fins to search for dragonflies with bulbous periscope eyes. The Pacific will still be there when our descendants flash past Pluto in ships whose science will not be discovered for another two centuries, with all the courage of those ancient Polynesians who sailed their wooden outriggers eastward into the Homeric dawn. There will be other worlds, other places for the human race to explore. There will be other oceans. But there is only one Earth, only one Pacific. Posterity will return to this world, tired from their travels in the lonely gulfs between the stars, and sit down on the shores of the Pacific. They will be grateful that people in our distant barbaric age, who lived before the birth of civilization, reached out in love to save the northern spotted owl of the Olympic Peninsula, the Siberian tiger of the Ussuri River, the wooly rhinoceros of coastal Sumatra from those who would destroy them out of greed and ignorance. The authors in this book are committed to that struggle. They know that the museums are full enough of ghosts, that words have power, and that even a small group of people working together can change the world. "O ke kanaka ke kuleano o ka moe," as the Hawaiian proverb goes. "The privilege of man is to dream."

◆—◆—◆—◆—◆

I

THE SOUTHERN PACIFIC

*June 10th [1832]—In the morning we made the best of our way
into the open Pacific. The western coast [of South America]
generally consists of low, rounded quite barren hills of granite and
greenstone . . . Outside the main islands, there are numberless
scattered rocks on which the long swell of the open ocean incessantly
rages. We passed out between the East and West Furies; and a little
farther northward there are so many breakers that the sea is called
the Milky Way. One sight of such a coast is enough to make a lands-
man dream for a week about shipwrecks, peril, and death; and with
this sight we bade farewell for ever to Tierra del Fuego.*
    Charles Darwin, *Journal of the Beagle*

*Thus it is that in the warm and equable climate of the tropics,
each available station is seized upon, and becomes the means of
developing new forms of life especially adapted to occupy it.*
    Alfred Russel Wallace, *The Malay Archipelago*

*"I am the ruler of the spirit world," said Singalang Burong,
"and have the power to make men successful. In all work you
undertake you must pay heed to the voices of the sacred birds."*
    Iban myth from the island of Borneo

1

LIFE ON THE ROCKS:

THE GALÁPAGOS

ANNIE DILLARD

First there was nothing, and although you know with your reason that nothing is nothing, it is easier to visualize it as a limitless slosh of sea—say, the Pacific. Then energy contracted into matter, and although you know that even an invisible gas is matter, it is easier to visualize it as a massive squeeze of volcanic lava spattered inchoate from the secret pit of the ocean and hardening mute and intractable on nothing's lapping shore—like a series of islands, an archipelago. Like: the Galápagos. Then a softer strain of matter began to twitch. It was a kind of shaped water; it flowed, hardening here and there at its tips. There were blue-green algae; there were tortoises.

The ice rolled up, the ice rolled back, and I knelt on a plain of lava boulders in the islands called Galápagos, stroking a giant tortoise's neck. The tortoise closed its eyes and stretched its neck to its greatest height and vulnerability. I rubbed that neck, and when I pulled away my hand, my palm was green with a slick of single-celled algae. I stared at the algae, and at the tortoise, the way you stare at any life on a lava flow, and thought: Well—here we all are.

Being here is being here on the rocks. These Galapagonian rocks, one of them seventy-five miles long, have dried under the equatorial sun between five and six hundred miles west of the South American continent; they lie at the latitude of the Republic of Ecuador, to which they belong.

There is a way a small island rises from the ocean affronting all reason. It is a chunk of chaos pounded into visibility *ex nihilo*: here rough, here smooth, shaped just so by a matrix of physical necessities too weird to contemplate, here instead of there, here instead of not at all. It is a fantastic utterance, as though I were to open my mouth and emit a French horn, or a vase, or a knob of tellurium. It smacks of folly, of first causes.

I think of the island called Daphnecita, little Daphne, on which I never set foot. It's in half of my few photographs, though, because it obsessed me: a dome of gray lava like a pitted loaf, the size of the Plaza Hotel, glazed with guano and crawling with red-orange crabs. Sometimes I attributed to this island's cliff face a surly, infantile consciousness, as though it were sulking in the silent moment after it had just shouted, to the sea and the sky, "I didn't ask to be born." Or sometimes it aged to a raging adolescent, a kid who's just learned that the game is fixed, demanding, "What did you have me for, if you're just going to push me around?" Daphnecita: again, a wise old island, mute, leading the life of pure creaturehood open to any antelope or saint. After you've blown the ocean sky-high, what's there to say? What if we the people had the sense or grace to live as cooled islands in an archipelago live, with dignity, passion, and no comment?

It is worth flying to Guayaquil, Ecuador, and then to Baltra in the

◆—◆—◆—◆—◆

Galápagos just to see the rocks. But these rocks are animal gardens. They are home to a Hieronymus Bosch assortment of windblown, stowaway, castaway, flotsam, and shipwrecked creatures. Most exist nowhere else on earth. These reptiles and insects, small mammals and birds, evolved unmolested on the various islands on which they were cast into unique species adapted to the boulder-wrecked shores, the cactus deserts of the lowlands, or the elevated jungles of the large islands' interiors. You come for the animals. You come to see the curious shapes soft proteins can take, to impress yourself with their reality, and to greet them.

You walk among clattering four-foot marine iguanas heaped on the shore lava, and on each other, like slag. You swim with penguins; you watch flightless cormorants dance beside you, ignoring you, waving the black nubs of their useless wings. Here are nesting blue-footed boobies, real birds with real feathers, whose legs and feet are nevertheless patently fake, manufactured by Mattel. The tortoises are big as stoves. The enormous land iguanas at your feet change color in the sunlight, from gold to blotchy red as you watch.

There is always some creature going about its beautiful business. I missed the boat back to my ship, and was left behind momentarily on uninhabited South Plaza Island, because I was watching the Audubon's shearwaters. These dark pelagic birds flick along pleated seas in stitching flocks, flailing their wings rapidly—because if they don't, they'll stall. A shearwater must fly fast, or not at all. Consequently it has evolved two nice behaviors which serve to bring it into its nest alive. The nest is a shearwater-sized hole in the lava cliff. The shearwater circles over the water, ranging out from the nest a quarter of a mile, and veers gradually toward the cliff, making passes at its nest. If the flight angle is precisely right, the bird will fold its wings at the hole's entrance and stall directly onto its floor. The an-

◆━◆━◆━◆━◆

gle is perhaps seldom right, however; one shearwater I watched made a dozen suicidal-looking passes before it vanished into a chink. The other behavior is spectacular. It involves choosing the nest hole in a site below a prominent rock with a downward-angled face. The shearwater comes careering in at full tilt, claps its wings, stalls itself into the rock, and the rock, acting as a backboard, banks it home.

The animals are tame. They have not been persecuted, and show no fear of man. You pass among them as though you were wind, spindrift, sunlight, leaves. The songbirds are tame. On Hood Island I sat beside a nesting waved albatross while a mockingbird scratched in my hair, another mockingbird jabbed at my fingernail, and a third mockingbird made an exquisite progression of pokes at my bare feet up the long series of eyelets in my basketball shoes. The marine iguanas are tame. One settler, Carl Angermeyer, built his house on the site of a marine iguana colony. The gray iguanas, instead of moving out, moved up on the roof, which is corrugated steel. Twice daily on the patio, Angermeyer feeds them a mixture of boiled rice and tuna fish from a plastic basin. Their names are all, unaccountably, Annie. Angermeyer beats on the basin with a long-handled spoon, calling, "Here AnnieAnnieAnnieAnnie"—and the spiny reptiles, fifty or sixty strong, click along the steel roof, finger their way down the lava boulder and mortar walls, and swarm round his bare legs to elbow into the basin and be elbowed out again smeared with a mash of boiled rice on their bellies and on their protuberant, black, plated lips.

The wild hawk is tame. The Galápagos hawk is related to North America's Swainson's hawk; I have read that if you take pains, you can walk up and pat it. I never tried. We people don't walk up and pat each other; enough is enough. The animals' critical distance and mine tended to coincide, so we could enjoy an easy sociability without threat of violence or unwanted intimacy. The hawk, which is not notably sociable, nevertheless endures even a blundering approach, and is apparently as content to perch on a scrub tree at your shoulder as anyplace else.

In the Galápagos, even the flies are tame. Although most of the land is Ecuadorian national park, and as such rigidly protected, I confess I gave the evolutionary ball an offsides shove by dispatching every fly that bit me, marveling the while at its pristine ignorance, its blithe failure to register a flight trigger at the sweep of my descending hand—an insouciance that was almost, but not quite, disarming. After you kill a fly, you pick it up and feed it to a lava lizard, a bright-throated four-inch lizard that scavenges everywhere in the arid lowlands. And you walk on, passing among the innocent mobs on every rock hillside; or you sit, and they come to you.

We are strangers and sojourners, soft dots on the rocks. You have walked along the strand and seen where birds have landed, walked, and flown; their tracks begin in sand, and go, and suddenly end. Our tracks do that: but we go down. And stay down. While we're here, during the seasons our tents are pitched in the light, we pass among each other crying "greetings" in a thousand tongues, and "welcome," and "good-bye." Inhabitants of uncrowded colonies tend to offer the stranger famously warm hospitality—and such are the Galápagos sea lions. Theirs is the greeting the first creatures must have given Adam—a hero's welcome, a universal and undeserved huzzah. Go, and be greeted by sea lions.

I was sitting with ship's naturalist Soames Summerhays on a sand beach under cliffs on uninhabited Hood Island. The white beach was a havoc of lava boulders black as clinkers, sleek with spray, and lambent as brass in the sinking sun. To our left a dozen sea lions were body-surfing in the long green combers that rose, translucent, half a mile offshore. When the combers broke, the shoreline boulders rolled. I could feel the roar in the rough rock on which I sat; I could hear the grate inside each long backsweeping sea, the rumble of a rolled million rocks muffled in splashes and the seethe before the next wave's heave.

To our right, a sea lion slipped from the ocean. It was a young bull; in another few years he would be dangerous, bellowing at intruders and biting off great dirty chunks of the ones he caught. Now this young bull, which weighed maybe 120 pounds, sprawled silhouetted in the late light, slick as a drop of quicksilver, his glistening whiskers radii of gold like any crown. He hauled his packed bulk toward us up the long beach; he flung himself with an enormous surge of fur-clad muscle onto the boulder where I sat. "Soames," I said—very quietly, "he's here because *we're* here, isn't he?" The naturalist nodded. I felt water drip on my elbow behind me, then the fragile scrape of whiskers, and finally the wet warmth and weight of a muzzle, as the creature settled to sleep on my arm. I was catching on to sea lions.

Walk into the water. Instantly sea lions surround you, even if none has been in sight. To say that they come to play with you is not especially anthropomorphic. Animals play. The bull sea lions are off patrolling their territorial shores; these are the cows and young, which range freely. A five-foot sea lion peers intently into your face, then urges her muzzle gently against your underwater mask and searches your eyes without blinking. Next she rolls upside down and slides along the length of your floating body, rolls again, and casts a long glance back at your eyes. You are, I believe, supposed to follow, and think up something clever in return. You can play games with sea lions in the water using shells or bits of leaf, if you are willing. You

◆ ◆ ◆ ◆

can spin on your vertical axis and a sea lion will swim circles around you, keeping her face always six inches from yours, as though she were tethered. You can make a game of touching their back flippers, say, and the sea lions will understand at once; somersaulting conveniently before your clumsy hands, they will give you an excellent field of back flippers.

And when you leave the water, they follow. They don't want you to go. They porpoise to the shore, popping their heads up when they lose you and casting about, then speeding to your side and emitting a choked series of vocal notes. If you won't relent, they disappear, barking; but if you sit on the beach with so much as a foot in the water, two or three will station with you, floating on their backs and saying, Urr.

Few people come to the Galápagos. Buccaneers used to anchor in the bays to avoid pursuit, to rest, and to lighter on fresh water. The world's whaling ships stopped here as well, to glut their holds with fresh meat in the form of giant tortoises. The whalers used to let the tortoises bang around on deck for a few days to empty their guts; then they stacked them below on their backs to live—if you call that living—without food or water for a year. When they wanted fresh meat, they killed one.

Early inhabitants of the islands were a desiccated assortment of grouches, cranks, and ships' deserters. These hardies shot, poisoned, and enslaved each other off, leaving behind a fecund gang of feral goats, cats, dogs, and pigs whose descendants skulk in the sloping jungles and take their tortoise hatchlings neat. Now scientists at the Charles Darwin Research Station, on the island of Santa Cruz, rear the tortoise hatchlings for several years until their shells are tough enough to resist the crunch; then they release them in the wilds of their respective islands. Today, some few thousand people live on three of the islands; settlers from Ecuador, Norway, Germany, and France make a livestock or pineapple living from the rich volcanic soils. The settlers themselves seem to embody a high degree of courteous and conscious humanity, perhaps because of their relative isolation.

On the island of Santa Cruz, eleven fellow passengers and I climb in an open truck up the Galápagos' longest road; we shift to horses, burros, and mules, and visit the lonely farm of Alf Kastdalen. He came to the islands as a child with his immigrant parents from Norway. Now a broad, blond man in his late forties with children of his own, he lives in an isolated house of finished timbers imported from the mainland, on four hundred acres he claimed from the jungle by hand. He raises cattle. He walks us round part of his farm, smiling expansively and meeting our chatter with a willing, open gaze and kind words. The pasture looks like any pasture—but the rocks under the grass are round lava ankle-breakers, the copses are a tangle of thorny bamboo and bromeliads, and the bordering trees dripping in epiphytes are breadfruit, papaya, avocado, and orange.

Kastdalen's isolated house is heaped with books in three languages. He knows animal husbandry; he also knows botany and zoology. He feeds us soup, chicken worth chewing for, green *naranjilla* juice, noodles, pork in big chunks, marinated mixed vegetables, rice, and bowl after bowl of bright mixed fruits.

And his isolated Norwegian mother sees us off; our beasts are ready. We will ride down the mud forest track to the truck at the Ecuadorian settlement, down the long road to the boat, and across the bay to the ship. I lean down to catch her words. She is gazing at me with enormous warmth. "Your hair," she says softly. I am blond. *Adiós.*

◆◆◆◆◆

II

Charles Darwin came to the Galápagos in 1835, on the *Beagle*; he was twenty-six. He threw the marine iguanas as far as he could into the water; he rode the tortoises and sampled their meat. He noticed that the tortoises' carapaces varied wildly from island to island; so also did the forms of various mockingbirds. He made collections. Nine years later he wrote in a letter, "I am almost convinced (quite contrary to the opinion I started with) that species are not (it is like confessing a murder) immutable." In 1859 he published *On the Origin of Species*, and in 1871 *The Descent of Man*. It is fashionable now to disparage Darwin's originality; not even the surliest of his detractors, however, faults his painstaking methods or denies his impact.

Darwinism today is more properly called neo-Darwinism. It is organic evolutionary theory informed by the spate of new data from modern genetics, molecular biology, paleobiology—from the new wave of the biologic revolution which spread after Darwin's announcement like a tsunami. The data are not all in. Crucial first appearances of major invertebrate groups are missing from the fossil record—but these early forms, sometimes modified larvae, tended to be fragile either by virtue of their actual malleability or by virtue of their scarcity and rapid variation into "hardened," successful forms. Lack of proof in this direction doesn't worry scientists. What neo-Darwinism seriously lacks, however, is a description of the actual mechanism of mutation in the chromosomal nucleotides.

In the larger sense, neo-Darwinism also lacks, for many, sheer plausibility. The triplet splendors of random mutation, natural selection, and Mendelian inheritance are neither energies nor gods; the words merely describe a gibbering tumult of materials. Many things are unexplained, many discrepancies unaccounted for. Ap-

◆—◆—◆—◆

pending a very modified neo-Lamarckism to Darwinism would solve many problems—and create new ones. Neo-Lamarckism holds, without any proof, that certain useful acquired characteristics may be inherited. Read C. H. Waddington, *The Strategy of the Genes*, and Arthur Koestler, *The Ghost in the Machine*. The Lamarckism/Darwinism issue is not only complex, hinging perhaps on whether DNA can be copied from RNA, but also politically hot. The upshot of it all is that while a form of Lamarckism holds sway in Russia, neo-Darwinism is supreme in the West, and its basic assumptions, though variously modified, are not overthrown.

So much for scientists. The rest of us didn't hear Darwin as a signal to dive down into the wet nucleus of a cell and surface with handfuls of strange new objects. We were still worried about the book with the unfortunate word in the title: *The Descent of Man*. It was dismaying to imagine great-grandma and great-grandpa effecting a literal, nimble descent from some liana-covered tree to terra firma, scratching themselves, and demanding bananas.

Fundamentalist Christians, of course, still reject Darwinism because it conflicts with the creation account in Genesis. Fundamentalist Christians have a very bad press. Ill feeling surfaces when, from time to time in small towns, they object again to the public schools' teaching evolutionary theory. Tragically, these people feel they have to make a choice between the Bible and modern science. They live and work in the same world as we, and know the derision they face from people whose areas of ignorance are perhaps different, who dismantled their mangers when they moved to town and threw out the baby with the straw.

Even less appealing in their response to the new evolutionary picture were, and are, the social Darwinists. Social Darwinists seized

◆—◆—◆—◆—◆

Herbert Spencer's phrase "the survival of the fittest," applied it to capitalism, and used it to sanction ruthless and corrupt business practices. A social Darwinist is unlikely to identify himself with the term; social Darwinism is, as the saying goes, not a religion but a way of life. A modern social Darwinist wrote the slogan "If you're so smart, why ain't you rich?" The notion still obtains, I believe, wherever people seek power: that the race is to the swift, that everybody is *in* the race, with varying and merited degrees of success or failure, and that reward is its own virtue.

Philosophy reacted to Darwin with unaccustomed good cheer. William Paley's fixed and harmonious universe was gone, and with it its meticulous watchmaker god. Nobody mourned. Instead philosophy shrugged and turned its attention from first and final causes to analysis of certain values here in time. "Faith in progress," the man-in-the-street philosophy, collapsed in two world wars. Philosophers were more guarded; pragmatically, they held a very refined "faith in process"—which, it would seem, could hardly lose. Christian thinkers, too, outside of Fundamentalism, examined with fresh eyes the world's burgeoning change. Some Protestants, taking their cue from Whitehead, posited a dynamic god who lives alongside the universe, himself charged and changed by the process of becoming. Catholic Pierre Teilhard de Chardin, a paleontologist, examined the evolution of species itself, and discovered in that flow a surge toward complexity and consciousness, a free ascent capped with man and propelled from within and attracted from without by god, the holy freedom and awareness that is creation's beginning and end. And so forth. Like flatworms, like languages, ideas evolve. And they evolve, as Arthur Koestler suggests, not from hardened final forms, but from the softest plasmic germs in a cell's heart, in the nub of a word's root, in the supple flux of an open mind.

◆

◆—◆—◆—◆

Darwin gave us time. Before Darwin (and Huxley, Wallace, et al.) there was in the nineteenth century what must have been a fairly nauseating period: people knew about fossils of extinct species, but did not yet know about organic evolution. They thought the fossils were litter from a series of past creations. At any rate, for many, this creation, the world as we know it, had begun in 4004 B.C., a date set by Irish Archbishop James Ussher in the seventeenth century. We were all crouched in a small room against the comforting back wall, awaiting the millennium which had been gathering impetus since Adam and Eve. Up there was a universe, and down here would be a small strip of man come and gone, created, taught, redeemed, and gathered up in a bright twinkling, like a sprinkling of confetti torn from colored papers, tossed from windows, and swept from the streets by morning.

The Darwinian revolution knocked out the back wall, revealing eerie lighted landscapes as far back as we can see. Almost at once, Albert Einstein and astronomers with reflector telescopes and radio telescopes knocked out the other walls and the ceiling, leaving us sunlit, exposed, and drifting—leaving us puckers, albeit evolving puckers, on the inbound curve of space-time.

III

It all began in the Galápagos, with these finches. The finches in the Galápagos are called Darwin's finches; they are everywhere in the islands, sparrowlike, and almost identical but for their differing beaks. At first Darwin scarcely noticed their importance. But by 1839, when he revised his *Journal* of the *Beagle* voyage, he added a key sentence about the finches' beaks: "Seeing this gradation and diversity of structure in one small, intimately related group of birds,

◆—◆—◆—◆

one might really fancy that from an original paucity of birds in this archipelago, one species had been taken and modified for different ends." And so it was.

The finches come when called. I don't know why it works, but it does. Scientists in the Galápagos have passed down the call: you say psssssh psssssh psssssh psssssh psssssh until you run out of breath; then you say it again until the island runs out of birds. You stand on a flat of sand by a shallow lagoon rimmed in mangrove thickets and call the birds right out of the sky. It works anywhere, from island to island.

Once, on the island of James, I was standing propped against a leafless *palo santo* tree on a semiarid inland slope, when the naturalist called the birds.

From other leafless *palo santo* trees flew the yellow warblers, speckling the air with bright bounced sun. Gray mockingbirds came running. And from the green prickly pear cactus, from the thorny acacias, sere grasses, bracken and manzanilla, from the loose black lava, the bare dust, the fern-hung mouths of caverns or the tops of sunlit logs—came the finches. They fell in from every direction like colored bits in a turning kaleidoscope. They circled and homed to a vortex, like a whirlwind of chips, like draining water. The tree on which I leaned was the vortex. A dry series of puffs hit my cheeks. Then a rough pulse from the tree's thin trunk met my palm and rang up my arm—and another, and another. The tree trunk agitated against my hand like a captured cricket: I looked up. The lighting birds were rocking the tree. It was an appearing act: before there were barren branches; now there were birds like leaves.

Darwin's finches are not brightly colored; they are black, gray, brown, or faintly olive. Their names are even duller: the large ground finch, the medium ground finch, the small ground finch; the

◆—◆—◆—◆—◆

large insectivorous tree finch; the vegetarian tree finch; the cactus ground finch, and so forth. But the beaks are interesting, and the beaks' origins even more so.

Some finches wield chunky parrot beaks modified for cracking seeds. Some have slender warbler beaks, short for nabbing insects, long for probing plants. One sports the long chisel beak of a woodpecker; it bores wood for insect grubs and often uses a twig or cactus spine as a pickle fork when the grub won't dislodge. They have all evolved, fanwise, from one bird.

The finches evolved in isolation. So did everything else on earth. With the finches, you can see how it happened. The Galápagos islands are near enough to the mainland that some strays could hazard there; they are far enough away that those strays could evolve in isolation from parent species. And the separate islands are near enough to each other for further dispersal, further isolation, and the eventual reassembling of distinct species. (In other words, finches blew to the Galápagos, blew to various islands, evolved into differing species, and blew back together again.) The tree finches and the ground finches, the woodpecker finch and the warbler finch, veered into being on isolated rocks. The witless green sea shaped those beaks as surely as it shaped the beaches. Now on the finches in the *palo santo* tree you see adaptive radiation's results, a fluorescent splay of horn. It is as though the archipelago were an arpeggio, a rapid series of distinct but related notes. If the Galápagos had been one unified island, there would be one dull note, one super-dull finch.

IV

Now let me carry matters to an imaginary, and impossible, extreme. If the earth were one unified island, a smooth ball, we would all be one species, a tremulous muck. The fact is that when you get down to this business of species formation, you eventually hit some form of reproductive isolation. Cells tend to fuse. Cells tend to engulf each other; primitive creatures tend to move in on each other and on us, to colonize, aggregate, blur. (Within species, individuals have evolved immune reactions, which help preserve individual integrity; you might reject my liver—or someday my brain.) As much of the world's energy seems to be devoted to keeping us apart as was directed to bringing us here in the first place. All sorts of different creatures can mate and produce fertile offspring: two species of snapdragon, for instance, or mallard and pintail ducks. But they don't. They live apart, so they don't mate. When you scratch the varying behaviors and conditions behind reproductive isolation, you find, ultimately, geographical isolation. Once the isolation has occurred, of course, forms harden out, enforcing reproductive isolation, so that snapdragons will never mate with pintail ducks.

Geography is the key, the crucial accident of birth. A piece of protein could be a snail, a sea lion, or a systems analyst, but it had to start somewhere. This is not science; it is merely metaphor. And the landscape in which the protein "starts" shapes its end as surely as bowls shape water.

We have all, as it were, blown back together like the finches, and it's hard to imagine the isolation from parent species in which we evolved. The frail beginnings of great phyla are lost in the crushed histories of cells. Now we see the embellishments of random chromosomal mutations selected by natural selection and preserved in geographically isolate gene pools as *faits accomplis*, as the differentiated fringe of brittle knobs that is life as we know it. The process is still going on, but there is no turning back; it happened, in the cells. Geographical determination is not the cow-caught-in-a-crevice business I make it seem. I'm dealing in imagery, working toward a picture.

◆━◆━◆━◆

Geography is life's limiting factor. Speciation—life itself—is ultimately a matter of warm and cool currents, rich and bare soils, deserts and forests, fresh and salt waters, deltas and jungles and plains. Species arise in isolation. A plaster cast is as intricate as its mold; life is a gloss on geography. And if you dig your fists into the earth and crumble geography, you strike geology. Climate is the wind of the mineral earth's rondure, tilt, and orbit modified by local geological conditions. The Pacific Ocean, the Negev Desert, and the rain forest in Brazil are local geological conditions. So are the slow carp pools and splashing trout riffles of any backyard creek. It is all, God help us, a matter of rocks.

The rocks shape life like hands around swelling dough. In Virginia, the salamanders vary from mountain ridge to mountain ridge; so do the fiddle tunes the old men play. All this is because it is hard to move from mountain to mountain. These are not merely anomalous details. This is what life is all about: salamanders, fiddle tunes, you and me and things, the split and burr of it all, the fizz into particulars. No mountains and one salamander, one fiddle tune, would be a lesser world. No continents, no fiddlers. No possum, no sop, no taters. The earth, without form, is void.

The mountains are time's machines; in effect, they roll out protoplasm like printers' rollers pressing out news. But life is already part of the landscape, a limiting factor in space; life too shapes life. Geology's rocks and climate have already become Brazil's rain forest, yielding shocking bright birds. To say that all life is an interconnected membrane, a weft of linkages like chain mail, is truism. But in this case, too, the Galápagos islands afford a clear picture.

On Santa Cruz island, for instance, the saddleback carapaces of tortoises enable them to stretch high and reach the succulent pads of prickly pear cactus. But the prickly pear cactus on that island, and on

◆◆◆◆◆

other tortoise islands, has evolved a treelike habit; those lower pads get harder to come by. Without limiting factors, the two populations could stretch right into the stratosphere.

Ça va. It goes on everywhere, tit for tat, action and reaction, triggers and inhibitors ascending in a spiral like spatting butterflies. Within life, we are pushing each other around. How many animal forms have evolved just so because there are, for instance, trees? We pass the nitrogen around, and vital gases; we feed and nest, plucking this and that and planting seeds. The protoplasm responds, nudged and nudging, bearing the news.

And the rocks themselves shall be moved. The rocks themselves are not pure necessity, given, like vast, complex molds around which the rest of us swirl. They heave to their own necessities, to stirrings and prickings from within and without.

The mountains are no more fixed than the stars. Granite, for example, contains much oxygen and is relatively light. It "floats." When granite forms under the earth's crust, great chunks of it bob up, I read somewhere, like dumplings. The continents themselves are beautiful pea-green boats. The Galápagos archipelago as a whole is surfing toward Ecuador; South America is sliding toward the Galápagos; North America, too, is sailing westward. We're on floating islands, shaky ground.

So the rocks shape life, and then life shapes life, and the rocks are moving. The completed picture needs one more element: life shapes the rocks.

Life is more than a live green scum on a dead pool, a shimmering scurf like slime mold on rock. Look at the planet. Everywhere freedom twines its way around necessity, inventing new strings of occasions, lassoing time and putting it through its varied and spirited paces. Everywhere live things lash at the rocks. Softness is vulnera-

◆—◆—◆—◆—◆

ble, but it has a will; tube worms bore and coral atolls rise. Lichens in delicate lobes are chewing the granite mountains; forests in serried ranks trammel the hills. Man has more freedom than other live things; anti-entropically, he batters a bigger dent in the given, damming the rivers, planting the plains, drawing in his mind's eye dotted lines between the stars.

The old ark's a moverin'. Each live thing wags its home waters, rumples the turf, rearranges the air. The rocks press out protoplasm; the protoplasm pummels the rocks. It could be that this is the one world, and that world is a bright snarl.

Like boys on dolphins, the continents ride their crustal plates. New lands shoulder up from the waves, and old lands buckle under. The very landscapes heave; change burgeons into change. Gray granite bobs up, red clay compresses; yellow sandstone tilts, surging in forests, incised by streams. The mountains tremble, the ice rasps back and forth, and the protoplasm furls in shock waves, up the rock valleys and down, ramifying possibilities, riddling the mountains. Life and the rocks, like spirit and matter, are a fringed matrix, lapped and lapping, clasping and held. It is like hand washing hand. It is like hand washing hand and the whole tumult hurled. The planet spins, rapt inside its intricate mists. The galaxy is a flung thing, loose in the night, and our solar system is one of many dotted campfires ringed with tossed rocks. What shall we sing?

What shall we sing, while the fire burns down? We can sing only specifics, time's rambling tune, the places we have seen, the faces we have known. I will sing you the Galápagos islands, the sea lions soft on the rocks. It's all still happening there, in real light, the cool cur-

◆ ◆ ◆ ◆

rents upwelling, the finches falling on the wind, the shearwaters looping the waves. I could go back, or I could go on; or I could sit down, like Kubla Khan:

> Weave a circle round him thrice,
>> And close your eyes with holy dread,
> For he on honey-dew hath fed,
>> And drunk the milk of Paradise.

2

LIFE AND DEATH

IN GALÁPAGOS

BARRY LOPEZ

og, melancholy as a rain-soaked dog, drifts through the highlands, beading my hair with moisture. On the path ahead a vermilion flycatcher, burning scarlet against the muted greens of the
cloud forest, bursts up in flight. He flies to a space just over my head
and flutters there furiously, an acrobatic stall, a tiny, wild commotion
that hounds me down the muddy trail, until I pass beyond the small
arena of his life. Soon another comes and leaves; and afterward another, tiny escorts on a narrow trail descending the forest.

I had not expected this, exactly. The day before, down below at
the airstrip, I'd looked out over a seared lava plain at the thin, desultory cover of leafless brush and thought *in this slashing light there
will be no peace.* How odd now, this damp, cool stillness. Balsa and
scalesia trees, festooned with liverworts and mosses, give on to
stretches of grassland where tortoises graze. Blue-winged teal glide
the surface of an overcast pond. The migrant fog opens on a flight of

doves scribing a rise in the land, and then, like walls sliding, it seals them off.

Beneath this canopy of trees, my eyes free of the shrill burden of equatorial light, my cheeks cool as the underside of fieldstone—I had not thought a day like this would come in Galápagos. I had thought, foolishly, only of the heat-dunned equator, of a remote, dragon-lair archipelago in the Pacific. I had been warned off any such refreshing scenes as these by what I had read. Since 1535 chroniclers have made it a point to mark these islands down as inhospitable, deserted stone blisters in a broad ocean, harboring no wealth of any sort. A French entrepreneur, M. de Beauchesne-Gouin, dismissed them tersely (and typically) in 1700: "*la chose du monde la plus affreuse*," the most horrible place on Earth. Melville, evoking images of holocaust and despair in *The Encantadas*, viewed the Galapagean landscape as the aftermath of a penal colony. A visiting scientist wrote in 1924 that Isla Santa Cruz, where I now wandered, "made Purgatory look like the Elysian Fields."

Obviously, I reflected, feeling the heft of the mist against the back of my hands and the brightness of bird song around me, our summaries were about to differ. And it was not solely because these writers had never ventured far inland, away from the bleak coasts. Singularly bent to other tasks—commercial exploitation, embroidering on darkness in a literary narrative, compiling names in the sometimes inimical catalogs of science—they had rendered the islands poorly for a visitor intent, as I was, on its anomalies, which by their irreducible contrariness reveal, finally, a real landscape.

Galápagos, an archipelago of thirteen large and six smaller islands and some forty exposed rocks and islets, occupies a portion of the eastern Pacific half the size of Maine. It lies on the equator, but oddly; the Humboldt Current, flowing up from the Antarctic

◆◆◆◆◆

Ocean, has brought penguins to live here amidst tropical fish, but its coolness inhibits the growth of coral; and the freshwater streams and sandy beaches of, say, equatorial Curaçao or Martinique are not to be found here. The Galápagos are black shield volcanoes, broadly round massifs that rise symmetrically to collapsed summits, called calderas. Their lightly vegetated slopes incline like dark slabs of grit to cactus-strewn plains of lava. The plains, a lay of rubble like a storm-ripped ocean frozen at midnight, run to precipitous coasts of gray basalt, where one finds, occasionally, a soothing strip of coastal mangrove. Reptiles and birds, the primitive scaled and feathered alone, abound here; no deer-like, no fox-like, no hare-like animal abides.

The tendency to dwell on the barrenness of the lowlands, and on the seeming reptilian witlessness of the tortoise, as many early observers did, or to diminish the landscape cavalierly as an "inglorious panorama"—an ornithologist's words—of Cretaceous beasts, was an inevitability, perhaps; but the notion founders on more than just the cloud forests of Santa Cruz. Pampas below many of the islands' calderas roll like English downs serenely to the horizon. Ingenious woodpecker finches pry beetle grubs from their woody chambers with cactus spines. The dawn voice of the dove is as plaintive here as in the streets of Cairo or São Paulo. Galápagos, the visitor soon becomes aware, has a kind of tenderness about it; its stern vulcanism, the Age of Dragons that persists here, eventually comes to seem benign rather than aberrant. The nobility that may occasionally mark a scarred human face gleams here.

Biologists call Galápagos "exceptional" and "truly extraordinary" among the world's archipelagos. They pay homage to its heritage by referring to it as "the Mt. Sinai of island biogeography." But these insular landscapes give more than just scientific or historical pause. With flamingos stretched out in lugubrious flight over its fur seal grottoes, flows of magma orange as a New Mexican sunset percolating from its active volcanoes, towering ferns nodding in the wind like trees from the Carboniferous, and with its lanky packs of bat-eared, feral dogs some two hundred generations removed from human contact, Galápagos proves unruly to the imagination.

A departing visitor typically recalls being astonished here by the indifference of animals to human superiority. Sea lions continue to doze on the beach as you approach, even as you come to stand within inches of their noses. Their eyes open with no more alarm at your presence than were you parent to their dozing child. Mockingbirds snatch at your hair and worry your shoelaces—you are to them but some odd amalgamation of nesting materials. While this "tameness" is not to be forgotten, and while it is an innocence that profoundly comforts the traveler, Galápagos imparts more important lessons, perhaps, about the chaos of life. A blue-footed booby chick, embraceable in its white down, stands squarely before an ocean breeze, wrestling comically with its new wings, like someone trying to fold a road map in a high wind. An emaciated sea lion pup, rudely shunned by the other adults, waits with resolute cheer for a mother who clearly will never return from the sea. You extend your fingers here to the damp, soft rims of orchids, blooming white on the flanks of dark volcanoes.

Santa Cruz, in whose highlands I had gone to hike, lies near the center of the archipelago, some 590 miles west of Ecuador. Almost half of Galápagos's permanent population of 10,000 lives here, on farms, in two small villages, and in the large town of Puerto Ayora. The geography of this island is typical of Galápagos; the character of the vegetation changes, rather sharply, as one gains altitude. Candelabra and prickly pear cactus, dominating the lowlands, give way to a transitional zone of dry brush. Higher up, this scrubland turns to

◆ ◆ ◆ ◆ ◆

forest, then to heath and open country, where sedges, grasses and ferns grow. It was while climbing up through these life zones on the slopes of an extinct volcano, hearing wet elephant grass swish against my pants, that I first became aware of my untempered pre-conception of Galápagos as desolate. And it was here, along a fence line meant to restrain cattle, that I initially encountered that immense and quintessential animal of Galápagos, the giant tortoise. In those first moments it seemed neither a dim nor a clumsy beast. In its saurian aloofness, in the wild shining of its eyes as it ceased its grazing to scrutinize my passage, I beheld a different realm of patience, of edification, than the one I knew. Tortoises hesitate and plunge across the highlands like stunned ursids. The spiritual essence of Galápagos clings to them.

It was also on Santa Cruz, in the streets of Puerto Ayora, that I first sensed the dimensions of something disturbingly ordinary—the difficulties the people of Galápagos confront today: an erratic economic development that has come with the growth of tourism, and the disaffection of local farmers, fishermen, and lobstermen with the distribution of wealth here.

Galápagos seduces the visitor with the complexity of its beauty; but, like any mecca of wonder in the modern era, its beauty, its capacity to heal the traveler from afar, is threatened by the traveler himself, and by the exigencies of modern society. In 1985 a huge, man-caused fire burned nearly a hundred square miles of forest and pampa on southern Isla Isabela. The fire began on the rim of Volcán Santo Tomás and burned for months before an international team of forest fire fighters finally put it out. The press in North America and Europe exaggerated the havoc (penguins, for example, did not flee before the flames, nor did flamingos turn gray from a fallout of ash)—and the exaggeration precipitated an indictment. While the cause of the fire remains undetermined, it was widely assumed in the

◆◆◆◆

United States and Europe that it was started, accidentally but perhaps on purpose, by residents of the small village of Santo Tomás. The charred landscape was viewed, by some, as a dark statement of economic frustration, of the village's irritation with officials of Galápagos National Park, who will not allow them to extend their croplands and small-scale ranching operations into the—to them—"unused" interior of the islands, or to cut timber there.

Two extreme views about the future of Galápagos have since emerged. Some scientists, already aware of the extensive damage done in the islands by domestic animals gone wild—there are presently 80,000 feral goats and 5,000 feral pigs on Isla Santiago alone—would like to see the resident population of Galápagos greatly reduced and most of the agricultural holdings bought out and incorporated into the park. Many colonists, on the other hand, want to see both tourism and town trade continue to expand, in order to supplement their relatively meager incomes from farming, ranching, fishing and odd jobs. (Galápagos has no indigenous people with prior land claims. The first colonists arrived in 1832, when Ecuador took possession of the islands.)

But these are extreme positions. Economic hardship is evident to anyone walking the dirt streets of Galápagos's villages; but, on Isla Santa Cruz at least, the accommodation achieved among colonists, scientists, and national park personnel seems, to one who inquires, of a relatively high order. Considering how recently principles of conservation, let alone land-use planning, have become part of village life in South America, the acquiescence of many farmers to park-service demands for conservation is striking. (In a gesture of reciprocal understanding, park managers recently began planting teak trees on private land, to compensate owners for the saw timber they are not allowed to take from the park.)

Galápagos has two indisputable, interrelated problems: eco-

◆◆◆◆◆

nomic development (farming, fishing, tourism) without any overall plan; and non-native plants and animals which continue to change the islands' ecology. The latter situation is dire, but no worse than it's been in recent memory. Programs to eliminate feral goats on some of the smaller islands have been successful, as have efforts to reintroduce tortoises to areas where their populations have been decimated by feral cats, dogs, pigs, and rats. (A new, current worry is that feral dogs may breach a rugged, waterless stretch of lava on Isabela called Perry Isthmus and begin to prey on the least-disturbed animal populations in the whole archipelago, those on northern Isabela.)

Galápagos National Park incorporates nearly 97 percent of Galápagos, a combined land mass the size of Connecticut. (Near-shore waters were recently declared a "marine resource reserve" by the Ecuadorian government. Tourism and commercial fisheries officials, the park service, and the Ecuadorian navy are currently working out a management agreement.) The other three percent of the land comprises several hundred square miles of farmstead, a few small settlements, and three large villages—Puerto Ayora, a base for tourism and scientific research on Santa Cruz; Puerto Baquerizo Moreno, the islands' administrative center on San Cristóbal; and Puerto Villamil, a farming and ranching community on Isabela. Agriculture in Galápagos has always been marginal, because of a lack of fresh water, poor soils, and periods of drought. Fishing offers an economic alternative, but Galapagean fishermen increasingly are of the view that profit lies with converting their work boats to touring yachts.

Changes in the Galapagean economy are directly related to a sharp rise in tourism. During the 1960s only a few thousand tourists a year visited the archipelago. When the numbers increased in the 1970s, a park committee suggested a limit—12,000 per year, later

◆ ◆ ◆ ◆ ◆

raised to 25,000. In 1986, for the first time, more than 26,000 came, severely straining hotel and restaurant facilities at Puerto Ayora and more limited facilities at Baquerizo Moreno, the two communities connected to the mainland by air. Officials are now looking for specific answers to three separate questions. How many visitors can the park itself absorb? How many visitors can the park service manage? And how many people can simultaneously be present at a single location in the park before a visitor's sense of the magical remoteness of Galápagos is lost?

Points of legal disembarkation in the park—seabird colonies, cactus forests, saltwater lagoons—are limited, currently to fifty; the tour I joined, therefore, took us to the very same spots other visitors see. Occasionally we did encounter another group, but what we saw or heard at nearly every site was so uncommon, so invigorating, that the intrusion of others rarely detracted. We snorkeled amid schools of brilliant sergeant majors and yellow-tailed surgeon fish at a place called Devil's Crown, off Isla Floreana. At tide pools on the coast of Santiago, octopuses stared at us askance, and small fish called blennies wriggled past, walking peg-leg on their fin tips from pool to pool over the rock. At Isla Española we stepped respectfully around blue-footed boobies nesting obdurately in the trail. At Punta Cormorant we watched a regatta of ghost crabs scurry off up the beach, a high-stepping whirr, two hundred or more of them, as if before a stiff breeze.

The genius of the management plan in Galápagos—its success in preserving a feeling of wilderness warrants the word—rests on three principles. The park, first, exercises a high degree of control over where visitors go, with whom, and what they do. No one may travel in the park without a licensed guide and guides can—and sometimes do—send visitors too cavalier about the environment back to

◆ ◆ ◆ ◆

the boat; trails are marked and bounds have been established at each visitor site; and touching or feeding the animals, wandering off on one's own, or pocketing so much as a broken sea-shell are all prohibited. Second, because the boat itself incorporates the services of a hotel, a restaurant, and a souvenir shop, there is no on-shore development aside from the villages. Last, the park works concertedly with the Charles Darwin Research Station, a nonprofit, international scientific program, to manage the islands and monitor their well-being.

As a result of these precautions, few sites appear overused. Occasionally you even have the illusion, because the animals don't flee at your approach, of being among the first to visit.

Galápagos gently, gradually, overpowers. As our small yacht made its long passage between islands at night (to put us at a new island at dawn), I would lie awake trying to remember some moment of the day just past. The very process of calling upon the details of color and sound was a reminder of how provocative the landscape is, to both the senses and the intellect. The sensual images I recalled in vivid bursts: the yellow-white incandescence of an iguana's head; a thick perfume, like the odor of frankincense, suspended through a grove of bursera trees. At the sheer headland on Islas Plazas, I watched swallow-tailed gulls rappel a violent draft of air, stall, quivering in the wind, then float slowly backward in the stream of it to land light as a sigh on their cliff nests. One afternoon while we drifted on a turquoise lagoon, Pacific green turtles rose continuously to the calm surface to glance at us, the stillness broken only by water tinkling from their carapaces. They drew surprised, audible breath and sank. Behind them a long hillside of leafless palo santo trees shot up, a cinder wall of Chinese calligraphy leaning into an azure sky.

The most enduring image in Galápagos for me, however, was

◆━◆━◆━◆

filled with terror rather than beauty. I stood an hour in a storm petrel colony, under heavy gray skies on the east coast of Tower Island. Galápagos and Madeiran petrels, adroit seabirds about the size of a robin but with thin, delicate legs, nested here in cracks and hollows on a flat expanse of barren lava. They were hunted down, even as I watched, by intense, compact lethal predators—short-eared owls. Wind had scattered the torn fragments of bone and feather like rubbish over the dark plain. Farther back from the sea, boobies and frigate birds had made nests in the first ranks of low *muyuyo* shrubs. The risk to these lives was apparent. Young birds dead of starvation, or victims of what ornithologists call sibling murder, lay crumpled on the bare ground like abandoned clothing. Detached wings hung like faded pennants in wickets of *Cordia lutea* bushes, the wreckage of fatal bad landings.

These deaths, one realizes, are all in the flow of natural selection; but the stark terror of it, like the sight of a sea lion's shark-torn flipper, makes the thought fresh and startling. Images of innocent repose and violence are never far apart in Galápagos and the visitor is nowhere spared the contrast. He or she scans the seascape and landscape at the storm petrel colony acutely aware of the light hold the biological has on the slow, brutal upheaval of the geological.

The first humans to visit Galápagos may have been Indians from the South American mainland, who arrived on ocean-going balsa rafts in the eleventh century and probably used the islands only as a base for fishing operations. In 1535 Fray Tomás de Berlanga, Bishop of Panama, sailing far off course, came on the islands by accident and gave them the name that later appeared in Abraham Ortelius's atlas of 1570—*Insulae de los Galapagos*. (The cleft fore-edge of a lowland tortoise's carapace resembles the sharply rising pommel of a sixteenth-century Spanish saddle, the old Spanish for which was

◆—◆—◆—◆—◆

galopego.) English buccaneers began using the islands as a raiding base late in the seventeenth century. Struck by the contrariness of local winds, they renamed the place *las encantadas*, the enchanted ones.

Early in the nineteenth century whalers began visiting Galápagos regularly. They came to hunt sperm whales west of Isabela but found they were also able to careen their boats easily on the beaches for repairs and to provision them quickly with live tortoises, a source of fresh meat. The whalers turned pigs and goats loose on most of the islands, food for anyone who came up shipwrecked, but, too, animals easy to hunt down on a return visit. They barreled fresh water in the odd year when it was readily available. They idly beat thousands of marine iguanas and Galápagos doves to death with clubs, marveling at how the animals "do not get out of our way." And they buried their dead among the stones.

The legacy of those frontier days of whaling (and later of sealing) is still evident in Galápagos. Only 15,000 of an original population of perhaps 200,000 tortoises remain; four of fifteen subspecies are extinct and another is on the verge of extinction. The fur seal population, almost hunted out, is making a slow recovery; and black rats (from the ships) long ago eliminated at least one species of rice rat, the lone native mammals on the islands, aside from bats. Foraging goats have radically altered the structure of some of the islands' plant communities.

In addition to the whalers and sealers, three other groups, historically, had an impact on the biology of Galápagos. During World War II, American soldiers stationed on Baltra shot virtually all the larger animals there, and scientists, during the late nineteenth and early twentieth centuries, collected extensively for zoos and museums. The most deleterious effects, however, were caused by colonists.

The history of colonization in Galápagos is marked to an unusual

◆━◆━◆━◆━◆

degree by violence and periods of wretched, bare subsistence. The early settlements, founded on the hope of trading agricultural products to the mainland, all failed. In due course, each was turned into a penal colony by the Ecuadorian government. Attempts to raise sugar cane, coffee, citrus fruits, melons, and sweet potatoes, and small-scale efforts to export sulfur, seal hides, and tortoise oil, or to make stock-ranching profitable, were all schemes that didn't take sufficiently into account the thinness of the volcanic soils, the undependable climate, or the vicissitudes of a trade-based economy.

Along with the farmers came resident fishermen who fared somewhat better. Utopian daydreamers, adventurers, and eccentrics followed, many of them poorly informed about the islands' climate, the extent of arable land, even their sovereign status. This pattern, in fact, carried far into the twentieth century.

The first scientific collectors in the islands, an expedition under the French, arrived in 1790. The next, under Captain FitzRoy in HMS *Beagle* in 1835, fixed the archipelago indelibly in the minds of all who read the subsequent reports of the ship's naturalist, Charles Darwin. In 1905–06 the California Academy of Sciences conducted the last major effort to collect in the islands, with an apparent excess of zeal—its leader killed the only tortoise ever recorded on Isla Fernandina.

The days when scientists trapped for zoos and collected indiscriminately are gone; settlers, however, still turn domestic animals loose to prey upon, and compete with, native animals, and residents still shoot Galápagos hawks as predators and occasionally poach tortoise meat. Colonists have also introduced nearly 250 exotic plants to the islands, some of which, in combination with the grazing of feral horses, goats, cattle, and donkeys, threaten several endemic plants with extinction. Scientists, too, sometimes contribute to al-

◆◆◆◆◆

terations in the islands' plant communities by bringing ashore food and equipment that harbor seeds or insects from the mainland, or from one of the other islands.

Anxiety about the islands' natural communities stems from scientific knowledge that each island's flora and fauna are unique. Remarkably, this remains essentially true today, despite plant introductions, damage by feral animals, and the loss of some native plant and animal populations. Researchers, in other words, can still find in Galápagos an evolutionary puzzle with relatively few pieces missing.

A desire to preserve a virtually undisturbed environment in the islands seems obsessive and unrealistic to some local villagers and farmers. Their pressing concerns are for food, a stable source of fresh water, and such things as raw building materials and supplementary income. (One encounters this basic difference in point of view, of course, with growing frequency in many countries—around the game parks of East Africa, for example, or in the rain forests of Guatemala.) In Galápagos, as elsewhere, things of the mind, including intellectual ramifications from evolutionary theory, and things of the spirit, like the feeling one gets from a Queen Anne's lace of stars in the moonless Galapagean sky, struggle toward accommodation with an elementary desire for material comfort. In Galápagos, however, the measure of accommodation is slightly different. Things of the mind and spirit exert more influence here because so many regard this archipelago as preëminently a terrain of the mind and spirit, a locus of biological thought and psychological rejuvenation. It represents the legacy of Charles Darwin, and the heritage of devotion to his thought.

The sheer strength alone of Darwin's insight into the development of biological life gently urges a visitor to be more than usually observant here—to notice, say, that while the thirteen Galapagean finches are all roughly the same hue, it is possible to separate them according to marked differences in the shapes of their bills and feeding habits. The eye catches similar nuances elsewhere—minor differences also separate eleven species of tortoise and fourteen species of scalesia tree. This close variety is tantalizing. Invariably, one begins to wonder why these related species look so much alike—and an encounter with adaptive radiation, with what Darwin called "descent with modification," becomes inevitable.

A vague intellectual current meanders continually through Galápagos, an ever-present musing one senses among a certain steady stream of visitors, if but faintly. Evolution, an elegantly simple perception, is clarified by exceedingly complex speculation; Darwin's heroic attempt to understand evolutionary change forms part of the atmospheric pressure in Galápagos. The idea that an elucidation of natural selection or genetic drift, mechanisms by which evolution might operate, could contribute to more than just a clearer understanding of the universe, that it might make humanity's place in it plainer, is never far off.

One has no need, of course, to know how natural selection might have directed their destinies to appreciate unadorned variety among Darwin's finches. The Galápagos penguin is no less startling, the turquoise eyes of the Galápagos cormorant no less riveting, for not knowing precisely how each might have evolved since it arrived. Nor is a visitor required to brood over the economic fate of farmers and villagers in Galápagos, while staring down into the wondrous blowhole of a dolphin riding the bow wave of a tour boat. But at the close of the twentieth century, not to turn to the complexities of evolution in a real place, to the metaphorical richness and utility of Darwin's

◆ ◆ ◆ ◆ ◆

thought, or to turn away from the economic aspirations of a local people, seems to risk much. Our knowledge of life is slim. The undisturbed landscapes are rapidly dwindling. And no plan has yet emerged for a kind of wealth that will satisfy all people.

As I sailed between the islands—at dawn from the sea they look like the heads of crows emerging from the ocean—I dwelled on the anomalies. Subsistence hunters pursue feral cattle high on the Sierra Negra with dogs and snares, the same cattle that are pursued by packs of resident feral dogs. What meat they get they sell in Puerto Villamil for thirteen cents a pound. From their mountain redoubt they watch the tour boats far below, streaming east along the coastal margin. The park's wardens work 364 days a year for $1,650, part of the time on twenty-day patrols in the arid, rugged interior, hunting down feral dogs and goats to purify the park. A young farmer, proud of his shrewdness, says he will grow a diversity of condiment crops on his small holding and so be in a strong and exclusive position to supply new restaurants which are sure to come to Puerto Ayora. I remember an afternoon sitting at the Darwin Research Station, reading formal descriptions of nearly a hundred scientific projects under way in the islands. What a concise presentation of the inexhaustible range of human inquiry, I thought, what invigorating evidence of the desire to understand.

The evening before I departed I stood on the rim of a lagoon on Isla Rabida. Flamingos rode on its dark surface like pink swans, apparently asleep. Small, curved feathers, shed from their breasts, drifted away from them over the water on a light breeze. I did not move for an hour. It was a moment of such peace, every troubled thread in a human spirit might have uncoiled and sorted itself into graceful order. Other flamingos stood in the shallows with diffident

◆—◆—◆—◆—◆

elegance in the falling light, not feeding but only staring off toward the ocean. They seemed a kind of animal I had never quite seen before.

2

I left for Quito with regrets. I had eaten the flesh of blue lobster and bacalao from Galápagos's waters and enjoyed prolonged moments of intimacy with the place; but I had not, as I had hoped, had the days to climb Volcán Alcedo, nor had I seen a shark or a violent thunderstorm. But I knew that I would be back. It was not the ethereal beauty of the flamingos, solely, or the dazzling appearance underwater of a school of blue-eyed damselfish that now pulled at me. It was the fastness of the archipelago, the fullness of its life; and the juxtaposition of violent death that signaled that more than scenery was here.

On the way to the Hotel Colón in Quito, the cab driver spoke about Galápagos with resignation and yearning. A number of Ecuadorians think of Galápagos the way Americans once dreamed of the West—a place where one might start life over, fresh. I told him about a young couple who had just opened a small restaurant on the hill above Puerto Ayora. I had had coffee there after a long hike. I sat by myself on the veranda, watching sunlight filter through the forest. Far in the distance I could see the pale ocean. I could hear bird song, which sharpened an irrational feeling of allegiance, of fierce camaraderie, with the trees, the wild tortoises I had seen that afternoon, the vermilion flycatchers that had followed me.

As we threaded our way through heavy traffic and billowing diesel exhaust from the municipal buses, the driver asked what sorts of birds I had seen. I told him. The litany made him gesture at the traffic, the different makes of vehicle pinning us in, and led him to smile ruefully.

¿Por qué quieres ir a las Galápagos? I asked. Why do you wish to go to Galápagos? For work? To buy a farm?

La paz, he said, turning to look at me, his thin, sharp face full of fervent belief. The peace.

Ah, Galápagos is not peaceful, I thought. It is full of the wild conflict that defines life. The groaning of the earth beneath fumaroles on Fernandina. Owl-dashed petrels. But what I reflected on wasn't what he meant at all. He meant a reprieve. Retreat. I thought to tell him, as I put the fare in his hand, of the flamingos at sunset on Rabida. People in Frankfurt and San Francisco, here in Quito, in Puerto Ayora, in Geneva, I wanted to assure him, are working to preserve such a retreat, a place out there in the ocean where men and women might gather themselves again. It would take wisdom and courtesy to effect, a certain understanding between those who wish fewer people would come and those who want to see more. An understanding that what is beautiful and mysterious belongs to no one, is in fact a gift.

But these were my own feelings, too presuming. What came out of me, as I nodded gratitude for a desultory conversation in an unfamiliar city, was *Hallar la paz, eso es sabio. . . .* To go there to find peace, that is very wise.

3

EASTER ISLAND

CAPTAIN JAMES COOK

CHAPTER VII

At eight o'clock in the morning on the 11th, land was seen, from the mast-head, bearing West; and at noon from the deck, extending from W. ¾ to W. by S., about twelve leagues distant. I made no doubt that this was Davis's Land, or Easter Island; as its appearance from this situation, corresponded very well with Wafer's account; and we expected to have seen the low sandy isle that Davis fell in with, which would have been a confirmation; but in this we were disappointed. At seven o'clock in the evening, the island bore from N. 62° West to North 87° West, about five leagues distant; in which situation we sounded without finding ground with a line of an hundred and forty fathoms. Here we spent the night, having alternately light airs and calms, till ten o'clock the next morning, when a breeze sprung up at W. S. W. With this we stretched in for the land; and by the help of our glass, discovered people, and some of those colossian statues or idols mentioned by the authors of Roggewin's

Voyage.* At four o'clock in the P. M. we were half a league S. S. E. and N. N. W. of the N. E. point of the island; and, on sounding, found thirty-five fathoms, a dark sandy bottom. I now tacked and endeavoured to get into what appeared to be a bay, on the West side of the point or S. E. side of the island; but before this could be accomplished, night came upon us, and we stood on and off, under the land, till the next morning; having soundings from seventy-five to an hundred and ten fathoms, the same bottom as before.

On the 13th, about eight o'clock in the morning, the wind, which had been variable most part of the night, fixed at S. E., and blew in squalls, accompanied with rain; but it was not long before the weather became fair. As the wind now blew right on the S. E. shore, which does not afford that shelter I at first thought, I resolved to look for anchorage on the West and N. W. sides of the island. With this view I bore up round the South point; off which lie two small islots; the one, nearest the point, high and peaked, and the other low and flattish. After getting round the point, and coming before a sandy beach, we found soundings thirty and forty fathoms, sandy ground, and about one mile from the shore. Here a canoe conducted by two men, came off to us. They brought with them a bunch of plantains, which they sent into the ship by a rope, and then they returned ashore. This gave us a good opinion of the islanders, and inspired us with hopes of getting some refreshments, which we were in great want of.

I continued to range along the coast, till we opened the northern point of the isle, without seeing a better anchoring-place than the one we had passed. We, therefore, tacked, and plied back to it; and, in the mean time, sent away the master, in a boat to sound the coast. He returned about five o'clock in the evening; and, soon after, we

* See Dalrymple's Collection of Voyages, vol. 2.

◆━◆━◆━◆━◆

came to an anchor in thirty-six fathoms water, before the sandy beach above mentioned. As the master drew near the shore with the boat, one of the natives swam off to her, and insisted on coming aboard the ship, where he remained two nights and a day. The first thing he did after coming aboard, was to measure the length of the ship, by fathoming her from the taffarel to the stern; and, as he counted the fathoms, we observed that he called the numbers by the same names that they do at Otaheite; nevertheless his language was, in a manner, wholly unintelligible to all of us.

Having anchored too near the edge of the bank, a fresh breeze from the land, about three o'clock the next morning, drove us off it; on which the anchor was heaved up, and sail made to regain the bank again. While the ship was plying in, I went ashore, accompanied by some of the gentlemen, to see what the island was likely to afford us. We landed at the sandy beach, where some hundreds of the natives were assembled, and who were so impatient to see us, that many of them swam off to meet the boats. Not one of them had so much as a stick or weapon of any sort in their hands. After distributing a few trinkets amongst them, we made signs for something to eat; on which they brought down a few potatoes, plantains, and sugar-canes, and exchanged them for nails, looking-glasses, and pieces of cloth.

We presently discovered that they were as expert thieves, and as tricking in their exchanges, as any people we had yet met with. It was with some difficulty we could keep the hats on our heads; but hardly possible to keep any thing in our pockets, not even what themselves had sold us; for they would watch every opportunity to snatch it from us, so that we sometimes bought the same thing two or three times over, and after all did not get it.

Before I sailed from England, I was informed that a Spanish ship had visited this isle in 1769. Some signs of it were seen among the

◆━◆━◆━◆━◆

people now about us; one man had a pretty good broad brimmed European hat on; another had a grego jacket; and another a red silk handkerchief. They also seemed to know the use of a musquet, and to stand in much awe of it; but this they probably learnt from Roggewin, who, if we are to believe the authors of that voyage, left them sufficient tokens.

Near the place where we landed, were some of those statues before mentioned, which I shall describe in another place. The country appeared barren and without wood; there were, nevertheless, several plantations of potatoes, plantains and sugar-canes; we also saw some fowls, and found a well of brackish water. As these were articles we were in want of, and as the natives seemed not unwilling to part with them, I resolved to stay a day or two. With this view, I repaired on board, and brought the ship to an anchor in thirty-two fathoms water; the bottom a fine dark sand. Our station was about a mile from the nearest shore, the South point of a small bay, in the bottom of which is the sandy beach before mentioned, being E. S. E., distant one mile and an half. The two rocky islots lying off the South point of the island, were just shut behind a point to the North of them; they bore South ¾ West, four miles distant; and the other extreme of the island bore N. 25° E., distant about six miles. But the best mark for this anchoring-place is the beach; because it is the only one on this side the island. In the afternoon, we got on board a few casks of water, and opened a trade with the natives for such things as they had to dispose of. Some of the gentlemen also made an excursion into the country to see what it produced; and returned again in the evening, with the loss only of a hat, which one of the natives snatched off the head of one of the party.

Early next morning, I sent Lieutenants Pickersgill and Edgcumbe with a party of men, accompanied by several of the gentlemen, to examine the country. As I was not sufficiently recovered from my late

◆—◆—◆—◆—◆

illness to make one of the party, I was obliged to content myself with remaining at the landing-place among the natives. We had, at one time, a pretty brisk trade with them for potatoes, which we observed they dug up out of an adjoining plantation; but this traffic, which was very advantageous to us, was soon put a stop to, by the owner (as we supposed) of the plantation coming down, and driving all the people out of it. By this we concluded, that he had been robbed of his property, and that they were not less scrupulous of stealing from one another, than from us, on whom they practised every little fraud they could think on, and generally with success; for we no sooner detected them in one, than they found out another. About seven o'clock in the evening, the party I had sent into the country returned, after having been over the greatest part of the island.

They left the beach about nine o'clock in the morning, and took a path which led across to the S. E. side of the island, followed by a great crowd of the natives, who pressed much upon them. But they had not proceeded far, before a middle-aged man, punctured from head to foot, and his face painted with a sort of white pigment, appeared with a spear in his hand, and walked along-side of them, making signs to his countrymen to keep at a distance, and not to molest our people. When he had pretty well effected this, he hoisted a piece of white cloth on his spear, placed himself in the front, and led the way, with his ensign of peace, as they understood it to be. For the greatest part of the distance across, the ground had but a barren appearance, being a dry hard clay, and every where covered with stones; but notwithstanding this, there were several large tracks planted with potatoes; and some plantain walks, but they saw no fruit on any of the trees. Towards the highest part of the South end of the island, the soil, which was a fine red earth, seemed much better; bore a longer grass; and was not covered with stones as in the other parts; but here they saw neither house nor plantation.

◆—◆—◆—◆—◆

On the East side, near the sea, they met with three platforms of stone-work, or rather the ruins of them. On each had stood four of those large statues, but they were all fallen down from two of them, and also one from the third; all except one were broken by the fall, or in some measure defaced. Mr. Wales measured this one, and found it to be fifteen feet in length, and six feet broad over the shoulders. Each statue had on its head a large cylindric stone of a red colour, wrought perfectly round. The one they measured, which was not by far the largest, was fifty-two inches high, and sixty-six in diameter. In some the upper corner of the cylinder was taken off in a sort of concave quarter-round; but in others the cylinder was entire.

From this place they followed the direction of the coast to the N. E., the man with the flag still leading the way. For about three miles they found the country very barren, and in some places stript of the soil to the bare rock, which seemed to be a poor sort of iron ore. Beyond this, they came to the most fertile part of the island they saw, it being interspersed with plantations of potatoes, sugar-canes, and plantain trees, and these not so much encumbered with stones as those which they had seen before; but they could find no water except what the natives twice or thrice brought them, which, though brackish and stinking, was rendered acceptable, by the extremity of their thirst. They also passed some huts, the owners of which met them with roasted potatoes and sugar-canes, and placing themselves ahead of the foremost of the party, (for they marched in a line in order to have the benefit of the path) gave one to each man as he passed by. They observed the same method in distributing the water which they brought; and were particularly careful that the foremost did not drink too much, least none should be left for the hindmost. But at the very time these were relieving the thirsty and hungry, there were not wanting others, who endeavoured to steal from them the very things which had been given them. At last, to prevent worse

◆◆◆◆◆

consequences, they were obliged to fire a load of small shot at one who was so audacious as to snatch from one of the men the bag which contained every thing they carried with them. The shot hit him on the back; on which he dropped the bag, ran a little way, and then fell; but he afterwards got up and walked, and what became of him they knew not, nor whether he was much wounded. As this affair occasioned some delay, and drew the natives together, they presently saw the man who had hitherto led the way, and one or two more, coming running towards them; but instead of stopping when they came up, they continued to run round them, repeating, in a kind manner, a few words, until our people set forwards again. Then their old guide hoisted his flag, leading the way as before, and none ever attempted to steal from them the whole day afterwards.

As they passed along, they observed on a hill a number of people collected together, some of whom had spears in their hands; but, on being called to by their countryman, they dispersed; except a few, amongst whom was one seemingly of some note. He was a stout well-made man, with a fine open countenance, his face was painted, his body punctured, and he wore a better *Ha hou*, or cloth, than the rest. He saluted them as he came up, by stretching out his arms, with both hands clinched, lifting them over his head, opening them wide, and then letting them fall gradually down to his sides. To this man, whom they understood to be the chief of the island, their other friend gave his white flag; and he gave it to another, who carried it before them the remainder of the day.

Towards the eastern end of the island, they met with a well whose water was perfectly fresh, being considerably above the level of the sea; but it was dirty, owing to the filthiness or cleanliness (call it which you will) of the natives, who never go to drink without washing themselves all over as soon as they have done; and if ever so many of them are together, the first leaps right into the middle of the hole, drinks, and washes himself without the least ceremony; after which another takes his place and does the same.

They observed that this side of the island was full of those gigantic statues so often mentioned; some placed in groupes on platforms of masonry; others single, fixed only in the earth, and that not deep; and these latter are, in general, much larger than the others. Having measured one, which had fallen down, they found it very near twenty-seven feet long, and upwards of eight feet over the breast or shoulders; and yet this appeared considerably short of the size of one they saw standing: its shade, a little past two o'clock, being sufficient to shelter all the party, consisting of near thirty persons, from the rays of the sun. Here they stopped to dine; after which they repaired to a hill, from whence they saw all the East and North shores of the isle, on which they could not see either bay or creek fit even for a boat to land in; nor the least signs of fresh water. What the natives brought them here was real salt water; but they observed that some of them drank pretty plentifully of it, so far will necessity and custom get the better of nature! On this account they were obliged to return to the last-mentioned well; where, after having quenched their thirst, they directed their route across the island towards the ship, as it was now four o'clock.

In a small hollow, on the highest part of the island, they met with several such cylinders as are placed on the heads of the statues. Some of these appeared larger than any they had seen before; but it was now too late to stop to measure any of them. Mr. Wales, from whom I had this information, is of opinion that there had been a quarry here, whence these stones had formerly been dug; and that it would have been no difficult matter to roll them down the hill after they were formed. I think this a very reasonable conjecture; and have no doubt that it has been so.

On the declivity of the mountain towards the West, they met with

◆—◆—◆—◆—◆

another well; but the water was a very strong mineral, had a thick green scum on the top, and stunk intolerably. Necessity, however, obliged some to drink of it; but it soon made them so sick, that they threw it up the same way it went down.

In all this excursion, as well as the one made the preceding day, only two or three shrubs were seen. The leaf and seed of one (called by the natives *Torromedo*) were not much unlike those of the common vetch; but the pod was more like that of a tamarind in its size and shape. The seeds have a disagreeable bitter taste; and the natives, when they saw our people chew them, made signs to spit them out; from whence it was concluded that they think them poisonous. The wood is of a redish colour, and pretty hard and heavy; but very crooked, small, and short, not exceeding six or seven feet in height. At the S. W. corner of the island, they found another small shrub, whose wood was white and brittle, and in some measure, as also its leaf, resembling the ash. They also saw in several places the Otaheitean cloth plant; but it was poor and weak, and not above two and a half feet high at most.

They saw not an animal of any sort, and but very few birds; nor indeed any thing which can induce ships that are not in the utmost distress, to touch at this island.

This account of the excursion I had from Mr. Pickersgill and Mr. Wales, men on whose veracity I could depend; and, therefore, I determined to leave the island the next morning, since nothing was to be obtained that could make it worth my while to stay longer; for the water which we had sent on board, was not much better than if it had been taken up out of the sea.

We had a calm till ten o'clock in the morning of the 16th, when a breeze sprung up at West, accompanied with heavy showers of rain, which lasted about an hour. The weather then clearing up, we got under sail, stood to sea, and kept plying to and fro, while an officer

◆━◆━◆━◆

was sent on shore with two boats, to purchase such refreshments as the natives might have brought down; for I judged this would be the case, as they knew nothing of our sailing. The event proved that I was not mistaken; for the boats made two trips before night; when we hoisted them in, and made sail to the N. W., with a light breeze at N. N. E.

CHAPTER VIII

I shall now give some farther account of this island, which is undoubtedly the same that admiral Roggewin touched at in April 1722; although the description given of it by the authors of that voyage does by no means agree with it now. It may also be the same that was seen by Captain Davis in 1686; for, when seen from the East, it answers very well to Wafer's description, as I have before observed. In short, if this is not the land, his discovery cannot lie far from the coast of America, as this latitude has been well explored from the meridian of 80° to 110°. Captain Carteret carried it much farther; but his track seems to have been a little too far South. Had I found fresh water, I intended spending some days in looking for the low sandy isle Davis fell in with, which would have determined the point. But as I did not find water, and had a long run to make before I was assured of getting any; and being in want of refreshments, I declined the search; as a small delay might have been attended with bad consequences to the crew, many of them beginning to be more or less affected with the scurvy.

No nation need contend for the honour of the discovery of this island; as there can be few places which afford less convenience for shipping than it does. Here is no safe anchorage; no wood for fuel; nor any fresh water worth taking on board. Nature has been exceedingly sparing of her favours to this spot. As every thing must be raised by dint of labour, it cannot be supposed the inhabitants plant much more than is sufficient for themselves; and as they are but few in number, they cannot have much to spare to supply the wants of visitant strangers. The produce is sweet potatoes, yams, taraoreddy root, plantains, and sugar-canes, all pretty good, the potatoes especially, which are the best of the kind I ever tasted. Gourds they have also; but so very few, that a cocoa-nut shell was the most valuable thing we could give them. They have a few tame fowls such as cocks and hens, small but well tasted. They have also rats, which, it seems, they eat; for I saw a man with some dead ones in his hand; and he seemed unwilling to part with them, giving me to understand they were for food. Land birds there were hardly any; and sea birds but few; these were, men of war, tropic, and egg birds, nodies, tern, &c. The coast seemed not to abound with fish; at least we could catch none with hook and line, and it was but very little we saw amongst the natives.

Such is the produce of Easter Island, or Davis's Land, which is situated in the latitude of 27° 5′ 30″ S., longitude 109° 46′ 20″ West. It is about ten or twelve leagues in circuit, hath a hilly and stony surface, and an iron bound shore. The hills are of such an height as to be seen fifteen or sixteen leagues: off the South end, are two rocky islots, lying near the shore: the North and East points of the island rise directly from the sea to a considerable height; between them, on the S. E. side, the shore forms an open bay, in which I believe the Dutch anchored. We anchored, as hath been already mentioned, on the West side of the island, three miles to the North of the South point, with the sandy beach bearing E. S. E. This is a very good road with easterly winds, but a dangerous one with westerly, as the other on the S. E. side must be with easterly winds.

For this, and other bad accommodations already mentioned, nothing but necessity will induce any one to touch at this isle, unless

◆—◆—◆—◆—◆

it can be done without going much out of the way; in which case touching here may be advantageous, as the people willingly and readily part with such refreshments as they have, and at an easy rate. We certainly received great benefit from the little we got; but few ships can come here without being in want of water, and this want cannot be here supplied. The little we took on board, could not be made use of; it being only salt water which had filtrated through a stony beach, into a stone well. This the natives had made for the purpose, a little to the southward of the sandy beach so often mentioned; and the water ebbed and flowed into it with the tide.

The inhabitants of this island do not seem to exceed six or seven hundred souls, and above two-thirds of those we saw were males. They either have but few females among them, or else many were restrained from making their appearance, during our stay; for though we saw nothing to induce us to believe the men were of a jealous disposition, or the women afraid to appear in public, something of this kind was probably the case.

In colour, features, and language, they bear such affinity to the people of the more western isles, that no one will doubt that they have had the same origin. It is extraordinary that the same nation should have spread themselves over all the isles in this vast ocean, from New Zealand to this island, which is almost one-fourth part of the circumference of the globe. Many of them have now no other knowledge of each other, than what is preserved by antiquated tradition; and they have, by length of time, become, as it were, different nations, each having adopted some peculiar custom, or habit, &c. Nevertheless, a careful observer will soon see the affinity each has to the other.

In general the people of this isle are a slender race. I did not see a man that would measure six feet; so far are they from being giants, as one of the authors of Roggewin's voyage asserts. They are brisk and active, have good features, and not disagreeable countenances, are friendly and hospitable to strangers, but as much addicted to pilfering as any of their neighbours.

Tatowing, or puncturing the skin, is much used here. The men are marked from head to foot, with figures all nearly alike; only some give them one direction, and some another, as fancy leads. The women are but little punctured; red and white paint is an ornament with *them*, as also with the men; the former is made of tamarick, but what composes the latter, I know not.

Their cloathing is a piece or two of quilted cloth about six feet by four, or a mat. One piece wrapped round their loins, and another over their shoulders, make a complete dress. But the men, for the most part, are in a manner naked, wearing nothing but a slip of cloth betwixt their legs, each end of which is fastened to a cord or belt they wear round the waist. Their cloth is made of the same materials as at Otaheite, viz. of the bark of the cloth-plant; but, as they have but little of it, our Otaheitean cloth, or indeed any sort of it, came here to a good market.

Their hair, in general, is black; the women wear it long, and sometimes tied up on the crown of the head; but the men wear it, and their beards, cropped short. Their head-dress is a round fillet adorned with feathers, and a straw bonnet something like a Scotch one; the former, I believe, being chiefly worn by the men, and the latter by the women. Both men and women have very large holes, or rather slits, in their ears, extended to near three inches in length. They sometimes turn this slit over the upper part, and then the ear looks as if the flap was cut off. The chief ear ornaments are the white down of feathers, and rings, which they wear in the inside of the hole, made of some elastic substance, rolled up like a watch-spring. I judged this was to keep the hole at its utmost extension. I do not remember seeing them wear any other ornaments, excepting amulets made of bone or shells.

As harmless and friendly as these people seem to be, they are not without offensive weapons, such as short wooden clubs, and spears; which latter are crooked sticks about six feet long, armed at one end with pieces of flint. They have also a weapon, made of wood, like the *Patoo patoo* of New Zealand.

Their houses are low miserable huts, constructed by setting sticks upright in the ground, at six or eight feet distance, then bending them towards each other, and tying them together at the top, forming thereby a kind of Gothic arch. The longest sticks are placed in the middle, and shorter ones each way, and at less distance asunder; by which means the building is highest and broadest in the middle, and lower and narrower towards each end. To these are tied others horizontally, and the whole is thatched over with leaves of sugarcane. The door-way is in the middle of one side, formed like a porch, and so low and narrow, as just to admit a man to enter upon all fours. The largest house I saw was about sixty feet long, eight or nine feet high in the middle, and three or four at each end; its breadth at these parts, was nearly equal to its height. Some have a kind of vaulted houses built with stone, and partly under ground; but I never was in one of these.

I saw no household utensils amongst them except gourds, and of these but very few. They were extravagantly fond of cocoa-nut shells; more so than of any thing we could give them. They dress their victuals in the same manner as at Otaheite; that is, with hot stones, in an oven or hole in the ground. The straw or tops of sugarcane, plantain heads, &c. serve them for fuel to heat the stones. Plantains, which require but little dressing, they roast under fires of straw, dried grass, &c.; and whole races of them are ripened or roasted in this manner. We frequently saw ten, or a dozen, or more, such fires in one place, and most commonly in the mornings and evenings.

Not more than three or four canoes were seen on the whole island; and these very mean, and built of many pieces sewed together with small line. They are about eighteen or twenty feet long, head and stern carved or raised a little, are very narrow, and fitted with out-riggers. They do not seem capable of carrying above four persons, and are, by no means, fit for any distant navigation. As small and as mean as these canoes were, it was a matter of wonder to us, where they got the wood to build them with. For in one of them was a board six or eight feet long, fourteen inches broad at one end, and eight at the other; whereas we did not see a stick on the island which would have made a board half this size; nor indeed was there another piece in the whole canoe half so big.

There are two ways by which it is possible they may have got this large wood: it might have been left here by the Spaniards; or it might have been driven on the shore of the island from some distant land. It is even possible that there may be some land in the neighbourhood, from whence they might have got it. We, however, saw no signs of any; nor could we get the least information on this head from the natives, although we tried every method we could think of, to obtain it. We were almost as unfortunate in our inquiries for the proper or native name of the island. For, on comparing notes, I found we had got three different names for it, viz. Tamareki, Whyhu, and Teapÿ. Without pretending to say which, or whether any of them, is right, I shall only observe, that the last was obtained by Oedidee, who understood their language much better than any of us, though even he understood it but very imperfectly.

It appears by the account of Roggewin's voyage, that these people had no better vessels than when he first visited them. The want of materials, and not of genius, seems to be the reason why they have made no improvement in this art. Some pieces of carving were found amongst them, both well designed and executed. Their plantations are prettily laid out by line, but not inclosed by any fence; indeed, they have nothing for this purpose but stones.

I have no doubt that all these plantations are private property, and that there are here, as at Otaheite, chiefs (which they call *Areekes*) to whom these plantations belong. But of the power or authority of these chiefs, or of the government of these people, I confess myself quite ignorant.

Nor are we better acquainted with their religion. The gigantic statues, so often mentioned, are not, in my opinion, looked upon as idols by the present inhabitants, whatever they might have been in the days of the Dutch; at least, I saw nothing that could induce me to think so. On the contrary, I rather suppose that they are burying-places for certain tribes or families. I, as well as some others, saw a human skeleton lying in one of the platforms, just covered with stones. Some of these platforms of masonry are thirty or forty feet long, twelve of sixteen broad, and from three to twelve in height; which last in some measure depends on the nature of the ground. For they are generally at the brink of the bank facing the sea, so that this face may be ten or twelve feet or more high, and the other may not be above three or four. They are built, or rather faced, with hewn stones of a very large size; and the workmanship is not inferior to the best plain piece of masonry we have in England. They use no sort of cement; yet the joints are exceedingly close, and the stones morticed and tenanted one into another, in a very artful manner. The side walls are not perpendicular, but inclining a little inwards, in the same manner that breast-works, &c. are built in Europe: yet had not all this care, pains, and sagacity, been able to preserve these curious structures from the ravages of all-devouring Time.

◆ ◆ ◆ ◆ ◆

The statues, or at least many of them, are erected on these platforms, which serve as foundations. They are, as near as we could judge, about half length, ending in a sort of stump at the bottom, on which they stand. The workmanship is rude, but not bad; nor are the features of the face ill formed, the nose and chin in particular; but the ears are long beyond proportion; and, as to the bodies, there is hardly any thing like a human figure about them.

I had an opportunity of examining only two or three of these statues, which are near the landing-place; and they were of a grey stone, seemingly of the same sort as that with which the platforms were built. But some of the gentlemen, who travelled over the island, and examined many of them, were of opinion that the stone of which they were made, was different from any other they saw on the island, and had much the appearance of being factitious. We could hardly conceive how these islanders, wholly unacquainted with any mechanical power, could raise such stupendous figures, and afterwards place the large cylindric stones, before mentioned, upon their heads. The only method I can conceive, is by raising the upper end by little and little, supporting it by stones as it is raised, and building about it till they got it erect; thus a sort of mount, or scaffolding, would be made; upon which they might roll the cylinder, and place it upon the head of the statue; and then the stones might be removed from about it. But if the stones are factitious, the statues might have been put together on the place, in their present position, and the cylinder put on by building a mount round them as above mentioned. But, let them have been made and set up, by this or any other method, they must have been a work of immense time, and sufficiently shew the ingenuity and perseverance of the islanders in the age in which they were built; for the present inhabitants have most certainly, had no hand in them, as they do not even repair the foundations of those which are going to decay. They give different names to them, such as Goto-

◆━◆━◆━◆━◆

moara, Marapate, Kanaro, Goway-too-goo, Matta Matta, &c. &c.; to which they sometimes prefix the word Moi, and sometimes annex Areekee. The latter signifies Chief; and the former, Burying, or Sleeping-place, as well as we could understand.

Besides the monuments of antiquity, which were pretty numerous, and no where but on or near the sea-coast, there were many little heaps of stones, piled up in different places, along the coast. Two or three of the uppermost stones in each pile were generally white; perhaps always so, when the pile is complete. It will hardly be doubted that these piles of stone had a meaning. Probably they might mark the place where people had been buried, and serve instead of the large statues.

The working-tools of these people are but very mean, and like those of all the other islanders we have visited in this ocean, made of stone, bone, shells, &c. They set but little value on iron or iron tools; which is the more extraordinary as they know their use; but the reason may be, their having but little occasion for them.

4

THE MARQUESAS

ISLANDS

HERMAN MELVILLE

I can never forget the eighteen or twenty days during which the light trade-winds were silently sweeping us towards the islands. In pursuit of the sperm whale, we had been cruising on the line some twenty degrees to the westward of the Gallipagos [Galápagos]; and all that we had to do, when our course was determined on, was to square in the yards and keep the vessel before the breeze, and then the good ship and the steady gale did the rest between them. The man at the wheel never vexed the old lady with any superfluous steering, but comfortably adjusting his limbs at the tiller, would doze away by the hour. True to her work, the *Dolly* headed to her course, and like one of those characters who always do best when let alone, she jogged on her way like a veteran old sea-pacer as she was.

What a delightful, lazy, languid time we had whilst we were thus gliding along! There was nothing to be done; a circumstance that happily suited our disinclination to do anything. We abandoned the fore-peak altogether, and spreading an awning over the forecastle, slept, ate, and lounged under it the live-long day. Every one seemed to be under the influence of some narcotic. Even the officers aft, whose duty required them never to be seated while keeping a deck watch, vainly endeavoured to keep on their pins; and were obliged invariably to compromise the matter by leaning up against the bulwarks, and gazing abstractedly over the side. Reading was out of the question; take a book in your hand, and you were asleep in an instant.

Although I could not avoid yielding in a great measure to the general languor, still at times I contrived to shake off the spell, and to appreciate the beauty of the scene around me. The sky presented a clear expanse of the most delicate blue, except along the skirts of the horizon, where you might see a thin drapery of pale clouds which never varied their form or colour. The long, measured, dirge-like swell of the Pacific came rolling along, with its surface broken by little tiny waves, sparkling in the sunshine. Every now and then a shoal of flying fish, scared from the water under the bows, would leap into the air, and fall the next moment like a shower of silver into the sea. Then you would see the superb albicore [*sic*], with his glittering sides, sailing aloft, and often describing an arc in his descent, disappear on the surface of the water. Far off, the lofty jet of the whale might be seen, and nearer at hand the prowling shark, that villainous footpad of the seas, would come skulking along, and, at a wary distance, regard us with his evil eye. At times, some shapeless monster of the deep, floating on the surface, would, as we approached, sink slowly into the blue waters, and fade away from the sight. But the most impressive feature of the scene was the almost unbroken silence that reigned over sky and water. Scarcely a sound could be heard but the occasional breathing of the grampus, and the rippling at the cut-water.

As we drew nearer the land, I hailed with delight the appearance

◆━◆━◆━◆━◆

of innumerable sea-fowl. Screaming and whirling in spiral tracks, they would accompany the vessel, and at times alight on our yards and stays. That piratical-looking fellow, appropriately named the man-of-war's-hawk, with his blood-red bill and raven plumage, would come sweeping round us in gradually diminishing circles, till you could distinctly mark the strange flashings of his eye; and then, as if satisfied with his observation, would sail up into the air and disappear from the view. Soon, other evidences of our vicinity to the land were apparent, and it was not long before the glad announcement of its being in sight was heard from aloft,—given with that peculiar prolongation of sound that a sailor loves—'Land ho!'

The captain, darting on deck from the cabin, bawled lustily for his spy-glass; the mate in still louder accents hailed the masthead with a tremendous 'where-away?' The black cook thrust his woolly head from the galley, and Boatswain, the dog, leaped up between the knight-heads, and barked most furiously. Land ho! Aye, there it was. A hardly perceptible blue irregular outline, indicating the bold contour of the lofty heights of Nukuheva.

This island, although generally called one of the Marquesas, is by some navigators considered as forming one of a distinct cluster, comprising the islands of Ruhooka, Ropo, and Nukuheva; upon which three the appellation of the Washington Group has been bestowed. They form a triangle, and lie within the parallels of 8° 38' and 9° 32' South latitude and 139° 20' and 140° 10' West longitude from Greenwich. With how little propriety they are to be regarded as forming a separate group will be at once apparent, when it is considered that they lie in the immediate vicinity of the other islands, that is to say, less than a degree to the northwest of them; that their inhabitants speak the Marquesan dialect, and that their laws, religion, and general customs are identical. The only reason why they were ever thus arbitrarily distinguished may be attributed to the singular fact that their existence was altogether unknown to the world until the year 1791, when they were discovered by Captain Ingraham, of Boston, Massachusetts, nearly two centuries after the discovery of the adjacent islands by the agent of the Spanish Viceroy. Notwithstanding this, I shall follow the example of most voyagers, and treat of them as forming part and parcel of the Marquesas.

Nukuheva is the most important of these islands, being the only one at which ships are much in the habit of touching, and is celebrated as being the place where the adventurous Captain Porter refitted his ships during the late war between England and the United States, and whence he sallied out upon the large whaling fleet then sailing under the enemy's flag in the surrounding seas. This island is about twenty miles in length and nearly as many in breadth. It has three good harbours on its coast; the largest and best of which is called by the people living in its vicinity 'Tyohee', and by Captain Porter was denominated Massachusetts Bay. Among the adverse tribes dwelling about the shores of the other bays, and by all voyagers, it is generally known by the name bestowed upon the island itself—Nukuheva. Its inhabitants have become somewhat corrupted, owing to their recent commerce with Europeans, but so far as regards their peculiar customs and general mode of life, they retain their original primitive character, remaining very nearly in the same state of nature in which they were first beheld by white men. The hostile clans, residing in the more remote sections of the island, and very seldom holding any communication with foreigners, are in every respect unchanged from their earliest known condition.

In the bay of Nukuheva was the anchorage we desired to reach. We had perceived the loom of the mountains about sunset; so that after running all night with a very light breeze, we found ourselves close in with the island the next morning, but as the bay we sought lay on its farther side, we were obliged to sail some distance along the shore, catching, as we proceeded, short glimpses of blooming valleys, deep glens, waterfalls, and waving groves, hidden here and there by projecting and rocky headlands, every moment opening to the view some new and startling scene of beauty.

Those who for the first time visit the South Sea generally are surprised at the appearance of the islands when beheld from the sea. From the vague accounts we sometimes have of their beauty, many people are apt to picture to themselves enamelled and softly swelling plains, shaded over with delicious groves, and watered by purling brooks, and the entire country but little elevated above the surrounding ocean. The reality is very different; bold rock-bound coasts, with the surf beating high against the lofty cliffs, and broken here and there into deep inlets, which open to the view thickly-wooded valleys, separated by the spurs of mountains clothed with tufted grass, and sweeping down towards the sea from an elevated and furrowed interior, form the principal features of these islands.

Towards noon we drew abreast the entrance to the harbour, and at last we slowly swept by the intervening promontory, and entered the bay of Nukuheva. No description can do justice to its beauty; but that beauty was lost to me then, and I saw nothing but the tri-coloured flag of France trailing over the stern of six vessels, whose black hulls and bristling broadsides proclaimed their warlike character. There they were, floating in that lovely bay, the green eminences of the shore looking down so tranquilly upon them, as if rebuking the sternness of their aspect. To my eye nothing could be more out of keeping than the presence of these vessels; but we soon learnt what brought them there. The whole group of islands had just been taken possession of by Rear-Admiral Du Petit Thouars, in the name of the invincible French nation.

This item of information was imparted to us by a most extraordinary individual, a genuine South-Sea vagabond, who came alongside of us in a whale-boat as soon as we entered the bay, and, by the aid of some benevolent persons at the gangway, was assisted on board, for our visitor was in that interesting stage of intoxication when a man is amiable and helpless. Although he was utterly unable to stand erect or to navigate his body across the deck, he still magnanimously proffered his services to pilot the ship to a good and secure anchorage. Our captain, however, rather distrusted his ability in this respect, and refused to recognize his claim to the character he assumed; but our gentleman was determined to play his part, for, by dint of much scrambling, he succeeded in getting into the weather-quarter boat, where he steadied himself by holding on to a shroud, and then commenced issuing his commands with amazing volubility and very peculiar gestures. Of course no one obeyed his orders; but as it was impossible to quiet him, we swept by the ships of the squadron with this strange fellow performing his antics in full view of all the French officers.

We afterwards learned that our eccentric friend had been a lieutenant in the English navy; but having disgraced his flag by some criminal conduct in one of the principal ports on the main, he had deserted his ship, and spent many years wandering among the islands of the Pacific, until accidentally being at Nukuheva when the French took possession of the place, he had been appointed pilot of the harbour by the newly constituted authorities.

As we slowly advanced up the bay, numerous canoes pushed off from the surrounding shores, and we were soon in the midst of quite a flotilla of them, their savage occupants struggling to get aboard of us, and jostling one another in their ineffectual attempts. Occasionally the projecting out-riggers of their slight shallops, running foul of one another, would become entangled beneath the water, threatening to capsize the canoes, when a scene of confusion would ensue

that baffles description. Such strange outcries and passionate gesticulations I never certainly heard or saw before. You would have
thought the islanders were on the point of flying at one another's
throats, whereas they were only amicably engaged in disentangling
their boats.

Scattered here and there among the canoes might be seen numbers of cocoanuts floating closely together in circular groups, and
bobbing up and down with every wave. By some inexplicable means
these cocoanuts were all steadily approaching towards the ship. As I
leaned curiously over the side, endeavouring to solve their mysterious movements, one mass far in advance of the rest attracted my attention. In its centre was something I could take for nothing else
than a cocoanut, but which I certainly considered one of the most
extraordinary specimens of the fruit I had ever seen. It kept twirling
and dancing about among the rest in the most singular manner, and
as it drew nearer I thought it bore a remarkable resemblance to the
brown shaven skull of one of the savages. Presently it betrayed a pair
of eyes, and soon I became aware that what I had supposed to have
been one of the fruit was nothing else than the head of an islander,
who had adopted this singular method of bringing his produce to
market. The cocoanuts were all attached to one another by strips of
the husk, partly torn from the shell and rudely fastened together.
Their proprietor, inserting his head into the midst of them, impelled
his necklace of cocoanuts through the water by striking out beneath
the surface with his feet.

I was somewhat astonished to perceive that among the number of
natives that surrounded us, not a single female was to be seen. At
that time I was ignorant of the fact that by the operation of the 'taboo'
the use of canoes in all parts of the island is rigorously prohibited to
the entire sex, for whom it is death even to be seen entering one

when hauled on shore; consequently, whenever a Marquesan lady voyages by water, she puts in requisition the paddles of her own fair body.

We had approached within a mile and a half perhaps of the foot of the bay, when some of the islanders, who by this time had managed to scramble aboard of us at the risk of swamping their canoes, directed our attention to a singular commotion in the water ahead of the vessel. At first I imagined it to be produced by a shoal of fish sporting on the surface, but our savage friends assured us that it was caused by a shoal of 'whihenies' (young girls), who in this manner were coming off from the shore to welcome us. As they drew nearer, and I watched the rising and sinking of their forms, and beheld the uplifted right arm bearing above the water the girdle of tappa, and their long dark hair trailing beside them as they swam, I almost fancied they could be nothing else than so many mermaids:—and very like mermaids they behaved too.

We were still some distance from the beach, and under slow headway, when we sailed right into the midst of these swimming nymphs, and they boarded us at every quarter; many seizing hold of the chain-plates and springing into the chains; others, at the peril of being run over by the vessel in her course, catching at the bob-stays, and wreathing their slender forms about the ropes, hung suspended in the air. All of them at length succeeded in getting up the ship's side, where they clung dripping with the brine and glowing from the bath, their jet-black tresses streaming over their shoulders, and half enveloping their otherwise naked forms. There they hung, sparkling with savage vivacity, laughing gaily at one another, and chattering away with infinite glee. Nor were they idle the while, for each one performed the simple offices of the toilette for the other. Their luxuriant locks, wound up and twisted into the smallest possible compass, were freed from the briny element; the whole person carefully dried, and from a little round shell that passed from hand to hand, anointed with a fragrant oil: their adornments were completed by passing a few loose folds of white tappa, in a modest cincture, around the waist. Thus arrayed they no longer hesitated, but flung themselves lightly over the bulwarks, and were quickly frolicking about the decks. Many of them went forward, perching upon the headrails or running out upon the bowsprit, while others seated themselves upon the taffrail, or reclined at full length upon the boats. What a sight for us bachelor sailors! How avoid so dire a temptation? For who could think of tumbling these artless creatures over board, when they had swum miles to welcome us?

Their appearance perfectly amazed me; their extreme youth, the light clear brown of their complexions, their delicate features, and inexpressibly graceful figures, their softly moulded limbs, and free unstudied action, seemed as strange as beautiful.

The *Dolly* was fairly captured; and never I will say was vessel carried before by such a dashing and irresistible party of boarders! The ship taken, we could not do otherwise than yield ourselves prisoners, and for the whole period that she remained in the bay, the *Dolly*, as well as her crew, were completely in the hands of the mermaids.

In the evening after we had come to an anchor the deck was illuminated with lanterns, and this picturesque band of sylphs, tricked out with flowers, and dressed in robes of variegated tappa, got up a ball in great style. These females are passionately fond of dancing, and in the wild grace and spirit of the style excel everything that I have ever seen. The varied dances of the Marquesan girls are beautiful in the extreme, but there is an abandoned voluptuousness in their character which I dare not attempt to describe.

Our ship was now wholly given up to every species of riot and debauchery. Not the feeblest barrier was interposed between the unholy passions of the crew and their unlimited gratification. The grossest licentiousness and the most shameful inebriety prevailed, with occasional and but short-lived interruptions, through the whole period of her stay. Alas for the poor savages when exposed to the influence of these polluting examples! Unsophisticated and confiding, they are easily led into every vice, and humanity weeps over the ruin thus remorselessly inflicted upon them by their European civilizers. Thrice happy are they who, inhabiting some yet undiscovered island in the midst of the ocean, have never been brought into contaminating contact with the white man.

CHAPTER FIFTEEN

All the inhabitants of the valley treated me with great kindness; but as to the household of Marheyo, with whom I was now permanently domiciled, nothing could surpass their efforts to minister to my comfort. To the gratification of my palate they paid the most unwearied attention. They continually invited me to partake of food, and when after eating heartily I declined the viands they continued to offer me, they seemed to think that my appetite stood in need of some piquant stimulant to excite its activity.

In pursuance of this idea, old Marheyo himself would hie him away to the sea-shore by the break of day, for the purpose of collecting various species of rare sea-weed; some of which among these people are considered a great luxury. After a whole day spent in this employment, he would return about nightfall with several cocoanut shells filled with different descriptions of kelp. In preparing these for use he manifested all the ostentation of a professed cook, although the chief mystery of the affair appeared to consist in pouring water in judicious quantities upon the slimy contents of his cocoanut shells.

The first time he submitted one of these saline salads to my criti-

◆—◆—◆—◆—◆

cal attention I naturally thought that anything collected at such pains must possess peculiar merits; but one mouthful was a complete dose; and great was the consternation of the old warrior at the rapidity with which I ejected his Epicurean treat.

How true it is, that the rarity of any particular article enhances its value amazingly. In some part of the valley—I know not where, but probably in the neighbourhood of the sea—the girls were sometimes in the habit of procuring small quantities of salt, a thimble-full or so being the result of the united labours of a party of five or six employed for the greater part of the day. This precious commodity they brought to the house, enveloped in multitudinous folds of leaves; and as a special mark of the esteem in which they held me, would spread an immense leaf on the ground, and dropping one by one a few minute particles of the salt upon it, invite me to taste them.

From the extravagant value placed upon the article, I verily believe, that with a bushel of common Liverpool salt all the real estate in Typee might have been purchased. With a small pinch of it in one hand, and a quarter section of a bread-fruit in the other, the greatest chief in the valley would have laughed at all luxuries of a Parisian table.

The celebrity of the bread-fruit tree, and the conspicuous place it occupies in a Typee bill of fare, induces me to give at some length a general description of the tree, and the various modes in which the fruit is prepared.

The bread-fruit tree, in its glorious prime, is a grand and towering object, forming the same feature in a Marquesan landscape that the patriarchal elm does in New England scenery. The latter tree it not a little resembles in height, in the wide spread of its stalwart branches, and in its venerable and imposing aspect.

The leaves of the bread-fruit are of great size, and their edges are cut and scolloped as fantastically as those of a lady's lace collar. As they annually tend towards decay, they almost rival in brilliant variety of their gradually changing hues the fleeting shades of the expiring dolphin. The autumnal tints of our American forests, glorious as they are, sink into nothing in comparison with this tree.

The leaf, in one particular stage, when nearly all the prismatic colours are blended on its surface, is often converted by the natives into a superb and striking head-dress. The principal fibre traversing its length being split open a convenient distance, and the elastic sides of the aperture pressed apart, the head is inserted between them, the leaf drooping on one side, with its forward half turned jauntily up on the brows, and the remaining part spreading laterally behind the ears.

The fruit somewhat resembles in magnitude and general appearance one of our citron melons of ordinary size; but, unlike the citron, it has no sectional lines drawn along the outside. Its surface is dotted all over with little conical prominences, looking not unlike the knobs on an antiquated church door. The rind is perhaps an eighth of an inch in thickness; and denuded of this at the time when it is in the greatest perfection, the fruit presents a beautiful globe of white pulp, the whole of which may be eaten, with the exception of a slender core, which is easily removed.

The bread-fruit, however, is never used, and is indeed altogether unfit to be eaten, until submitted in one form or other to the action of fire.

The most simple manner in which this operation is performed, and I think, the best, consists in placing any number of the freshly plucked fruit, when in a particular state of greenness, among the embers of a fire, in the same way that you would roast a potato. After the lapse of ten or fifteen minutes, the green rind embrowns and cracks, showing through the fissures in its sides the milk-white interior. As soon as it cools the rind drops off, and you then have the

◆◆◆◆◆

soft round pulp in its purest and most delicious state. Thus eaten, it has a mild and pleasing flavour.

Sometimes after having been roasted in the fire, the natives snatch it briskly from the embers, and permitting it to slip out of the yielding rind into a vessel of cold water, stir up the mixture, which they call 'bo-a-sho'. I never could endure this compound, and indeed the preparation is not greatly in vogue among the more polite Typees.

There is one form, however, in which the fruit is occasionally served, that renders it a dish fit for a king. As soon as it is taken from the fire the exterior is removed, the core extracted, and the remaining part is placed in a sort of shallow stone mortar, and briskly worked with a pestle of the same substance. While one person is performing this operation, another takes a ripe cocoanut, and breaking it in halves, which they also do very cleverly, proceeds to grate the juicy meat into fine particles. This is done by means of a piece of mother-of-pearl shell, lashed firmly to the extreme end of a heavy stick, with its straight side accurately notched like a saw. The stick is sometimes a grotesquely-formed limb of a tree, with three or four branches twisting from its body like so many shapeless legs, and sustaining it two or three feet from the ground.

The native, first placing a calabash beneath the nose, as it were, of his curious-looking log-steed, for the purpose of receiving the grated fragments as they fall, mounts astride of it as if it were a hobby-horse, and twirling the inside of his hemispheres of cocoanut around the sharp teeth of the mother-of-pearl shell, the pure white meat falls in snowy showers into the receptacle provided. Having obtained a quantity for his purpose, he places it in a bag made of the net-like fibrous substance attached to all cocoanut trees, and compressing it over the bread-fruit, which being now sufficiently pounded, is put into a wooden bowl—extracts a thick creamy milk.

◆—◆—◆—◆

The delicious liquid soon bubbles round the fruit, and leaves it at last just peeping above its surface.

This preparation is called 'kokoo', and a most luscious preparation it is. The hobby-horse and the pestle and mortar were in great requisition during the time I remained in the house of Marheyo, and Kory-Kory had frequent occasion to show his skill in their use.

But the great staple articles of food into which the bread-fruit is converted by these natives are known respectively by the names of Amar and Poee-Poee.

At a certain season of the year, when the fruit of the hundred groves of the valley has reached its maturity, and hangs in golden spheres from every branch, the islanders assemble in harvest groups, and garner in the abundance which surrounds them. The trees are stripped of their nodding burdens, which, easily freed from the rind and core, are gathered together in capacious wooden vessels, where the pulpy fruit is soon worked by a stone pestle, vigorously applied, into a blended mass of a doughy consistency, called by the natives 'Tutao'. This is then divided into separate parcels, which, after being made up into stout packages, enveloped in successive folds of leaves, and bound round with thongs of bark, are stored away in large receptacles hollowed in the earth, from whence they are drawn as occasion may require.

In this condition the Tutao sometimes remains for years, and even is thought to improve by age. Before it is fit to be eaten, however, it has to undergo an additional process. A primitive oven is scooped in the ground, and its bottom being loosely covered with stones, a large fire is kindled within it. As soon as the requisite degree of heat is attained, the embers are removed, and the surface of the stones being covered with thick layers of leaves, one of the large packages of Tutao is deposited upon them and overspread with another layer of leaves. The whole is then quickly heaped up with earth, and forms a sloping mound.

The Tutao thus baked is called Amar; the action of the oven having converted it into an amber-coloured caky substance, a little tart, but not at all disagreeable to the taste.

By another and final process the Amar is changed into Poee-Poee. This transition is rapidly effected. The Amar is placed in a vessel, and mixed with water until it gains a proper pudding-like consistency, when, without further preparation, it is in readiness for use. This is the form in which the Tutao is generally consumed. The singular mode of eating it I have already described.

Were it not that the bread-fruit is thus capable of being preserved for a length of time, the natives might be reduced to a state of starvation; for owing to some unknown cause the trees sometimes fail to bear fruit; and on such occasions the islanders chiefly depend upon the supplies they have been enabled to store away.

This stately tree, which is rarely met with upon the Sandwich Islands, and then only of a very inferior quality, and at Tahiti does not abound to a degree that renders its fruit the principal article of food, attains its greatest excellence in the genial climate of the Marquesan group, where it grows to an enormous magnitude, and flourishes in the utmost abundance.

CHAPTER SEVENTEEN

Day after day wore on, and still there was no perceptible change in the conduct of the islanders towards me. Gradually I lost all knowledge of the regular recurrence of the days of the week, and sunk insensibly into that kind of apathy which ensues after some violent outburst of despair. My limb suddenly healed, the swelling went down, the pain subsided, and I had every reason to suppose I should soon completely recover from the affliction that had so long tormented me.

As soon as I was enabled to ramble about the valley in company with the natives, troops of whom followed me whenever I sallied out of the house, I began to experience an elasticity of mind which placed me beyond the reach of those dismal forebodings to which I had so lately been a prey. Received wherever I went with the most deferential kindness; regaled perpetually with the most delightful fruits; ministered to by dark-eyed nymphs, and enjoying besides all the services of the devoted Kory-Kory, I thought that, for a sojourn among cannibals, no man could have well made a more agreeable one.

To be sure there were limits set to my wanderings. Toward the sea my progress was barred by an express prohibition of the savages; and after having made two or three ineffectual attempts to reach it, as much to gratify my curiosity as anything else, I gave up the idea. It was in vain to think of reaching it by stealth, since the natives escorted me in numbers wherever I went, and not for one single moment that I can recall to mind was I ever permitted to be alone.

The green and precipitous elevations that stood ranged around the head of the vale where Marheyo's habitation was situated effectually precluded all hope of escape in that quarter, even if I could have stolen away from the thousand eyes of the savages.

But these reflections now seldom obtruded upon me; I gave myself up to the passing hour, and if ever disagreeable thoughts arose in my mind, I drove them away. When I looked around the verdant recess in which I was buried, and gazed up to the summits of the lofty eminence that hemmed me in, I was well disposed to think that I was in the 'Happy Valley', and that beyond those heights there was naught but a world of care and anxiety.

◆ ◆ ◆ ◆ ◆

As I extended my wanderings in the valley and grew more familiar with the habits of its inmates, I was fain to confess that, despite the disadvantages of his condition, the Polynesian savage, surrounded by all the luxurious provisions of nature, enjoyed an infinitely happier, though certainly a less intellectual existence than the self-complacent European.

The naked wretch who shivers beneath the bleak skies, and starves among the inhospitable wilds of Tierra-del-Fuego, might indeed be made happier by civilization, for it would alleviate his physical wants. But the voluptuous Indian, with every desire supplied, whom Providence has bountifully provided with all the sources of pure and natural enjoyment, and from whom are removed so many of the ills and pains of life—what has he to desire at the hands of Civilization? She may 'cultivate his mind'—may 'elevate his thoughts,'—these I believe are the established phrases—but will he be the happier? Let the once smiling and populous Hawaiian Islands, with their now diseased, starving, and dying natives, answer the question. The missionaries may seek to disguise the matter as they will, but the facts are incontrovertible; and the devoutest Christian who visits that group with an unbiased mind, must go away mournfully asking—'Are these, alas! the fruits of twenty-five years of enlightening?'

In a primitive state of society, the enjoyments of life, though few and simple, are spread over a great extent, and are unalloyed; but Civilization, for every advantage she imparts, holds a hundred evils in reserve;—the heart-burnings, the jealousies, the social rivalries, the family dissensions, and the thousand self-inflicted discomforts of refined life, which make up in units the swelling aggregate of human misery, are unknown among these unsophisticated people.

But it will be urged that these shocking unprincipled wretches are cannibals. Very true; and a rather bad trait in their character it must

◆—◆—◆—◆—◆

be allowed. But they are such only when they seek to gratify the passion of revenge upon their enemies; and I ask whether the mere eating of human flesh so very far exceeds in barbarity that custom which only a few years since was practised in enlightened England:—a convicted traitor, perhaps a man found guilty of honesty, patriotism, and suchlike heinous crimes, had his head lopped off with a huge axe, his bowels dragged out and thrown into a fire; while his body, carved into four quarters, was with his head exposed upon pikes, and permitted to rot and fester among the public haunts of men!

The fiend-like skill we display in the invention of all manner of death-dealing engines, the vindictiveness with which we carry on our wars, and the misery and desolation that follow in their train, are enough of themselves to distinguish the white civilized man as the most ferocious animal on the face of the earth.

His remorseless cruelty is seen in many of the institutions of our own favoured land. There is one in particular lately adopted in one of the States of the Union which purports to have been dictated by the most merciful considerations. To destroy our malefactors piecemeal, drying up in their veins, drop by drop, the blood we are too chicken-hearted to shed by a single blow which would at once put a period to their sufferings, is deemed to be infinitely preferable to the old-fashioned punishment of gibbeting—much less annoying to the victim, and more in accordance with the refined spirit of the age; and yet how feeble is all language to describe the horrors we inflict upon these wretches, whom we mason up in the cells of our prisons, and condemn to perpetual solitude in the very heart of our population.

But it is needless to multiply the examples of civilized barbarity; they far exceed in the amount of misery they cause the crimes which

◆—◆—◆—◆—◆

we regard with such abhorrence in our less enlightened fellow-creatures.

The term 'Savage' is, I conceive, often misapplied, and indeed, when I consider the vices, cruelties, and enormities of every kind that spring up in the tainted atmosphere of a feverish civilization, I am inclined to think that so far as the relative wickedness of the parties is concerned, four or five Marquesan Islanders sent to the United States as Missionaries might be quite as useful as an equal number of Americans despatched to the Islands in a similar capacity.

I once heard it given as an instance of the frightful depravity of a certain tribe in the Pacific that they had no word in their language to express the idea of virtue. The assertion was unfounded; but were it otherwise, it might be met by stating that their language is almost entirely destitute of terms to express the delightful ideas conveyed by our endless catalogue of civilized crimes.

In the altered frame of mind to which I have referred, every object that presented itself to my notice in the valley struck me in a new light, and the opportunities I now enjoyed of observing the manners of its inmates tended to strengthen my favourable impressions. One peculiarity that fixed my admiration was the perpetual hilarity reigning through the whole extent of the vale. There seemed to be no cares, griefs, troubles, or vexations, in all Typee. The hours tripped along as gaily as the laughing couples down a country dance.

There were none of those thousand sources of irritation that the ingenuity of civilized man has created to mar his own felicity. There were no foreclosures of mortgages, no protested notes, no bills payable, no debts of honour in Typee; no unreasonable tailors and shoemakers, perversely bent on being paid; no duns of any description; no assault and battery attorneys, to foment discord, backing their clients up to a quarrel, and then knocking their heads together; no poor relations, everlastingly occupying the spare bed-chamber, and diminishing the elbow room at the family table; no destitute widows with their children starving on the cold charities of the world; no beggars; no debtors' prisons; no proud and hard-hearted nabobs in Typee; or to sum up all in one word—no Money! 'That root of all evil' was not to be found in the valley.

In this secluded abode of happiness there were no cross old women, no cruel step-dames, no withered spinsters, no lovesick maidens, no sour old bachelors, no inattentive husbands, no melancholy young men, no blubbering youngsters, and no squalling brats. All was mirth, fun, and high good humour. Blue devils, hypochondria, and doleful dumps went and hid themselves among the nooks and crannies of the rocks.

Here you would see a parcel of children frolicking together the live-long day, and no quarrelling, no contention, among them. The same number in our own land could not have played together for the space of an hour without biting or scratching one another. There you might have seen a throng of young females, not filled with envyings of each other's charms, nor displaying the ridiculous affectations of gentility, nor yet moving in whalebone corsets, like so many automatons, but free, inartificially happy, and unconstrained.

There were some spots in that sunny vale where they would frequently resort to decorate themselves with garlands of flowers. To have seen them reclining beneath the shadows of one of the beautiful groves, the ground about them strewn with freshly gathered buds and blossoms, employed in weaving chaplets and necklaces, one would have thought that all the train of Flora had gathered together to keep a festival in honour of their mistress.

With the young men there seemed almost always some matter of diversion or business on hand that afforded a constant variety of enjoyment. But whether fishing, or carving canoes, or polishing their ornaments, never was there exhibited the least sign of strife or contention among them.

As for the warriors, they maintained a tranquil dignity of demeanour, journeying occasionally from house to house, where they were always sure to be received with the attention bestowed upon distinguished guests. The old men, of whom there were many in the vale, seldom stirred from their mats, where they would recline for hours and hours, smoking and talking to one another with all the garrulity of age.

But the continual happiness, which so far as I was able to judge appeared to prevail in the valley, sprang principally from that all-pervading sensation which Rousseau has told us he at one time experienced, the mere buoyant sense of a healthful physical existence. And indeed in this particular the Typees had ample reason to felicitate themselves, for sickness was almost unknown. During the whole period of my stay I saw but one invalid among them; and on their smooth skins you observed no blemish or mark of disease.

The general repose, however, upon which I have just been descanting, was broken in upon about this time by an event which proved that the islanders were not entirely exempt from those occurrences which disturb the quiet of more civilized communities.

Having now been a considerable time in the valley, I began to feel surprised that the violent hostility subsisting between its inhabitants, and those of the adjoining bay of Happar, should never have manifested itself in any warlike encounter. Although the valiant Typees would often by gesticulations declare their undying hatred against their enemies, and the disgust they felt at their cannibal propensities; although they dilated upon the manifold injuries they had received at their hands, yet with a forbearance truly commendable, they appeared to sit down under their grievances, and to refrain from making any reprisals. The Happars, entrenched behind their mountains, and never even showing themselves on their summits, did not appear to me to furnish adequate cause for that excess of animosity evinced towards them by the heroic tenants of our vale, and I was inclined to believe that the deeds of blood attributed to them had been greatly exaggerated.

On the other hand, as the clamours of war had not up to this period disturbed the serenity of the tribe, I began to distrust the truth of those reports which ascribed so fierce and belligerent a character to the Typee nation. Surely, thought I, all these terrible stories I have heard about the inveteracy with which they carried on the feud, their deadly intensity of hatred and the diabolical malice with which they glutted their revenge upon the inanimate forms of the slain, are nothing more than fables, and I must confess that I experienced something like a sense of regret at having my hideous anticipations thus disappointed. I felt in some sort like a 'prentice boy who, going to the play in the expectation of being delighted with a cut-and-thrust tragedy, is almost moved to tears of disappointment at the exhibition of a genteel comedy.

I could not avoid thinking that I had fallen in with a greatly traduced people, and I moralized not a little upon the disadvantage of having a bad name, which in this instance had given a tribe of savages, who were as pacific as so many lambkins, the reputation of a confederacy of giant-killers.

But subsequent events proved that I had been a little too premature in coming to this conclusion. One day about noon, happening to be at the Ti, I had lain down on the mats with several of the chiefs, and had gradually sunk into a most luxurious siesta, when I was awakened by a tremendous outcry, and starting up beheld the natives seizing their spears and hurrying out, while the most puissant of the chiefs, grasping the six muskets which were ranged against

◆—◆—◆—◆—◆

the bamboos, followed after, and soon disappeared in the groves. These movements were accompanied by wild shouts, in which 'Happar, Happar,' greatly predominated. The islanders were now seen running past the Ti, and striking across the valley to the Happar side. Presently I heard the sharp report of a musket from the adjoining hills, and then a burst of voices in the same direction. At this the women who had congregated in the groves set up the most violent clamours, as they invariably do here as elsewhere on every occasion of excitement and alarm, with a view of tranquillizing their own minds and disturbing other people. On this particular occasion they made such an outrageous noise, and continued it with such perseverance, that for a while, had entire volleys of musketry been fired off in the neighboring mountains, I should not have been able to have heard them.

When this female commotion had a little subsided I listened eagerly for further information. At last, bang went another shot, and then a second volley of yells from the hills. Again all was quiet, and continued so for such a length of time that I began to think the contending armies had agreed upon a suspension of hostilities; when pop went a third gun, followed as before with a yell. After this, for nearly two hours nothing occurred worthy of comment, save some straggling shouts from the hillside, sounding like the halloos of a parcel of truant boys who had lost themselves in the woods.

During this interval I had remained standing on the piazza of the Ti, which directly fronted the Happar mountain, and with no one near me but Kory-Kory and the old superannuated savages I have described. These latter never stirred from their mats, and seemed altogether unconscious that anything unusual was going on.

As for Kory-Kory, he appeared to think that we were in the midst of great events, and sought most zealously to impress me with a due sense of their importance. Every sound that reached us conveyed some momentous item of intelligence to him. At such times, as if he were gifted wth second sight, he would go through a variety of pantomimic illustrations, showing me the precise manner in which the redoubtable Typees were at that very moment chastising the insolence of the enemy. 'Mehevi hanna pippee nuee Happar,' he exclaimed every five minutes, giving me to understand that under that distinguished captain the warriors of his nation were performing prodigies of valour.

Having heard only four reports from the muskets, I was led to believe that they were worked by the islanders in the same manner as the Sultan Solyman's ponderous artillery at the siege of Byzantium, one of them taking an hour or two to load and train. At last, no sound whatever proceeding from the mountains, I concluded that the contest had been determined one way or the other. Such appeared, indeed, to be the case, for in a little while a courier arrived at the Ti, almost breathless with his exertions, and communicated the news of a great victory having been achieved by his countrymen: 'Happar poo arva!—Happar poo arva!' (the cowards had fled). Kory-Kory was in ecstasies, and commenced a vehement harangue, which, so far as I understood it, implied that the result exactly agreed with his expectations, and which, moreover, was intended to convince me that it would be a perfectly useless undertaking, even for an army of fire-eaters, to offer battle to the irresistible heroes of our valley. In all this I of course acquiesced, and looked forward with no little interest to the return of the conquerors, whose victory I feared might not have been purchased without cost to themselves.

But here I was again mistaken; for Mehevi, in conducting his warlike operations, rather inclined to the Fabian than to the Bonapartean tactics, husbanding his resources and exposing his troops to no unnecessary hazards. The total loss of the victors in this obstinately contested affair was, in killed, wounded, and missing—one forefin-

◆ ◆ ◆ ◆ ◆

ger and part of a thumb-nail (which the late proprietor brought along with him in his hand), a severely contused arm, and a considerable effusion of blood flowing from the thigh of a chief, who had received an ugly thrust from a Happar spear. What the enemy had suffered I could not discover, but I presume they had succeeded in taking off with them the bodies of their slain.

Such was the issue of the battle, as far as its results came under my observation: and as it appeared to be considered an event of prodigious importance, I reasonably concluded that the wars of the natives were marked by no very sanguinary traits. I afterwards learned how the skirmish had originated. A number of the Happars had been discovered prowling for no good purpose on the Typee side of the mountain; the alarm sounded, and the invaders, after a protracted resistance, had been chased over the frontier. But why had not the intrepid Mehevi carried the war into Happar? Why had he not made a descent into the hostile vale, and brought away some trophy of his victory—some materials for the cannibal entertainment which I had heard usually terminated every engagement? After all, I was much inclined to believe that these shocking festivals must occur very rarely among the islanders, if, indeed, they ever take place.

For two or three days the late event was the theme of general comment; after which the excitement gradually wore away, and the valley resumed its accustomed tranquillity.

5

TAHITI

CHARLES DARWIN

October 20th.—The survey of the Galápagos Archipelago being concluded, we steered towards Tahiti and commenced our long passage of 3200 miles. In the course of a few days we sailed out of the gloomy and clouded ocean district which extends during the winter far from the coast of South America. We then enjoyed bright and clear weather, while running pleasantly along at the rate of about 60 miles a day before the steady trade-wind. The temperature of this more central part of the Pacific is higher than near the American shore. The thermometer in the poop cabin, by night and day, ranged between 80° and 83°, which feels very pleasant; but with one degree or two higher, the heat becomes oppressive. We passed through the Low or Dangerous Archipelago, and saw several of those most curious rings of coral land, just rising above the water's edge, which have been called Lagoon Islands. A long and brilliantly-white beach is capped by a margin of green vegetation; and the strip, looking either way, rapidly narrows away in the distance and sinks beneath the horizon. From the masthead a wide expanse of smooth water can be seen within the ring. These low hollow coral islands bear no proportion to the vast ocean out of which they abruptly rise; and it seems wonderful that such weak invaders are not overwhelmed by the all-powerful and never-tiring waves of that great sea, miscalled the Pacific.

November 15th.—At daylight, Tahiti, an island which must for ever remain classical to the voyager in the South Sea, was in view. At a distance the appearance was not attractive. The luxuriant vegetation of the lower part could not yet be seen, and as the clouds rolled past, the wildest and most precipitous peaks showed themselves towards the centre of the island. As soon as we anchored in Matavai Bay, we were surrounded by canoes. This was our Sunday, but the Monday of Tahiti; if the case had been reversed, we should not have received a single visit; for the injunction not to launch a canoe on the Sabbath is rigidly obeyed. After dinner we landed to enjoy all the delights produced by the first impressions of a new country, and that country the charming Tahiti. A crowd of men, women, and children was collected on the memorable Point Venus, ready to receive us with laughing, merry faces. They marshalled us towards the house of Mr Wilson, the missionary of the district, who met us on the road, and gave us a very friendly reception. After sitting a short time in his house, we separated to walk about, but returned there in the evening.

The land capable of cultivation is scarcely in any part more than a fringe of low alluvial soil, accumulated round the base of the mountains, and protected from the waves of the sea by a coral reef, which encircles the entire line of coast. Within the reef there is an expanse of smooth water, like that of a lake, where the canoes of the natives can ply with safety and where ships anchor. The low land which comes down to the beach of coral-sand, is covered by the most beautiful productions of the intertropical regions. In the midst of bananas, orange, cocoa-nut, and bread-fruit trees, spots are cleared where yams, sweet potatoes, the sugar-cane, and pine-apples are cultivated. Even the brushwood is an imported fruit-tree—namely, the guava—which from its abundance has become as noxious as a weed. In Brazil I have often admired the varied beauties of the bananas, palms, and orange-trees contrasted together; and here we also have the bread-fruit, conspicuous from its large, glossy, and deeply digitated leaf. It is admirable to behold groves of a tree, sending forth its branches with the vigour of an English oak, loaded with large and most nutritious fruit. However seldom the usefulness of an object can account for the pleasure of beholding it, in the case of these beautiful woods, the knowledge of their high productiveness no doubt enters largely into the feeling of admiration. The little winding paths, cool from the surrounding shade, led to the scattered houses; the owners of which everywhere gave us a cheerful and most hospitable reception.

I was pleased with nothing so much as with the inhabitants. There is a mildness in the expression of their countenances which at once banishes the idea of a savage, and an intelligence which shows that they are advancing in civilisation. The common people, when working, keep the upper part of their bodies quite naked: and it is then that the Tahitians are seen to advantage. They are very tall, broad-shouldered, athletic, and well-proportioned. It has been remarked, that it requires little habit to make a dark skin more pleasing and natural to the eye of a European than his own colour. A white man bathing by the side of a Tahitian was like a plant bleached by the gardener's art compared with a fine dark green one growing vigorously in the open fields. Most of the men are tatooed, and the ornaments follow the curvature of the body so gracefully that they have a very elegant effect. One common pattern, varying in its details, is somewhat like the crown of a palm-tree. It springs from the central line of the back, and gracefully curls round both sides. The simile may be a fanciful one, but I thought the body of a man thus ornamented was like the trunk of a noble tree embraced by a delicate creeper.

Many of the elder people had their feet covered with small figures, so placed as to resemble a sock. This fashion, however, is partly gone by, and has been succeeded by others. Here, although fashion is far from immutable, every one must abide by that prevailing in his youth. An old man has thus his age for ever stamped on his body, and he cannot assume the airs of a young dandy. The women are tatooed in the same manner as the men, and very commonly on their fingers. One unbecoming fashion is now almost universal—namely, shaving the hair from the upper part of the head, in a circular form, so as to leave only an outer ring. The missionaries have tried to persuade the people to change this habit; but it is the fashion, and that is a sufficient answer at Tahiti as well as at Paris. I was much disappointed in the personal appearance of the women; they are far inferior in every respect to the men. The custom of wearing a white or scarlet flower in the back of the head, or through a small hole in each ear, is pretty. A crown of woven cocoa-nut leaves is also worn as a shade for the eyes. The women appear to be in greater want of some becoming costume even than the men.

Nearly all the natives understand a little English—that is, they know the names of common things; and by the aid of this, together with signs, a lame sort of conversation could be carried on. In returning in the evening to the boat, we stopped to witness a very pretty scene. Numbers of children were playing on the beach, and had lighted bonfires, which illuminated the placid sea and surrounding trees; others, in circles, were singing Tahitian verses. We seated ourselves on the sand, and joined their party. The songs were impromptu, and I believe related to our arrival: one little girl sang a line, which the rest took up in parts, forming a very pretty chorus. The whole scene made us unequivocally aware that we were seated on the shores of an island in the far-famed South Sea.

November 17th.—This day is reckoned in the log-book as Tuesday the 17th, instead of Monday the 16th, owing to our, so far, successful chase of the sun. Before breakfast the ship was hemmed in by a flotilla of canoes; and when the natives were allowed to come on board I suppose there could not have been less than two hundred. It was the opinion of every one that it would have been difficult to have picked out an equal number from any other nation who would have given so little trouble. Everybody brought something for sale: shells were the main article of trade. The Tahitians now fully understand the value of money, and prefer it to old clothes or other articles. The various coins, however, of English and Spanish denomination puzzle them, and they never seemed to think the small silver quite secure until changed into dollars. Some of the chiefs have accumulated considerable sums of money. One chief, not long since, offered 800 dollars (about 160 pounds sterling) for a small vessel; and frequently they purchase whale-boats and horses at the rate of from 50 to 100 dollars.

After breakfast I went on shore, and ascended the nearest slope to a height of between two and three thousand feet. The outer mountains are smooth and conical, but steep; and the old volcanic rocks, of which they are formed, have been cut through by many profound ravines, diverging from the central broken parts of the island to the coast. Having crossed the narrow low girt of inhabited and fertile land, I followed a smooth steep ridge between two of the deep ravines. The vegetation was singular, consisting almost exclusively of small dwarf ferns, mingled, higher up, with coarse grass; it was not very dissimilar from that on some of the Welsh hills, and this so close above the orchard of tropical plants on the coast was very surprising.

◄━●━●━●━●

At the highest point which I reached trees again appeared. Of the three zones of comparative luxuriance, the lower one owes its moisture, and therefore fertility, to its flatness; for, being scarcely raised above the level of the sea, the water from the higher land drains away slowly. The intermediate zone does not, like the upper one, reach into a damp and cloudy atmosphere, and therefore remains sterile. The woods in the upper zone are very pretty, tree-ferns replacing the cocoa-nuts on the coast. It must not, however, be supposed that these woods at all equal in splendour the forests of Brazil. The vast number of productions which characterise a continent cannot be expected to occur in an island.

From the highest point which I attained there was a good view of the distant island of Eimeo, dependent on the same sovereign with Tahiti. On the lofty and broken pinnacles white massive clouds were piled up, which formed an island in the blue sky, as Eimeo itself did in the blue ocean. The island, with the exception of one small gateway, is completely encircled by a reef. At this distance a narrow but well-defined brilliantly white line was alone visible, where the waves first encountered the wall of coral. The mountains rose abruptly out of the glassy expanse of the lagoon included within this narrow white line, outside which the heaving waters of the ocean were dark-coloured. The view was striking: it may aptly be compared to a framed engraving, where the frame represents the breakers, the marginal paper the smooth lagoon, and the drawing the island itself. When in the evening I descended from the mountain, a man, whom I had pleased with a trifling gift, met me, bringing with him hot roasted bananas, a pine-apple, and cocoa-nuts. After walking under a burning sun, I do not know anything more delicious than the milk of a young cocoa-nut. Pine-apples are here so abundant that the people eat them in the same wasteful manner as we might turnips. They are of an excellent flavour—perhaps even better than those

◆◆◆◆◆

cultivated in England; and this I believe is the highest compliment which can be paid to any fruit. Before going on board, Mr Wilson interpreted for me to the Tahitian who had paid me so adroit an attention that I wanted him and another man to accompany me on a short excursion into the mountains.

November 18th.—In the morning I came on shore early, bringing with me some provisions in a bag, and two blankets for myself and servant. These were lashed to each end of a long pole, which was alternately carried by my Tahitian companions on their shoulders. These men are accustomed thus to carry, for a whole day, as much as fifty pounds at each end of their poles. I told my guides to provide themselves with food and clothing; but they said that there was plenty of food in the mountains, and for clothing, that their skins were sufficient. Our line of march was the valley of Tia-auru, down which a river flows into the sea by Point Venus. This is one of the principal streams in the island, and its source lies at the base of the loftiest central pinnacles, which rise to a height of about 7000 feet. The whole island is so mountainous that the only way to penetrate into the interior is to follow up the valleys. Our road at first lay through woods which bordered each side of the river; and the glimpses of the lofty central peaks, seen as through an avenue, with here and there a waving cocoa-nut tree on one side, were extremely picturesque. The valley soon began to narrow, and the sides to grow lofty and more precipitous. After having walked between three and four hours, we found the width of the ravine scarcely exceeded that of the bed of the stream. On each hand the walls were nearly vertical; yet from the soft nature of the volcanic strata, trees and rank vegetation sprang from every projecting ledge. These precipices must have been some thousand feet high; and the whole formed a mountain gorge far more magnificent than anything which I had ever before beheld. Until the mid-day sun stood vertically over the ravine, the air felt cool and damp, but now it became very sultry. Shaded by a ledge of rock, beneath a façade of columnar lava, we ate our dinner. My guides had already procured a dish of small fish and freshwater prawns. They carried with them a small net stretched on a hoop; and where the water was deep and in eddies, they dived, and, like otters, with their eyes open, followed the fish into holes and corners, and thus caught them.

The Tahitians have the dexterity of amphibious animals in the water. An anecdote mentioned by Ellis shows how much they feel at home in this element. When a horse was landing for Pomare in 1817, the slings broke, and it fell into the water; immediately the natives jumped overboard, and by their cries and vain efforts at assistance almost drowned it. As soon, however, as it reached the shore, the whole population took to flight, and tried to hide themselves from the man-carrying pig, as they christened the horse.

A little higher up the river divided itself into three little streams. The two northern ones were impracticable, owing to a succession of waterfalls which descended from the jagged summit of the highest mountains; the other to all appearance was equally inaccessible, but we managed to ascend it by a most extraordinary road. The sides of the valley were here nearly precipitous; but, as frequently happens with stratified rocks, small ledges projected, which were thickly covered by wild bananas, liliaceous plants, and other luxuriant products of the tropics. The Tahitians, by climbing amongst these ledges, searching for fruit, had discovered a track by which the whole precipice could be scaled. The first ascent from the valley was very dangerous; for it was necessary to pass a steeply-inclined face of naked rock by the aid of ropes which we brought with us. How any person discovered that this formidable spot was the only point where the side of the mountain was practicable, I cannot imagine. We then cautiously walked along one of the ledges till we came to one of the three streams. This ledge formed a flat spot, above which a beautiful cascade, some hundred feet in height, poured down its waters, and beneath, another high cascade fell into the main stream in the valley below. From this cool and shady recess we made a circuit to avoid the overhanging waterfall. As before, we followed little projecting ledges, the danger being partly concealed by the thickness of the vegetation. In passing from one of the ledges to another there was a vertical wall of rock. One of the Tahitians, a fine active man, placed the trunk of a tree against this, climbed up it, and then by the aid of crevices reached the summit. He fixed the ropes to a projecting point, and lowered them for our dog and luggage, and then we clambered up ourselves. Beneath the ledge on which the dead tree was placed the precipice must have been five or six hundred feet deep; and if the abyss had not been partly concealed by the overhanging ferns and lilies my head would have turned giddy, and nothing should have induced me to have attempted it. We continued to ascend, sometimes along ledges, and sometimes along knife-edged ridges, having on each hand profound ravines. In the Cordillera I have seen mountains on a far grander scale, but for abruptness, nothing at all comparable with this. In the evening we reached a flat little spot on the banks of the same stream which we had continued to follow, and which descends in a chain of waterfalls: here we bivouacked for the night. On each side of the ravine there were great beds of the mountain-banana, covered with ripe fruit. Many of these plants were from twenty to twenty-five feet high, and from three to four in circumference. By the aid of strips of bark for rope and the stems of bamboos for rafters and the large leaf of the banana for a thatch, the Tahitians in a few minutes built us an excellent house; and with withered leaves made a soft bed.

They then proceeded to make a fire and cook our evening meal. A light was procured by rubbing a blunt-pointed stick in a groove

◆ ◆ ◆ ◆ ◆

made in another, as if with the intention of deepening it, until by the friction the dust became ignited. A peculiarly white and very light wood (the *Hibiseus tiliaceus*) is alone used for this purpose: it is the same which serves for poles to carry any burden, and for the floating outriggers to their canoes. The fire was produced in a few seconds; but to a person who does not understand the art it requires, as I found, the greatest exertion; but at last, to my great pride, I succeeded in igniting the dust. The Gaucho in the Pampas uses a different method: taking an elastic stick about eighteen inches long, he presses one end on his breast, and the other pointed end into a hole in a piece of wood, and then rapidly turns the curved part, like a carpenter's centre-bit. The Tahitians, having made a small fire of sticks, placed a score of stones, of about the size of cricket-balls, on the burning wood. In about ten minutes the sticks were consumed, and the stones hot. They had previously folded up in small parcels of leaves, pieces of beef, fish, ripe and unripe bananas, and the tops of the wild arum. These green parcels were laid in a layer between two layers of the hot stones, and the hole then covered up with earth, so that no smoke or steam could escape. In about a quarter of an hour, the whole was most deliciously cooked. The choice green parcels were now laid on a cloth of banana leaves, and with a cocoa-nut shell we drank the cool water of the running stream; and thus we enjoyed our rustic meal.

I could not look on the surrounding plants without admiration. On every side were forests of banana; the fruit of which, though serving for food in various ways, lay in heaps decaying on the ground. In front of us there was an extensive brake of wild sugarcane; and the stream was shaded by the dark-green knotted stem of the ava,—so famous in former days for its powerful intoxicating effects. I chewed a piece, and found that it had an acrid and unpleasant taste, which would have induced any one at once to have pronounced it poisonous. Thanks to the missionaries, this plant now thrives only in these deep ravines, innocuous to every one. Close by I saw the wild arum, the roots of which, when well baked, are good to eat, and the young leaves better than spinach. There was the wild yam, and a liliaceous plant called Ti, which grows in abundance, and has a soft brown root, in shape and size like a huge log of wood: this served us for dessert, for it is as sweet as treacle, and with a pleasant taste. There were, moreover, several other wild fruits and useful vegetables. The little stream, besides its cool water, produced eels and cray-fish. I did indeed admire this scene, when I compared it with an uncultivated one in the temperate zones. I felt the force of the remark, that man, at least savage man, with his reasoning powers only partly developed, is the child of the tropics.

As the evening drew to a close, I strolled beneath the gloomy shade of the bananas up the course of the stream. My walk was soon brought to a close by coming to a waterfall between two and three hundred feet high; and again above this there was another. I mention all these waterfalls in this one brook, to give a general idea of the inclination of the land. In the little recess where the water fell, it did not appear that a breath of wind had ever blown. The thin edges of the great leaves of the banana, damp with spray, were unbroken, instead of being, as is so generally the case, split into a thousand shreds. From our position, almost suspended on the mountain-side, there were glimpses into the depths of the neighbouring valleys; and the lofty points of the central mountains, towering up within sixty degrees of the zenith, hid half the evening sky. Thus seated, it was a sublime spectacle to watch the shades of night gradually obscuring the last and highest pinnacles.

Before we laid ourselves down to sleep, the elder Tahitian fell on his knees, and with closed eyes repeated a long prayer in his native tongue. He prayed as a Christian should do, with fitting reverence, and without the fear of ridicule or any ostentation of piety. At our meals neither of the men would taste food without saying beforehand a short grace. Those travellers who think that a Tahitian prays only when the eyes of the missionary are fixed on him should have slept with us that night on the mountain-side. Before morning it rained very heavily; but the good thatch of banana-leaves kept us dry.

◆━◆━◆━◆━◆

6

UNDER THE MOUNTAIN WALL

PETER MATTHIESSEN

When the sun was high, a party of men under the leadership of Nilik, kain of the Walilo, went west quickly and quietly to the albizzia forest in the country of the Kosi-Alua. From there they moved toward the north side of the Waraba, slipping through low woodland. From the wood they crept down along the banks of a small stream which flows between the Waraba and the Siobara. They were nearly a hundred, including Husuk and his men and a band of Wilil under the leadership of Tegearek. Siba was there, and Tuesike, reserved and quiet, and Aloro, the lame man.

Sometimes their women weep when the raiders go, for the raid is very dangerous, and on hearing the women, the men may sing this song:

> See, we will set an ambush in the gardens of the Wittaia,
> But we are afraid,
> For if caught, we shall be killed.

The raiders slipped through the brush and sedge grass, crossing the deep sloughs of the April rains in water to their chests. A Wittaia lookout outlined on the crest of the Siobara failed to see them, for they kept close to the bottom of the hill, and they were hidden as well from the sentries on the grassy ridge off to the southward.

It was a quiet morning, overcast. The Kurelu women worked stolidly in the fields, and sentries climbed into the kaios. In the woods of Homuak a dove called dolefully. Dull light reflected from the smoke of fires, from the leaden water of the ditches, from the banks of white quartz sand on the hills of the Wittaia. On the savanna between the gardens and Homuak the yegerek fought noisily with spears of grass, but the men were nowhere to be seen. Two egrets which frequent the Place of Fear sat still as white flowers in the distance, just west of a tall bush which, in the few days past, had burst into orange flame.

In the early afternoon the Kurelu crossed the frontier of the Wittaia. The main party had been left in hiding in the wood by the Waraba, while thirty or more young warriors led by Tegearek crept forward. They were stalking a kaio and the surrounding fields of a village south of the Siobara.

There was a sentry in the kaio tower; he did not see the attackers until they were at the field edge. There were no warriors in the shelter, and but a solitary man, named Huwai, working in the gardens. The man on the kaio scrambled down and fled, shouting the alarm. Huwai was not fast enough. The war party surged out of the brush and rushed upon him; he was run down and speared to death by the wild-faced, shaggy-haired son of the war kain Wereklowe.

The raiding party returned quickly through the woods and climbed onto the rocks of the Waraba. There they were joined by the others, and the rest of the Kurelu came forward from the kaios, prepared for war.

◆ ◆ ◆ ◆ ◆

The Wittaia came quickly, shouting out their rage, and challenged the Kurelu to a battle on a grassy meadow just below the Waraba and to the south of it. Though badly outnumbered, this advance party of the Wittaia fought with ferocity and drove the Kurelu back among the rocks; a man of the Kosi-Alua was speared through the calf, and Tuesike of Wuperainma caught an arrow in the stomach, just one inch to the right side of his navel. The Wittaia moved into the rocks of the Siobara, awaiting reinforcements, while the Kurelu perched on the gray boulders which lie tumbled along the crest of the Waraba. The spears of both sides wavered on the sky like spines.

Tuesike was carried back on the powerful shoulders of Siba and put down in the shelter of some bushes on the north flank of the ridge. He was in terrible pain and in a little while passed into a state of shock. Siba supported him from behind, grasping his hair to hold his head upright. Tuesike's horim was gone, and his blood ran down his stomach onto the grass. The wound was not bleeding badly, for the arrow shaft had broken off inside, and the point was in too far to be withdrawn on the field. Tuesike panted tightly, harshly, as his brown face, draining, turned to gray. He was half conscious, and the others stared at him like awed children who have hurt one of their friends by accident. Tuesike, whose name means "Bird Bow," closed his eyes.

The Wittaia continued to gather on the Siobara and in an open area between the Waraba and the kaio near which Huwai had been killed. There a grass fire had been lit to burn away his blood. Wereklowe and other kains sat on the highest rock, observing, and now the Wittaia called out to the Kurelu across the way, confirming that Huwai had died. At this the Kurelu raised a shout, rushing forward to mass in a large body at the west end of the ridge. Some went farther, down onto the middle ground, and danced and shouted insults at

◆━◆━◆━◆━◆

the enemy. The Kurelu wanted war, but, strangely, the Wittaia now refused it. They sat in dead silence on the rocks and would not take up the challenge. Opposite, on the knolls and boulders of the Waraba, the Kurelu awaited them.

The Waraba, shaped in an L, is a rock garden of strewn boulders, set about with ferns and orchids and shining islets of wild sugar cane. Old gardens dance in the wild flowering below its flanks, for in the corner of the L, in years of peace, had been a village; banana fronds gleam in the low forest, a sparkling varnished gleam which turns to silver in the western light.

The horizon beyond is a dark mid-mountain landscape, dark with cloud shadows, distant thunderheads, dense tropic greens of montane forest, high black walls. But the darkness is muted by the soft colors of the gardens, by the green velvet of low marshy swales. The gold grass of the old fields draws the light, and rays of white break the green weight of the distances—a sprinkling of vivid whites, like snow patches. In the dawn of certain days true snow is visible, a scraggy outcropping near the peak of Arolik at fifteen thousand feet; for a few moments, on these days, the peak casts back the clouds. Soft white smoke rolls from the garden fires, soft as the mists on the horizons of far rains. And there are the blaze of sands on the flanks of Siobara, the alabaster statues of egrets, the shower of rhododendron. . . .

The Wittaia rose out of their silence, filed away.

At this the shouting was renewed, more strongly than before. The wild dancing of etai began, a whirling and prancing in which the men leapt high in the air or in a circle, driving both heels against the ground, or performed an odd taunting shuffle in which the feet are still, the knees pushed in and out, the hips and shoulders cocked in turn, and the arms darted snakily forward; the effect is one of lewd, jeering enticement, though it is a joyful dance, performed out of the

◆—◆—◆—◆—◆

wild high spirits brought about by a death among the enemy and the knowledge that no further risk will come that day.

Only the Aloros and a few others enjoy the risk, though all enjoy the war. At the first shout Aloro, alone among the warriors around Tuesike, had seized his bow and hobbled desperately toward a battle not destined to take place.

In a forest of spears the Kurelu were streaming back along the ridge, their stamping thunderous, their voices soaring. *O-o-A-i-i-A-y-y—WU! O-o-A-i-i-O-o—WAH!* Other voices, in simultaneous high counterpoint, howled, *WUA, WUA, WUA!* The egret wands and whisks of cassowary twirled like bright maddened insects, and the white of plumes and shells and boars' tusks flashed in the surging brown. At the edges of the tide ran yegerek, setting fire with thatch torches to the grass tops. Here and there bobbed a spot of brilliant red—the feathers of a parakeet, or a crown of the red ginger flower. These colors spun, and the weathered grays and greens of the ancient land lay still.

There came a shout, and Weaklekek with two of his men ran from the Waraba. They crossed the swamp and plunged through the reeds on the far side of the Tokolik, sprinting across the field toward Puakaloba. Once again the Wittaia had set fire to the shelter, which was burning fast. Apparently the enemy had been scared off, for the kaio itself still stood.

The warriors stopped to dance again. Some of them charged in a great circle, while others swayed and shimmied, *way-o-way-y—YO, lay-o-lay-y—AH!* to an answering din of hootings and wild high shrieks. In the middle of one group U-mue, resplendent in his clean bright ornaments of white, stood looking off into the distance, leaning on his spear, for he keeps his own counsel even in time of celebration.

A few women had collected from the fields, and these had begun their own slow sensual dropping of alternate knees, a swaying of the shoulders, while their arms shivered in and out, palms upward. One tall woman danced alone, far out in front of the rest, wearing a mikak shell above her breasts; in her splendor, she dominated a grassy hillside between the men and the women. This was the wife of Wereklowe's son, who had killed Huwai. Wereklowe came and danced beside her, but in a little while he went away again, and she swayed on, as if rooted to the landscape.

Soon the warriors ran down the slope, passing the bushes where Tuesike sat upon the ground and moving into the swamp of brush and sedge grass which separates the Waraba from the Tokolik. At the Tokolik they assembled to dance again, before moving on to the etai field called Liberek.

Tuesike was lifted painfully onto a stretcher. Siba and Asok-meke and Tegearek—the men of his pilai—were helped by a few elege like Siloba and Yonokma. Siloba winced himself, for, in the curing of an arrow wound which he carried in his left collarbone, his stomach had been lanced in several places and blood drawn; while the arrow wound had healed itself, the places of his cure had become infected and still hurt him.

Together the men hoisted the stretcher and entered the low ground. Tuesike was unconscious, and his body and face had been covered with green straw. The procession wound slowly through the black water of the swamp and, crossing the Tokolik, entered the home territory. It disappeared once more into the heavy swale of reeds and in a little while emerged, near the kaio which guards the outermost of the fields. Already, at the Liberek, dancing had started, and the chants of triumph did not cease at dark but rose and fell throughout the evening, from all the villages below the mountain.

◆◆◆◆

7

THE BIRD

OF PARADISE

EDWARD O. WILSON

ome with me now to another part of the living world. The role
of science, like that of art, is to blend exact imagery with more
distant meaning, the parts we already understand with those given
as new into larger patterns that are coherent enough to be acceptable
as truth. The biologist knows this relation by intuition during the
course of field work, as he struggles to make order out of the infinitely varying patterns of nature.

Picture the Huon Peninsula of New Guinea, about the size and
shape of Rhode Island, a weathered horn projecting from the
northeastern coast of the main island. When I was twenty-five, with
a fresh Ph.D. from Harvard and dreams of physical adventure in far-
off places with unpronounceable names, I gathered all the courage I
had and made a difficult and uncertain trek directly across the pen-
insular base. My aim was to collect a sample of ants and a few other
kinds of small animals up from the lowlands to the highest part of the

mountains. To the best of my knowledge I was the first biologist to take this particular route. I knew that almost everything I found would be worth recording, and all the specimens collected would be welcomed into museums.

Three days' walk from a mission station near the southern Lae coast brought me to the spine of the Sarawaget range, 12,000 feet above sea level. I was above treeline, in a grassland sprinkled with cycads, squat gymnospermous plants that resemble stunted palm trees and date from the Mesozoic Era, so that closely similar ancestral forms might have been browsed by dinosaurs 80 million years ago. On a chill morning when the clouds lifted and the sun shone brightly, my Papuan guides stopped hunting alpine wallabies with dogs and arrows, I stopped putting beetles and frogs in bottles of alcohol, and together we scanned the rare panoramic view. To the north we could make out the Bismarck Sea, to the south the Markham Valley and the more distant Herzog Mountains. The primary forest covering most of this mountainous country was broken into bands of different vegetation according to elevation. The zone just below us was the cloud forest, a labyrinth of interlocking trunks and branches blanketed by a thick layer of moss, orchids, and other epiphytes that ran unbroken off the tree trunks and across the ground. To follow game trails across this high country was like crawling through a dimly illuminated cave lined with a spongy green carpet.

A thousand feet below, the vegetation opened up a bit and assumed the appearance of typical lowland rain forest, except that the trees were denser and smaller and only a few flared out into a circle of blade-thin buttresses at the base. This is the zone botanists call the mid-mountain forest. It is an enchanted world of thousands of species of birds, frogs, insects, flowering plants, and other organisms, many found nowhere else. Together they form one of the richest and most nearly pure segments of the Papuan flora and fauna. To visit the mid-mountain forest is to see life as it existed before the coming of man thousands of years ago.

The jewel of the setting is the male Emperor of Germany bird of paradise (*Paradisaea guilielmi*), arguably the most beautiful bird in the world, certainly one of the twenty or so most striking in appearance. By moving quietly along secondary trails you might glimpse one on a lichen-encrusted branch near the tree tops. Its head is shaped like that of a crow—no surprise because the birds of paradise and crows have a close common lineage—but there the outward resemblance to any ordinary bird ends. The crown and upper breast of the bird are metallic oil-green and shine in the sunlight. The back is glossy yellow, the wings and tail deep reddish maroon. Tufts of ivory-white plumes sprout from the flanks and sides of the breast, turning lacy in texture toward the tips. The plume rectrices continue on as wirelike appendages past the breast and tail for a distance equal to the full length of the bird. The bill is blue-gray, the eyes clear amber, the claws brown and black.

In the mating season the male joins others in leks, common courtship arenas in the upper tree branches, where they display their dazzling ornaments to the more somberly caparisoned females. The male spreads his wings and vibrates them while lifting the gossamer flank plumes. He calls loudly with bubbling and flutelike notes and turns upside down on the perch, spreading the wings and tail and pointing his rectrices skyward. The dance then reaches a climax as he fluffs up the green breast feathers and opens out the flank plumes until they form a brilliant white circle around his body, with only the head, tail, and wings projecting beyond. The male sways gently from side to side, causing the plumes to wave gracefully as if caught in an errant breeze. Seen from a distance his body now resembles a spinning and slightly out-of-focus white disk.

This improbable spectacle in the Huon forest has been fashioned by millions of generations of natural selection in which males competed and females made choices, and the accouterments of display were driven to a visual extreme. But this is only one trait, seen in physiological time and thought about at a single level of causation. Beneath its plumed surface, the Emperor of Germany bird of paradise possesses an architecture culminating an ancient history, with details exceeding those that can be imagined from the naturalist's simple daylight record of color and dance.

Consider one such bird for a moment in the analytic manner, as an object of biological research. Encoded within its chromosomes is the developmental program that led with finality to a male *Paradisaea guilielmi*. The completed nervous system is a structure of fiber tracts more complicated than any existing computer, and as challenging as all the rain forests of New Guinea surveyed on foot. A microscopic study will someday permit us to trace the events that culminate in the electric commands carried by the efferent neurons to the skeletal-muscular system and reproduce, in part, the dance of the courting male. This machinery can be dissected and understood by proceeding to the level of the cell, to enzymatic catalysis, microfilament configuration, and active sodium transport during electric discharge. Because biology sweeps the full range of space and time, there will be more discoveries renewing the sense of wonder at each step of research. By altering the scale of perception to the micrometer and millisecond, the laboratory scientist parallels the trek of the naturalist across the land. He looks out from his own version of the mountain crest. His spirit of adventure, as well as personal history of hardship, misdirection, and triumph, are fundamentally the same.

Described this way, the bird of paradise may seem to have been turned into a metaphor of what humanists dislike most about science: that it reduces nature and is insensitive to art, that scientists are conquistadors who melt down the Inca gold. But bear with me a

◆━◆━◆━◆

minute. Science is not just analytic; it is also synthetic. It uses artlike intuition and imagery. In the early stages, individual behavior can be analyzed to the level of genes and neurosensory cells, whereupon the phenomena have indeed been mechanically reduced. In the synthetic phase, though, even the most elementary activity of these biological units creates rich and subtle patterns at the levels of organism and society. The outer qualities of *Paradisaea guilielmi*, its plumes, dance, and daily life, are functional traits open to a deeper understanding through the exact description of their constituent parts. They can be redefined as holistic properties that alter our perception and emotion in surprising and pleasant ways.

There will come a time when the bird of paradise is reconstituted by the synthesis of all the hard-won analytic information. The mind, bearing a newfound power, will journey back to the familiar world of seconds and centimeters. Once again the glittering plumage takes form and is viewed at a distance through a network of leaves and mist. Then we see the bright eye open, the head swivel, the wings extend. But the familiar notions are viewed across a far greater range of cause and effect. The species is understood more completely; misleading illusions have given way to light and wisdom of a greater degree. One turn of the cycle of intellect is then complete. The excitement of the scientist's search for the true material nature of the species recedes, to be replaced in part by the more enduring responses of the hunter and poet.

What are these ancient responses? The full answer can only be given through a combined idiom of science and the humanities, whereby the investigation turns back into itself. The human being, like the bird of paradise, awaits our examination in the analytic-synthetic manner. As always by honored tradition, feeling and myth can be viewed at a distance through physiological time, idiosyncratically, in the manner of traditional art. But they can also be penetrated more deeply than ever was possible in the prescientific age, to their physical basis in the processes of mental development, the brain structure, and indeed the genes themselves. It may even be possible to trace them back through time past cultural history to the evolutionary origins of human nature. With each new phase of synthesis to emerge from biological inquiry, the humanities will expand their reach and capability. In symmetric fashion, with each redirection of the humanities, science will add dimensions to human biology.

◆—◆—◆—◆—◆

8

MAUKI

JACK LONDON

He weighed one hundred and ten pounds. His hair was kinky and negroid, and he was black. He was peculiarly black. He was neither blue-black nor purple-black, but plum-black. His name was Mauki, and he was the son of a chief. He had three *tambos*. *Tambo* is Melanesian for *taboo*, and is first cousin to that Polynesian word. Mauki's three *tambos* were as follows: first, he must never shake hands with a woman, nor have a woman's hand touch him or any of his personal belongings; secondly, he must never eat clams nor any food from a fire in which clams had been cooked; thirdly, he must never touch a crocodile, nor travel in a canoe that carried any part of a crocodile even if as large as a tooth.

Of a different black were his teeth, which were deep black, or, perhaps better, *lamp*-black. They had been made so in a single night, by his mother, who had compressed about them a powdered mineral which was dug from the landslide back of Port Adams. Port Adams is a salt-water village on Malaita, and Malaita is the most savage island in the Solomons—so savage that no traders nor planters have yet gained a foothold on it; while, from the time of the earliest *bêche-de-mer* fishers and sandalwood traders down to the latest labor recruiters equipped with automatic rifles and gasoline engines, scores of white adventurers have been passed out by tomahawks and soft-nosed Snider bullets. So Malaita remains to-day, in the twentieth century, the stamping ground of the labor recruiters, who farm its coasts for laborers who engage and contract themselves to toil on the plantations of the neighboring and more civilized islands for a wage of thirty dollars a year. The natives of those neighboring and more civilized islands have themselves become too civilized to work on plantations.

Mauki's ears were pierced, not in one place, nor two places, but in a couple of dozen places. In one of the smaller holes he carried a clay pipe. The larger holes were too large for such use. The bowl of the pipe would have fallen through. In fact, in the largest hole in each ear he habitually wore round wooden plugs that were an even four inches in diameter. Roughly speaking, the circumference of said holes was twelve and one-half inches. Mauki was catholic in his tastes. In the various smaller holes he carried such things as empty rifle cartridges, horseshoe nails, copper screws, pieces of string, braids of sennit, strips of green leaf and, in the cool of the day, scarlet hibiscus flowers. From which it will be seen that pockets were not necessary to his well-being. Besides, pockets were impossible, for his only wearing apparel consisted of a piece of calico several inches wide. A pocket knife he wore in his hair, the blade snapped down on a kinky lock. His most prized possession was the handle of a china cup, which he suspended from a ring of turtle-shell, which, in turn, was passed through the partition-cartilage of his nose.

But in spite of embellishments, Mauki had a nice face. It was really a pretty face, viewed by any standard, and for a Melanesian it was a remarkably good-looking face. Its one fault was its lack of

◆ ◆ ◆ ◆

strength. It was softly effeminate, almost girlish. The features were small, regular and delicate. The chin was weak, and the mouth was weak. There was no strength nor character in the jaws, forehead and nose. In the eyes only could be caught any hint of the unknown quantities that were so large a part of his make-up and that other persons could not understand. These unknown quantities were pluck, pertinacity, fearlessness, imagination and cunning; and when they found expression in some consistent and striking action, those about him were astounded.

Mauki's father was chief over the village at Port Adams, and thus, by birth a salt-water man, Mauki was half amphibian. He knew the way of the fishes and oysters, and the reef was an open book to him. Canoes, also, he knew. He learned to swim when he was a year old. At seven years he could hold his breath a full minute and swim straight down to bottom through thirty feet of water. And at seven years he was stolen by the bushmen, who cannot even swim and who are afraid of salt water. Thereafter Mauki saw the sea only from a distance, through rifts in the jungle and from open spaces on the high mountain sides. He became the slave of old Fanfoa, head chief over a score of scattered bush-villages on the range-lips of Malaita, the smoke of which, on calm mornings, is about the only evidence the seafaring white men have of the teeming interior population. For the whites do not penetrate Malaita. They tried it once, in the days when the search was on for gold, but they always left their heads behind to grin from the smoky rafters of the bushmen's huts.

When Mauki was a young man of seventeen, Fanfoa got out of tobacco. He got dreadfully out of tobacco. It was hard times in all his villages. He had been guilty of a mistake. Suo was a harbor so small that a large schooner could not swing at anchor in it. It was surrounded by mangroves that overhung the deep water. It was a trap, and into the trap sailed two white men in a small ketch. They were after recruits, and they possessed much tobacco and trade-goods, to say nothing of three rifles and plenty of ammunition. Now there were no salt-water men living at Suo, and it was there that the bush-men could come down to the sea. The ketch did a splendid traffic. It signed on twenty recruits the first day. Even old Fanfoa signed on. And that same day the score of new recruits chopped off the two white men's heads, killed the boat's crew and burned the ketch. Thereafter, and for three months, there was tobacco and trade-goods in plenty and to spare in all the bush-villages. Then came the man-of-war that threw shells for miles into the hills, frightening the people out of their villages and into the deeper bush. Next the man-of-war sent landing parties ashore. The villages were all burned, along with the tobacco and trade-stuff. The coconuts and bananas were chopped down, the taro gardens uprooted, and the pigs and chickens killed.

It taught Fanfoa a lesson, but in the meantime he was out of to-bacco. Also, his young men were too frightened to sign on with the recruiting vessels. That was why Fanfoa ordered his slave, Mauki, to be carried down and signed on for half a case of tobacco advance, along with knives, axes, calico and beads, which he would pay for with his toil on the plantations. Mauki was sorely frightened when they brought him on board the schooner. He was a lamb led to the slaughter. White men were ferocious creatures. They had to be, or else they would not make a practice of venturing along the Malaita coast and into all harbors, two on a schooner, when each schooner carried from fifteen to twenty blacks as boat's crew, and often as high as sixty or seventy black recruits. In addition to this, there was always the danger of the shore population, the sudden attack and the cut-ting off of the schooner and all hands. Truly, white men must be ter-rible. Besides, they were possessed of such devil-devils—rifles that shot very rapidly many times, things of iron and brass that made the schooners go when there was no wind, and boxes that talked and laughed just as men talked and laughed. Ay, and he had heard of one white man whose particular devil-devil was so powerful that he could take out all his teeth and put them back at will.

Down into the cabin they took Mauki. On deck, the one white man kept guard with two revolvers in his belt. In the cabin the other white man sat with a book before him, in which he inscribed strange marks and lines. He looked at Mauki as though he had been a pig or a fowl, glanced under the hollows of his arms, and wrote in the book. Then he held out the writing stick and Mauki just barely touched it with his hand, in so doing pledging himself to toil for three years on the plantations of the Moongleam Soap Company. It was not explained to him that the will of the ferocious white men would be used to enforce the pledge, and that, behind all, for the same use, was all the power and all the warships of Great Britain.

Other blacks there were on board, from unheard-of far places, and when the white man spoke to them, they tore the long feather from Mauki's hair, cut that same hair short, and wrapped about his waist a lava-lava of bright yellow calico.

After many days on the schooner, and after beholding more land and islands than he had ever dreamed of, he was landed on New Georgia, and put to work in the field clearing jungle and cutting cane grass. For the first time he knew what work was. Even as a slave to Fanfoa he had not worked like this. And he did not like work. It was up at dawn and in at dark, on two meals a day. And the food was tiresome. For weeks at a time they were given nothing but sweet potatoes to eat, and for weeks at a time it would be nothing but rice. He cut out the coconut from the shells day after day; and for long days and weeks he fed the fires that smoked the copra, till his eyes got sore and he was set to felling trees. He was a good axe-man, and later he was put in the bridge-building gang. Once, he was punished by being put in the road-building gang. At times he served as boat's crew in the whale-boats, when they brought in copra from distant beaches or when the white men went out to dynamite fish.

Among other things he learned *bêche-de-mer* English, with which he could talk with all white men, and with all recruits who otherwise would have talked in a thousand different dialects. Also, he learned certain things about the white men, principally that they kept their word. If they told a boy he was going to receive a stick of tobacco, he got it. If they told a boy they would knock seven bells out of him if he did a certain thing, when he did that thing seven bells invariably were knocked out of him. Mauki did not know what seven bells were, but they occurred in *bêche-de-mer*, and he imagined them to be the blood and teeth that sometimes accompanied the process of knocking out seven bells. One other thing he learned: no boy was struck or punished unless he did wrong. Even when the white men were drunk, as they were frequently, they never struck unless a rule had been broken.

Mauki did not like the plantation. He hated work, and he was the son of a chief. Furthermore, it was ten years since he had been stolen from Port Adams by Fanfoa, and he was homesick. He was even homesick for the slavery under Fanfoa. So he ran away. He struck back into the bush, with the idea of working southward to the beach and stealing a canoe in which to go home to Port Adams. But the fever got him, and he was captured and brought back more dead than alive.

A second time he ran away, in the company of two Malaita boys. They got down the coast twenty miles, and were hidden in the hut of a Malaita freeman, who dwelt in that village. But in the dead of night two white men came, who were not afraid of all the village people and who knocked seven bells out of the three runaways, tied them like pigs and tossed them into the whaleboat. But the man in whose

◆◆◆◆◆

house they had hidden—seven times seven bells must have been knocked out of him from the way the hair, skin and teeth flew, and he was discouraged for the rest of his natural life from harboring run-away laborers.

For a year Mauki toiled on. Then he was made a house-boy, and had good food and easy times, with light work in keeping the house clean and serving the white men with whiskey and beer at all hours of the day and most hours of the night. He liked it, but he liked Port Adams more. He had two years longer to serve, but two years were too long for him in the throes of homesickness. He had grown wiser with his year of service, and, being now a house-boy, he had opportunity. He had the cleaning of the rifles, and he knew where the key to the store-room was hung. He planned the escape, and one night ten Malaita boys and one boy from San Cristoval sneaked from the barracks and dragged one of the whale-boats down to the beach. It was Mauki who supplied the key that opened the padlock on the boat, and it was Mauki who equipped the boat with a dozen Winchesters, an immense amount of ammunition, a case of dynamite with detonators and fuse, and ten cases of tobacco.

The northwest monsoon was blowing, and they fled south in the night-time, hiding by day on detached and uninhabited islets, or dragging their whale-boat into the bush on the large islands. Thus they gained Guadalcanar, skirted halfway along it, and crossed the Indispensable Straits to Florida Island. It was here that they killed the San Cristoval boy, saving his head and cooking and eating the rest of him. The Malaita coast was only twenty miles away, but the last night a strong current and baffling winds prevented them from gaining across. Daylight found them still several miles from their goal. But daylight brought a cutter, in which were two white men, who were not afraid of eleven Malaita men armed with twelve rifles. Mauki and his companions were carried back to Tulagi, where lived the great white master of all the white men. And the great white master held a court, after which, one by one, the runaways were tied up and given twenty lashes each, and sentenced to a fine of fifteen dollars. Then they were sent back to New Georgia, where the white men knocked seven bells out of them all around and put them to work. But Mauki was no longer house-boy. He was put in the road-making gang. The fine of fifteen dollars had been paid by the men from whom he had run away, and he was told that he would have to work it out, which meant six months' additional toil. Further, his share of the stolen tobacco earned him another year of toil.

Port Adams was now three years and a half away, so he stole a canoe one night, hid on the islets in Manning Straits, passed through the Straits, and began working along the eastern coast of Ysabel, only to be captured, two-thirds of the way along, by the white men on Meringe Lagoon. After a week, he escaped from them and took to the bush. There were no bush natives on Ysabel, only salt-water men, who were all Christians. The white men put up a reward of five hundred sticks of tobacco, and every time Mauki ventured down to the sea to steal a canoe he was chased by the salt-water men. Four months of this passed when, the reward having been raised to a thousand sticks, he was caught and sent back to New Georgia and the road-building gang. Now a thousand sticks are worth fifty dollars, and Mauki had to pay the reward himself, which required a year and eight months' labor. So Port Adams was now five years away.

His homesickness was greater than ever, and it did not appeal to him to settle down and be good, work out his four years, and go home. The next time, he was caught in the very act of running away. His case was brought before Mr Haveby, the island manager of the Moongleam Soap Company, who adjudged him an incorrigible. The Company had plantations on the Santa Cruz Islands, hundreds of miles across the sea, and there it sent its Solomon Islands' incorrigibles. And there Mauki was sent, though he never arrived. The schooner stopped at Santa Anna, and in the night Mauki swam ashore, where he stole two rifles and a case of tobacco and got away in a canoe to Cristoval. Malaita was now to the north, fifty or sixty miles away. But when he attempted the passage, he was caught by a light gale and driven back to Santa Anna, where the trader clapped him in irons and held him against the return of the schooner from Santa Cruz. The two rifles the trader recovered, but the case of tobacco was charged up to Mauki at the rate of another year. The sum of years he now owed the Company was six.

On the way back to New Georgia, the schooner dropped anchor in Marau Sound, which lies at the southeastern extremity of Guadalcanar. Mauki swam ashore with handcuffs on his wrists and got away to the bush. The schooner went on, but the Moongleam trader ashore offered a thousand sticks, and to him Mauki was brought by the bushmen with a year and eight months tacked on to his account. Again, and before the schooner called in, he got away, this time in a whale-boat accompanied by a case of the trader's tobacco. But a northwest gale wrecked him upon Ugi, where the Christian natives stole his tobacco and turned him over to the Moongleam trader who resided there. The tobacco the natives stole meant another year for him, and the tale was now eight years and a half.

'We'll send him to Lord Howe,' said Mr Haveby. 'Bunster is there, and we'll let them settle it between them. It will be a case, I imagine, of Mauki getting Bunster, or Bunster getting Mauki, and good riddance in either event.'

If one leaves Meringe Lagoon, on Ysabel, and steers a course due north, magnetic, at the end of one hundred and fifty miles he will lift the pounded coral beaches of Lord Howe above the sea. Lord Howe is a ring of land some one hundred and fifty miles in circumference, several hundred yards wide at its widest, and towering in

◆—◆—◆—◆—◆

places to a height of ten feet above sea-level. Inside this ring of sand is a mighty lagoon studded with coral patches. Lord Howe belongs to the Solomons neither geographically nor ethnologically. It is an atoll, while the Solomons are high islands; and its people and language are Polynesian, while the inhabitants of the Solomons are Melanesian. Lord Howe has been populated by the westward Polynesian drift which continues to this day, big outrigger canoes being washed upon its beaches by the southeast trade. That there has been a slight Melanesian drift in the period of the northwest monsoon, is also evident.

Nobody ever comes to Lord Howe, or Ontong-Java as it is sometimes called. Thomas Cook & Son do not sell tickets to it, and tourists do not dream of its existence. Not even a white missionary has landed on its shore. Its five thousand natives are as peaceable as they are primitive. Yet they were not always peaceable. The *Sailing Directions* speak of them as hostile and treacherous. But the men who compile the *Sailing Directions* have never heard of the change that was worked in the hearts of the inhabitants, who, not many years ago, cut off a big bark and killed all hands with the exception of the second mate. This survivor carried the news to his brothers. The captains of three trading schooners returned with him to Lord Howe. They sailed their vessels right into the lagoon and proceeded to preach the white man's gospel that only white men shall kill white men and that the lesser breeds must keep hands off. The schooners sailed up and down the lagoon, harrying and destroying. There was no escape from the narrow sand-circle, no bush to which to flee. The men were shot down at sight, and there was no avoiding being sighted. The villages were burned, the canoes smashed, the chickens and pigs killed, and the precious coconut-trees chopped down. For a month this continued, when the schooners sailed away; but the fear of the white man had been seared into the souls of the islanders and never again were they rash enough to harm one.

Max Bunster was the one white man on Lord Howe, trading in the pay of the ubiquitous Moongleam Soap Company. And the Company billeted him on Lord Howe, because, next to getting rid of him, it was the most out-of-the-way place to be found. That the Company did not get rid of him was due to the difficulty of finding another man to take his place. He was a strapping big German, with something wrong in his brain. Semi-madness would be a charitable statement of his condition. He was a bully and a coward, and a thrice-bigger savage than any savage on the island. Being a coward, his brutality was of the cowardly order. When he first went into the Company's employ, he was stationed on Savo. When a consumptive colonial was sent to take his place, he beat him up with his fists and sent him off a wreck in the schooner that brought him.

Mr Haveby next selected a young Yorkshire giant to relieve Bunster. The Yorkshire man had a reputation as a bruiser and preferred fighting to eating. But Bunster wouldn't fight. He was a regular little lamb—for ten days, at the end of which time the Yorkshire man was prostrated by a combined attack of dysentery and fever. Then Bunster went for him, among other things getting him down and jumping on him a score or so of times. Afraid of what would happen when his victim recovered, Bunster fled away in a cutter to Guvutu, where he signalized himself by beating up a young Englishman already crippled by a Boer bullet through both hips.

Then it was that Mr Haveby sent Bunster to Lord Howe, the falling-off place. He celebrated his landing by mopping up half a case of gin and by thrashing the elderly and wheezy mate of the schooner which had brought him. When the schooner departed, he called the kanakas down to the beach and challenged them to throw him in a wrestling bout, promising a case of tobacco to the one who succeeded. Three kanakas he threw, but was promptly thrown by a fourth, who, instead of receiving the tobacco, got a bullet through his lungs.

And so began Bunster's reign on Lord Howe. Three thousand people lived in the principal village, but it was deserted, even in broad day, when he passed through. Men, women and children fled before him. Even the dogs and pigs got out of the way, while the king was not above hiding under a mat. The two prime ministers lived in terror of Bunster, who never discussed any moot subject, but struck out with his fists instead.

And to Lord Howe came Mauki, to toil for Bunster for eight long years and a half. There was no escaping from Lord Howe. For better or worse, Bunster and he were tied together. Bunster weighed two hundred pounds. Mauki weighed one hundred and ten. Bunster was a degenerate brute. But Mauki was a primitive savage. While both had wills and ways of their own.

Mauki had no idea of the sort of master he was to work for. He had had no warnings, and he had concluded as a matter of course that Bunster would be like other white men, a drinker of much whiskey, a ruler and a lawgiver who always kept his word and who never struck a boy undeserved. Bunster had the advantage. He knew all about Mauki, and gloated over the coming into possession of him. The last cook was suffering from a broken arm and a dislocated shoulder, so Bunster made Mauki cook and general house-boy.

And Mauki soon learned that there were white men and white men. On the very day the schooner departed he was ordered to buy a chicken from Samisee, the native Tongan missionary. But Samisee had sailed across the lagoon and would not be back for three days. Mauki returned with the information. He climbed the steep stairway (the house stood on piles twelve feet above the sand), and en-

◆◆◆◆◆

tered the living-room to report. The trader demanded the chicken. Mauki opened his mouth to explain the missionary's absence. But Bunster did not care for explanations. He struck out with his fist. The blow caught Mauki on the mouth and lifted him into the air. Clear through the doorway he flew, across the narrow veranda, breaking the top railing, and down to the ground. His lips were a contused, shapeless mass, and his mouth was full of blood and broken teeth.

'That'll teach you that back talk don't go with me,' the trader shouted, purple with rage, peering down at him over the broken railing.

Mauki had never met a white man like this, and he resolved to walk small and never offend. He saw the boat-boys knocked about, and one of them put in irons for three days with nothing to eat for the crime of breaking a rowlock while pulling. Then, too, he heard the gossip of the village and learned why Bunster had taken a third wife—by force, as was well known. The first and second wives lay in the graveyard, under the white coral sand, with slabs of coral rock at head and feet. They had died, it was said, from beatings he had given them. The third wife was certainly ill-used, as Mauki could see for himself.

But there was no way by which to avoid offending the white man, who seemed offended with life. When Mauki kept silent, he was struck and called a sullen brute. When he spoke, he was struck for giving back talk. When he was grave, Bunster accused him of plotting and gave him a thrashing in advance; and when he strove to be cheerful and to smile, he was charged with sneering at his lord and master and given a taste of stick. Bunster was a devil. The village would have done for him, had it not remembered the lesson of the three schooners. It might have done for him anyway, if there had been a bush to which to flee. As it was, the murder of the white man, of any white man, would bring a man-of-war that would kill the offenders and chop down the precious coconut-trees. Then there were the boat-boys, with minds fully made up to drown him by accident at the first opportunity to capsize the cutter. Only Bunster saw to it that the boat did not capsize.

Mauki was of a different breed, and, escape being impossible while Bunster lived, he was resolved to get the white man. The trouble was that he could never find a chance. Bunster was always on guard. Day and night his revolvers were ready to hand. He permitted nobody to pass behind his back, as Mauki learned after having been knocked down several times. Bunster knew that he had more to fear from the good-natured, even sweet-faced, Malaita boy than from the entire population of Lord Howe; and it gave added zest to the programme of torment he was carrying out. And Mauki walked small, accepted his punishments and waited.

All other white men had respected his *tambos*, but not so Bunster. Mauki's weekly allowance of tobacco was two sticks. Bunster passed them to his woman and ordered Mauki to receive them from her hand. But this could not be, and Mauki went without his tobacco. In the same way he was made to miss many a meal, and to go hungry many a day. He was ordered to make chowder out of the big clams that grew in the lagoon. This he could not do, for clams were *tambo*. Six times in succession he refused to touch the clams, and six times he was knocked senseless. Bunster knew that the boy would die first, but called his refusal mutiny, and would have killed him had there been another cook to take his place.

One of the trader's favorite tricks was to catch Mauki's kinky locks and bat his head against the wall. Another trick was to catch Mauki unawares and thrust the live end of a cigar against his flesh. This Bunster called vaccination, and Mauki was vaccinated a number of times a week. Once, in a rage, Bunster ripped the cup handle from Mauki's nose, tearing the hole clear out of the cartilage.

'Oh, what a mug!' was his comment, when he surveyed the damage he had wrought.

The skin of a shark is like sandpaper, but the skin of a ray fish is like a rasp. In the South Seas the natives use it as a wood file in smoothing down canoes and paddles. Bunster had a mitten made of ray fish skin. The first time he tried it on Mauki, with one sweep of the hand it fetched the skin off his back from neck to armpit. Bunster was delighted. He gave his wife a taste of the mitten, and tried it out thoroughly on the boat-boys. The prime ministers came in for a stroke each, and they had to grin and take it for a joke.

'Laugh, damn you, laugh!' was the cue he gave.

Mauki came in for the largest share of the mitten. Never a day passed without a caress from it. There were times when the loss of so much cuticle kept him awake at night, and often the half-healed surface was raked raw afresh by the facetious Mr Bunster. Mauki continued his patient wait, secure in the knowledge that sooner or later his time would come. And he knew just what he was going to do, down to the smallest detail, when the time did come.

One morning Bunster got up in a mood for knocking seven bells out of the universe. He began on Mauki, and wound up on Mauki, in the interval knocking down his wife and hammering all the boat-boys. At breakfast he called the coffee slops and threw the scalding contents of the cup into Mauki's face. By ten o'clock Bunster was shivering with ague, and half an hour later he was burning with fever. It was no ordinary attack. It quickly became pernicious, and developed into black-water fever. The days passed, and he grew weaker and weaker, never leaving his bed. Mauki waited and watched, the while his skin grew intact once more. He ordered the boys to beach the cutter, scrub her bottom, and give her a general overhauling. They thought the order emanated from Bunster, and they obeyed. But Bunster at the time was lying unconscious and giving no orders. This was Mauki's chance, but still he waited.

When the worst was past, and Bunster lay convalescent and conscious, but weak as a baby, Mauki packed his few trinkets, including the china cup handle, into his trade box. Then he went over to the village and interviewed the king and his two prime ministers.

'This fella Bunster, him good fella you like too much?' he asked.

They explained in one voice that they liked the trader not at all. The ministers poured forth a recital of all the indignities and wrongs that had been heaped upon them. The king broke down and wept. Mauki interrupted rudely.

'You savve me—me big fella marster my country. You no like 'm this fella white marster. Me no like 'm. Plenty good you put hundred coconut, two hundred coconut, three hundred coconut along cutter. Him finish, you go sleep 'm good fella. Altogether kanaka sleep 'm good fella. Bime by big fella noise along house, you no savve hear 'm that fella noise. You altogether sleep strong fella too much.'

In like manner Mauki interviewed the boat-boys. Then he ordered Bunster's wife to return to her family house. Had she refused, he would have been in a quandary, for his *tambo* would not have permitted him to lay hands on her.

The house deserted, he entered the sleeping-room, where the trader lay in a doze. Mauki first removed the revolvers, then placed the ray fish mitten on his hand. Bunster's first warning was a stroke of the mitten that removed the skin the full length of his nose.

'Good fella, eh?' Mauki grinned, between two strokes, one of which swept the forehead bare and the other of which cleaned off one side of his face. 'Laugh, damn you, laugh.'

Mauki did his work thoroughly, and the kanakas, hiding in their

◆◆◆◆◆

houses, heard the 'big fella noise' that Bunster made and continued to make for an hour or more.

When Mauki was done, he carried the boat compass and all the rifles and ammunition down to the cutter, which he proceeded to ballast with cases of tobacco. It was while engaged in this that a hideous, skinless thing came out of the house and ran screaming down the beach till it fell in the sand and mowed and gibbered under the scorching sun. Mauki looked toward it and hesitated. Then he went over and removed the head, which he wrapped in a mat and stowed in the stern-locker of the cutter.

So soundly did the kanakas sleep through that long hot day that they did not see the cutter run out through the passage and head south, close-hauled on the southeast trade. Nor was the cutter ever sighted on that long tack to the shores of Ysabel, and during the tedious head-beat from there to Malaita. He landed at Port Adams with a wealth of rifles and tobacco such as no one man had ever possessed before. But he did not stop there. He had taken a white man's head, and only the bush could shelter him. So back he went to the bush-villages, where he shot old Fanfoa and half a dozen of the chief men, and made himself the chief over all the villages. When his father died, Mauki's brother ruled in Port Adams, and, joined together, salt-water men and bushmen, the resulting combination was the strongest of the ten score fighting tribes in Malaita.

More than his fear of the British government was Mauki's fear of the all-powerful Moongleam Soap Company; and one day a message came up to him in the bush, reminding him that he owed the Company eight and one-half years of labor. He sent back a favorable answer, and then appeared the inevitable white man, the captain of the schooner, the only white man during Mauki's reign who ventured the bush and came out alive. This man not only came out, but he brought with him seven hundred and fifty dollars in gold sovereigns—the money price of eight years and a half of labor plus the cost price of certain rifles and cases of tobacco.

Mauki no longer weighs one hundred and ten pounds. His stomach is three times its former girth, and he has four wives. He has many other things—rifles and revolvers, the handle of a china cup, and an excellent collection of bushmen's heads. But more precious than the entire collection is another head, perfectly dried and cured, with sandy hair and a yellowish beard, which is kept wrapped in the finest of fibre lava-lavas. When Mauki goes to war with villages beyond his realm, he invariably gets out this head, and, alone in his grass palace, contemplates it long and solemnly. At such times the hush of death falls on the village, and not even a pickaninny dares make a noise. The head is esteemed the most powerful devil-devil on Malaita, and to the possession of it is ascribed all of Mauki's greatness.

◆◆◆◆◆

9

THE ORANGUTAN

OF BORNEO

ALFRED RUSSEL WALLACE

One of my chief objects in coming to stay at Simunjon was to see the Orang-utan (or great man-like ape of Borneo) in his native haunts, to study his habits, and obtain good specimens of the different varieties and species of both sexes, and of the adult and young animals. In all these objects I succeeded beyond my expectations, and will now give some account of my experience in hunting the Orang-utan, or "Mias," as it is called by the natives; and as this name is short, and easily pronounced, I shall generally use it in preference to *Simia satyrus*, or Orang-utan.

Just a week after my arrival at the mines, I first saw a Mias. I was out collecting insects, not more than a quarter of a mile from the house, when I heard a rustling in a tree near, and, looking up, saw a large red-haired animal moving slowly along, hanging from the branches by its arms. It passed on from tree to tree till it was lost in the jungle, which was so swampy that I could not follow it. This mode of progression was, however, very unusual, and is more characteristic of the Hylobates than of the Orang. I suppose there was some individual peculiarity in this animal, or the nature of the trees just in this place rendered it the most easy mode of progression.

About a fortnight afterwards I heard that one was feeding in a tree in the swamp just below the house, and, taking my gun, was fortunate enough to find it in the same place. As soon as I approached, it tried to conceal itself among the foliage; but I got a shot at it, and the second barrel caused it to fall down almost dead, the two balls having entered the body. This was a male, about half-grown, being scarcely three feet high. On April 26th, I was out shooting with two Dyaks, when we found another about the same size. It fell at the first shot, but did not seem much hurt, and immediately climbed up the nearest tree, when I fired, and it again fell, with a broken arm and a wound in the body. The two Dyaks now ran up to it, and each seized hold of a hand, telling me to cut a pole, and they would secure it. But although one arm was broken, and it was only a half-grown animal, it was too strong for these young savages, drawing them up towards its mouth notwithstanding all their efforts, so that they were again obliged to leave go, or they would have been seriously bitten. It now began climbing up the tree again; and, to avoid trouble, I shot it through the heart.

On May 2nd, I again found one on a very high tree, when I had only a small 80-bore gun with me. However, I fired at it, and on seeing me, it began howling in a strange voice like a cough, and seemed in a great rage, breaking off branches with its hands and throwing them down, and then soon made off over the tree-tops. I did not care to follow it, as it was swampy, and in parts dangerous, and I might easily have lost myself in the eagerness of pursuit.

On the 12th of May I found another, which behaved in a very similar manner, howling and hooting with rage, and throwing down branches. I shot at it five times, and it remained dead on the top of the tree, supported in a fork in such a manner that it would evidently not fall. I therefore returned home, and luckily found some Dyaks, who came back with me, and climbed up the tree for the animal. This was the first full-grown specimen I had obtained; but it was a female, and not nearly so large or remarkable as the full-grown males. It was, however, 3ft. 6in. high, and its arms stretched out to a width of 6ft. 6in. I preserved the skin of this specimen in a cask of arrack, and prepared a perfect skeleton, which was afterwards purchased for the Derby Museum.

Only four days afterwards some Dyaks saw another Mias near the same place, and came to tell me. We found it to be a rather large one, very high up on a tall tree. At the second shot it fell rolling over, but almost immediately got up again and began to climb. At a third shot it fell dead. This was also a full-grown female, and while preparing to carry it home, we found a young one face downwards in the bog. This little creature was only about a foot long, and had evidently been hanging to its mother when she first fell. Luckily it did not appear to have been wounded, and after we had cleaned the mud out of its mouth it began to cry out, and seemed quite strong and active. While carrying it home it got its hands in my beard, and grasped so tightly that I had great difficulty in getting free, for the fingers are habitually bent inwards at the last joint so as to form complete hooks. At this time it had not a single tooth, but a few days afterwards it cut its two lower front teeth. Unfortunately, I had no milk to give it, as neither Malays, Chinese, nor Dyaks ever use the article, and I in vain inquired for any female animal that could suckle my little infant. I was therefore obliged to give it rice-water from a bottle with a quill in the cork, which after a few trials it learned to suck very well. This was very meagre diet, and the little creature did not thrive well on it, although I added sugar and cocoa-nut milk occasionally, to make it more nourishing. When I put my finger in its mouth it sucked with great vigour, drawing in its cheeks with all its might in the vain effort to extract some milk, and only after persevering a long time would it give up in disgust, and set up a scream very like that of a baby in similar circumstances.

When handled or nursed, it was very quiet and contented, but when laid down by itself would invariably cry; and for the first few nights was very restless and noisy. I fitted up a little box for a cradle, with a soft mat for it to lie upon, which was changed and washed every day; and I soon found it necessary to wash the little Mias as well. After I had done so a few times, it came to like the operation, and as soon as it was dirty would begin crying, and not leave off till I took it out and carried it to the spout, when it immediately became quiet, although it would wince a little at the first rush of the cold water and make ridiculously wry faces while the stream was running over its head. It enjoyed the wiping and rubbing dry amazingly, and when I brushed its hair seemed to be perfectly happy, lying quite still with its arms and legs stretched out while I thoroughly brushed the long hair of its back and arms. For the first few days it clung desperately with all four hands to whatever it could lay hold of, and I had to be careful to keep my beard out of its way, as its fingers clutched hold of hair more tenaciously than anything else, and it was impossible to free myself without assistance. When restless, it would struggle about with its hands up in the air trying to find something to take hold of, and, when it had got a bit of stick or rag in two or three of its hands, seemed quite happy. For want of something else, it would often seize its own feet, and after a time it would constantly cross its arms and grasp with each hand the long hair that grew just below the opposite shoulder. The great tenacity of its grasp soon diminished, and I was obliged to invent some means to give it exercise and strengthen its limbs. For this purpose I made a short ladder of three or four rounds, on which I put it to hang for a quarter of an hour at a time. At first it seemed much pleased, but it could not get all four hands in a comfortable position, and, after changing about several times, would leave hold of one hand after the other, and drop on to the floor. Sometimes, when hanging only by two hands, it would loose one, and cross it to the opposite shoulder, grasping its own hair; and, as this seemed much more agreeable than the stick, it would then loose the other and tumble down, when it would cross both and lie on its back quite contentedly, never seeming to be hurt by its numerous tumbles. Finding it so fond of hair, I endeavoured to make an artificial mother, by wrapping up a piece of buffalo-skin into a bundle, and suspending it about a foot from the floor. At first this seemed to suit it admirably, as it could sprawl its legs about and always find some hair, which it grasped with the greatest tenacity. I was now in hopes that I had made the little orphan quite happy; and so it seemed for some time, till it began to remember its lost parent, and try to suck. It would pull itself up close to the skin, and try about everywhere for a likely place; but, as it only succeeded in getting mouthfuls of hair and wool, it would be greatly disgusted, and scream violently, and after two or three attempts, let go altogether. One day it got some wool into its throat, and I thought it would have choked, but after much gasping it recovered, and I was obliged to take the imitation mother to pieces again, and give up this last attempt to exercise the little creature.

After the first week I found I could feed it better with a spoon, and give it a little more varied and more solid food. Well-soaked biscuit mixed with a little egg and sugar, and sometimes sweet potatoes, were readily eaten; and it was a never-failing amusement to observe the curious changes of countenance by which it would express its approval or dislike of what was given to it. The poor little thing would lick its lips, draw in its cheeks, and turn up its eyes with an expression

◆◆◆◆◆

of the most supreme satisfaction when it had a mouthful particularly to its taste. On the other hand, when its food was not sufficiently sweet or palatable, it would turn the mouthful about with its tongue for a moment as if trying to extract what flavour there was, and then push it all out between its lips. If the same food was continued, it would set up a scream and kick about violently, exactly like a baby in a passion.

After I had had the little Mias about three weeks, I fortunately obtained a young hare-lip monkey (*Macacus cynomolgus*), which, though small, was very active, and could feed itself. I placed it in the same box with the Mias, and they immediately became excellent friends, neither exhibiting the least fear of the other. The little monkey would sit upon the other's stomach, or even on its face, without the least regard to its feelings. While I was feeding the Mias, the monkey would sit by, picking up all that was spilt, and occasionally putting out its hands to intercept the spoon; and as soon as I had finished would pick off what was left sticking to the Mias's lips, and then pull open its mouth and see if any still remained inside; afterwards lying down on the poor creature's stomach as on a comfortable cushion. The little helpless Mias would submit to all these insults with the most exemplary patience, only too glad to have something warm near it, which it could clasp affectionately in its arms. It sometimes, however, had its revenge; for when the monkey wanted to go away, the Mias would hold on as long as it could by the loose skin of its back or head, or by its tail, and it was only after many vigorous jumps that the monkey could make his escape.

It was curious to observe the different actions of these two animals, which could not have differed much in age. The Mias, like a very young baby, lying on its back quite helpless, rolling lazily from side to side, stretching out all four hands into the air, wishing to grasp something, but hardly able to guide its fingers to any definite

◆━◆━◆━◆━◆

object; and when dissatisfied, opening wide its almost toothless mouth, and expressing its wants by a most infantine scream. The little monkey, on the other hand, in constant motion; running and jumping about wherever it pleased, examining everything around it, seizing hold of the smallest objects with the greatest precision, balancing itself on the edge of the box, or running up a post, and helping itself to anything eatable that came in its way. There could hardly be a greater contrast, and the baby Mias looked more baby-like by the comparison.

When I had had it about a month, it began to exhibit some signs of learning to run alone. When laid upon the floor it would push itself along by its legs, or roll itself over, and thus make an unwieldy progression. When lying in the box it would lift itself up to the edge into almost an erect position, and once or twice succeeded in tumbling out. When left dirty, or hungry, or otherwise neglected, it would scream violently till attended to, varied by a kind of coughing or pumping noise, very similar to that which is made by the adult animal. If no one was in the house, or its cries were not attended to, it would be quiet after a little while, but the moment it heard a footstep would begin again harder than ever.

After five weeks it cut its two upper front teeth, but in all this time it had not grown the least bit, remaining both in size and weight the same as when I first procured it. This was no doubt owing to the want of milk or other equally nourishing food. Rice-water, rice, and biscuits were but a poor substitute, and the expressed milk of the cocoa-nut which I sometimes gave it did not quite agree with its stomach. To this I imputed an attack of diarrhœa from which the poor little creature suffered greatly, but a small dose of castor-oil operated well, and cured it. A week or two afterwards it was again taken ill, and this time more seriously. The symptoms were exactly those of intermittent fever, accompanied by watery swellings on the feet and head. It lost all appetite for its food, and, after lingering for a week a most pitiable object, died, after being in my possession nearly three months. I much regretted the loss of my little pet, which I had at one time looked forward to bringing up to years of maturity, and taking home to England. For several months it had afforded me daily amusement by its curious ways and the inimitably ludicrous expression of its little countenance. Its weight was three pounds nine ounces, its height fourteen inches, and the spread of its arms twenty-three inches. I preserved its skin and skeleton, and in doing so found that when it fell from the tree it must have broken an arm and a leg, which had, however, united so rapidly that I had only noticed the hard swellings on the limbs where the irregular junction of the bones had taken place.

10

ON THE REEF,

DARKLY

KENNETH BROWER

Geerat Vermeij sat in a spare, termite-ridden apartment built above a small biology laboratory in the Palau Archipelago of Micronesia, seven degrees north of the equator. The room was littered with shells of all descriptions, some loose on the tabletops like spare change, others wet and drying on the sink, still more wrapped in toilet paper and jammed by the dozen into plastic bags. Vermeij found two snails to demonstrate the problems in distinguishing species. He held up the first.

"Here's a shell that superficially, to me, looks very much like a young morula," he said. "In fact, when I picked it up the first time, I thought it *was* a young morula. But I know that it isn't. It's a nassarius. It's a young *Nassarius graniferus*. It has very, very similar sculpture on top to a young morula."

The morula in Vermeij's palm was black. The nassarius was white.

"Of course someone with eyesight would know right away," I suggested.

"Of course," he agreed. "The morula is dark, and the nassarius is white."

Vermeij is twenty-eight years old. He is lean and in a fragile way handsome. His face in thought is ascetic. It's a Dutch face, and in Palau, not far from the old Netherlands New Guinea, it seemed to have a historical rightness. It was a face from Joseph Conrad. It looked correct under coconut palms and trade-wind cumuli. Vermeij's goatee is sparse and boyish, his features youthful in their enthusiasms. He moves with a trace of the brittleness of the blind, forever anticipating a bump. He has a questing stride with just a hint of reserve to it. He will gladly show you how far he can broad-jump, if you point him in a safe direction. The legs are full of spring and they take him an amazing distance.

Vermeij's was the first juvenile case of glaucoma in his province of the Netherlands. He was born blind, or nearly so. He could see colors and vague outlines until he was three, then the light went out. It will never come back; his present set of eyes are plastic. The last color he saw was yellow.

The Vermeij family left the Netherlands when Geerat was eight, partly for his sake. "At that time," he says, "Holland did not have particularly good education for the blind. They made you go to one of these hideous institutions. The discipline was awful. I spent three years in such places. I think if I stayed I would have gone nuts."

In Holland Vermeij did have one teacher, a Miss Mooy, whom he remembers as extraordinary. She took Geerat and his classmates into the heath and showed them things. He began collecting acorns, shells, leaves, and such, with the approval of his father, an avid am-

◆◆◆◆◆

ateur naturalist. When the Vermeijs moved to New Jersey, one of the three states then known for enlightened programs for the blind, Miss Mooy's place was taken by Mrs. Caroline Colberg. Geerat was a ten-year-old in Mrs. Colberg's fourth-grade class when she brought in some shells from Florida. They were semitropical, like nothing he had felt before. His fingers traced the extravagant sculpture, the glassy involutions, and encountered there the first intimations of their genius.

"I got to see helmet shells," he says. "Helmet shells are very different from anything you see in Holland. The *smoothness*. It's nice smooth stuff with good, even sculpture on it. I thought it was gorgeous. Most shells in Holland are kind of rough and calcareous. All northern shells are that way."

The sensation was epochal. Vermeij's consuming interest, since the helmet shells, has been the tropics.

The town of Koror, Palau's capital, woke at six-thirty to the siren on top of the police station. Geerat Vermeij was up forty minutes before that to take his morning shower, because at six o'clock the public works shuts the water off. The shower was cold, a fine way to start the tropical day. Afterward Vermeij sat and waited for breakfast, listening to the town waking. There was no glass in the windows, and the morning sounds entered through the screens easily.

Somewhere below a child asked a question. Sleepy, rising inflection. A woman answered irritably. A rooster crowed. Conversation began to stir, a question here, a declaration there. A pig squealed, then subsided. Tires crunched on the crushed-coral road surface. They rolled over the tips of staghorn corals, the tubes of pipe-organ corals, the convolutions of a brain coral, half-buried, a *memento mori* of the reef. Alas, poor brain coral. They rolled too over mollusks that came up with the corals in the dredge. Cone shells are imbedded in

Koror's roads, *Conus magus* and *imperialis* and *tessulatus* and *textile,*
their patterns long since faded. The fluted shells of *Tridacna,* the
giant clam, curve above the earth like the tips of buried boulders.
The tires rolled over trochus, thais, murexes, mitrids. The car
slowed to take the corner, then the coralline-molluscan mumble of
the tires diminished. Another rooster crowed. A shorebird skimmed
the laboratory lawn, braked, and gave a cry as it landed. A group of
children were on the move, the locus of their voices traveling downhill. Several dogs got very excited about something. The siren
sounded. "Breakfast!" said Dr. Edith Vermeij, and Dr. Geerat Vermeij bounded up from his chair.

Vermeij earned his B.S. in three years and his Ph.D. in three. He is
now an associate professor at the University of Maryland. In recent
years he has collected shells in Jamaica, Puerto Rico, Netherlands
Antilles, Guadeloupe, Panama, Costa Rica, Ecuador, Peru, Chile,
Brazil, Senegal, Ivory Coast, Ghana, Sierra Leone, Kenya, Mada-
gascar, Singapore, Philippines, Hawaii, Guam, Saipan, and Palau.
He has become a biogeographer. The patterns that interest him are
global.

When he refers, shell in hand, to his mental globe, his journey
there is tactile and auditory. In Vermeij's geography, all continents
are dark. When he thinks of Senegal, he remembers the dryness, the
sounds and smells of the city of Dakar, and a couple of large limpets.
When he thinks of Israel he remembers the dry heat, the friendli-
ness, and a couple of species of *Drupa.* The features that leap at Vermeij from his mental globe are not land masses but shorelines. His
world is littoral.

"How do you do it?" I asked Vermeij one morning. "Show me exactly how you tell them apart."

He agreed to try, and picked up two unwrapped shells at random

◆◆◆◆◆

from the table. They were reasonably similar. One was *Thais armigera,* the other *Vasum turbinellus.* He held up the thais.

"Okay," he said. "The first thing you notice about *Thais armigera* is that it's knobby." He hesitated. "But so is *Vasum.* What *do* I do when I pick up a shell? I sort of know right away. For one thing, the thais has a widish aperture." He began again. This time he lifted the vasum.

"Okay. *Vasum* and *Thais.* They're similar. They both have big knobs. *Thais* has a wide aperture, *Vasum* has a narrow aperture. They both have short spines, they both have knobs. But with the knobs on the vasums, at least the Palauan vasums, by far the largest knobs are closer to the suture between adjacent whorls."

He picked up the thais again.

"Whereas on this shell it's . . . it's true also, but much less so. Somewhat less so. This second row of spines is still pretty strong, I'll admit."

He began again.

"*Vasum turbinellus* has the posteriormost row of knobs much the strongest. And they gradually become smaller as you go anterior, except for this very anterior set of knobs, which is again longer. Whereas on the thais it's . . . it's a little different. The description actually would be the same, because here again the anterior knobs get continually shorter. But there's a difference. The large spines on the thais point move backward, a little bit." He lifted the vasum. "On this one . . . on this one they . . . they point backward too. So that doesn't work either. It's just a . . ."

He paused, perplexed.

"You seemed to know them right away . . . as soon as you touched them," I offered. "What was the first clue?"

"It was probably the more triangular nature of this vasum. As opposed to the somewhat more expanded aperture of the thais."

◆━◆━◆

I waited, but Vermeij didn't seem to want to say more on the subject. "I'm amazed that they're in different genera," I said.

"Families," he answered. "In fact, I think they're in different suborders."

I decided, then, not to ask him about subspecies. On Ilha Fernando de Noronha, off the coast of Brazil, he had discovered a new subspecies of nerite, distinguishing it from the subspecies that were its cousins. I was doubtful now that he could tell me how.

The smell of dead mollusks was strongest outside Vermeij's kitchen door. It was there, in a deep outdoor sink, that he gave his shells their first washing. The larger shells never came inside. They remained by the back door, propped against the walls. Vermeij spent hours each day removing the inhabitants with pins and washing out their houses. As he handled the shells, he thought about them. "There's a lot of drudgery," he admitted once, "but there's also a lot of learning. I get to see the shells in detail again."

Dr. Vermeij had spent so much time at the splashing sink, up to his elbows in the phylum Mollusca, that he smelled of it. He was redolent of dying gastropods. And of fish stomachs, which he opened regularly for evidence of fish predation of mollusks. The apartment's aroma of molluscan death reached its apogee not in the scattered piles of mollusks, but in the malacologist.

When a shell falls into Geerat Vermeij's hand, at the sink or elsewhere, it is caught up in a kind of dance. It revolves, flips, cants one way or another as his fingertips count whorls, gauge thicknesses, measure spires.

Most mollusks are identifiable by shape, according to Vermeij. Cone shells present problems for him, because color pattern distinguishes them more than their forms, which are all very similar. But cones are hard for everyone, he says. Their designs are often obscured by growths. Vermeij has trouble, too, with shells smaller than

◆━◆━◆━◆━◆

five millimeters. With shells approaching that limit he uses his thumbnail instead of his fingertips. His chitinous nail, sending up a private Morse code of clicks from the minute landscape of calcium carbonate, tells him what he's holding.

"I've been handling shells for twenty years, and I've never gotten tired of it," Vermeij mused as he handled still another. Through the intermediaries of his fingers, he rolled and rolled the shell with his mind, wondering what the shape meant. What, Vermeij asks himself continually, is the adaptive significance?

"This is *Fragum fragum,* a sand-dwelling bivalve," he told me. "Run your hand from the umbo—which is this thing on top—down to this edge here, and then back again. You'll notice it's sharper one way." I did as he advised. In one direction the shell was rough, like a cat's tongue; in the other it was smooth. "When it burrows," said Vermeij, "and it's a very fast burrower, its foot goes down and forward. It is exactly in that direction that the spines are least resistant. The most resistance is when you try to pull them out. It's a wonderful adaptation that an awful lot of sand animals have."

This was, of course, a Dick and Jane exercise in shell contemplation. Vermeij's more serious thoughts run to the geometry of shell shape and the adaptive function of that. He considers himself foremost a shell geometrician. *The angle of elevation of the coiling axis relative to the plane of the aperture* and a host of other angles and figures preoccupy him.

Vermeij applies the word "geometry" broadly. ("Organ music is the only loud music I like. It has a whole different geometrical effect for me. You sit in a room and you're entirely surrounded by music.") For Vermeij geometry has become more than a science.

One day he set a shell down on the apartment table and leaned back proudly.

"Logarithmic spiral," he said. "This is the figure that is gener-

◆—◆—◆—◆

ated when shape does not change with size. It's the most beautiful shape in nature, I think."

The nearly perpetual splashing of the outdoor sink, then, though it sounded tedious to me, for Vermeij was not. For him it was drowned out by organ music. At the sink he was lost in his digital ruminations. The shapes of shells were his sunsets.

Quietly, so quietly that I suspected Vermeij had not heard, one, then two, then three small Palauan boys began pulling themselves in slow motion up onto the ledge outside his window. They pressed black faces to the screen—seven of them, finally—and they watched Vermeij from three feet away.

"You have some spectators," I informed him.

"I know," he said.

The room had suddenly become dark. The boys, jammed as they were in the window, shut out the light. That made no difference to Vermeij, of course. Expressionless, the boys watched him work. There wasn't a clue on their faces as to what they made of him. After five minutes they began conferring among themselves, exchanging short sentences in the Palauan tongue, a polysyllabic and often guttural language. Their voices had the pleasant huskiness common to Palauan children. The Palauan language is full of changes in pitch, and Vermeij likes it. Monotonous languages and voices irritate him.

"What's this?" asked one boy finally, in English.

"It's writing. It's braille," said Vermeij, eager at the chance to communicate. He held up the heavy brown braille paper, the stylus, and the braille slate, and he showed the boys how he wrote from right to left. The boys watched him gravely and said nothing more.

Vermeij worked on for five minutes. Then the boys' silence at last got to him, and he began to feel like something in a zoo. Decisively he set his writing things aside. "All right, that's all," he said. "I'm done. All finished. Why don't you go play somewhere else." The boys did not get the idea at first, but when they did, they departed as silently as they had come.

Vermeij moved to the kitchen sink and began washing shells. An electronic noise made by some insect came, as usual, from a tree outside the kitchen window. The tree hummed as if a transformer were hidden in the epiphytes that bearded its branches. Below the hilltop a girls' softball game was in progress, and the shrieks of the players and of the audience carried up. The shrieks came regularly, like breathing. It sounded like the most exciting softball game in history, but in truth Palauan girls scream at the softest grounder, the shallowest fly, the most routine play at first.

The tree hummed, the girls screamed, Vermeij's sink splashed, the noon siren sounded.

To date, Vermeij's principal contribution to his science bas been, he believes, his discovery of certain differences between Pacific and Atlantic shells. He has found that Pacific shells are more heavily armored than Atlantic. They show a higher incidence of antipredatory devices—obstructed apertures, inflexible opercula, low spires, and strong external shell sculpture. The reason, Vermeij believes, is that the Pacific has had a longer history without major geological perturbation. Predator–prey relationships have evolved without as much interruption in the Pacific and have become more complex. Survival for mollusks there has become a neater trick.

Vermeij does not want to spend the rest of his career developing this theory, as he probably should. He is leery of specialization. Until his final year of graduate school, his preoccupation with mollusks was total, but in that last year he broadened his reading. He is now a

◆━◆━◆━◆

student of all invertebrates, and of biochemistry. He has written a paper on vines. He is interested in slow muscle and fast muscle in the claws of crabs.

In Palau one evening we watched him root through the garbage and come up with a fish head that Edith, his wife, had boiled for soup. He knows little about fish, but he was fascinated by the teeth. He kept running his fingers over the strange, rounded molars, indulging in pure, uninformed speculation. Though he remains most knowledgeable about mollusks, especially snails and nerites, he likes to think it may not always be so. He is one of those scientists who want to be free—as Newton was, and as Newton put it—to pick up "a smoother pebble or prettier shell than ordinary, whilst the great ocean of truth lay all undiscovered before me."

The reef curved away to either side of where we stood. Long white combers broke on it, marking it as far as I could see. On the arc to the south was a distant wreck. The tide was low. Our shins were awash.

Vermeij turned and started north along the slight ridge of coral stones that made the spine of the reef. He stepped carefully among the reef's irregular vertebrae, hunting the line that divides lagoon from ocean. The surf broke forty yards offshore, and the Pacific, its energy spent, lapped the rocks in a gentle current and rippled past our ankles. The sun was radiant on our shoulders, though a cool wind allowed us to believe it wasn't. The sea smell was strong.

Vermeij soon tired of the higher rocks, left the reef's spine, and walked toward the ocean. The reef shelved very gradually under sea, in that direction. He collected for a time in knee-deep water, turning stones and searching their bottom surfaces. When his fingers encountered a snail, they pulled it off and dropped it in the bucket. They rolled the snail in transit, identifying it somewhere along its parabola to the pail.

◆◆◆◆◆

"A new species of *Thais*," he said, bucketing a specimen. "New for this trip, anyway."

He crouched in the water and began collecting on his haunches, so that his arms could sweep a wider area. His loins were in the Pacific. He heard the incoming waves and avoided them with a water-ouzel motion, straightening his knees but dipping his torso, so that the work of his hands could go on uninterrupted. He moved in nice synchrony with the waves, rising just in time, with a shorebird's sense of the sea's rhythm.

He brought up a cobalt-blue, slender-armed starfish. He tucked his pail between his knees to free his hands, and he patted down the undersides of the animal's rays, two at a time, from base to tip, feeling for any molluscan parasites. The starfish was clean, and he tossed it away. "Blue starfish," he said, and he gave the Latin name.

He moved on. For a time he worked in silence. Then I saw him smile tightly. "Fire coral here," he said.

"Sting you?" I asked.

"A little, on the knuckle."

The hydroid corals, called fire corals or stinging corals, are common on Indo-Pacific reefs. They are protean, forming saucers, blades, and branches. They encrust other corals, taking their shape, or grow over old bottles and wrecks, rendering these rich and strange, but disguising themselves in the process. For this reason, and because they vary in color, they are hard to recognize, but Vermeij knows instantly when he has found one.

The pressure of his knuckle had tripped the triggers of thousands of nematocysts, or stinging cells, on the coral's surface. Within the capsule of each nematocyst was a coiled tube armed with folded barbs. The opercula of the capsules sprang open, the tubes uncoiled, their barbs unfolded and stabbed Vermeij. The poison-filled hollow in which each tube had reposed emptied its contents into him. The poison contained 5-hydroxytryptamine, a potent pain-producer and histamine-releaser, which worked directly on pain receptors in his skin. Vermeij made the identification even faster than with the gastropods he knows so well. The problem was never presented formally to his brain; it was intercepted by his sympathetic nervous system, which mindlessly gave its readout. "FIRE CORAL," it said.

Vermeij is stung regularly by fire corals, and he accepts their nettlesomeness casually, as a mild reprimand. There are worse things around. The seas Vermeij has chosen for his work are the most venomous in the world. He has been stung by fire-worms, hydroids, sea urchins, Portuguese men-of-war.

"See this coral here?" Vermeij asked. "Jesus! Lovely!"

He didn't linger at the lovely coral, but left it and moved on. He found something he could not identify. It was under a rock, and he was unable to scrape it off. He smelled his fingers, making use of another sense.

"What is it?" I asked.

"I don't know. But it has a very peculiar smell, like iodine."

He moved on again, without having resolved the problem. The sun was hot on our shoulders and I shifted the shirt that I had draped across mine. I realized that I was a little sunsick. Vermeij worked on, dark, like Samson, amid the blaze of noon. He turned rocks and shifted them. If a rock did not move easily, he abandoned it for the next.

"I never look in the sand underneath the rocks, after turning them over," he said. "There are a lot of dangerous things down there. Cones. Some very dangerous fish."

Despite his precaution, Vermeij occasionally does pick up a cone shell. He knows instantly what he has found, and the knowledge is electric, but he does not drop his catch. He quickly shifts his fingers to the apex, where the cone's proboscis cannot immediately find them, and he deposits the animal in his bucket.

The teeth of a cone are long, fine, chitinous, and hollow. In the species *Conus striatus* they are designed exactly like Eskimo harpoons, but are perfectly transparent, and as lovely as harpoons by Steuben. Cone teeth are miniatures on a scale that no glass-carver could achieve. Their barbs are as sharp as ice crystals, and for the tropical worms, snails, small fish, and shell collectors that they strike, the teeth do have an arctic chill. An early symptom of their venom is numbness.

One night in Palau Vermeij dreamed he was stung by a cone he had collected. The numbness spread from his hand to his arm and shoulder, and then he woke up. Symptoms are, as in Vermeij's dream, first a stinging sensation, then numbness, then a spreading paralysis. The victim loses sensation in his limbs and has difficulty speaking and swallowing. If he is to live, his recovery begins after about six hours. Otherwise his sight is affected, his respiratory muscles begin to fail, he loses consciousness, and he dies.

I put on my face mask, lay in the water, and watched Vermeij's fingers work. They were ghostly underwater and they moved ceaselessly, meandering, then marching over the coral stones, pausing in crannies, moving on. They completed their scans so quickly that I found them hard to follow. When fingers met something animate, they retracted for a cautious instant, then returned, and in a flurry of touches they felt the thing out. Sometimes, after heavy collecting, Vermeij's fingers are so roughened that they slow his reading to a crawl. Scanning braille notes with fingers full of sponge spicules and coral cuts is like reading by moonlight through a bad prescription.

Vermeij turned over rocks for fifteen minutes without either of us speaking. For all he knew, he was alone on the reef. He did not care.

"Nice coral here. Pretty," he said at last. He directed his words to the reef at large, for he no longer knew where I stood.

Lying in perfect camouflage along Palau's reefs, in places just like this, was *Synanceja horrida*, the stonefish. Sluggish, big-mouthed, bug-eyed, covered with warts and debris, abysmally ugly, the stonefish is armed with spines that produce probably the most excruciating pain known to man. Swimming slowly among the same corals, all lace and frills and bands of color, wildly beautiful, is *Pterois volitans*, the lionfish. A victim of the lionfish, like that of the stonefish, thrashes, screams, and loses consciousness. His skin reddens, swells, and sloughs away. "Cardiac failure," writes Bruce Halstead, a student of marine venoms, "delirium, convulsions, various nervous disturbances, nausea, vomiting, lymphangitis, lymphadenitis, joint aches, fever, respiratory distress and convulsions may be present, and death may occur."

Yellow sea snakes, yellow-lipped sea kraits, annulated sea snakes, reef sea snakes, banded small-headed sea snakes, graceful small-headed sea snakes, elegant sea snakes, wandering sea snakes, beaked sea snakes, Darwin's, Gray's, Grey's, blue-banded, broad-banded sea snakes, and thirty-odd other species hunt the tropical waters where Vermeij collects. The sea snakes have the most toxic venom in the snake kingdom. Their poison works with an odd gentleness. The fangs are painless, or nearly so. If the victim realizes at all that he has been bitten, it is in a slight stinging sensation. There is no swelling or unusual bleeding. The affected part may become sensitive to touch briefly, then a local anesthesia sets in. There is a latent period of an hour or two. Then the victim begins to feel sluggish. He has increasing difficulty moving his limbs and special trouble opening his mouth. His urine turns red. His tendon reflexes diminish, then disappear. The muscles of his eyelids become paralyzed. He feels a kind of false drowsiness, then a real drowsiness. Soon he is motionless, eyes closed, and he appears to be sleeping. He is not. Survivors report that they remained conscious but unable to move, or to open their eyes or mouths. For many victims, of course, the false sleep becomes real and final.

On the sandy patches of reef where Vermeij probes for the long-spired snails that live buried in sand, stingrays, too, lie buried. When stepped upon or handled, stingrays whip their tails across their backs and strike with the retro-barbed sawblades of their stings. The venom works directly on the heart and vascular system.

"Look at all this *Caulerpa*," Vermeij said.

He was running his fingers through a green patch of the edible algae that Palauans sometimes come to the reef to gather. *Caulerpa* sways in the current like soft coral, but it is not. It's a real plant in a realm of animals that masquerade as such. In the midst of the reef's sharp edges it felt soft and wonderful. But Vermeij moved on.

He worked his way steadily deeper, toward the breaking surf. He was thigh-deep now, heading southwest. In that direction there was nothing but ocean, and, five hundred miles away, New Guinea. He continued still deeper, until he was collecting with his cheek beside the swells, his arm extended full length, his fingers exploring. The secondary waves rolled in bigger here, and Vermeij, warned by the sound they made as they began to break, straightened just ahead of them, with his shorebird's distaste for wasted motion. He left off his hunting not a moment too soon.

The wave that finally hit him was arrhythmic. It did not break, and followed closely a wave that did. It hid from him in the noise of its predecessor and socked him in the chest. He regained his balance with a small smile of surprise.

The ocean threw several more sneak punches at him in the course

◆—◆—◆—◆

of the day. The collecting pail never went under, I noticed. He bore it like a standard, and the ocean never trod on it.

Night was coming on, the tree frogs were warming up their instruments, the rice was cooking on the stove. Edith Vermeij went to the cupboard and poured rum and Coke for everyone. Vermeij broke off his work. He washed up, left the sink, and crossed to his chair, his arms held slightly out before him. When he had located the chair with a shin, he turned and fell back into it with abandon, as was his habit. He sat with his heels on the edge of the seat, knees under chin, and he began to smile oddly.

The malacologist's mind, when it is not in gear professionally, keeps itself idling in plays on words. When he has nothing to do, as on airplane trips—an especially deadly time for him—he does simple anagrams, "top" becoming "opt" and so on, or he plays similar games of his own invention. He was playing some such game tonight, or working on a pun. Vermeij puns compulsively and with a crazy delight.

Outside the frogs sang like strident battalions of telegraphers all sending the same message. A toad soloed against it. The rapid mellow drumming was a jungle-movie sound, like someone beating a tattoo on a long slender log. The first toad stopped and another began. The toads sometimes seemed to repect each other's songs and not interrupt, but now two toads started drumming together, making a single noise with a resonating pulse.

A gecko on the screen made its scolding noise, as if with a mechanical birdcall. Three of the high-pitched barks, Palauans say, mean that someone is to visit. Tonight the geckos all made long speeches, and no one called on us. Now and again the squeak of a bat came down from the dark, slipping to a pitch that our human ears could register. The high note was a reminder that we were hearing

◆ ◆ ◆ ◆

only a slice of the night. Hundreds of bats were hunting the air above the laboratory hilltop. In full spectrum the night must have truly roared.

A squall approached, sending ahead of it a gust that buffeted the screen. Vermeij had moved already to the window, sensing some sort of insensible gust before the gust, and he stood ready for the wind's cool benediction. I had seen him do that several times before. The gust rattled the screen, bringing with it for a moment, in its coolness and its smell of distance, the recollection of another latitude. The first scattered drops hit, then the sky dumped and the tin roof thundered.

Vermeij nodded upward at the violence on the roof.

"I've been in the tropics for years now, and I've never got used to it," he said.

The nine o'clock siren sounded. The rain fell harder and soon it seemed to beat a circular pattern on the tin. The toads, wet and happy, all began to drum together, their percussion pulsing, and the whole night swirled and eddied with sound.

The sun of a new day was directly overhead. It was not yet ten, but the white ball had raced already to zenith, where it would hang until late afternoon, then plunge precipitously. I studied Vermeij in the perfect saturation of its light.

He crouched chest-deep in the lagoon, his back to me. He was perfectly still and listed slightly to one side, like a statue undermined by the sea. I knew from experience that underwater he was moving, working tirelessly, scanning the sand and corals at his sides, then circling behind to scan what lay at his heels. I had watched it often enough to see without watching. His fingers now were walking palely through the most lavish colors in nature. There are no hues on earth like those of a tropical coral reef. A school of opalescent fusi-

◆━◆━◆━◆

liers turned away in perfect unison, deflected by the motion of his hand. An angelfish outlined in electric blue, as if struck just now by lightning, studied his forearm and moved on. Feather worms buried in coral heads snapped their circular fans shut as his fingers drew near. A clown fish, painted for the circus, ran from him to its anemone and did its dance among the tentacles. Cleanerfish with blue-green stripes that glowed like neon, bold with the privilege of their office, hunted his toes for parasites. They gave him tiny, insensible, fishy kisses, were disappointed, and moved on. A Spanish mackerel circled in from deeper water, then out again, and as it turned the light scattered prismatically from its sides.

Vermeij moved sideways to a new spot and became a statue again. In front of him the shallows were turquoise, the deeper passages dark blue and serpentine. Across the channel, the adjacent island rose mountainous and green. Against the green two white terns, blinding in the sun, spiraled upward, then dropped a little, but above the island's summit a great tropical cumulus continued their ascent, climbing up and up, as tropical clouds do, all banners and battlements, with the albedo nearly of the birds, into a blue sky.

"Here's a coral I've never seen before," Vermeij said, to his wife, or to himself, or to the great ocean of truth that lay all undiscovered before him.

11

TO ISLANDS ON
WINGS AND WIND

ANDREW MITCHELL

*You lie on a mat in a cool Samoan hut, and look out on the white
sand under the high palms, and a gentle sea, and the black line of
the reef a mile out, and moonlight over everything... It is sheer
beauty, so pure that it is difficult to breathe in.*
  Rupert Brooke, *Collected Poems*, 1918

There is often an uneasy calm preceding a hurricane's touch.
Light airs are scooped from warm seas into the upper atmosphere, and pressure near the surface drops like a stone. Beyond the
horizon, the sky darkens to a bruise. Warm, moist winds rush in to
fill the rising vacuum, the anvil-tops of a hundred storms join arms,
and the air of the whole region begins to turn, slowly at first, then
gathering momentum and strength until a vortex is born, writhing
at its centre and producing sucking winds far stronger than any gale.
Like a slowly revolving Medusa the cyclone advances, flicking the

sea into a foam, churning the surface of the Pacific swells into a car-pet of twisting spume and the waves themselves into cliffs. Latent heat oozes from smoke-grey clouds as they rise, cool, and condense into sheets of rain. Soon the first tendrils of the hurricane begin to cast a shadow across the green peaks of an island in its path. Fresh-ening breezes begin to tumble through the sturdy rainforest trees, enveloping the palms swaying urgently above the sand.

With cracks like pistol shots the palms begin to snap, and as the wind turns to the hillside, the buttress roots of mightier trees are torn apart; tall crowns topple to the sound of thunder. Lightning moves across a scene of growing devastation. Whole hillsides are laid waste. The air is filled with a fleece of leaves, flowers and fruits, stripped from a million branches. Unable to cling to the buffeting forest, a flycatcher foolishly takes to the air. Its tiny wings are no match for the cyclone's energy and it is swept far out to sea. Over the mountains the wind collects an ever-increasing detritus of small in-sects, spiders, organisms too small to see; the dust of life is swept from stream banks, branches and the seashore. Pastel-pink pigeons and bright-green lorikeets are swept hopelessly upwards into the vortex and joined by clumsy bats, tumbled from their daytime roosts in their hundreds unable to cling to the branches, some carrying young, some yet to give birth. All try uselessly to fly against the force which carries them from the land.

When the wind has moved on and the branches stand bare, birds and bats alike will begin to starve in the forest, and fall to struggle on the ground. Weeks will pass before the trees grow fruits again. Meanwhile, far out to sea, sucked into the atmosphere and swept on the uncaring hand of the wind, are the seeds of new life, the spawn of a dying forest, the colonizers of new islands.

Exactly where most birds have come from that brighten the for-ests of the remote Pacific Islands is a question that keeps biogeog-

◆ ◆ ◆ ◆ ◆

raphers arguing long into the night. With the exception of a few species in Hawaii and those on the eastern Pacific Island groups of Juan Fernandez, Easter Island and Galápagos, none of the land birds of the South Pacific is of American origin. There are, of course, many sea birds which wander freely thoughout the world's tropical and subtropical seas, and in addition migratory species which pass through the islands on their way to or from their feeding grounds. Of these the now extinct Tahiti sandpiper *Prosobonia leucoptera*, found by Captain Cook but not seen again since, and a similar species which still exists on the numerous atolls of the Tuamotus, may have colonized the islands from the Arctic. Turnstones, bristle-thighed curlews, and wandering tattlers are still to be seen probing the muds and sands of the South Pacific each year, having flown south from their Arctic breeding grounds. It is in the beautiful Palauan Islands just east of the Philippines and in the Mariana Islands that the greatest Asian influence is to be found. The yellow bittern *Ixobrychus sinensis* is prominent in the marshes while the jungle nightjar may have island-hopped down the Mariana chain to Palau from northern China or Japan. Reed warblers also took this northern route through Micronesia and now eight species and many subspecies are found scattered across the ocean as far as the eastern Pacific. Swiftlets, woodswallows, short-eared owls and several rails may have entered Micronesia from the Philippines and Indonesia, though some could have an Australian origin.

Most of the Pacific's ancestral birds journeyed from New Guinea. Even the most distant islands such as Pitcairn and Hawaii have birds which came from here. Their colonizing route across the Pacific seems to have taken them from New Guinea to the Bismarck Archipelago, on to the Solomons, Vanuatu and New Caledonia, to Fiji and Samoa, east to the Society Islands, and lastly north to the Tuamotus and Marquesas. The megapodes, fruit pigeons, kingfishers, white-eyes, weaver finches, cuckoo shrikes and honey-eaters all came this way. As usual their numbers dwindled as they flew eastwards; in Tahiti there are just twelve land birds while an island of similar size in the Solomons or Vanuatu might support forty. The birds of New Zealand, New Caledonia and Vanuatu appear to be of Australian origin, as do some of those in the Solomons and Fiji. Only in New Zealand, Hawaii and the Galápagos Islands are there endemic families of birds, indicating their long separation. Almost all other Pacific birds belong to genera related to those of New Guinea or found there.

A number of birds in the Pacific are flightless, yet their ancestors probably flew there. The rails, inconspicuous brown birds with long beaks and longer legs that carry their outstretched bodies rapidly across roads to vanish silently into the undergrowth, can barely fly. The cormorant of the Galápagos Islands holds out wings to dry in the sun which are pathetically small compared to those of its fish-eating relatives elsewhere in the world. To fly requires such great effort that once wings are no longer needed to forage for food or to escape predators they are, in evolutionary terms, quickly dispensed with.

In the vaults of the most prestigious museum in the world, the British Museum of Natural History, there is the skin of a bird named after a Scotsman. It was collected over 130 years ago on the island of Gau by a Dr F. M. Rayner on an expedition to the Lomaviti Islands in the Fiji group aboard HMS *Herald.* It was sent in a box to London where it was named MacGillivray's petrel after the ship's naturalist who, unknown to the closeted museum taxonomist who described it, had left the expedition under a cloud. The bird is related to the albatross, but possesses a dark plumage and probably nests on cliff tops; since the day it was discovered it has never been

◆—◆—◆—◆—◆

collected again. The name has persisted but the bird has not—or has it?

A seabird restricted to a single island is very unusual; most travel widely in the Pacific. The specimen in the British Museum, a juvenile, showed that the birds may have bred in the month of October, when the fledgling was collected. Petrels tend to nest on inaccessible cliff tops emerging from the forest in the centre of remote islands. Gau was just such a place, and in October 1983 ornithologist Dick Watling set out to try to find the elusive bird. Petrels tend only to fly at night, and after an exhausting march into the mountains in the centre of Gau, the search began by the light of a powerful lamp. After hours of fruitless scrambling over branches on the treacherous cliff tops, Watling was amazed when a large bird suddenly flew into the torch beam, collided with his head, and fell stunned to the ground. After 128 years, MacGillivray's petrel had been found. The story illustrates the ridiculous state of our knowledge about the rapidly disappearing birdlife of the Pacific.

Dick and I sat on the rush mats spread over the floor of his house in Suva, the capital of Fiji. I had known him since we had tramped round the rainforests of Sulawesi in Indonesia together in 1981. Now he had returned to Fiji, where he had been brought up, and earned a living as an environmental consultant.

"The landbirds in this part of the world are some of the most beautiful I've seen, yet there's no one studying them, and I can't cover them all. I'm not a millionaire. More grog?" He offered me a coconut full of *kava* which I downed with customary claps.

"The islands are too remote and complicated to reach and half the species will be extinct due to land clearance and the mongoose before we know anything about them." The mongoose had been imported to Fiji from India to kill rats but turned on the native birds instead. Eight species have been extinguished on Viti Levu and Vanua Levu alone.

The pigeons of the Pacific are some of the most spectacular in the world. They have enchanting names such as the many-coloured fruit dove, which looks as though an artist has thrown colours at it with his palette knife, the crimson-crowned fruit dove, the golden dove and the friendly ground dove. All but the last belong to the *Ptilinopus* genus of pigeons which have evolved into species with arresting bright colours and unusual voices, and are restricted to just a few islands in Fiji, Tonga or Samoa. Of their nesting habits, diet or numbers, almost nothing is known. By far the most superb of these pigeons was the dove reputed to fly like a flickering flame. I was determined to see one.

"The best place to search for them is Taveuni," Dick told me. "The mongoose hasn't reached that island so most of the original species are still around. It's called the flame dove because it looks like a flickering flame as it flies the forest. The silktail's also there. Nobody knows what that is; it looks a bit like a small bird of paradise. If you see anything with a white bum flying about low down in the forest, that'll be it."

Taveuni is known as the garden island of Fiji. It is 16 kilometres long and the young volcanic hills in the interior rise to 1,241 metres at the summit of Mount Uluiggalau. Volcanism ceased on the island less than 2,000 years ago, but since then it has been colonized by a rich flora. Abundant rainfall produces some spectacular waterfalls in its forest, the branches of which are festooned with ferns and orchids as well as the indigenous *Medinilla spectabilis* which hangs in clusters of small red bells from the trees. High in the centre of the island is Lake Tagimaucia which is famous for its red and white *tagimaucia* flowers (*M. waterhousei*), growing by the lakeside. Legend has it that the flowers, which resemble tears in the morning dew, are

◆ ◆ ◆ ◆ ◆

those of a girl whose irritable father wished her to marry an old man whom she did not love. She fled to the lake for solitude and her tears turned into glistening flowers. When her father found her and saw the delicate flowers, his heart was softened, and the girl was reunited with her lover.

A circular rainbow pursued us through a patch of leaden clouds above the Koro Sea as I flew towards the islands. Near the coast lies the Chiefly Island of Bau, the inhabitants of which are still accorded almost royal status. Further north the large volcanic island of Ovalau slipped under our port wing. On its east coast is Levuka, a former whaling settlement and the colonial capital, where the agreement for the annexation of the Fijian islands by Great Britain was signed. To the south lay Gau island, a distant shadow in the mist, and then below us the island of Koro came into view, surrounded by the aquamarine of its coral reefs. Forty minutes more passed before the Twin Otter, decked out in the royal blue and white colours of Fiji Air, swooped into Matei airstrip and bounced on to the grass.

In the small hut which served as the airport lounge, Indian taxi drivers jostled for business. The one I chose drove with customary terrifying speed down the beachside track though the mangrove forests to Somosomo, capital of the island and home of Sir Ratu Ganilau, Paramount Chief and the Governor General of all Fiji. I purchased some *waka* and descended on Kelera's father, Elio, a seventy-year-old veteran of the Solomon Islands war, which had cost him an eye. He kindly agreed to find me a guide and the following day I set off up the mountain accompanied by the tall half-Tongan, half-Gujerati "Jim Boy" to search for the flame dove.

Jim Boy spoke excellent English but had a somewhat melancholy air. He had travelled widely before settling as an Indonesian chef at the Java Restaurant in Suva. He surprised me by indicating that he now had eleven wives—which he later modified to eleven women

◆—◆—◆—◆—◆

and a child from each of them. Now he lived on Taveuni and had only a taro patch, but time to show people around.

As we climbed up through hillsides cleared of trees by a large bulldozer operated by a nameless German, we passed collections of young coffee plants waiting to replace them. A Fiji goshawk settled on a stump before wheeling into the sunshine, its "weeeee-weeee" calls floating on the cool morning breeze. This elegant bird is a frequent sight in open wooded country, but only in Fiji; it is found nowhere else. Its slaty wings outstretched, it flew with a combination of wing beats and glides across the clearing, its salmon-pink breast contrasting with a grey head and yellow eye. Near the forest edge a male Vanikoro broadbill suddenly sped outwards, gunmetal-blue head prominent on dark-blue wings and rufous orange breast. It seemed the goshawk had seen it and turned as if to strike but the broadbill flew up at it and fearlessly attacked. The noble goshawk wheeled and turned, and eventually flew away.

The Vanikoro broadbill is one of the few birds to have adapted well to the breaking up of Fiji's forests and is commonly seen in town gardens and suburbs. It is a form of flycatcher which flits through the forest picking caterpillars and beetles from the undersides of leaves, hovering before them as it does so. It is an artistic nest-builder, creating a small cup of grass stems and fine fibres decorated with lichens, pieces of moss and the odd leaf. The whole thing is bound with silk from spiders' webs. Horse and cattle hair furnish the lining into which two speckled white eggs will be laid. The bird's only relative is found on the Santa Cruz Islands in the Solomons. Within Fiji it has a number of subspecies on different islands, all varying slightly in size or colour. Even though the broadbill must somehow have reached Fiji from lands further west, the short distances between islands in the Fiji group have been sufficient to isolate each population. This kind of reproductive isolation—even over com-

◆◆◆◆◆

paratively short distances—can often lead to the creation of completely new species which, though all related to the ancestral stock, may appear quite different in shape or colour. This is the kind of process which gave rise to Darwin's varied finches in the Galápagos, and which has resulted in Fiji's magnificent *Ptilinopus* pigeons of which the flame dove is but one.

It still eluded me. We climbed higher, at last reaching the line of undamaged forest, entering the cool shade with relief and beginning the scramble over tree roots, pushing aside tree ferns and tangled vines as we pushed up the small track towards Lake Tagimaucia. On the way I narrowly missed brushing against the large leaves of the *salato*, one of the few poisonous plants in the Pacific Islands. This is like a nettle the size of a tree, with fine hairs over its leaves which contain poison. If injected, this causes frightening welts and intense pain which recurs for weeks. Fortunately the islands of the South Pacific have few such plants as well as few snakes and biting insects.

Rounding a bend in the track, we came to a clearing filled with squawking and guttural sounds which could only come from the Taveuni parrot. A number of them were walking backwards and forwards along the branches of a fig tree, while another pair were demonstrating their abilities as trapeze artists on hanging vines. The musk parrots of the Fijian Islands are quite simply the most handsome parrots in the world. *Prosopeia tabuensis taviunensis* is confined to the islands of Taveuni and Quamea alone, and four of them were cavorting in front of me, quite indifferent to the fact that I was there. Their backs and wings were an iridescent emerald green rimmed in sky blue. The undersides of their tails were black, while the heads and breasts were the deepest maroon. As they gathered at the base of a large bough to watch, bobbing and chortling, they looked like a collection of distinguished gentlemen in their smoking jackets

◆━◆━◆━◆━◆

swapping jokes at the club. Another species found only on Kadavu has a brilliant red head and breast with a sky-blue collar, a feature distinguishing it from other parrots on Vanua Levu and elsewhere. Formerly, the sulphur-breasted musk parrot *P. personata*, which is similar but with a black face and bright-yellow breast feathers, was the only large parrot on Vanua Levu, but the red-breasted species was introduced there many years ago.

Sometimes these birds will gather in feeding flocks of forty or more to reach for mangoes, guavas or fruits of the *ivi* tree. Unlike pigeons, parrots are generally predators of seeds, tending to crack them in their powerful bills to reach the kernels and so destroy their chances of germination. Only the seeds of figs and other such soft and small-seeded fruits are likely to be consumed and then distributed around the forest in droppings. Fig trees are an important source of food for many forest birds in the Pacific. They grow to an enormous size, though the fig tree starts out as a tiny epyphytic plant sprouting in the branches of a host tree into which its seed may have been dropped by a passing bird or bat. Its roots descend to the ground and, once there, swell with the moisture and nutrients the soil provides. Eventually these will completely encase the host tree and strangle it to death. The banyan fig eventually stands on the curtains of roots it has sent to the ground. Fortunately these trees are hard to cut down, and are consequently left alone by commercial loggers and farmers alike, providing food for the diminished population of remaining birds.

Ahead the path steepened through the tall trees, and I began to feel the weight of the small pack on my back. It was now well into the morning and Jim Boy beckoned me to quicken my pace. My vision was soon obscured by biting trickles of sweat, and I could feel the first coatings of damp moss on vines and branches as we made our way higher up the mountain's flanks. Numerous small birds tanta-

◆ ◆ ◆ ◆ ◆

lized us with their calls but refused to be identified, merely offering a flash of yellow or iridescent blue as they disappeared through the undergrowth. Worst of all, I could not hear the "tock-tock-tock," like the dripping of a tap, which would announce that a flame dove was nearby. A casserole-sized bird took off in a blur of wings from a tree crown: a Pacific pigeon. It settled in a tree below us, the distinctive blue-black knob prominent on its beak. It looked jerkily in our direction for further signs of danger, with good reason. Jim Boy explained that the pigeons were attracted by smoke. A small fire beneath a tree would bring in three or four which he could readily despatch for the pot with his .22 rifle. I wondered that there were any left.

In Fiji the barking or Peale's pigeon is confined to the larger islands alone, while the equally large Pacific pigeon tends to be found on the smaller islands. The latter is known as a "tramp" species because of its habit of wandering between islands. It is a nonspecialist, finding food where it can from a variety of trees and vines. This ability has enabled it to colonize the tropical Pacific from the Bismarcks east to the Cook Islands. In Micronesia another large pigeon with a handsome green back, white head, and rust-coloured underparts reigns supreme. Tahiti and the Marquesas each have their own endemic species of these large, heavy pigeons as well. *Ducula goliath*, an enormous chestnut-brown pigeon found only on the island of New Caledonia, must be the largest I have seen; it would make a satisfying meal for any aspiring David.

Savai'i and Upolu in Western Samoa are the only places in the world where you will find the tooth-billed pigeon. It is rare, extremely hard to find and must be in danger of disappearing from the world. When Ramsey Peale first described the curious pigeon he found in Samoa in 1848, he was so struck by its beak, which resembled that of the dodo, that he named it *Didunculus* or "little dodo."

Since then others have believed the bird to be related to parrots because of its eating habits and apparent ability to hold food in its feet. In fact, this is not so. The tooth-billed pigeon has evolved in a similar way to parrots, but it is still a pigeon. Only its beak resembles that of a dodo; nothing else. The large orange beak and chestnut back serve to distinguish it from all other pigeons on Samoa. It feeds almost exclusively on the fruits of the *Dysoxylum* tree. These tall trees produce clusters of round green fruits a little smaller than ping-pong balls. Grasping the fruit with the upper half of its beak, the pigeon moves the lower half backwards and forwards like a saw. It is able to cut even hard, unripe fruit, to get at the four seeds inside. Once the fruit is open, the highly mobile top mandible manoeuvres the seeds into the bird's mouth.

Almost certainly the survival of the *Dysoxylum* tree is as intimately connected to this pigeon as that of the *Calvaria* tree was to the dodo. For almost three centuries following the dodo's extinction no *Calvaria* trees germinated on Mauritius. No bird on the islands appeared capable of opening the enormous hard-shelled fruits so that the seeds could germinate. Scientists concluded that the dodo must have been responsible for this task in the past. The handsome *Calvaria* trees, for which the island was famous, seemed doomed. Only when seeds from the last remaining trees were fed in desperation to turkeys, which had crops strong enough to weaken the seed casings, did the first seedlings grow: the tree was thus saved. Many birds, including pigeons in the Pacific's dwindling forest, have a job to do; they do not exist simply to grace the hunter's table. Evolution has charged them with the means to distribute the offspring of trees and so ensure the survival of both tree and bird. To harm one half of such a partnership is often to threaten the survival of the other.

A secondary invasion of birds may eclipse the first colonizers by competing with them for food, reducing the original species to mere

◆━◆━◆━◆━◆

relicts on isolated islands. It may be that the tooth-billed pigeon represents just such an early invader now living in reduced circumstances. Once a species has become established on an island, it might disperse to others, each of which gives rise to its own unique form. If there is no competition, the initial colonizer might evolve into many species, adapted to exploit the variety of niches on one island or several; each one will be quite different in colour, shape and form from the original colonizing ancestor. In the Pacific, all of these things have happened.

It was early afternoon before Jim Boy and I reached a cleared look-out some distance from the summit of the mountain. As the *tagimaucia* flowers did not bloom until December, there seemed little point in continuing to the crater lake where they are found. Instead I took time to rest against the blood-red leaves of young ferns which grew there. Disappointed that I had not managed to see a single flame dove from my high spot, I called to Jim Boy and we set off down the mountain. By four o'clock we were about to emerge from the forest when I heard a sound, a single penetrating "tock." In the forest many birds seem to have the qualities of a ventriloquist; their calls appear to come first from the left and then from the right, making them very hard to locate. I craned up into the treetops, scanning the branches with my binoculars, and suddenly I saw it. No photographs exist of this pigeon and the paintings I had seen left me quite unprepared for the brightness of its plumage. It was a fluorescent orange, which stood out against the leaves like a traffic signal. The bird was male; a slight tinge of green dusts the male's head, whereas the females are a dark olive-green all over. Soon other males joined it in trees nearby and the canopy was filled with intermittent "tocks," each delivered at the apex of an imperial bow, as the birds displayed. I was overjoyed, but more was to come. As I squatted in the undergrowth another of Taveuni's specialities revealed itself, sporting a bright white rump in contrast with black almost fur-like feathers: a silktail, stopping on a branch not ten feet away as it paused before vanishing into the undergrowth of the only island where it has evolved.

Not all creatures that have wings are as powerful fliers as birds. The Pacific Islands are full of insects, including attractive butterflies, beetles and flies, which would certainly never have set out intentionally on long inter-island journeys. Many of them also have bats, which prefer to confine themselves to forests and caves. Some islands in the west Pacific enjoy the attentions of small insectivorous bats; these have failed to reach the islands of the Central Pacific, though one species appears to have colonized Hawaii from America. The islands of the South Pacific are the domain of some of the largest bats in the world, the Pacific flying foxes. One species has reached as far east as the Cook Islands, though it was almost certainly carried there by Tongans in their canoes. Another is mainly restricted to the islands of Samoa; this species is one of the most endangered. How the Samoan flying fox got there remains a mystery, though it is almost certain it could not have done so by using its wings alone. I went to Samoa to see if I could find out more.

Polynesians arrived here more than a thousand years B.C. In A.D. 950, the Tongans invaded and ruled Samoa for three centuries. Six hundred years later new, more subtle invaders had arrived. The first was the Reverend John Williams aboard the *Messenger of Peace*, from the London Missionary Society. Williams brought religious influence and influenza. The Germans followed and developed commerce and copra, while the Americans, eager for new territories, imported a consul and a Constitution. In 1875 the British sent a gunboat and attempted to remove them both. Civil war then raged.

On 16 March 1889, the U.S. warships *Trenton*, *Nipsic* and *Vanda-*

lia faced the German *Alder* and *Eber* in Apia harbour on the north coast of Upolu in what is today Western Samoa. The British had also ordered HMS *Calliope* to enter the capital's harbour to add weight to their claim on the territory. While the Germans, Americans and British postured for power and sovereignty over a small and defenceless tropical island in the South Pacific, an even greater storm was brewing offshore. A terrible hurricane was about to strike Apia.

Despite warnings of worsening weather, none of the captains wished to leave the harbour for the safety of the open ocean lest another might take the island. Almost too late, the British captain sensed the danger. At the last minute, he ordered his ship to weigh anchor and the *Calliope* began to turn into the rising sea.

Walking along Beach Road on the Apia waterfront today there is nothing to be seen of the hurricane which buffeted the town a century ago or of the wrecks of the German and American ships which littered the harbour then. The *Trenton* and *Nipsic* were thrown on to the reefs, the *Vandalia* sank, the *Alder* turned upside down, and 200 lives were lost. Only the *Calliope* survived by bravely beating out to sea in the face of the storm. Apia is now a pretty town dominated from the sea by the twin white towers of its Catholic cathedral set in a line of low colonial bungalows, gracious government buildings and a few smart hotels, backed by steep green mountains rising from the coast. More than 33,000 people live in the capital now. The Germans finally raised their flag over the islands ten years after the hurricane, before being pushed out by the New Zealand Expeditionary Force at the beginning of the First World War. In 1962 Samoa was the first Polynesian nation to gain independence, and His Highness Malietoa Tanumafili II, Paramount Chief of Samoa, has been Head of State ever since.

Tradition is all important to the *matai* or chiefs of Western Samoa. They police the two large islands of Upolu and Savai'i which comprise the Samoan nation and make all decisions of high office. They alone can stand for seats in Parliament; just two remain open to non-Samoan residents. The Fa'a Samoa, or Samoan Way, has persisted despite a Government on the verge of bankruptcy and dependent on aid from Japan, Australia and New Zealand, with little to export other than copra, taro and cocoa. Samoans are proud, tall, and honey-skinned. They have black wavy hair and, unlike the islanders of Fiji, they are Polynesians; the Maoris of New Zealand are the only Polynesians to outnumber them. Adherence to tribal protocol is almost feudal, religious customs are vehemently observed, success and wealth are attributes of the communal *aiga* or family, and individual success outside the Chiefly system is frowned upon.

Air travel has enabled more Samoans to exist outside the islands than in them, principally in the U.S. and New Zealand. A consumer boom is fuelled by television from Pago Pago in the neighbouring American Samoan Islands. These were annexed by the United States in 1900 for Tutuila's magnificent harbour, something the U.S. has never let go. The contrasts between American Samoa and Western Samoa are stark. Pago Pago is a miserable town where people move in fear of insanely driven trucks, and unsmiling Samoan youths hide behind mirrored sunglasses and clutch ghetto-blasters blaring American funk. Traditional canoes have been replaced by sleek American-owned tuna catchers which assemble here from all over the Pacific. As a result Paradise stinks of putrefying fish from the processing factory across the bay.

While both groups of islands retain many traditions away from the towns, it is in Western Samoa that they are strongest, and so the conflict with modern desires is greatest here. Western Samoa is still a paradise, yet its young show one of the highest suicide rates in the world, a symptom of the trauma which taints this beautiful land.

◆━━◆━━◆━━◆

Many are educated in New Zealand, and once they have experienced the freedoms that the Western world provides, cannot come to terms with the restrictions tradition dictates in their own. Faced with years of virtual slavery to their families' will, and no honourable way out, many succumb to depression and take their own lives with Paraquat; this is the ridiculous paradox of a land occupied by what Brooke called "the loveliest people in the world."

It was a bright sunny day as I strode past small shops selling aluminium pots and pans, postcards and carvings, or bright cottons of red and blue *lavalava* shirts printed with hibiscus flowers, exchanging the occasional *"talofa!"* with smiling passers-by. A cool coastal wind blew away most of the humidity, picking up a little white dust from the roadside as I walked past the Prime Minister's office and the immigration office at 'Ifi 'Ifi Street. Aggie Grey's famous hotel lured me inside for a thirst-quenching beer among the green palms and tastefully traditional furnishings and traditionally tasteless tourists. Then I turned left into Falealili Street to begin the longish climb to Robert Louis Stevenson's resting place on Mount Vaea four miles inland.

It comes as something of a surprise to discover that the author of *Treasure Island* lies on the edge of Samoa's forests on Mt. Vaea overlooking Apia. *Tusitala,* the teller of tales, as Stevenson was known, bought the land for his home at Vailima in the same year as the terrible hurricane. Five years later he died of a stroke on the veranda of his house, which survives today as Government House. I trudged up the path cut by two hundred Samoans as they carried Stevenson up the hill to the site where he had wanted to be buried.

Sadly, I noticed that a few taro patches had been cut from the lower slopes of the Stevenson Reserve, eating into the forest. Higher up a small grey bird accompanied me, hopping busily around the branches, occasionally singing a pretty lilting song, then swinging

◆━◆━◆━◆

its tail, spread like a small grey fan, to the left and right so vigorously that I thought it might twist itself off its perch. It was a Samoan fantail, unique to Upolu and Savai'i. I searched for its distinctive nest, woven from grasses and shaped like a cup with a long tapering tail, but found none. Higher up, the heat of the morning brought out rivulets of sweat on my brow as I scrambled over the red earth and twisted roots along the path. Then there was blue sky through the overhanging canopy and a last effort brought me out into a grassy clearing the size of a small terrace. In the centre was a simple tomb of white cement and on the side in bronze Stevenson's still-living words:

> Under the wide and starry sky,
> Dig the grave and let me lie.
> Glad did I live and gladly die
> > And I laid me down with a will
>
> This be the verse you grave for me:
> *Here he lies where he longs to be;*
> *Home is the sailor, home from the sea,*
> > *And the hunter home from the hill.*

The white paint on the tomb is scratched with graffiti now, but that can do nothing to diminish the place. The view is magnificent. Large forested hills sweep in from the right on the other side of Vaisigano valley. On the flat bottom majestic groves of palms dominate the encroaching aluminium roofs of Apia. Looking north I could see over the town to the sea and the white ring of surf outlining the reefs. In the flame trees beneath the neatly-cropped grassy platform, wattled honey-eaters searched for nectar in the clusters of flowers shaped like lobsters' claws.

Lying on my back in the warm grass above Vailima I wondered

◆━◆━◆━◆

why so many writers and painters found so little happiness or inspiration in Paradise. The mystery of the islands has attracted many of them to Polynesia: Rupert Brooke, Herman Melville, Pierre Loti, Jack London, Somerset Maugham and of course Gauguin. It is almost as if the beauty of the surroundings saps the creative will. The natural world offers a parallel: some creatures, once vibrant and energetic colonizers, having landed on an island home suited to their needs, have evolved into simpler forms.

Darkness was falling about Stevenson's tomb before I thought of returning to Apia. New creatures emerged from the gloom of the hillside behind, gliding on monstrous blackened wings and turning into the breeze with such speed that their wing membranes vibrated loudly like the skins of kites. The flying foxes, on wings as wide as my arms, descended on to the croplands below to gorge themselves on papaya, guava, or the pollen of kapok flowers which open at night. This was a good spot from which to count their silhouettes against the sea as they emerged to feed. I watched them clumsily fluttering around the trees and methodically beating their way across the valley below, and wondered how they could have colonized Samoa so far out into the Pacific. Fruit bats cannot fly as well as birds, and rarely fly long distances from land.

There are stories of lizards and frogs falling on the islands from the sky after cyclones. Often there is an almost invisible rain of spiders, beetles and flies, pollen, seeds and spores that drift on the passing winds once the storm has passed. Most fall into the sea and die, but some reach new islands and evolve. It is much easier to reach islands if you have wings. After a passing cyclone, many birds and bats find themselves out of sight of land. Flying for days at a time is no difficulty for birds used to long migrations such as long-tailed cuckoos, which fly to the South Pacific Islands from New Zealand each year, or golden plovers which do so from North America, or

◆━◆━◆━◆

even great seabirds such as the albatross, which wanders oceans at will. It has a wingspan of up to three and a half metres which enables it to fly everywhere in the Pacific but the Doldrums. It has no difficulty crossing water gaps to reach islands, though it may have a hard time finding a place secure enough to breed in; it therefore confines itself to the more remote atolls and islands.

Less elegant and more bulky is the giant petrel, which has a wingspan of about two metres. Its heavy bill and savage habits have earned this bird the name "vulture of the seas." It will occasionally land on the nest sites of other seabirds, seizing chicks from unwary parents as well as feeding on carrion. Unlike the smaller petrels and shearwaters, which feed on squid and crustaceans at the sea surface and breed on many of the islands of the tropical Pacific, the giant petrel is a rare visitor to these waters. But for birds used to forested valleys and sheltered bays, the open sea is a desert. These will fly until their last reserves of energy are used up—a day, three days, at most a week—then simply flutter into the sea and drown. Every mariner has encountered the friendly bird at sea which refuses to leave and seems quite unafraid; exhaustion is easily mistaken for tameness.

Most that manage to reach land will probably die there, without the correct food supply or without a mate. Eventually, however, a pair might arrive together, or a clutch of eggs might be fertile, and a flycatcher, kingfisher, pigeon or bat population can begin. Such a colonizing event might never happen again.

I journeyed across the mountains of Upolu to the O Le Pupu-Pu'e National Park on the southern coast. At 258 square kilometres, this is the only major forest park in the South Pacific. It runs from Upolu's highest volcanic peak, Mount Fito at 1,100 metres, down steep forest-covered slopes, growing over brown lava-field boulders to the coast. Here two of the world's largest bats, with wingspans ap-

◆—◆—◆—◆—◆

proaching a metre and a half, are to be found. One species, named *Pteropus tonganus,* the Tongan fruit bat, after the island where it was first found, is in fact much more common in Samoa. These bats spend the day in colonial roosts high in trees, a habit which has earned them the local name *Pea taulaga* or town bat. They are handsome creatures with fox-like faces, upright ears, deep-brown eyes, and manes of soft tan-coloured fur over their shoulders. The second type is known as *Pea vao,* the forest bat. This is supposed to have reddish fur over its shoulders but is otherwise similar to the Tongan bat. It enjoys the scientific name of *Pteropus samoensis,* the Samoan bat. This was the species I particularly wanted to see, as it is surrounded by mystery and confusion. Local mammalogists on the island had told me that it did not exist, and was merely a young Tongan bat. Some believed it to be rare and in danger of dying out; others thought it common. Most extraordinary of all, it lived alone in the forest and flew not at night but during the day. My first introduction to one was unexpected.

Outside his modern forestry department house, styled like a traditional Samoan *fale,* Tatua, head of the Samoan family with which I was staying, tossed some newly-skinned fruit bats on to the wire mesh over the fire. As I watched their leathery wings twist and shrink, he turned to me with a huge grin and said, "You said you liked to see bats, so I shot you some."

Tatua was to some extent a poacher turned gamekeeper—a hunter who was sent to Bulolo Forestry College in Papua New Guinea and returned to work in the Forestry Department in Samoa. Orange flames flickered over his hugely plump and almost naked body. From knees to hips, his legs were minutely decorated in fine indigo tattoos, precise geometric patterns depicting battles and great past events. To wound the body in this way takes weeks; the pain and blood endured is the mark of a true Samoan man.

◆━◆━◆━◆━◆

Plucking a well-roasted bat from the flames, Tatua thrust two fingers under its ribs, scooped out the guts, and swept them into his mouth, closing his eyes with relish. Samoans regard these as a delicacy; being largely filled with pulpy fruit, they have a sweet flavour. He gestured to a carcass and said, "Try some." The meat tasted gamey, rather like a roasted pigeon. It was tough but delicious.

Tatua loved to sing and dance and it was not long before he rose, cheered by the other Samoans around the fire, to bob and weave with arms outstretched like a bird of the forest, delicately changing the angle of his palms, then slapping his intricately decorated thighs and gazing up towards the stars, hooting and howling into the night. They insisted I dance too, and the pair of us revolved around the fire, crouching and stamping like a pair of alcohol-crazed demons. Inadvertently I stamped my foot on the burning embers, but filled with the energy of a Polynesian warrior, I never even noticed.

The following day we set off into the park past the beautiful Togitogiga Falls, a favourite picnic spot for Samoans, and into the forest scrabbling over the uneven lava boulders in search of bats. We found no roosts, but after several hours we arrived at a large cave in the pouring rain, where Tatua assured me there would be bats. It was a lava tube. Volcanoes do not always throw their lava into the sky. Sometimes it flows down tunnels beneath the mountainside. These "lava tubes" are created when the molten rock hardens on the surface but continues to flow beneath. It is so hot that when the source ceases, the cavern empties, leaving a hollow tunnel sometimes many miles long, scoured with lines from ancient lava flows like rings around a bath.

I expected small cave-living insectivorous bats to be huddling in the roof, but instead found birds which behave like bats and are often mistaken for them; they were white-rumped swiftlets. These small birds can echolocate their way around caves, where they prefer to

◆—◆—◆—◆—◆

nest, in total darkness, using small clicks and twitters like bats. They make small cup-sized nests out of plant fibres glued together with their own saliva. A couple of small chicks snuggle inside each one on a lining of moss and lichens. In Asia the nests of their cousins are used to make bird's-nest soup, but those of the white-rumped swiftlet are considered too fibrous.

The bat roosts had eluded us, but that evening I was able to count more than 4,000 fruit bats flying across the road from the southern portion of the park to their feeding grounds in the north in the forty minutes just before dusk fell. Each evening this phenomenon repeats itself, as perhaps it has done for thousands of years. Some of the bats appeared to be flying south; they flew differently, were larger and had differently shaped wings: the elusive *Pea vao?* Suddenly shots began to split the night. The bats weaved and turned and some fell. Further away, the sound of gunshots, more frequent now, rang out along the road as far as I could hear. As the bats fell to the road, limbs broken and bleeding, the hunters grabbed their wings and swung them in an arc over their shoulders, smashing their heads on the road. The carnage continued for perhaps an hour until it was too dark, then the guns fell silent. The war on these harmless bats is not waged to provide food for the Samoan hunter's family, nor is it designed to prevent the bats from gorging themselves on the Samoan farmer's crops. It is to satisfy the traditional greed of gourmets thousands of miles away on the island of Guam.

Guam is the southernmost island in the chain known as the Mariana Islands in the Western Pacific region of Micronesia. The indigenous Chamorro islanders have been subjected to a succession of invaders—Spanish, German, Japanese, and finally American. The Americans currently own the island, and once used it as a base from which to bomb the paddy fields and jungles of Vietnam. The Chamorro, now mostly Americanized, have retained one aspect of their

◆━◆━◆━◆

traditional culture: a love of bat soup. On feast days, fruit bats are simmered, fur, wings and all, in a broth of coconut milk and then eaten with relish. To Chamorro Indians, bats are a treat, and if you are poor you can even buy them on U.S. welfare stamps.

The Second World War wiped out most of the forests on Guam, which is now covered largely with military bases, asphalt and huge creeping automobiles, so the supply of local bats was quickly used up. Hunters scoured the islands to the north so well that the Mariana Islands fruit bat, *Pteropus marianus,* is now on the endangered species list. Hungry for new killing grounds, the trade has crept across Micronesia, reducing the bat populations on numerous islands. As I stood in the dark beside the O Le Pupu-Pu'e National Park I knew that it had reached as far into the Pacific as Samoa, and that the bats there could now be doomed.

Thousands of bats are now illegally sent frozen from Samoa to gourmets in Guam in polystyrene boxes packed with ice. I asked Ray Tulafono, a senior member of the Forestry Department in Apia, about it and he told me that a law already exists to prevent the trade from Samoa, but that the Government has neither the resources, nor it seems the will, to prevent it. Middlemen provide free cartridges and a day's pay to the hunters who shoot the bats. They are given export licenses and certificates of authenticity without which the bats cannot enter Guam. American Samoa also sends bats to Guam. Though there are supposed to be restrictions, no precise record is kept of the number exported. Hunters merely report the numbers shot, without providing proof. In Guam the bats will fetch anything up to $US35 each. At present there seem to be enough Tongan bats to withstand a limited trade; they thrive in the secondary forest and croplands which are gradually replacing Samoa's original jungle. How long will it be before these flying foxes are

◆—◆—◆—◆—◆

added to the list of the world's endangered species? And what of the mysterious Samoan bat, which depends on untouched forests?

This giant bat perhaps already merits that status, and to find it I had to travel to the last remaining area of extensive lowland forest left on the neighbouring volcanically active island of Savai'i. Surprisingly the ferry left on time from Mulifanua on Upolu's western tip. A couple of hours later we were docked at Salelologa and I took the long bus-ride along the southern coast, past the spectacular blowholes at Cape Asuisui where the surf bursts like geysers through fissures in the lava cliffs, sending rainbows across the sky. We turned inland from the palms and tangled overgrown taro gardens towards Asau Bay on the north side of the island. Several miles to the east of Asau lie huge raw lava fields, similar to those of Hawaii, remnants of the last great eruptions from Mount Elietoga and Mount Silisili in 1905 and 1911. The Faleolupo peninsula is at the north-western end of Savai'i. The forests there are some of the best I saw in the South Pacific Islands. The trees reached the height of twenty-storey buildings, and a number of the species are unique to this area. They have only recently been identified—by Paul Cox, an American researcher who has been studying the area for a number of years. He believes it to be the last potential stronghold of the Samoan flying fox.

From a hillside overlooking the undulating canopy of trees I was able to see these bats well for the first time. They fly quite differently from the other large species on the island, with fewer beats, and their shape is a less pronounced *W*. I could occasionally follow them with my binoculars as they spread giant wings over the forest in the sunlight, soaring on rising air thermals like birds of prey. Most bats do not soar; these were the most impressive I had ever seen. Elsewhere I found evidence which explained Paul Cox's concern. Plans to log this forest are well under way, supervised by representatives from the New Zealand Forestry Service. I met none in Samoa who knew anything about the ecology of tropical forests or the role of a pigeon or a bat. Though meaning well, they can only see the forest in terms of timber management, mostly learnt in the temperate forests of New Zealand to which they would secretly like to return. Survey lines had been cut; chainsaw gangs were already at work. Moving along their tracks deeper into the forest was profoundly disturbing. Houses and banana plantations soon gave way to a wall of seemingly wild forest, but behind this a battleground was revealed. Trees sprawled drunkenly in all directions, stumps grey and twisted pointing to the sky. All the larger trees had been felled. Those smaller specimens left standing appeared throttled with climbers and epiphytes which were racing up their trunks, feeding on the abundant light now available to them. On the ground there was new growth, but not of the original forest. Elephant taro, young banana palms, and coconut grew quickly on soil scheduled for new trees. Crushed branches littered the ground.

Landowners here, unlike those in many other areas, often do not want their forests cut. In March 1986 Salelologa's farmers burnt two million dollars' worth of logging equipment belonging to the South Korean South Pacific Development Corporation. They also dug up the graves of relatives of the Chief, who had capriciously signed away their trees against their wishes while living in Hawaii. In Faleolupo they were forced into an agreement to log when the Government threatened to close their old school for lack of maintenance. They needed $US25,000 for a new one, and the villagers could not raise it until the logging began. Only then would the bank give them a loan, guaranteed by the royalties they received (the bank would benefit additionally, of course, from deposits from the loggers). Not surprisingly the royalty offered by the Government precisely

◆ ◆ ◆ ◆

matched the funds required. The villagers relented for their children's sake and now the forests which they would have inherited are being destroyed, along with the unique creatures and trees they contain. Such tragedies are significant on a world scale. Savai'i's forests exist nowhere else. To remove the mix of species unique to an island is to remove them from the world altogether; there is no chance of importing them again from elsewhere. Samoa's remarkable bats, tooth-billed pigeon, friendly ground dove and forests teeter in the face of oblivion.

I visited one place in the Pacific where bats are safe by royal decree: the Kingdom of Tonga. There King Taufa'ahau Tupou IV (who, it is rumoured, has recently reduced his weight from 36 stone to a mere 25) rules with an almost feudal charm through Polynesia's oldest and only remaining monarchy. His dominions stretch across 1,000 kilometres of the Pacific from Niuafo'ou in the north to the ancient island of 'Eua in the south. Essentially the kingdom consists of three large groups of atolls, Vava'u to the north, then Ha'apai, then Tongatapu in the south. Only 37 of the 170 islands are inhabited. The first Polynesians arrived here more than 3,000 years ago, and developed into a powerful seafaring nation with an empire covering islands as far west as Rotuma, part of Fiji, and as far east as Samoa and Niue. The first European to reach Tongatapu was the Dutchman Abel Tasman in 1643. Cook followed 130 years later, presenting the Tu'i Tonga with a giant tortoise collected during *Endeavour*'s visit to the Galápagos Islands. It survived in the Royal Gardens at Nuku'alofa, the island's capital, until 1966. Overwhelmed by the hospitality he received, Cook named the islands the Friendly Islands.

Tongatapu is a small flat island shaped like a seahorse and barely thirty kilometres long. Two-thirds of the Tongan nation live here. Though there is little of the original forest left, the island supports a

◆—◆—◆—◆

number of thriving Tongan flying-fox colonies and none is more spectacular than the one occupying the *Casuarina* trees down the main street of Kolovai village on the western tip of the island. The bats here are not shot at, so they are very tame and will not fly away if approached; indeed the whole hustle and bustle of village life continues beneath them while they watch with interest, twisting their chocolate-brown faces to and fro to watch buses and bicyclists, children and large Tongan ladies. It is a delight to see such harmony here. Despite the damage to the fruit crops that the bats undoubtedly cause, most people I spoke to welcomed them. They gave the village a certain amount of fame and brought in many valuable tourists. Watching the furry creatures from the roof of the local church, I was captivated by their flying skill as they came in to land on the topmost branches, often in strong winds. They would either fly over a branch, catching it with the claws on their hind feet, lurching to a stop like a fighter on a carrier's deck, or do a 180° turn as they approached and grasp the branch behind as expertly as a circus performer. Large mature males occupied the trees in the centre of the village, above a cemetery filled with sand graves. They spent most of the day attempting to mate with the females; a precarious occupation, the least danger of which is falling off your perch. A female bat who does not wish to be molested is a fearsome sight; she delivers a constant rain of blows and screeching rebuffs which one would have thought were sufficient to deter the most ardent suitor. Only when his loved one's wings are firmly gripped by his own can the male grasp her furry mane with his teeth and achieve success.

Less mature males and females were strung out along the high street to the east. The males here were no less determined but lacked the finesse of their elders, and seemed more easily put off. Those furthest away had given up all hope, and hung apparently asleep, wrapped behind dark leathery wings. In all I counted 6,500

◆ ◆ ◆ ◆ ◆

bats in the colony, an increase of 1,500 over a census carried out four years before. Mafi, an old man of the village and the keeper of its ancient traditions, explained how these bats reached Kolovai. His story added another piece to the colonization jigsaw.

It seemed that many years ago, the King of Samoa at Apia invited the King of Tonga to participate in some games. The King sent his finest navigator, who excelled himself and was spotted by the Samoan King's daughter. She gave him a pair of bats and he returned with them to Tongatapu and kept them in his house. It so happened that the Chief of Kolovai was critically ill, and hearing that the bats had magical powers, he called for them and put them in a tree outside his house. Miraculously, he was cured, and the Chief asked that the bats should remain there, which they have done to this day. This story, which in essence is probably true, reveals that the Tongans were able to carry creatures long distances in their huge double-hulled canoes. In the Cook Islands I heard stories of how Tongans had brought bats there; elsewhere they had traded parrots and lorikeets across the sea for their scarlet feathers. Man and nature were once again entwined in the flow of creatures across the Pacific archipelagos.

There is a gentle pace of life in Kolovai, an understanding perhaps of the value of nature to modern man. Tongans, like most Polynesians, bring a spirit of enjoyment to life; there is always time to play cricket amongst the palms, to sing a song, to admire the rainbow colours of fish brought ashore as the sun sets. Nowhere is this demonstrated better than in their delight in feasts. These are a celebration of abundance and good nature. Their preparation binds villages to their King; they are to be admired as well as consumed. Such a feast, once attended, is never forgotten.

Great processions of lorries trundled towards the eastern tip of the island. Each contained four or five roasted pigs, nose to tail on a trestle shrouded behind white lace, supported on arches of smooth branches. The pigs' feet were decorated for the occasion with small pyramids of taro, and on to this were placed baked crabs, boiled crayfish blushing along their backs, fish, taro leaves, tinned meats, bananas, coconuts and sweet potatoes. At the feasting ground, a square of leaf shelters had been constructed for the thousands of guests. Schoolchildren enacted vigorous *kailao* war dances in skirts of long leaves mottled in red and green, rings of nuts rattling around their ankles, white plumes dancing on their heads as they stamped to the beat of drums and thrust a hundred spears up into the perfect blue sky. With shrieks of delight vast Tongan women rushed forward and thrust *pa'anga* notes into the dancers' shorts; young men stuck them to the girls' oiled bodies.

The trestles of roasted meat and trimmings were set out; there were 2,500 pigs awaiting the King's arrival. He emerged finally from a large blue sedan, in a knee-length black leather overcoat and a pair of skiing goggles. He walked slightly unsteadily on a walking stick to his pavilion, and sat cross-legged on the ground behind a table burdened with food fit for twenty kings. He had just opened the college's new chapel and was feeling a trifle hungry.

◆—◆—◆—◆—◆

12

THE REEF

EDWARD ABBEY

For me, the journey to Australia began with an abstract siege of time and space in a QANTAS (Queensland and Northern Territory Air Service) 707. It was more a process than a flight. We started in the dark at San Francisco's International Airport in the midst of an oppressive metallic uproar—jets like wounded dinosaurs bellowing around us—then lunged upward into deeper darkness where we hung, not moving at all for all I knew, for about three and a half hours until we descended into the clammy balm of Honolulu. A pause. After the stop, the processing was resumed through the longest night anyone ever paid good money to endure. We sat or lounged or lay huddled in this darkened aluminum cigar-shaped capsule while the space transformers whined steadily beyond the insulated walls. From Honolulu's vernal eve across the equatorial circle into the night of the Southern Hemisphere, we submitted, my fellow passengers and I, like docile patients in an intensive-treatment ward, to the ministrations of the machine. Not a journey, not a flight, but simply the transference of human bodies from one point to another by geometrical theorem, or what Ortega y Gasset called "the annihilation of distance." By which process some small but maybe critical element of the human spirit is also annihilated (how annihilate distance without damaging time?), day and night extinguished by our crossing of the international date line. There is no sensation of significant movement in such a mode of transportation; therefore, no sense of travel.

What we have accomplished through jet-engine aircraft is the abolition of the journey. Next time I'll go by sea—or not go at all. Why I've seen more of the world in a subway train from Hoboken to Brooklyn than I saw in that aerial shuttle through the Pacific night.

At dawn we landed in Brisbane. Nothing had changed. I could have sworn I was still in the States, in some familiar town the name of which I had, for the moment, forgotten. The people looked the same. The buildings looked the same, except for some of the older homes and hotels, tropical-style bungalows perched on stilts above the ground, many with wrought-iron balconies that recalled New Orleans. Even the money came in dollars and cents, though the bills were bright with color, not so serious as ours. The heavy motor traffic, under the nostalgic pall of smog, looked the same. Only the language was different; when my taxi driver opened his mouth and began to talk to me in the dialect known as Strine, I realized for the first time that I was in a country full of foreigners.

My hosts, Stan and Kay Breeden, however, whom I met later on that first day, made me feel at home, as did Ed Hegerl, to whom they referred me for the latest information concerning the Great Barrier Reef. (First I would inspect the reef—then the interior.) The Breedens, writers and photographers, have produced several books on the flora, fauna, and geography of Australia, but think of themselves

◆ ◆ ◆ ◆

primarily as "inlanders." Ed Hegerl, on the other hand, is a specialist in marine biology, a transplanted American whose early interest in the coral beds of his native Florida has become a passionate enthusiasm for what he believes are the even greater wonders of Australia's barrier reef. It was the reef, in fact, which had attracted him to the University of Queensland in the first place, and he has since spent so much time and effort in the struggle to save the reef from its many enemies that he has not yet completed his academic studies. Only twenty-four years old, he is one of the founders of the Queensland Littoral Society, preeminent among defenders of the Queensland coastal area.

We talked of the dangers to the barrier reef: the crown of thorns starfish (*Acanthaster planci*), which has multiplied to plague proportions in recent years and is devouring the living coral polyps of the reef; the threat of oil drilling by a consortium of British, Japanese, and American oil companies; proposals to mine the limestone from parts of the reef; pollution from coastal cities, industry, and agriculture; an excessive development of commercial tourism on the islands of the reef; oil spillage, both deliberate and accidental, from seagoing tankers in the area; commercial and amateur shell collectors; dredging and filling operations along the coast; even proposals to blast (with nuclear power) deeper channels through parts of the reef.

"What about whales?" I asked. The barrier reef was once famous as a nursery for the migrant humpback whale.

"No problem," said Ed. "Hardly any whales left. The industry took care of them years ago."

To me it sounded like a familiar story. I asked young Hegerl what he thought would be the optimum population for a country like Australia.

"Three hundred thousand aborigines," he replied.

◆━◆━◆━◆

We shook hands on that. At the far end of the Pacific, in the dim illumination of a Brisbane (pronounced *Bris*-bun) bar, across a generation gap of twenty years, two fanatics had found each other.

The next morning I rented a car and drove north along the coast to observe a bit of the reef with my own antennae. I was lucky to get out of Brisbane. Not only was the steering wheel mounted on the wrong side of the car, but all the motorists except myself, as I quickly discovered, were driving on the wrong side of the road. I caused a traffic jam in the center of the city when I confronted, head-on, a massive wall of opposing traffic, but soon got the knack of the thing and escaped the city without killing anybody or catching the notice of a policeman.

Finding the main highway leading north was not easy. Brisbane has no freeway system, I am happy to report, but the good inhabitants are eager to advise a stranger on how to find his way. I learned first that the road I was seeking had several names—Bruce Highway, Gympie Road, Pacific Coast Highway, Route 1, etc.—and that in beginning from the center of the city there is a mathematically infinite number of different routes by which to reach it, so that opinions on the *best* way naturally differed. One man advised me to "follow the main traffic north until you come to this big gum tree in the middle of the street, go around it and turn right at the first Ampol petrol station you see, follow that till you come to the railway, go over the bridge, turn left at the chemist's shop, keep on that street till you find the Shell station, stop there, and get more directions."

He was right. Soon enough I found myself out of the city and deep in rural Queensland, which resembles, in a general way, the America of forty years ago: narrow winding roads, scattered villages, isolated farms, open fields, unfenced cattle range, woods and forest everywhere. The hills were dry now, in Australia's early autumn; the land

◆◆◆◆◆

had a lovely golden glow upon it. I saw many birds, mostly strange to me: cockatoos and kookaburras and flocks of what looked like crows but sounded like magpies. When I lay down in the eucalyptus woods that first night, somewhere 200 miles north of Brisbane, and drew the hood of my mummy bag over my head—for the clear air became quite cold after sundown—I heard the raucous squabble of more exotic birds fighting for roosts in the trees nearby. I looked at the stars and saw only one familiar constellation—mighty Orion, upside down, far in the north.

I'm in Australia, I told myself. I didn't quite believe it. The differences between the world I saw here and the America I remembered from childhood were too dreamlike to be real. Australia seemed to me not so much another country as my own country in another time.

But that perception was only half-true. The forces that are fouling up America are hard at work in Australia too. I dreamed that night of a planetary starfish enclosing our earth in its thorny, mindless, hungry embrace. Seventeen arms. Lop one off and a new one grows in its place. Give it an inch and it spawns between 12 million and 24 million eggs. Each year. Every year.

Next day I reached the town of Gladstone and took the launch to Heron Island, seventy miles offshore. Heron Island is the southern anchor of the Great Barrier Reef and also, according to my friend Hegerl, the best surviving example of a typical reef island.

The sky was bright and sunny, the sea a deep dark blue. Dolphins escorted the boat for a mile or two, once we'd left Gladstone Harbor behind. There seem to be plenty of them left, the boat captain told me, but not so many as before. Dolphins have a tendency, he explained, to get trapped in the shark nets that have been set up around popular beaches; once trapped, they drown. Another problem is that dolphins are thought to chase away big-game fish such as black marlin and tarpon. So fishermen shoot them on sight. Had he seen any whales? Not for several years, he answered. And the crocodiles? They're up north around Cape York, he said, but becoming rare. And the sea cow or dugong, a mammal much like Florida's manatee? They too are getting into trouble with man and his works.

These shallow reef waters are also the home of the giant clam, a 500-pound bivalve reputed to have the ability to close on an unwary diver's foot and drown him. This belief was put to empirical test by a fisheries researcher. Deliberately, he put his foot into a giant clam. The clam snapped shut, holding the researcher fast by one ankle. After fifty seconds, he reported, the clam's muscle relaxed for a moment, allowing him to withdraw his foot—by acting quickly. The tide was out at the time, so the experimenter had been able to keep his head above water. What did the test prove? That the giant clam might drown a man? Yes. But only by raising an equally interesting question: Who could be stupid enough or so inattentive as to step into the brilliantly mantled mouth of a giant clam?

Heron Island appeared on the horizon. A true coral island, or cay, it lay flat against the sky, green with pisonia trees, coconut palms, pandanus palms, surrounded by the pale aquamarine waters of the reef. From this point the reef extends some 1,250 miles north at varying distances off the coast at Queensland—from the Tropic of Capricorn to Cape York and beyond to the southern shore of Papua, near the Equator, where, as my Queensland map says, "Kennedy [an early explorer] speared by blacks hereabout, 1848."

The launch entered a narrow channel leading to the island's sole landing place, a rough coral beach. The channel was marked on one side by buoys, on the other by the hulk of an iron ship, rich with rust, crusty with barnacles, half-sunken, condemned, its crew a flock of seagulls perched on the sagging rails.

On the beach was a circular concrete pad for helicopters. A plan to construct a modern landing field for fixed-wing aircraft had been

◆◆◆◆◆

averted a year before. The strip, if constructed, would clear a wide swath through the center of Heron Island for most of the island's length. Heron is a small island. About half of it is a national park. It is also the site of a scientific research station, winter home of the shearwater—a bird that migrates annually from here to Siberia and back—and a rookery for the noddy tern. Here too comes the great green turtle, *Chelonia mydas*, a 300-pound reptile in a shell, to lay its eggs in the warm sands of Australia's February summer.

As with so much else concerning the reef, there is a lot still unknown about this giant turtle. An herbivorous animal, it spends most of each year a thousand miles to the north in the warm tropical waters of the Coral Sea, where the feeding grounds are more to its liking, but comes south once every four years to bury its eggs in the sandy beaches of Heron Island. Why the journey? And how does the turtle find its way back to the same tiny island in the vast Pacific? The answer is hypothetical: The northern coastline and island are largely enclosed by tangled mangrove swamps, unsuitable for egg hatcheries; therefore, the green turtle comes south. And what guides it? A combination, perhaps, of solar-compass capacity and the ability to smell (in the ocean currents) traces of material from the target island.

The female green turtle swims onto the reef, waits for nightfall, then comes ashore. In the water she is a swift and agile creature, but on land slow, clumsy, vulnerable. Nevertheless, she has no option: The eggs must be deposited in a sandy beach if they are to hatch. Obeying this instinctive command, she digs a pit in the sand well above the high-water line, lays her eggs—usually about a hundred in a clutch—covers them, lumbers back to sea. In earlier times she might never have made it to the water, but would have been caught by man, killed, turned into turtle soup. Now the green turtle is protected by the state of Queensland and has a fair chance of survival.

In other parts of the world, as in the South Atlantic and Caribbean Sea, the green turtle is close to extinction.

The laying of the eggs is only the first part of the green turtle drama. After hatching, the two-inch-long baby turtles begin at once a return to the sea, attracted and guided apparently by the radiance of the surf. From each nest a hundred or more hatchlings come scrambling and start a hasty crawl toward the waves. They have good reason for haste: There are enemies along the way. The young turtles are attacked by gulls or scooped up by the big spiderlike ghost crabs and dragged off to the crabs' burrows, there to be vivisected and devoured. The survivors reaching the water become the prey of fish, sharks, stingrays. From each clutch of turtle hatchlings it is estimated that only two or three will live to maturity.

Time for a firsthand look at the reef itself. So far, I had seen it only when the tide was in, the water high enough to cover the coral boulders and the open sandy spaces between. Now, as the tide retreated, I armed myself with a fossicking pole, put on a pair of canvas shoes, and walked out onto the open reef. By keeping to the sand, it was possible to avoid walking directly on the living coral. The purpose of the pole is to test your footing and to turn over the small "boulders" or clusters of coral to see what's living and going on underneath. Fossicking etiquette requires that you return the coral to its original position; otherwise, the living organisms exposed to the air would die. So, in this way, I was privileged to see such things as the bêche-de-mer, a wormlike creature six to ten inches long; diminutive hermit crabs peering at me out of purloined seashells; small clams embedded hinge downward that closed with a smart snap when I touched them, squirting seawater at me; and occasional small fish suspended in the clear water, gliding away when I came near. Something like a shadow drifted before me, slowly moving its broad wings—a stingray.

◆—◆—◆—◆—◆

Approaching the edge of the reef, where the coral cliffs and valleys and canyons begin, I put on flippers, goggles, and snorkel and drifted out over the deeper waters. Here was the true coral wonderland, a complex array of varied forms and subtle, pastel colors. It looked at first glance like some fantastic garden, but here the flowers are living animals—anemones swaying back and forth with the slow surge of the sea, each waving strand having the ability to capture and kill appropriate prey; the amazing variety of coral, some like lacy fronds, others like antlers or like cholla cactus; still others resembling huge disembodied lavender brains four or five feet in diameter.

Each of these objects, whatever its size and color, is a colony, many individual polyps bound together by calcareous secretions to a common base. Transforming calcium from the seawater into limestone, the coral colonies shape themselves outward and upward, each generation forming the base of the next. There are said to be hundreds of varieties of coral here; each one has a distinctive shape and color. Taken all together, over a period of a million years, they have created the largest animal-made structure on earth—the Great Barrier Reef.

Some might say the reef is the most beautiful nature-made structure on earth. Gazing down at the half-tame, gorgeously banded schools of fish drifting over and within the coral caverns, I felt what someone—was it Cousteau?—has called "the euphoria of the deep." The fish themselves seemed to share such a feeling. We hear of the struggle for survival; we see it every day in the streets and cells of a human city. But among these brilliantly enameled fish, swaying in unison with the currents of the water, drifting soundlessly among the fans and veils and candelabra of the coral, that struggle seemed to have been forgotten. They moved past one another, little fish and big fish, like creatures in a trance, in a state of solemn enchantment, indifferent to me floating above as well as to one another. Surely an

◆◆◆◆◆

illusion. Surely, when my eyes were turned elsewhere, something was rending something.

I looked for starfish and saw a few of the small, ordinary, five-armed kind. But not the famous crown of thorns. Later, on another day, I paid a visit to the research station on Heron Island and learned more about the starfish question.

The crown of thorns starfish has attacked the barrier reef from the north, spreading and multiplying southward. When I was on the reef the plague had been observed as far south as Townsville, half the distance from Cape York to Heron Island. It seemed to be continuing in a southerly direction, although the rate of advance was not known.

The starfish invasion was first noticed in the middle 1960s. Later, it was discovered that the crown of thorns was destroying coral reefs in other parts of the Pacific—Guam, Fiji, Borneo, and Majuro. Some marine biologists believe that the starfish swarm is a cyclical event; others, that it follows from human interference with the ecology of the coral reef.

One of the leading proponents of the latter theory is Dr. Robert Endean, professor of zoology at the University of Queensland and chairman of the Great Barrier Reef Committee, an international organization of scientists interested in the welfare of the reef. Dr. Endean proposes that the starfish is multiplying because one of its natural enemies, the shellfish called giant triton (*Charonia tritonis*), has been drastically reduced in number as a result of commercial and amateur shell collecting. Among collectors and souvenir hunters, the ornate, trumpet-shaped, large (as long as eighteen inches) shell of the triton is considered a prize. Following the advent of mass tourism in the sixties this shell and the snaillike mollusk that creates and inhabits it began to become rare. Although the triton seems to attack and kill no more than one crown of thorns starfish per week, this may be sufficient to make the difference between a stable population of starfish and an exponentially expanding one.

Attempts to verify the triton hypothesis have so far failed. The tritons are hard to find, hard to keep track of in their underwater environment; skilled divers are needed to do the work, and the money to pay them is not available. The starfish themselves are difficult to follow because they cannot be tagged, dyed, or "earmarked." If tagged, the starfish soon rids itself of wire or metal by shedding its own tissue; if dyed, the dye fades away too soon to be of any use; if spines or arms are cut off, the starfish regenerates them, making identification doubtful. All that is known with certainty is that the triton will destroy starfish—but not often.

How does the starfish destroy the coral? By embracing and digesting the individual coral animal. Attacked, the coral polyp—itself a carnivorous little beast—withdraws into the cup of limestone that is its self-secreted home. Not good enough. The starfish extrudes its stomach through its own mouth into the polyp's cavern, surrounds the living tissue with stomach lining, and reduces the polyp to a mucous soup by the action of digestive juices. When the starfish descend upon the coral colonies by the hundreds of thousands, as they were now doing, they cover portions of a reef with a tangle of thorny arms, spiny backs, industrious stomachs. When the coral life is wiped out, the starfish move on to another reef, leaving behind the bare skeletons of their prey. Lifeless, the coral reef begins to break up and dissolve under the pounding of the waves. Meanwhile, the crown of thorns starfish, once a year, lift their arms and release through gonadal ducts clouds of eggs, eggs by the million, which are thoroughly circulated among the reefs and islands by the movement of water currents.

The triton is not the only enemy of the starfish. The giant clams, legendary menace to divers, consume large amounts of plankton—

◆—◆—◆—◆—◆

plankton that contains, among other organisms, the larvae and fertilized eggs of the starfish. But like most large, conspicuous inhabitants of the barrier reef ecosystem, the giant clams are themselves being subjected to intensive predation by humans. The clams are considered a delicacy by Asiatics, and clam hunters in powerboats are raiding the reef from places as far away as China.

One of the checks on growth of the *A. planci* starfish population is, or was, the same animal that is now its prey—the coral. Among the many species of microfauna that the polyp captures and stings and ingests are the larvae of the crown of thorns starfish.

Now, in a turnabout, the adult and juvenile starfish are destroying a former enemy. How did this happen? One among the many hypotheses is that another variety of human interference—dredging of ship channels, seismic blasting in oil exploration—by destroying the reef filter feeders, including coral, has opened the way to the expansion of the starfish population. Pollution, too, in its many forms, from city sewage to residual pesticides and herbicides washed down the coastal rivers from agriculture areas, has probably contributed to the disturbance of the barrier reef.

The theory that the plague is a natural episodic event, from which the coral in the course of time will make a natural recovery, has, like the others, one serious flaw: absence of conclusive supporting evidence. It also has one serious advantage: If true, no corrective action is needed. This theory appeals to Australian citizens and politicians reluctant to spend the enormous amounts of money necessary for further research or remedial action.

Until further knowledge establishes the exact cause of the starfish plague, the only remedy is the crude but simple one of employing an army of skin divers to go into the water after the crown of thorns one by one, destroying them *in situ* with injections of formalin or removing them from the coral, bringing them to the surface, loading them

◆ ◆ ◆ ◆ ◆

in boats, and dumping them on shore to die by exposure. Either method would be expensive; estimated costs run into millions of dollars. Confused by contradictory reports from various investigators, neither the State of Queensland nor the Commonwealth of Australia has appropriated the funds for a war against *Acanthaster planci*.

Maybe the starfish menace will go away, with or without man's intervention. But other dangers to the integrity and life diversity of the Great Barrier Reef remain: excessive tourism, pollution from coastal sources, mining of limestone and mineral-bearing sands, extermination of endangered species by uncontrolled big-game hunting and fishing, the seashell business, and other forms of industrial development on the Queensland coast, especially oil.

Extensive oil prospecting has already been carried out on the reef. The identification of commercially profitable petroleum deposits is said to be "promising." At present all drilling has been halted by a state moratorium until a royal commission of scientists, government officials, and laymen appointed jointly by the Australian Commonwealth and the State of Queensland, completes an inquiry.

The debate on oil drilling follows familiar lines. Supported by the Queensland state government, whose premier, Johannes Bjelke-Petersen, is alleged to hold a $700,000 interest in the oil consortium called Japex (Japan and Texas—a logical pair), the backers of the oil companies argue that oil discoveries will provide a great shot in the arm to the Queensland economy, now suffering (as usual) from a recession. Many Australian scientists, especially geologists and mining engineers, support the position that controlled exploitation of the barrier reef's mineral resources can be carried on without "seriously" damaging the reef "as a whole." This is, in fact, the position taken by the Great Barrier Reef Committee. And if this is so, developers contend, it is economic folly not to utilize the mineral wealth available in the reef and surrounding waters of the continental shelf.

Opponents of oil and other mineral development take the line that any amount of oil drilling presents risks to the reef that outweigh the immediate financial benefits. The conservationists do not agree that parts of the reef can be drilled, blasted, dredged, and mined without harm to the remainder. They believe that the web of life in the region is so intricate, specialized, and diversified that harm to any part will harm the whole.

Defenders of the reef invoke the specter of thousands of drilling rigs in operation, as off the coast of Louisiana. Blowouts and oil spills mean certain death to much of the bird life and marine life of the reef, more vulnerable to such contaminants than a place like the Santa Barbara Channel. There are 1,150 different species of fish in the waters off Heron Island alone. There are hundreds of species of coral in the barrier reef; the Caribbean has only about 40.

What are the effects of oil spills? The effect on bird life is well known. Of the 7,800 birds rescued and treated after the wreck of the tanker *Torrey Canyon* off the coast of England, only 443 survived. The wreck of the *Tampico Maru* off Baja California destroyed for a time all life in the tidal pools except one species of anemone and one of periwinkle.

The harm done by oil goes below the surface. The soluble constituents of oil, such as benzene, toluene, and other hydrocarbons, which may escape cleaning-up operations, are highly toxic to fish. Bacterial life too is destroyed by these compounds, except for certain aerobic species that have the capacity to digest oil. Being aerobic, they reduce the oxygen content of the water, endangering the fish population.

In view of these dangers, the Queensland Littoral Society has advocated that the entire barrier reef area be set aside as a national reserve, that oil and gas drilling operations be deferred until the technology of the industry is so advanced that complete safety for the life community of the reef can be assured. This would mean, in all likelihood, no drilling in the near future. Maybe never.

It was an immense pleasure to forget for a while the troubles of the Great Barrier Reef, to walk the coral shore of Heron Island and swim in that dazzling Pacific sea. Out there above the coral gardens where the fish drift back and forth in their amazing grace and unforeseeable color, I found it possible to think that all was yet well in this enchanted chamber of humankind's ancestral home. The crown of thorns was 800 miles to the north, the sharks out of sight, the stingray and fatal stonefish nowhere to be seen. Through crystal water I gazed at open polyps below, like red and yellow daisies, filtering their supper from the rich sea that sustains them.

13

SOUTH PACIFIC

FOLKLORE

AS COLLECTED BY R. H. CODDINGTON

THE SHARK AND THE SNAKE (LEPERS' ISLAND)

This is about the Shark and the Snake. They quarrelled, and the Shark told the Snake to come down into the sea, that the Shark might eat him. The Snake said to him, They will kill you, and I shall eat a bit of you. Now when they killed the Shark, the Snake went down into the sea and ate the Shark.

THE HEN AND
HER CHICKENS
(LEPERS' ISLAND)

This is about a Hen that had ten Chickens. So they went about seeking their food, and they fell in with the tuber of a wild yam, a *gigimbo*.

After a while the tuber got up and ate one of the chickens. They called to a Kite, which said to the Hen, Put them under me. So they got there and stayed. Presently the Tuber came and asked the Kite, Where are they? *He-i,* said he, I don't know. So the Tuber scolded the Kite; and the Kite flew down and took it up from the ground, and hovered with it in the sky, and then let it drop down to the ground. Then another took it up, and hovered in turn in the sky, and dropped it, and it fell down and broke in two. So the two Kites divided the Tuber between them; therefore some of the tubers are good, and some are bad. We call the name of the good tuber *nggeremanggeggneni.*

THE ORIGIN OF POISONED
ARROWS (AURORA ISLAND)

I have often heard them telling the story about it in this way. They say that in old times there was no fighting. But there was an old man whose name was Muesarava, who was blind and used to stay doing nothing in the house; and he heard a pigeon calling, and took a bow and broad-headed arrow and went under the tree; and the pigeon let drop a bit of the fruit it was eating, and that blind man shot at a venture into the tree, and hit the pigeon without seeing it. And he took it up, and went and put it into the oven together with the yams, and sat down and sang a song. But two young fellows came along and quietly opened that old man Muesarava's oven, and ate up his pigeon with some of his yams. Then they went to another place, and sang back a song to him; and he heard it, and went back to eat his pigeon, but found when he uncovered the oven that it was eaten up, and that something not good had been put in its place. Then he was exceeding angry, and plotted a fight against the people of the place whence the two young men had come who had stolen and eaten Muesarava's food. And now Muesarava began to make fighting arrows of men's bones. Muesarava went and grubbed up with his hands a boy who had died, and took his bones, and beat them to splinters and rubbed them sharp. But his enemies on their side knew nothing of that, they only cut wood into shape, or bones of fish or birds, and fixed them in their arrows, while Muesarava on his side prepared men's bones. And when they fought they shot at him and hit, but he did not die; and he shot them and they could not live, but died outright all of them. And they fought again and shot at him, and hit him and he did not die; but Muesarava shot at them and hit, and they all died. So it often happened, and they saw that they died in very great numbers; and they asked Muesarava why it was that they shot him and he did not die, while he shot them and they all of them died. Therefore he told them and said, Go and grub up one of the dead men I have shot, and scrape his bones, and point your arrows with that. Upon this they listened to his counsel and did as he had said to them; and when they fought again they shot him, and he straightway died.

And that thing, the dead man's bone that Muesarava ground to a point for himself with his own hand, still remains, and has not yet been spoilt; the reed-shaft has been spoilt and replaced over and over again, but that dead man's bone still remains; I have seen it myself in my brother's possession; it still remains. The people think a great deal of it, thinking that there is supernatural power, *mana*, in that *toto* arrow. If there is heard a rumour of fighting, and that is pointed in the direction whence it comes, the fighting comes to nothing.

◆━◆━◆━◆

HOW TAGARO MADE THE
SEA (AURORA ISLAND)

They say that he made the sea, and that in old times the sea was quite small, like a common pool upon the beach, and that this pool was at the back of his house, and that there were fish in the pool, and that he had built a stone wall round it. And Tagaro was gone out to look at the various things he had made, and his wife was in the village, and his two children were at home, whom he had forbidden to go to the back of the house. So when he was gone the thought entered into the mind of those two, Why has our father forbidden us to go there? And they were shooting at lizards and rats; and after a while one said to the other, Let us go and see what that is he has bid us keep away from. So they went and saw the pool of salt-water with many fish crowding together in it. And one of the boys stood on the stones Tagaro had built up, and he sees the fish, and he shoots at one and hits it; and as he runs to catch hold of it he threw down a stone, and then the water ran out. And Tagaro heard the roaring of the water and ran to stop it; and the old woman laid herself down in the way of it, but nothing could be done; those two boys who had thrown down the stone took clubs like knives and prepared a passage for the sea, one on one side and the other on the other side of the place, and the sea followed as it flowed. And they think that the old woman turned into a stone, and lies now on the part of Maewo near Raga.

THE WOMAN AND THE EEL
(AURORA ISLAND)

A woman went to lay pandanus leaves to weave mats with in the water, and she laid them there in the evening and went home. In the morning she went to take the leaves from the water; and when she

◆—◆—◆—◆—◆

went to take them out, behold, they were turned into an eel. Then she ran back and told it to some men who were engaged in the *suqe*, and they ran down and tied a cord to the eel and dragged it up to the village. But there was a lame man who could not go with them, and he lay in the *gamal*, club-house; and by the side of the *gamal* there was a croton-tree; and as they dragged up that eel it curled its tail round the croton, and the croton was nearly broken, and the lame man saw it. But they dragged hard at the eel and it loosed its tail from the croton, and they brought it into the village, and laid it at the entrance of the *gamal*. So when they ran off for fire-wood and banana leaves to cook it with, the eel said to the lame man, When they are eating don't you eat; they shall eat by themselves. Consequently the lame man did not eat; but they put the eel to be cooked in the oven of the *suqe*, and covered in the oven. And when they opened the oven they all took up pieces of the eel, every one of them a piece, and when the great man said to them, Now put them ready, then they all put them ready; and after that he said again, Now let us eat, and they all took a bite at once. But as they bit once their legs turned into eels; and they bit a second time and the bodies of them all turned into eels; and they bit again, and they were all eels; and the great man glided away first, and they all followed him into the water.

◆◆◆◆◆

14

THE ICEBERGS

OF ANTARCTICA

JOHN MURRAY

cebergs.—Sir James Ross, in his celebrated voyage, having discovered Victoria Land, sailed along its coast to the southward as far as the 76th parallel, where he was stopped by an icy barrier extending upwards of 300 miles east and west, the perpendicular cliffs of which attained an altitude of from 150 to 200 feet, whilst the depth of water close outside these cliffs ranged between 180 and 410 fathoms. This icy barrier began at the foot of Mounts Erebus and Terror, which appear to be the southern peaks of a range of hills stretching irregularly to the northward at moderate distances from the coast as far as Cape North, in lat. 71° 30′ S. Off the coast of this high land there was pack ice; and here and there, descending from the ravines of the mountain ranges, were glaciers which extended some distance into the sea, and ended in perpendicular cliffs of considerable height, but there was no such barrier as extended west from the foot of Mount Terror.

◆◆◆◆◆◆◆◆◆◆◆◆◆◆◆◆◆◆◆◆◆◆◆◆

That the edge of the icy barrier seen by Ross is nearly, if not quite, water-borne, and therefore just in a condition to generate icebergs is evident, for the height of the ice cliffs above the water-line varies from 150 to 200 feet (mean 175 feet), whilst the depth of water within a mile of them is 260 fathoms. Now, supposing the specific gravity of ice at 32° to be 0.92, and that of sea water at the same temperature to be 1.027 (distilled water at 39° being equal to 1), an iceberg floating will have 89.6 per cent of its volume immersed, that is supposing it to be of the same temperature and consistency throughout, or in round numbers 90 per cent of volume will be under water, and 10 per cent above. Taking this as the basis of calculation, it is found that the icy cliffs of the barrier will be water-borne at 260 fathoms, or precisely the depth found by Ross close to them. This also will be the draught of water of a tabular iceberg detached from the barrier whose height above water is 175 feet. This uniform height, about 175 feet, of the tabular icebergs in high latitudes cannot fail to strike even the most ordinary observer, and can only be accounted for by supposing them to have been generated by the icy barrier.

The highest berg seen by Cook was in lat. 59° S., long. 92° E., 300 to 400 feet high, but was only half a mile round. Ross does not mention any very high iceberg, and Wilkes estimates his highest at 500 feet, but this was not a tabular berg, and although very high tabletopped icebergs have been seen far north, they were always in a rapid state of dissolution. In fact they sometimes break up in high latitudes, for Biscoe observed one fall asunder in lat. 65° S., long. 116° W.

The icebergs met with in the *Challenger* were usually from a quarter to half a mile in diameter, and about 200 feet high; the highest measured was 248 feet, but it was evidently an old berg floating on a large base. The largest, which was seen farthest south in latitude 66°

40′, was 3 miles in length, and was accompanied by several others nearly as large. It is remarkable how few were fallen in with to the westward of the 80th meridian of east longitude, or to the northward of the pack ice there, which was probably a detached pack, similar to that sailed through by Ross in 1841.

To the eastward of the meridian of 92° E. icebergs were very numerous, and continued so as the ship ran to the eastward even at a distance from the pack. Their absence farther to the westward, between 70° and 80° E. longitude, except when close to the pack edge, was so marked that, coupled with their absence on the same meridians in lower latitudes as shown by the ice chart, it seems to indicate that there can be no land for a considerable distance south in that neighbourhood, and that a very high latitude could be gained there if desired.

The pack ice consisted chiefly of small salt water ice pieces, which could scarcely be called floes, from 30 to 50 feet in diameter; 100 miles within the pack edge Ross found them to be 600 feet in diameter. The single season's ice was about 3 feet in thickness, the hummocky ice, formed by several layers heaped one upon another and frozen compactly together, was from 7 to 8 feet thick, the upper surface of each piece being covered by a layer of snow about a foot in thickness. Scattered about in the pack were a few blue coloured berg pieces of all sizes, some of them frozen into the salt water ice. All the latter was much honey-combed by melting, but the ice was evidently still of sufficient strength to give a very dangerous blow if impelled against a vessel's side, or to a vessel forcing her way through the pack. A properly fortified ship could nevertheless have easily made way through it.

In the pack were numerous icebergs, but they were not in greater numbers than in the open water, and certainly not numerous enough by themselves to create the nucleus for the pack to form around.

A very large proportion of the bergs were, as stated, flat-topped and maintained their original balance. Very many were bounded by a single range of cliffs washed by the waves all round. In some these ranges were evidently old and very much indented. Many were highly complex, combining two stories, lines of caves, talus slopes, and evidences of having been tilted to various angles from the original line of flotation once or twice; some were excessively worn and weathered, having apparently been long in warmer regions, and were pinnacled and broken up by deep gullies or channels bounded often by rounded ridges projecting at their mouths on either side. One much weathered pinnacled berg was passed which had its entire surface shining and polished as if it had recently toppled, and no fresh snow had fallen since this had occurred. Several were seen with the parts which had been below water partially exposed by tilting; the surfaces of these were always polished and smooth; but no berg was seen to tilt or turn over during the voyage. One was noticed divided into three separate columnar masses so far as the part above water was concerned, no connection between the columns being visible.

The platforms under water at the bases of the bergs often run out into spurs and irregular projections, and these may be dangerous to ships going too near. Soundings were taken on one of these platforms and gave 7 fathoms at some distance from the berg and 3½ fathoms nearer in. Nearly all the flat-topped bergs showed numerous crevasses in their cliffs near their summits, and these were always widest towards the summits, and were irregularly perpendicular in general direction. The flat tops of the bergs had usually rather uneven surfaces, being covered with small hillocks, apparently formed by the drifting of snow, or showing irregularities where they covered over the mouths of crevasses. The surfaces in fact, looked just like those of the "Firn" or "Névé," the cracked snowfields at the heads of European glaciers, and appeared as if they would be equally dangerous to traverse, except by a party roped together. The second stories of bergs were always covered with snow, which had fallen on them after their emergence.

The stratified structure of the bergs is best seen in the case of flat-topped rectangular bergs, where an opportunity is afforded of examining at a corner two vertical cliff faces meeting one another at a right angle. The entire mass shows a well-marked stratification, being composed of alternate layers of white opaque-looking, and blue, more compact and transparent, ice. The late Dr. E. L. Moss, R.N., Staff-Surgeon on the recent Arctic Expedition, describes a similar stratification as occurring in Arctic ice. He had opportunities of examining the ice closely at leisure, and describes each stratum as consisting of an upper white part merging into a lower blue part, the colour depending on the greater or less number and size of the air-cells in the ice.*

Towards the lower part of the cliffs, the strata are seen to be extremely fine and closely pressed, whilst they are thicker with the blue lines wider apart, in proportion as they are traced towards the summits of the cliffs. In the lower regions of the cliffs the strata are remarkably even and horizontal, whilst towards the summit, where not subjected to pressure, slight curvings are to be seen in them corresponding to the inequalities of the surface and drifting of the snow. In one berg there was in the strata at one spot the appearance of complex bedding, somewhat resembling that shown in the Æolian calcareous sand formations of Bermuda. The strata were often curved in places, but always in their main line of run, horizontal, *i.e.*, parallel to the original flat top of the berg. The strata in the cliff at the level of the wash-line of a rectangular berg 80 feet in height were so

* Observations on Arctic Sea Water and Ice, *Proc. Roy. Soc. Lond.*, vol. xxvii. p. 547, 1878.

◆—◆—◆—◆—◆

thin and closely packed that they looked almost like the leaves of a huge book at a distance, for by the lap of the waves the softer layers had been to some extent dissolved out from between the harder. In one berg where the face of the cliff was very flat and seen quite closely with a powerful glass, the fine blue bands were seen to be grouped, the groups being separated by bands in which no lines were visible, or where these were obscured by the ice fracturing with a rougher surface, not with a perfectly even and polished one, as existed where the blue bands showed out. The cliff surfaces, where freshly fractured, showed an irregular jointing and cleavage of the entire mass, very like that shown in a cliff of compact limestone. In one or two bergs a fine cleavage lamination was noticed like that of slate or shale, the laminæ being parallel to the face of the cliff, and breaking up at their edges with a zigzag fracture, resembling diamond cleavage of slate; this condition may have been produced by a peculiar exertion of pressure in these particular bergs.

When the lower cliff of a two-storied berg had a shot fired into it, large masses of ice fell, raising a considerable swell in the sea. The pieces of the cliff split off in flat masses parallel to the face of the cliff, just as was noticed in the case of the splitting of the glacier cliffs at Heard Island, and did not tumble forward but slid down the face of the cliff, keeping their upper edges, parts of the old plateau surface, horizontal. The ice floated round the ship in some quantity; it was opaque and white-looking, somewhat like white porcelain, and the shattered fragments had remarkably sharp angular edges, showing that the ice was very hard and compact, far more so than its appearance in mass would lead one to suppose, since it looked at a distance as if it were hardly consolidated, but merely closely pressed snow. Its manner of cleavage only gives evidence at a distance of its very compact nature. Many of the floating fragments were traversed by parallel veins of transparent ice, those which, when seen on a cliff surface, looked blue.

During the short time that the ship was amongst the icebergs not one was met with that bore upon it any moraines or rocks which could with certainty be determined as such, but on the 24th February a large rock was reported on one. The scarcity of such appearances has been remarked by former voyagers. Nevertheless, there are numerous instances in which observers have met with rocks on southern bergs. Wilkes and Ross saw many; and the latter on one occasion landed a party on a berg on which there was a volcanic rock weighing many tons, and covered with mud and stones.* Mr. Darwin published a note on a rock seen on an Antarctic iceberg in lat. 61° S.† Dr. Wallich‡ remarks on the similar scarcity of the appearance of stones or gravel on northern bergs; not one in a thousand shows dirt, stones, or rocks. He attributes this to the very small disturbance of their centres of gravity which icebergs undergo when floating freely. Stones and gravel may be present in most cases, but generally remain invisible under water in the lower parts of the bergs.

On three occasions discolorations of bergs were seen. In one case there was a light yellow band on one surface of a cliff high up, possibly the result of birds' dung which had fallen on the snow when the layer was formed, or it might have been due to a fall of volcanic dust; it was too high up to be due to Diatoms. On another occasion two bergs were passed at a distance, which showed conspicuous black-looking bands, apparently dirt bands. In one of the bergs there were

* Ross's Antarctic Voyage, vol. i. p. 173, London, 1847.
† C. Darwin, Notes on a Rock Seen on an Iceberg in lat. 61° S., *Geogr. Soc. Journ.*, vol. ix. pp. 528, 529, 1839; see also Journal of Researches during the Voyage of H.M.S. "Beagle," p. 251, ed. 1879.
‡ G. C. Wallich, The North Atlantic Sea Bed, pt. i. p. 56, London, 1862.

two or three such bands, very broad, parallel to the blue bands, and separated by considerable intervals, in which the berg showed the usual stratification. In another two black bands existed at one end of the berg and one at the other. Both were parallel in direction to the blue bands, but the stratification at the end where the two black bands were situated was inclined at an angle to that of the remainder of the berg, as if a dislocation of a part of the berg had taken place. These bergs were too far distant to allow of the exact nature of the black bands being determined.

In none of the numerous bergs was there seen any bending or curved vertical bands, giving evidence of a former differential motion in the mass, such as are to be seen on every land glacier. How far the absence of these characteristic lines of motion may be explained by the fact that only about the uppermost tenth of the entire height of the bergs is seen, it is difficult to say.

The colouring of the southern bergs is magnificent. The general mass has an appearance like loaf sugar, with a slight bluish tint, except where fresh snow resting on the tops and ledges is absolutely white. On this ground colour there are parallel streaks of cobalt blue, of various intensities, and more or less marked effect, according to the distance at which the berg is viewed. Some bergs with the blue streaks very definitely marked have, when seen quite close, exactly the appearance of the common marbled blue soap. The colouring of the crevasses, caves, and hollows is of the deepest and purest azure blue possible. None of the artists on board was able to approach a representation of its intensity; it seemed a much more powerful colour than that which is to be seen in the ice of Swiss glaciers. In the case of the bergs with all their sides exposed, no doubt a greater amount of light is able to penetrate than in glaciers where the light can usually only enter at the top. A large berg full of caves and crevasses, seen on a bright day, is a most beautiful and striking object.

◆◆◆◆

One small berg was passed at a distance which was of a remarkable colour; it looked just like a huge crystal of sulphate of copper, being all intensely blue, but it seemed as if attached to, and forming part of, another berg of normal colour. Possibly it was part of the formerly submerged base, and of more than ordinary density. Only one other such berg was seen. The intensity of the blue light received from the bergs is ordinarily such that the grey sky behind them appears distinctly reddened, assuming the complementary tint, and the reddening appears most intense close to the berg. At night bergs appear as if they had a very slight luminous glow, suggesting that they are to a very small extent phosphorescent. The sea at the foot of the bergs usually looks of a dark indigo colour, partly, no doubt, in contrast to the brighter blue of the ice. Where spurs and platforms run out under water from the bases of the berg cliffs, the shallow water is seen to be lighted up by reflection of the light from them.

The surf beats on an iceberg as on a rocky shore, and washes and dashes in and out of the gullies and caverns, and up against the cliffs. Washing in and out of the caves, it makes a resounding roar, which, when many bergs surround the ship, is very loud. So heavy is the surf on the bergs, and so steep are they as a rule, that none was seen on which landing could have been effected from a boat. As the waves wash up into the wash-lines of the bergs they form icicles, which are to be seen hanging in rows from the upper border of these grooves. A line of fragments is always to be seen drifting away from a large berg; these are termed wash-pieces. They are very instructive as showing the vast relative extent of submerged ice required to float a small portion above water, the parts of the fragments below water being visible from a ship's deck.

The scenic effects produced by large numbers of icebergs, some in the foreground, others scattered at all distances to the horizon and beyond it, are very varied and remarkable, depending on the varying effects of light and atmosphere. On one occasion, as the pack ice was being approached, some distant bergs were seen to assume a most intense black colour. This was due to their being thrown in shade by clouds passing between them and the sun, and the heightening of this effect by the contrast with brilliantly lighted up bergs around them. They looked like rocks of basalt.

15

ADMIRALTY BAY

DAVID CAMPBELL

The summer's flower is to the summer sweet,
Though to itself it only live and die.
    William Shakespeare

I spent three summers in Antarctica, in places beyond the horizon of most of the rest of my species. The journeys all took place during that single long day that begins in October and ends in March. Sometimes, in the sere, glaciated interior of the continent, Antarctica seemed to be a prebiotic place, as the world must have been before the broth of life bubbled and popped into whales and tropical forests—and humans. I was as lonely as an astronaut walking on the moon. But at other times, during the short, erotic summer along the ocean margins of the continent, Antarctica seemed to be a celebration of everything living, of unchecked DNA in all its procreative frenzy, transmuting sunlight and minerals into life itself, hatching, squabbling, swimming, and soaring on the sea wind.

Most of my journeys have been to the Antarctic Peninsula, a spine

◆-◆-◆-◆-◆-◆-◆-◆-◆-◆-◆-◆-◆-◆-◆-◆-◆-◆

of rock and ice at the bottom of the Western Hemisphere that rambles north toward South America from the glacial fastness of the southern continent and then bends eastward, as if submitting to the prevailing westerly winds and currents of the Drake Passage. This is the "maritime" Antarctic, where the extremes of temperature are modulated by the sea. Explorers who have been to the frigid interior of the continent call the peninsula and its nearby islands the "Banana Belt" of Antarctica. It rains frequently during the summer, and once, in late January, I watched the thermometer climb to 9° centigrade. The rest of the continent, ice-fast and arid, is a true desert and is mostly lifeless.

Northwest of the peninsula are the South Shetlands, an ocean-sculpted arc of islands, some with active volcanoes, that reminded the first homesick and frightened Scottish sealers of those treeless, windblown islands of the North Sea. The sealers named the new islands Clarence, Elephant, King George, Nelson, Greenwich, Livingston, and Snow, after various monarchs, captains, mammals, meteorological events, and hometowns. Set off from the archipelago is aptly named Deception Island, an active volcano with a secret caldera where ash-blackened snow mimics rock. These islands of ice and black basalt, now and then tinged russet or blue by oozings of iron or copper, rise over 600 meters. Their hearts are locked under deep glaciers, a crystal desert forever frozen in terms of our short life spans, but transient in their own time scale. Sometimes one sees only the cloud-marbled glacial fields, high in the sun above hidden mountain slopes and sea fog, Elysian planes that seem as insubstantial as vapor. The interiors of the glaciers, glimpsed through crevasses, are neon blue. Sliding imperceptibly on their bellies, the glaciers carve their own valleys through the rock, and when they pass over rough terrain they have the appearance of frozen rapids, which is in fact what they are, cascading at the rate of a centimeter a

◆◆◆◆◆

day. Sudden cold gusts, known as katabatic winds, tumble down their icefalls to the shore; sometimes the coast snaps from tranquility to tempest in just a few minutes. Just as quickly the glacial winds abate, and there is calm. Where they reach the sea, the glaciers give birth to litters of icebergs, which usually travel a short distance and, at the next low tide, run aground on hidden banks. Most of the ice-free land is close to shore, snuggled near the edge of the warm sea in places that are buffeted by both sea wind and land wind, where rain changes to snow and back. There is no plant taller than a lichen here, no animal larger than a midge. Biological haiku. But on protected slopes, where the snow melts on warm summer days and glacial meltwater nourishes the soil, lichens and mosses dust the hills a pale gray-green, and the islands take on a tenuous verdancy.

The Pacific and Atlantic oceans meet at the South Shetland Islands. Indeed, all of the world's oceans mix in the Southern Ocean, the circumpolar sea that so absolutely isolates Antarctica from the other continents. Only a few small islands fleck this globe-girdling sea, and the westerly spiral storms that orbit the Earth at these latitudes, unimpeded by land masses and ever sucking energy from the sea, develop the anger of hurricanes. These zones are the "roaring forties" and "screaming fifties," which have commanded the respect and fear of sailors since the time of Francis Drake. Today satellite photographs show these low-pressure zones, spiraling clockwise, regularly spaced, separated by several hundred kilometers of calm sea—a flowered anklet on the planet Earth. But the Southern Ocean is a manic sea, and between the tempests there is tranquility and light. To the land-bound on the Shetland Islands, the distance between cyclones is measured in time, three to five days apart.

If the bright ice and dark rock are the canvas of these desert islands, then light is the medium, and the Southern Ocean, ever

◆—◆—◆—◆—◆

fickle, often angry, is the artist. She swathes the islands in mist, or snow, or clarid sea-light, depending on her moods. Sometimes the sea rages for days, and you can lean against the wind, rubbery and firm. The wind lifts the round pebbles from the beach and flings them like weapons at hapless beachcombers. The cyclonic winds march around the compass, so at one moment they will herd the icebergs against the shore in a groaning cluster, and a few hours later waft them out to sea like feathers on a pond. At other times there will be a clammy calm, a disquieting purple grayness that smothers light and sound, punctuated only by the distant, muffled crack of a calving glacier. The days one anticipates are the tranquil ones that break the long captivity of cabin fever, when the sky is a transparent blue, and the deep, clear sea scintillates with shafts of sunlight.

King George Island lies in the middle of the South Shetland archipelago. Like the Antarctic Peninsula, 96 kilometers to the east across Bransfield Strait, it seems to bend slightly to the westerly currents. Ninety-five percent of the island is permanently covered with ice. The smooth domes of glaciers are the highest places on the island, all above 580 meters. Echo-sounding has proved that some of these glaciers have their feet at sea level. Along the shore the temperature is more or less constant, no more than 5° or 6° C above or below freezing, winter and summer. The seasonal and daily cycles of freeze and thaw create a disheveled landscape of wet landslides and cleaved rocks. Some rocks are shattered in leaves, like sliced bread. There is precipitation three hundred days a year, and an equal probability of rain and snow during all months of the year. The northern shore of King George Island takes the full brunt of the wind and the sea; the breakers arrive unimpeded all the way from Tasmania. The coast is flecked by numerous rocky islets and scalloped by crescent bays. Many features are uncharted and unnamed. Others bear

◆—◆—◆—◆—◆

names of fancy: Sinbad Rock, Jagged Island, Tartar Island, Hole Rock, Venus Bay; or of tragedy: Destruction Bay.

On the north face of King George Island, the outer edge of Antarctica, cliffs of ice act as giant airfoils, pushing the sea wind up their faces onto the frozen, white plateau of the island. Once, during a blizzard, I walked along this shore and watched fat snowflakes fly skyward in seeming defiance of gravity. In the dark ocean below, the ricocheting swells converged on unseen banks, and the sea seemed to be spontaneously erupting. On clear days the summer sunlight refracts in these sea-lenses and the ocean appears to be glowing from within. In the half-moon bays below the cliffs, the volcanic basalt is ground to smooth pebbles. During the austral summer the seafaring flotillas of juvenile penguins come ashore to rest, and their white bellies look like stranded icebergs on the black beaches. The elephant seals, like huge grubs, wallow in their own oily excrement. If you walk amid the shuffle of broken algae and limpet shells, where the pebbles boom with each breaking swell and the icebergs ping and crackle offshore, you smell none of the familiar seashore odor of decomposition of more temperate climes, no beach flies or scuttling crabs. Everything remains frozen, immutable.

The southern, leeward shore of King George Island is not as rugged and steep as the north, and most ships arriving across the stormy Drake Passage from the tip of South America, 970 kilometers to the north, hie to shelter there. They skirt the North Foreland, on the eastern edge of the island closest to South America, and sail past Cape Melville, Sherratt Bay, Three Sisters Point, Penguin Island, and King George Bay, where in 1819 William Smith, commanding the brigantine *Williams*, planted the Union Jack and named the island after his distant and unknowing sovereign. And then a vast anvil-shaped bay opens to the northwest and invades the

◆◆◆◆◆

heart of the island. This is Admiralty Bay, a three-fingered fjord that is one of the safest anchorages in all of Antarctica. It is also perhaps the prettiest place in Antarctica. The bay splits into three deep inlets: Mackellar, which suffers a southern exposure and is sometimes chopped by storm and wave; Escurra, which is scoured by sudden katabatic winds; and Martel, which offers safe anchorage in winds from all directions. All three inlets terminate in glaciers that flow down from the heart of the island, nudging spongy moraines along their flanks, and during the summer cluttering the bay with icebergs. The bay itself was born of fire and ice. A tectonic fault line, where two plates scrape against each other, is buried in its cold and dark heart five hundred meters deep. The flanks of the bay were carved from timeless rock by the huge ice sheets of the Pleistocene ice ages, when sea levels were lower than they are today. Admiralty Bay may be a microcosm of all Antarctica. It is oceanic, it is terrestrial, and its heart is glaciated, but during the summer its shores are warm and rainy.

During the ever-bright Antarctic summer day, the sun marches around the northern horizon and only briefly dips from sight. The nights never really blacken but are long and often pastel twilights. The summer bay is a huge nursery, denizened with all manner of life: humpback whales, elephant and leopard seals, giant petrels, skuas and terns. The Weddell seals spend the winter in the bay, chewing breathing holes in the pack ice. By October the females have climbed onto the ice to give birth, and for a few days the ice is stained red with natal blood. The penguins—first the Adélies and gentoos and then the chinstraps—arrive from September to December. The males stake out their little plots and shortly after are joined by the females. By the time I arrive in mid-November, it is already late spring. The big-eyed elephant seal pups are six weeks old and weaned. They lounge on the beaches, mustering the courage to venture into the sea for the first time. The Weddell seal pups, although still nursing, are not far behind.

In the mouth of the bay, which is five kilometers wide and subject to the passions of the open sea, penguins weave through the swells on their way to nesting colonies on the shore, looking like small piebald porpoises. The whole western entrance of the bay, from Demay Point to Point Thomas, is a guanoed penguin metropolis. During the summer amorous penguins, each pair defending a modest cairn of pebbles, position themselves over the low hills and beaches with geometrical precision, exactly one pecking length in every direction from their neighbors. The rookeries are a cacophonous bustle of activity: bickerings, ecstatic displays, pebble robbing. By December the low volcanic hills are buffed pink with guano, and when the wind is westerly, the stench of the rookery wafts kilometers out to sea.

Behind the penguin rookery, the shoulders of the mountains rise in tiers of snow and black scree, capped with ever-present glacier. The Antarctic terns, black-headed and sharp-winged, lay their eggs in the shelter of these wind-roamed rocks. They course over the beach and sea, screaming at intruders, on their way to clip fish and krill from the bay. From prominent vantage points behind the penguin rookery, the skuas have set up their vigil for unguarded eggs and early chicks. They fly low and fast, just above the upturned heads of the nesting penguins, trying to evoke an inopportune lurch or other distraction to snatch away a hatchling and take it to the edge of the rookery, where two of them, tugging at the squealing baby, will tear it apart and eat it.

The bay has gradually warmed during the past century. Some of the glaciers have been reduced to small patches, isolated from the snowy interior of the island, and are evaporating, leaving in their slow wakes ablation moraines. Most of the ground surface is permafrost, but on warm summer days, earthflows of saturated soil and

◆—◆—◆—◆—◆

rock, upheaved by the cycle of freeze and thaw, ooze down the slopes. The stable areas of the mountain slopes are cloaked with fruticose, or branching, lichens. These are species of *Usnea,* and although only six centimeters tall, some individuals may be hundreds, perhaps thousands, of years old. *Usnea,* fretted and complex, look like basket sea stars at the bottom of a tropical ocean, and if it is snowing on the hillside—the big, moist, ephemeral snowflakes of summer—the flakes get caught in the tangle and are held, for a moment, until they melt. Relieved of the burden of winter snow, the plants expand rapidly in the wet early-summer days. The new tissue of the growing edge of fungus is pale white-green, but the more mature spikes are dark green, and the very old, dead spikes are black.

Other parts of the bay have no beaches or mountain flanks but steep, cerulean glacial walls thirty meters tall. You risk your life taking a small boat near these facades, for they disintegrate without warning. The bay changes color according to the wind and the amount of wash from the glaciers. When the wind blows from the land, the water is rich in suspended sediments and is a pastel chalky green, but when the wind pushes choppy ocean water into the bay, the water is dark and clear. The ocean currents also bring swarms of krill, followed by the minke and humpback whales that graze on that pink bounty. Sometimes the humpbacks will loiter just offshore, indolently waving their white pectorals in the air and slapping the water.

The summer pulse of procreation lasts only a few months. By February the baby seals are independent, and the fledged penguin chicks, after long contemplation on the beach, are making their first forays into the sea. Fat and buoyant, they are easy prey for marauding leopard seals. Hard times set in for the skuas, which scavenge and bicker over scraps on the beaches, and by April the terns and the whales have migrated north. Once I lingered until late March and at

◆ ◆ ◆ ◆ ◆

last found darkness. Others have spent the winter in Admiralty Bay. Some winters the bay never freezes, but in most years snow begins to accumulate in March or April, and by late May the bay begins to glaze with ice, starting at the foot of the glaciers, where the water is freshest and coldest. At first the brisk glacial winds sweep the new ice out to sea, but by July the pack ice forms and the bay freezes solid. Now the day is a long twilight and the nights are black. The mountains that surround the bay become hoary with snow; only the tips of the volcanic nunataks and the sharp edges of the mountains remain brown. The penguins follow the expanding edge of the pack ice far out into the Southern Ocean. The terns migrate to the warmer margins of Africa and the Americas. The skuas soon follow, although a few may stay the winter, especially near human habitations, where they can feed on garbage. During July, August, and September, the bay is dead and white.

Beyond the hilly penguin rookery at Point Thomas, across a green, mossy plain, is Arctowski, the Polish research station. Sheltered in the rock at the point itself is a wooden Madonna who stares unblinking at the snow-dusted sea. Her face is sorrowful. The rocky beach is strewn with crates and oil drums. The station, behind a cockscomb of Polish, Russian, and Belgian flags, declaring the nationality of the scientists working there, is a series of rambling wooden buildings, standing on stilts above the permafrost, which intersect in a communal dining hall and kitchen. Once, sitting at the long dining table there, I sensed an unspoken tension between the Poles and the Russians. "We are all scientists and indifferent to politics here," a Polish biologist told me, between mouthfuls of *pierogi*. But he was wearing a *Solidarinosc* T-shirt.

Indeed, the primary purpose of every nation's Antarctic stations is political; the science (even good science) is just an excuse for a

◆◆◆◆

presence on the continent. Britain, Argentina, and Chile all claim the South Shetland Islands and the Antarctic Peninsula as their territories or dependencies. Regardless, since the 1960s Antarctica, with unknown but potentially vast resources, has become a free-for-all, and King George Island, only a three-day sail from South America and surrounded by a sea that is ice-free for much of the year, is the easiest place to invade. In the 1960s and 1970s Chile, Argentina, Great Britain, the Soviet Union, Poland, the United States, and Italy all established (and in some cases quickly abandoned) bases or refuges on the island. And in the first six years of the 1980s, Brazil, Uruguay, Peru, South Korea, and the People's Republic of China, all nations with negligible Antarctic heritage, also invaded King George Island. By necessity all of these facilities were built on the five percent of the island's coast that is not glaciated.

Parts of King George Island are rapidly becoming the urban slum of Antarctica. Some people, optimistically, consider it a sacrifice so that other areas may remain pristine. The worst hit is the Fildes Peninsula, on the southwest tip of the island, where once there were extensive meadows of lichens and important breeding colonies of penguins. It was one of the largest ice-free areas in all of Antarctica, and large areas of the peninsula were designated to be specially protected according to the terms of the Antarctic Treaty. But then came the Russian invasion. In 1964, having failed to establish a station farther south on inclement Peter I Island, and with winter fast approaching, the Russians hastily threw together a station on the Fildes Peninsula, smack in the middle of a specially protected area. (The next year the treaty was modified and, in true Soviet tradition, history was rewritten.) They named the station after Admiral Thaddeus Bellingshausen, the pioneering Russian explorer who sailed in these waters in 1821. It was not a happy place. During my visits to Bellingshausen I sensed a spirit of burdensome exile, of hierarchy

◆◆◆◆◆

and pecking order. The corridors were long and empty. The only perceptible scientific activity was at the weather station, which received and printed photos taken by Soviet and American satellites. In the recreation hall, a gloomy portrait of Lenin peered down at the pool table, as if he were calculating angles and shots.

Next to Bellingshausen, across a seasonal creek, are Base Frei, the Chilean meteorological station; Teniente Marsh, the Chilean air force base; and La Villa de las Estrellas (Village of the Stars), the Chilean Antarctic colony. Frei Base was constructed in 1965 during the Marxist government of Salvador Allende at the invitation of the Russians, who considered the Chileans to be comrades in socialism. But then the neighborhood changed, and the two stations have since endured a chilly proximity. The Fildes Peninsula was doomed. The Chileans built a long airstrip, able to accommodate four-engine C-130's, with adjacent hangars that sheltered a small air force of Twin Otters and helicopters. A hotel and cafeteria were built for the workers. Vast areas of the peninsula were graded for roads. And then came the colonists, hoisting the standard of Chilean nationalism. Their ranks include mothers and children, the families of the base officers, who sign up for two-year stints. They are Antarctic pioneers. The children, muffed in red parkas, bring the strange squeals of youth to the Antarctic. But they aren't exactly roughing it; the base has a bank, hotel, and gift shop, and a suburb of comfortable, rambling ranch houses with satellite TV. One evening that I spent at the hotel, the guests gathered in the salon to watch "Miami Vice."

I first sailed into Admiralty Bay on a sun-swept day in late November 1982 and made a landing deep in the interior of the bay at Martel Inlet, on the shore of the Keller Peninsula. Across the inlet was the Ternyck Needle, a nunatak of brown basalt that punched a hole in

◆━◆━◆━◆━◆

the glacier and rose 90 meters above the ice cap. The wind had scooped a trench 25 meters deep and 45 meters wide in front of the nunatak, which seemed incongruous and disturbingly out of place, an alien rock in the field of ice. Keller Peninsula was a spine of extinct, eroded volcanos, 600 meters high, that emerged from the glaciated interior of the island. To the east was Stenhouse Glacier, which originated in the ice dome of the island's interior and slid down a valley of its own making to the sea. Like all of the glaciers on King George Island, it was shrinking, calving icebergs and evaporating faster than the snow could accumulate on the ice dome above. Years before, British glaciologist G. Hattersley-Smith journeyed on dog sleds and skis over this glacier in order to measure its rate of travel. He found that it varied during the summer from 23 centimeters per day high up on its heavily crevassed slopes to over 100 centimeters per day where the ice is warmed and softened by the summer sea. During the winter, when Martel Inlet is shaded by the spine of the island and the sea froze, the glacier stops calving and rests.

Behind the beach was Flagstaff Mountain, an extinct volcano 600 meters high, and on its flank a vestigial glacier of the same name. Flagstaff Glacier was only a few hundred meters across and was not joined to the ice cap in the interior of the island, nor to the sea. With no new mass flowing into it, its only crevasse choked with snow, it was slowly evaporating. On this summer afternoon it was dusted with pink snow algae.

I discovered two derelict huts on Keller Peninsula: Argentine and British meteorological stations. Both were built in 1947 during a squabble over Antarctic territories. The Argentine station was abandoned in 1954, but the British station, which bore the uninspiring name of Base G, remained occupied, summer and winter, until 1962. The boards used to construct the base were scavenged

◆◆◆◆◆

from the old whaling station at Deception Island. The grain of the wooden planks was so etched by wind-blow ice and dust that every detail of the knots and whorls stood out. The hut's windows and doors were stove in and its rooms were filled with snow. Rotten wooden tables and chairs, rusting bed springs, canned food with peeling labels, molten paperbacks, dissected motor parts, and tools were all frozen in their places, just as in the moment of abandonment twenty years before. On the floor of the hut was a dilapidated plaque that read:

> The preservation, care and maintenance of
> these historic ruins has been undertaken
> hereinafter upon the aforsaid [sic] schedule
> by the ministry of Perks [sic].
> Permission to view from
> the Chief Magistrate

Behind the stations on the first ridge of rocks that overlooked the pastel bay were two freshwater ponds fed by melting snow. I peered into one of them. The water was dancing with copepods. Above the ponds four lonely crosses, memorials to casualties of the British station, were etched silently against the horizon. They coldly endowed the peninsula with a feeling of being peopled; one never felt quite alone there. I hiked up the ridge to read their inscriptions. On the first cross was written:

> IN MEMORY OF
> DENNIS RONALD BELL
> BORN 15·7·34
> WHO WHILST SERVING WITH F.I.D.S.
> DIED ACCIDENTALLY AT BASE 'G' ON
> 26·7·59

◆–◆–◆–◆

The second cross:

> ERIC PLATT
> GEOLOGIST
> BASE LEADER
> F.I.D.S.
> DIED ON DUTY
> 10 X 1 1948
> AGED 22 YEARS
> R.I.P.

On the third:

> IN MEMORY OF
> ALAN SHARMAN
> BORN 29·12·36
> WHO, WHILST SERVING WITH F.I.D.S.
> DIED ACCIDENTALLY AT BASE "G" ON
> 23·4·59

I realized that these explorers, who had died on the rim of the earth, were just boys. This nursery bay, lovely on that still afternoon, could take life as well as bestow it.

The fourth cross was so eroded that it read only:

> R   G.   N
>   B   L
>   F.I.D.S.
>   B
>   L

The hero's name had been lost to the wind, erased by blowing needles of sand and ice.

The pebble beach in front of the huts was littered with stranded icebergs, sculpted into fantastic shapes by the spring thaw, and a covered wooden boat that had been used to haul water a half-century earlier by whalers who took shelter in the bay. Its iron chains were decomposed and bleeding rust, but the wooden rivets that bound the hull were still preserved. What I remember most, though, were the hundreds of whale bones—skulls, ribs, and vertebrae, looking like a giant child's scattered jacks on the beach. They were far more permanent than any human-made structure. To the north, beyond the Argentine station, the twenty-meter-long skeleton of a baleen whale, a composite of many individuals of several species, had been reconstructed on a bed of moss behind the beach by Jacques Cousteau and the crew of the *Calypso,* which occupied Base G during the summer of 1972–73. The whale's deflated ribs were splayed on the ground, its vertebrae looking like a white picket fence. It was late spring, and a shelf of melting snow and ice covered the beach below the whale. The silence was absolute, except when an iceberg calved from Stenhouse Glacier with a reverberation that ricocheted across the bay and the white snowbanks of Ullman Spur. This was followed moments later by a small tsunami, which surged onto the beach and shuffled the icebergs.

Two years later, when I next visited the bay, the Brazilian research station had popped up like a cluster of metal and plastic mushrooms on the beach, behind the highest tide mark, between the Argentine hut and Base G. Events in Brasília, 4,800 kilometers to the north, had motivated the politicians and generals to declare that tropical Brazil had a national interest in Antarctica. An illuminated crucifix had been hauled to the top of Flagstaff Mountain, transforming it into a miniature Corcovado. A pumphouse had been built next to one of the freshwater lakes to provide the station with water, carefully filtered of copepods (at the other end of the cycle, the sewage was pumped into a deep well). The station consisted of eight insu-

◆——◆——◆——◆

lated tractor-trailer containers, painted pale green, assembled during the summer of 1984. The green and yellow Brazilian flag, bearing a globe on which was inscribed "Ordem e Progresso" (Order and Progress), shuffled in the wind from a mast on the beach. Behind it was a soccer field.

During the austral summer of 1987 I was invited to the Brazilian station to conduct marine biological research. By then it had grown to fifty-one prefabricated tractor-trailer containers linked by narrow corridors much like railroad cars, giving it a boxy, unfinished appearance. Huge rubber bladders of fuel wallowed on the beach, oozing oil into the bay. The industrial age had come to Admiralty Bay. The tranquility that I so vividly remembered from five years before was gone. A diesel generator, which ran twenty-four hours a day, shredded the silence, and I had to walk beyond the old Argentine station, 200 meters south, to be free of the noise. The generator was the metabolic heart of the station, an artificial sun that kept the personnel warm, incinerated their garbage, and provided the power to link them with the outside world.

"Polar exploration is at once the cleanest and most isolated way of having a bad time which has been devised," wrote Apsley Cherry-Garrard more than a half-century ago. But we had fun. Visitors affectionately nicknamed the Brazilian station "Little Copacabana." Its spirit was buoyant and welcoming. Just inside the door, one stripped off boots and woolen clothing in an arid, hot foyer and hung one's clothing on the wall. The walls are lined with hooks, each designating someone's little vertical territory: a pair of boots, a red parka, gloves and a hat. Three hooks were reserved for visitors. As in any Brazilian household, the kitchen was the center of social activity. Coconut snacks and sugary *cafezinho*, served in demitasses, were always available on a wide counter covered by a plastic tablecloth printed with Santa Clauses. The automatic dough-kneading ma-

◆ ◆ ◆ ◆ ◆

chine plodded like a metronome, filling the air with yeast smells. A traditional Saturday feast of *feijoada completa*, a Cariocan dish of black beans, sausage, and pig's ears, was simmering on the stove. Behind the kitchen was the radio room, where a squawking box linked the station with the disembodied voices of lovers, children, and bureaucrats in the crowded parts of the world. In the central dining room and lounge, on a cluster of sofas, a group of scientists watched a video of *Back to the Future*, and in another corner, someone was playing a kung-fu game on a Brazilian clone of the Apple II computer. The electronic imitation of karate kicks became a constant acoustical backdrop at the station during my visit. The walls were paved with the emblems of ships that had visited the station, the banners of Rotary and Lions clubs, portraits of station members over the years. On the western wall was an oil portrait of Comandante Ferraz, one of the first Brazilians to travel to Antarctica, after whom the station was named. In the far corner was the bar, which also served as a post office (you canceled your own letters and they were picked up every two months). It was stacked neatly with crystal brandy snifters to be used only for special events, which, because of the Brazilian *joie de vivre*, occurred often. The bar also stored the accordion, drums, and tambourines. Parties often lasted all night, and *Carnival* lasted three days. Behind the bar was mounted a fossil leaf of a southern beech tree, 16 million years old, found at Point Hennequin across the bay. One eastern window of the lounge had been shattered by a tempest-flung rock, and the shards had been shattered by a tempest-flung rock, and the shards had been colored with cellophane and rearranged in the form of a *papagayo*, the cloth and bamboo parrot kite of Copacabana Beach.

Beyond the lounge was a warren of sleeping modules, each equipped with a set of bunk beds, a small table, and a double-paned window. A central module contained the toilets and showers, men's

on the north, women's on the south. The water was heated to scalding by the exhaust of the generator. Only the commander, Queiroz,
who by tradition was a navy captain, had a private module and bath.
Next to his module was the gym, the only structure that was not
modular, with tall windows overlooking the expanse of black beach.
It was cluttered with mountaineering equipment, skis, barbells, and
weights. At its center was a snooker table, plenty of chalk and cues,
and a slate blackboard with a system of numbered beads for keeping
score. The clack of billiard balls was another pervading sound of the
station.

During the summer Little Copacabana was a favorite stop for the
tourist ships, which would disgorge legions of passengers, all clad in
red parkas so that their leaders could keep track of them. Most visits
lasted only an hour or two, and the tourists didn't learn, or see,
much. After the obligatory pose for a portrait with Cousteau's whale
skeleton, they shuffled into the station to buy stamps, postcards, key
rings, and other mementos utterly irrelevant to Antarctica. Some
offered barter T-shirts and other wampum with the station personnel, as if they were primitive tribesmen. Snuffling and sneezing, the
tourists usually left colds in their wake. Regardless, the hospitable
Brazilians had a limitless tolerance for these intrusions. Often they
would organize a soccer game with the ship's crew and break out the
cachaça and the accordion.

The tourists were innocuous and friendly, but the visitors who
made us truly uneasy were those from Greenpeace, which had a ship
patrolling the area. Ready with criticism and armed with video cameras, Greenpeace has brought to world attention many environmental problems in Antarctic stations and has advocated the concept of
an Antarctic world park. "If they come, don't offer them any information," cautioned Queiroz. "Let them ask first." When Greenpeace visited Comandante Ferraz in April 1987, the Brazilians, true

◆ ◆ ◆ ◆ ◆

to their nature, threw them a party. Greenpeace reported that "the Brazilian station is one of the tidiest seen.... It is obvious that they not only took good care of their base, but also the surrounding environment."

The hospital, aquarium, and biology laboratories were separate from the living modules, under a gloomy metal roof that protected them from drifting snow. The base physician, deputy commander, and postal clerk was Dutra, an urbane doctor from Rio de Janeiro, who kept the operating room scrubbed and instrument-ready for sudden emergencies.

I spent much of each day, and the long bright night, in the three biology modules. We had to wear warm parkas while working in the aquarium module, which was kept at near-freezing in order not to poach the heat-sensitive organisms that we were studying. On some nights, while manipulating the cold steel knobs of the microscope, I would wear gloves. On very windy days the module would shake so much that it was impossible to use the microscope. It was a damp, cold, noisy place, filled with the gurgle of filters and the hiss of water jets, which were continually charged with seawater pumped through a black PVC pipe that snaked over the rock beach from the bay. The water supply had to be constantly monitored to keep it from freezing. If the catch had been good that week, the nets and baited traps not snarled by drifting ice or, worse yet, lost, the aquariums were populated with all manner of marine organisms from the bay: brown antifreeze fish, big-mouthed, nacreous icefish, starfish, sea anemones, isopods, amphipods, sea spiders, and krill. A few of the krill were forced to swim against an artificial current in a physiological chamber, their oxygen consumption measured by instruments that periodically tasted the water. This corner belonged to Phan, a Vietnamese-Brazilian physiologist. The Brazilian station lacked the trawl nets and swift boats necessary to capture krill on the open sea.

◆─◆─◆─◆─◆

But Phan had devised a system of high-powered lights that attracted krill (and myriad other organisms) close to shore in front of the station, where they could be conveniently caught in hand nets. At the opposite corner of the laboratory were the glass aquariums used for behavioral studies. This was Claude's corner. He spent long hours staring into the aquariums to observe the feeding strategies and food preferences of captive amphipods, trying to imagine what they would be doing on the unseen bottom of the bay.

The two other labs were under a sheltering canopy and therefore slightly warmer, but you still needed to wear a heavy coat inside. These contained more microscopes, dissecting tables, cupboards of chemicals, scales, plates of agar, and sinks with hot and cold running fresh water. On the days the nets were brought in, the labs reeked of formaldehyde. Renato, the veterinarian, worked here. It was Renato who had invited me to work at the station as part of a team trying to figure out the life cycles of parasites that live in seals, fish, and crustaceans.

The station had a homey ambience the summer I was there. But we were probably just lucky. Crews for Antarctic stations are like classrooms full of students: each has its own, unpredictable collective personality. But the psychological stress of prolonged confinement, with minimal privacy, in modules crowded in a hostile environment, often gets to even the strongest individuals. Antarctic workers frequently develop a dazed, almost autistic condition known as "big eye." Therefore the screening of candidates for the stations is serious business, particularly for the personnel who will endure the long, dark winter. At one of the Soviet Antarctic stations a worker killed another with an axe in a dispute over a chess game. During the autumn of 1983, the staff doctor at the Argentine station Almirante Brown, on the edge of Paradise Harbor, 400 kilometers

◆─◆─◆─◆

south of King George Island, forced his own rescue by burning the base down.

Candidates for the Brazilian Antarctic program were evaluated according to fifteen criteria, including "resistance to long periods of confinement, resistance to frustration, capacity for prolonged sexual abstinence and capacity to sustain long separation from one's family." How the evaluator could possibly ascertain this information was beyond me. In addition to the eight support personnel from the navy, all men, Ferraz Base had twenty-one scientists, five of whom were women. In many ways the station personnel become a surrogate family, and, like all families, they may be supportive or abusive. The Brazilians were wonderfully supportive, and we hugged and cried at the end of the summer in one *grande tristeza* of homesickness that lingers even now, two years after.

It was sometimes easy to forget, in that snug station on the edge of a blue bay, that we were living in an alien environment, beyond the edge of the habitable earth. Only the generator and a few membranes of metal and cloth prevented us from freezing to death. But the station, although necessary for our survival in Antarctica, was an upstart intruder in a timeless, frozen place. We were scientists who had come to study more enduring things: fossils and glaciers, the ebb and flow of seasons, wind and albatrosses, metropolises of penguins, and the crowded, unseen Antarctic underwater realm, which brims with life as no other sea on Earth. We were pilgrims in the last new land on Earth.

◆◆◆◆◆

II

THE NORTHERN PACIFIC

At the equinox when the earth was veiled in a late rain,
wreathed with wet poppies, waiting spring,
The ocean swelled for a far storm, and beat its boundary,
the ground-swell shook the beds of granite.
    Robinson Jeffers, from "Continent's End"

Our house was in Togiya-cho, close to where the atom bomb fell and my mother
was burned into white bones while praying before our family Buddhist altar.
    Sachiko Habu, writing in the fifth grade of the Hiroshima
    bombing that occurred when she was five years old

Coming is the dark cloud and the rainbow;
Wildly comes the rain and the wind;
    Whirlwinds sweep over the earth;
    Rolling down are the rocks of the ravines;
    The red mountain-streams are rushing to the sea.
Here the waterspouts;
Tumbled about are the clustering clouds of heaven;
Gushing forth are the springs of the mountains.
    One eye has the god;
    Two, four eyes, that he may see clearly behind him.
    Greatly revered be the voice of my god in heaven.
    Hawaiian Prayer to Lono

16

A VISIT TO THE

GREAT VOLCANOES

MARK TWAIN

CHAPTER 69

Bound for Hawaii (a hundred and fifty miles distant) to visit the great volcano and behold the other notable things which distinguish that island above the remainder of the group, we sailed from Honolulu on a certain Saturday afternoon, in the good schooner *Boomerang*.

The *Boomerang* was about as long as two streetcars, and about as wide as one. She was so small (though she was larger than the majority of the interisland coasters) that when I stood on her deck I felt but little smaller than the Colossus of Rhodes must have felt when he had a man-of-war under him. I could reach the water when she lay over under a strong breeze. When the captain and my comrade (a Mr. Billings), myself, and four other persons were all assembled on the little after portion of the deck which is sacred to the cabin passengers, it was full—there was not room for any more quality folks. Another section of the deck, twice as large as ours, was full of natives of both sexes, with their customary dogs, mats, blankets, pipes, calabashes of poi, fleas, and other luxuries and baggage of minor importance. As soon as we set sail the natives all lay down on the deck as thick as Negroes in a slave pen, and smoked, conversed, and spit on each other, and were truly sociable.

The little low-ceiled cabin below was rather larger than a hearse and as dark as a vault. It had two coffins on each side—I mean two bunks. A small table, capable of accommodating three persons at dinner, stood against the forward bulkhead, and over it hung the dingiest whale-oil lantern that ever peopled the obscurity of a dungeon with ghostly shapes. The floor room unoccupied was not extensive. One might swing a cat in it, perhaps, but not a long cat. The hold forward of the bulkhead had but little freight in it, and from morning till night a portly old rooster, with a voice like Baalam's ass, and the same disposition to use it, strutted up and down in that part of the vessel and crowed. He usually took dinner at six o'clock, and then, after an hour devoted to meditation, he mounted a barrel and crowed a good part of the night. He got hoarser and hoarser all the time, but he scorned to allow any personal consideration to interfere with his duty and kept up his labors in defiance of threatened diphtheria.

Sleeping was out of the question when he was on watch. He was a source of genuine aggravation and annoyance. It was worse than useless to shout at him or apply offensive epithets to him—he only took these things for applause and strained himself to make more noise. Occasionally, during the day, I threw potatoes at him through an aperture in the bulkhead, but he only dodged and went on crowing.

The first night, as I lay in my coffin, idly watching the dim lamp

◆—◆—◆—◆—◆

swinging to the rolling of the ship, and snuffing the nauseous odors of bilge water, I felt something gallop over me. I turned out promptly. However, I turned in again when I found it was only a rat. Presently something galloped over me once more. I knew it was not a rat this time, and I thought it might be a centipede, because the captain had killed one on deck in the afternoon. I turned out. The first glance at the pillow showed me a repulsive sentinel perched upon each end of it—cockroaches as large as peach leaves—fellows with long, quivering antennae and fiery, malignant eyes. They were grating their teeth like tobacco worms, and appeared to be dissatisfied about something. I had often heard that these reptiles were in the habit of eating off sleeping sailors' toenails down to the quick, and I would not get in the bunk anymore. I lay down on the floor. But a rat came and bothered me, and shortly afterward a procession of cockroaches arrived and camped in my hair. In a few moments the rooster was crowing with uncommon spirit and a party of fleas were throwing double somersaults about my person in the wildest disorder, and taking a bite every time they struck. I was beginning to feel really annoyed. I got up and put my clothes on and went on deck.

The above is not overdrawn; it is a truthful sketch of interisland schooner life. There is no such thing as keeping a vessel in elegant condition when she carries molasses and Kanakas.

It was compensation for my sufferings to come unexpectedly upon so beautiful a scene as met my eye—to step suddenly out of the sepulchral gloom of the cabin and stand under the strong light of the moon—in the center, as it were, of a glittering sea of liquid silver—to see the broad sails straining in the gale, the ship keeled over on her side, the angry foam hissing past her lee bulwarks, and sparkling sheets of spray dashing high over her bows and raining upon her decks; to brace myself and hang fast to the first object that presented itself, with hat jammed down and coattails whipping in the breeze,

◆-◆-◆-◆

and feel that exhilaration that thrills in one's hair and quivers down his backbone when he knows that every inch of canvas is drawing and the vessel cleaving through the waves at her utmost speed. There was no darkness, no dimness, no obscurity there. All was brightness, every object was vividly defined. Every prostrate Kanaka; every coil of rope; every calabash of poi; every puppy; every seam in the flooring; every bolthead; every object, however minute, showed sharp and distinct in its every outline; and the shadow of the broad mainsail lay black as a pall upon the deck, leaving Billings' white, upturned face glorified and his body in a total eclipse.

Monday morning we were close to the island of Hawaii. Two of its high mountains were in view—Mauna Loa and Hualalai. The latter is an imposing peak, but being only ten thousand feet high is seldom mentioned or heard of. Mauna Loa is said to be sixteen thousand feet high. The rays of glittering snow and ice, that clasped its summit like a claw, looked refreshing when viewed from the blistering climate we were in. One could stand on that mountain (wrapped up in blankets and furs to keep warm), and while he nibbled a snowball or an icicle to quench his thirst he could look down the long sweep of its sides and see spots where plants are growing that grow only where the bitter cold of winter prevails; lower down he could see sections devoted to productions that thrive in the Temperate Zone alone; and at the bottom of the mountain he could see the home of the tufted coconut palms and other species of vegetation that grow only in the sultry atmosphere of eternal summer. He could see all the climes of the world at a single glance of the eye, and that glance would only pass over a distance of four or five miles as the bird flies!

By and by we took boat and went ashore at Kailua, designing to ride horseback through the pleasant orange and coffee region of Kona, and rejoin the vessel at a point some leagues distant. This journey is well worth taking. The trail passes along on high ground—say a thousand feet above sea level—and usually about a mile distant from the ocean, which is always in sight, save that occasionally you find yourself buried in the forest in the midst of a rank tropical vegetation and a dense growth of trees, whose great bows overarch the road and shut out sun and sea and everything, and leave you in a dim, shady tunnel, haunted with invisible singing birds and fragrant with the odor of flowers. It was pleasant to ride occasionally in the warm sun, and feast the eye upon the ever-changing panorama of the forest (beyond and below us), with its many tints, its softened lights and shadows, its billowy undulations sweeping gently down from the mountain to the sea. It was pleasant also, at intervals, to leave the sultry sun and pass into the cool, green depths of this forest and indulge in sentimental reflections under the inspiration of its brooding twilight and its whispering foliage.

We rode through one orange grove that had ten thousand trees in it! They were all laden with fruit.

At one farmhouse we got some large peaches of excellent flavor. This fruit, as a general thing, does not do well in the Sandwich Islands. It takes a sort of almond shape, and is small and bitter. It needs frost, they say, and perhaps it does; if this be so, it will have a good opportunity to go on needing it, as it will not be likely to get it. The trees from which the fine fruit I have spoken of, came, had been planted and replanted *sixteen times,* and to this treatment the proprietor of the orchard attributed his success.

We passed several sugar plantations—new ones and not very extensive. The crops were, in most cases, third rattoons. [NOTE.— The first crop is called "plant cane"; subsequent crops which spring from the original roots, without replanting, are called "rattoons."] Almost everywhere on the island of Hawaii sugar cane matures in twelve months, both rattoons and plant, and although it ought to be taken off as soon as it tassels, no doubt, it is not absolutely necessary

◆—◆—◆—◆

to do it until about four months afterward. In Kona, the average yield of an acre of ground is *two tons* of sugar, they say. This is only a moderate yield for these islands, but would be astounding for Louisiana and most other sugar-growing countries. The plantations in Kona being on pretty high ground—up among the light and frequent rains—no irrigation whatever is required.

CHAPTER 73

At noon, we hired a Kanaka to take us down to the ancient ruins at Honaunau in his canoe—price two dollars—reasonable enough, for a sea voyage of eight miles, counting both ways.

The native canoe is an irresponsible-looking contrivance. I cannot think of anything to liken it to but a boy's sled runner hollowed out, and that does not quite convey the correct idea. It is about fifteen feet long, high and pointed at both ends, is a foot and a half or two feet deep, and so narrow that if you wedged a fat man into it you might not get him out again. It sits on top of the water like a duck, but it has an outrigger and does not upset easily, if you keep still. This outrigger is formed of two long bent sticks like plow handles, which project from one side, and to their outer ends is bound a curved beam composed of an extremely light wood, which skims along the surface of the water and thus saves you from an upset on that side, while the outrigger's weight is not so easily lifted as to make an upset on the other side a thing to be greatly feared. Still, until one gets used to sitting perched upon this knifeblade, he is apt to reason within himself that it would be more comfortable if there were just an outrigger or so on the other side also.

I had the bow seat, and Billings sat amidships and faced the Kanaka, who occupied the stern of the craft and did the paddling. With the first stroke the trim shell of a thing shot out from the shore like an arrow. There was not much to see. While we were on the shallow water of the reef, it was pastime to look down into the limpid depths at the large bunches of branching coral—the unique shrubbery of the sea. We lost that, though, when we got out into the dead blue water of the deep. But we had the picture of the surf, then, dashing angrily against the crag-bound shore and sending a foaming spray high into the air. There was interest in this beetling border, too, for it was honeycombed with quaint caves and arches and tunnels, and had a rude semblance of the dilapidated architecture of ruined keeps and castles rising out of the restless sea. When this novelty ceased to be a novelty, we turned our eyes shoreward and gazed at the long mountain with its rich green forests stretching up into the curtaining clouds, and at the specks of houses in the rearward distance and the diminished schooner riding sleepily at anchor. And when these grew tiresome we dashed boldly into the midst of a school of huge, beastly porpoises engaged at their eternal game of arching over a wave and disappearing, and then doing it over again and keeping it up—always circling over, in that way, like so many well-submerged wheels. But the porpoises wheeled themselves away, and then we were thrown upon our own resources. It did not take many minutes to discover that the sun was blazing like a bonfire and that the weather was of a melting temperature. It had a drowsing effect, too.

In one place we came upon a large company of naked natives, of both sexes and all ages, amusing themselves with the national pastime of surf bathing. Each heathen would paddle three or four hundred yards out to sea (taking a short board with him), then face the shore and wait for a particularly prodigious billow to come along; at the right moment he would fling his board upon its foamy crest and himself upon the board, and here he would come whizzing by like a bombshell! It did not seem that a lightning express train could shoot along at a more hair-lifting speed. I tried surf bathing once, subsequently, but made a failure of it. I got the board placed right, and at the right moment, too; but missed the connection myself. The board struck the shore in three-quarters of a second, without any cargo, and I struck the bottom about the same time, with a couple of barrels of water in me. None but natives ever master the art of surf bathing thoroughly.

At the end of an hour, we had made the four miles, and landed on a level point of land, upon which was a wide extent of old ruins, with many a tall coconut tree growing among them. Here was the ancient City of Refuge—a vast enclosure, whose stone walls were twenty feet thick at the base and fifteen feet high; an oblong square, a thousand and forty feet one way and a fraction under seven hundred the other. Within this enclosure, in early times, had been three rude temples; each two hundred and ten feet long by one hundred wide, and thirteen high.

In those days, if a man killed another anywhere on the island the relatives were privileged to take the murderer's life; and then a chase for life and liberty began—the outlawed criminal flying through pathless forests and over mountain and plain, with his hopes fixed upon the protecting walls of the City of Refuge, and the avenger of blood following hotly after him! Sometimes the race was kept up to the very gates of the temple, and the panting pair sped through long files of excited natives, who watched the contest with flashing eye and dilated nostril, encouraging the hunted refugee with sharp, inspiriting ejaculations, and sending up a ringing shout of exultation when the saving gates closed upon him and the cheated pursuer sank exhausted at the threshold. But sometimes the flying criminal fell under the hand of the avenger at the very door, when one more brave stride, one more brief second of time would have brought his feet upon the sacred ground and barred him against all harm. Where did these isolated pagans get this idea of a City of Refuge—this ancient Oriental custom?

This old sanctuary was sacred to all—even to rebels in arms and invading armies. Once within its walls, and confession made to the priest and absolution obtained, the wretch with a price upon his head could go forth without fear and without danger—he was *tabu*, and to harm him was death. The routed rebels in the lost battle for idolatry fled to this place to claim sanctuary, and many were thus saved.

Close to the corner of the great enclosure is a round structure of stone, some six or eight feet high, with a level top about ten or twelve in diameter. This was the place of execution. A high palisade of coconut piles shut out the cruel scenes from the vulgar multitude. Here criminals were killed, the flesh stripped from the bones and burned, and the bones secreted in holes in the body of the structure. If the man had been guilty of a high crime, the entire corpse was burned.

The walls of the temple are a study. The same food for speculation that is offered the visitor to the Pyramids of Egypt he will find here—the mystery of how they were constructed by a people unacquainted with science and mechanics. The natives have no invention of their own for hoisting heavy weights, they had no beasts of burden, and they have never even shown any knowledge of the properties of the lever. Yet some of the lava blocks quarried out, brought over rough, broken ground, and built into this wall, six or seven feet from the ground, are of prodigious size and would weigh tons. How did they transport and how raise them?

Both the inner and outer surfaces of the walls present a smooth front and are very creditable specimens of masonry. The blocks are of all manner of shapes and sizes, but yet are fitted together with the neatest exactness. The gradual narrowing of the wall from the base upward is accurately preserved.

No cement was used, but the edifice is firm and compact and is capable of resisting storm and decay for centuries. Who built this temple, and how was it built, and when, are the mysteries that may never be unraveled.

Outside of these ancient walls lies a sort of coffin-shaped stone eleven feet four inches long and three feet square at the small end (it would weigh a few thousand pounds), which the high chief who held sway over this district many centuries ago brought thither on his shoulder one day to use as a lounge! This circumstance is established by the most reliable traditions. He used to lie down on it, in his indolent way, and keep an eye on his subjects at work for him and see that there was no "soldiering" done. And no doubt there was not any done to speak of, because he was a man of that sort of build that incites to attention to business on the part of an employee. He was fourteen or fifteen feet high. When he stretched himself at full length on his lounge, his legs hung down over the end, and when he snored he woke the dead. These facts are all attested by irrefragable tradition.

On the other side of the temple is a monstrous seven-ton rock, eleven feet long, seven feet wide, and three feet thick. It is raised a foot or a foot and a half above the ground, and rests upon half a dozen little stony pedestals. The same old fourteen-footer brought it down from the mountain, merely for fun (he had his own notions about fun), and propped it up as we find it now and as others may find it a century hence, for it would take a score of horses to budge it from its position. They say that fifty or sixty years ago the proud Queen Kaahumanu used to fly to this rock for safety, whenever she had been making trouble with her fierce husband, and hide under it

◆ ◆ ◆ ◆ ◆

until his wrath was appeased. But these Kanakas will lie, and this statement is one of their ablest efforts—for Kaahumanu was six feet high—she was bulky—she was built like an ox—and she could no more have squeezed herself under that rock than she could have passed between the cylinders of a sugar mill. What could she gain by it, even if she succeeded? To be chased and abused by a savage husband could not be otherwise than humiliating to her high spirit, yet it could never make her feel so flat as an hour's repose under that rock would.

We walked a mile over a raised macadamized road of uniform width; a road paved with flat stones and exhibiting in its every detail a considerable degree of engineering skill. Some say that wise old pagan, Kamehameha I, planned and built it, but others say it was built so long before his time that the knowledge of who constructed it has passed out of the traditions. In either case, however, as the handiwork of an untaught and degraded race it is a thing of pleasing interest. The stones are worn and smooth, and pushed apart in places, so that the road has the exact appearance of those ancient paved highways leading out of Rome which one sees in pictures.

The object of our tramp was to visit a great natural curiosity at the base of the foothills—a congealed cascade of lava. Some old forgotten volcanic eruption sent its broad river of fire down the mountainside here, and it poured down in a great torrent from an overhanging bluff some fifty feet high to the ground below. The flaming torrent cooled in the winds from the sea, and remains there today, all seamed, and frothed and rippled, a petrified Niagara. It is very picturesque, and withal so natural that one might almost imagine it still flowed. A smaller stream trickled over the cliff and built up an isolated pyramid about thirty feet high, which has the semblance of a mass of large gnarled and knotted vines and roots and stems intricately twisted and woven together.

◆◆◆◆

CHAPTER 76

We rode horseback all around the island of Hawaii (the crooked road making the distance two hundred miles), and enjoyed the journey very much. We were more than a week making the trip, because our Kanaka horses would not go by a house or a hut without stopping— whip and spur could not alter their minds about it, and so we finally found that it economized time to let them have their way. Upon inquiry the mystery was explained: the natives are such thoroughgoing gossips that they never pass a house without stopping to swap news, and consequently their horses learn to regard that sort of thing as an essential part of the whole duty of man, and his salvation not to be compassed without it. However, at a former crisis of my life I had once taken an aristocratic young lady out driving, behind a horse that had just retired from a long and honorable career as the moving impulse of a milk wagon, and so this present experience awoke a reminiscent sadness in me in place of the exasperation more natural to the occasion. I remembered how helpless I was that day, and how humiliated; how ashamed I was of having intimated to the girl that I had always owned the horse and was accustomed to grandeur; how hard I tried to appear easy, and even vivacious, under suffering that was consuming my vitals; how placidly and maliciously the girl smiled, and kept on smiling, while my hot blushes baked themselves into a permanent blood pudding in my face; how the horse ambled from one side of the street to the other and waited complacently before every third house two minutes and a quarter while I belabored his back and reviled him in my heart; how I tried to keep him from turning corners, and failed; how I moved heaven and earth to get him out of town, and did not succeed; how he traversed the entire settlement and delivered imaginary milk at a hundred and sixty-two different domiciles, and how he finally brought

◆ ◆ ◆ ◆ ◆

up at a dairy depot and refused to budge further, thus rounding and completing the revealment of what the plebian service of his life had been; how, in eloquent silence, I walked the girl home, and how, when I took leave of her, her parting remark scorched my soul and appeared to blister me all over: she said that my horse was a fine, capable animal, and I must have taken great comfort in him in my time—but that if I would take along some milk tickets next time, and appear to deliver them at the various halting places, it might expedite his movements a little. There was a coolness between us after that.

In one place in the island of Hawaii we saw a laced and ruffled cataract of limpid water leaping from a sheer precipice fifteen hundred feet high; but that sort of scenery finds its stanchest ally in the arithmetic rather than in spectacular effect. If one desires to be so stirred by a poem of Nature wrought in the happily commingled graces of picturesque rocks, glimpsed distances, foliage, color, shifting lights and shadows, and falling water, that the tears almost come into his eyes so potent is the charm exerted, he need not go away from America to enjoy such an experience. The Rainbow Fall, in Watkins Glen, New York, on the Erie railway, is an example. It would recede into pitiable insignificance if the callous tourist drew an arithmetic on it; but left to compete for the honors simply on scenic grace and beauty—the grand, the august, and the sublime being barred the contest—it could challenge the old world and the new to produce its peer.

In one locality, on our journey, we saw some horses that had been born and reared on top of mountains, above the range of running water, and consequently they had never drank that fluid in their lives, but had been always accustomed to quenching their thirst by eating dew-laden or shower-wetted leaves. And now it was destructively funny to see them sniff suspiciously at a pail of water, and then put in their noses and try to take a *bite* out of the fluid, as if it were a

◆—◆—◆—◆

solid. Finding it liquid, they would snatch away their heads and fall to trembling, snorting, and showing other evidences of fright. When they became convinced at last that the water was friendly and harmless, they thrust in their noses up to their eyes, brought out a mouthful of the water, and proceeded to *chew* it complacently. We saw a man coax, kick, and spur one of them five or ten minutes before he could make it cross a running stream. It spread its nostrils, distended its eyes, and trembled all over, just as horses customarily do in the presence of a serpent—and for aught I know it thought the crawling stream *was* a serpent.

In due course of time our journey came to an end at Kawaihae (usually pronounced To-a-*hi*—and before we find fault with this elaborate orthographical method of arriving at such an unostentatious result, let us lop off the *ugh* from our word "though"). I made this horseback trip on a mule. I paid ten dollars for him at Kau (Kahoo), added four to get him shod, rode him two hundred miles, and then sold him for fifteen dollars. I mark the circumstances with a white stone (in the absence of chalk—for I never saw a white stone that a body could mark anything with, though out of respect for the ancients I have tried it often enough); for up to that day and date it was the first strictly commercial transaction I had ever entered into and come out a winner. We returned to Honolulu, and from thence sailed to the island of Maui, and spent several weeks there very pleasantly. I still remember, with a sense of indolent luxury, a picnicking excursion up a romantic gorge there, called the Iao Valley. The trail lay along the edge of a brawling stream in the bottom of the gorge—a shady route, for it was well roofed with the verdant domes of forest trees. Through openings in the foliage we glimpsed picturesque scenery that revealed ceaseless changes and new charms with every step of our progress. Perpendicular walls from one to three thousand feet high guarded the way, and were sumptuously plumed

◆—◆—◆—◆—◆

with varied foliage, in places, and in places swathed in waving ferns. Passing shreds of cloud trailed their shadows across these shining fronts, mottling them with blots; billowy masses of white vapor hid the turreted summits, and far above the vapor swelled a background of gleaming green crags and cones that came and went, through the veiling mists, like islands drifting in a fog; sometimes the cloudy curtain descended till half the canyon wall was hidden, then shredded gradually away till only airy glimpses of the ferny front appeared through it—then swept aloft and left it glorified in the sun again. Now and then, as our position changed, rocky bastions swung out from the wall, a mimic ruin of castellated ramparts and crumbling towers clothed with mosses and hung with garlands of swaying vines, and as we moved on they swung back again and hid themselves once more in the foliage. Presently a verdure-clad needle of stone, a thousand feet high, stepped out from behind a corner and mounted guard over the mysteries of the valley. It seemed to me that if Captain Cook needed a monument, here was one ready made— therefore, why not put his sign here and sell out the venerable coconut stump?

But the chief pride of Maui is her dead volcano of Haleakala— which means, translated, "The House of the Sun." We climbed a thousand feet up the side of this isolated colossus one afternoon; then camped, and next day climbed the remaining nine thousand feet, and anchored on the summit, where we built a fire and froze and roasted by turns all night. With the first pallor of dawn we got up and saw things that were new to us. Mounted on a commanding pinnacle, we watched Nature work her silent wonders. The sea was spread abroad on every hand, its tumbled surface seeming only wrinkled and dimpled in the distance. A broad valley below appeared like an ample checkerboard, its velvety-green sugar plantations alternating with dun squares of barrenness and groves of trees

◆—◆—◆—◆—◆

diminished to mossy tufts. Beyond the valley were mountains picturesquely grouped together; but bear in mind, we fancied that we were looking *up* at these things—not down. We seemed to sit in the bottom of a symmetrical bowl ten thousand feet deep, with the valley and the skirting sea lifted away into the sky above us! It was curious; and not only curious, but aggravating; for it was having our trouble all for nothing, to climb ten thousand feet toward heaven and then have to look *up* at our scenery. However, we had to be content with it and make the best of it; for all we could do we could not coax our landscape down out of the clouds. Formerly, when I had read an article in which Poe treated of this singular fraud perpetrated upon the eye by isolated great altitudes, I had looked upon the matter as an invention of his own fancy.

I have spoken of the outside view—but we had an inside one, too. That was the yawning dead crater, into which we now and then tumbled rocks, half as large as a barrel, from our perch, and saw them go careering down the almost perpendicular sides, bounding three hundred feet at a jump; kicking up dust clouds wherever they struck; diminishing to our view as they sped farther into distance; growing invisible, finally, and only betraying their course by faint little puffs of dust; and coming to a halt at last in the bottom of the abyss, two thousand five hundred feet down from where they started! It was magnificent sport. We wore ourselves out at it.

The crater of Vesuvius, as I have before remarked, is a modest pit about a thousand feet deep and three thousand in circumference; that of Kilauea is somewhat deeper, and *ten miles* in circumference. But what are either of them compared to the vacant stomach of Haleakala? I will not offer any figures of my own, but give official ones— those of Commander Wilkes, USN, who surveyed it and testifies that it is *twenty-seven miles in circumference!* If it had a level bottom it would make a fine site for a city like London. It must have afforded a spectacle worth contemplating in the old days when its furnaces gave full rein to their anger.

Presently vagrant white clouds came drifting along, high over the sea and the valley; then they came in couples and groups, then in imposing squadrons; gradually joining their forces, they banked themselves solidly together, a thousand feet under us, and *totally shut out land and ocean*—not a vestige of *anything* was left in view but just a little of the rim of the crater, circling away from the pinnacle whereon we sat (for a ghostly procession of wanderers from the filmy hosts without had drifted through a chasm in the crater wall and filed round and round, and gathered and sunk and blended together till the abyss was stored to the brim with a fleecy fog). Thus banked, motion ceased, and silence reigned. Clear to the horizon, league on league, the snowy floor stretched without a break—not level, but in rounded folds, with shallow creases between, and with here and there stately piles of vapory architecture lifting themselves aloft out of the common plain—some near at hand, some in the middle distances, and others relieving the monotony of the remote solitudes. There was little conversation, for the impressive scene overawed speech. I felt like the Last Man, neglected of the judgment, and left pinnacled in mid-heaven, a forgotten relic of a vanished world.

While the hush yet brooded, the messengers of the coming resurrection appeared in the east. A growing warmth suffused the horizon, and soon the sun emerged and looked out over the cloud waste, flinging bars of ruddy light across it, staining its folds and billow caps with blushes, purpling the shaded troughs between, and glorifying the massy vapor palaces and cathedrals with a wasteful splendor of all blendings and combinations of rich coloring.

It was the sublimest spectacle I ever witnessed, and I think the memory of it will remain with me always.

◆━◆━◆━◆

17

DECLINE

OF A LAGOON

JOHN CULLINEY

Eastern Oahu fronts on the sea with extensive fringing reefs. These extend almost continuously from the island's northern tip at Kahuku Point southeastward past Kaaawa, a straight-line distance of sixteen miles. This is the windward side of the island, and from the perspective of an *iwa* (frigate bird) high in the northeast trades, the white breakers on the shallow coral rim trace a much longer meandering line, broken only where major stream valleys intersect the coast.

At Kaaawa, however, the simple coralline shelf is interrupted dramatically. A wide marine lagoon extends far into the land beneath dramatic heights toward the main Koolau Range. This is Kaneohe Bay, a unique Hawaiian lagoon of approximately twenty square miles of calm water. It is protected across a wide sea entrance by a three-mile-long barrier reef, the only one in the main Hawaiian Islands. To a latter-day explorer afloat on the bay, this is a coastal setting that despite creeping urbanization and a nearby military base is still steeped in beauty. Sadly, the same can no longer be said of much of the environment below the surface of the bay, which once included some of the richest and loveliest of Hawaiian reef lands.

Kaneohe Bay had its origins in the last ice age as a coalescence of stream valleys cut into a wide windward coastal plain. In those millennia of far-away, ice-covered continents, the sea had receded from the island. Its edge was well to the east and some 300 feet lower than its present position. Freshwater runoff reached this late Pleistocene shoreline mainly via river channels off either end of the present bay. Long, low bluffs, possibly capped by sand dunes, spanned the wide front of this region between the two main river channels. Behind this frontal barrier, the rivers carved channels and sloughs in the present basin areas of the bay and left behind smaller bluffs and promontories that stood well above the valley floors. Then, with the melting of the great continental glaciers beginning about 15,000 years ago, the sea rose, and on Oahu it progressively drowned the Kaneohe region's river channels and valley floors and finally began to creep over the basin promontories behind the central rise.

Perhaps 8,000 years ago, the sea rose above the last of the land barrier fronting the bay, and from then on conditions over the area would have been predominantly marine. Within a few centuries, framework corals must have built substantial foundations on the front ridge and on many of the drowned promontories in the basin. Upward growth of the reef with the incremental transgression of the Holocene sea accounts for the present coralline barrier across the mouth of the bay. The same process has produced tiny islets, expanses of intertidal sandbars, and the many small patch reefs that stud the basin area like miniature, barely submerged atolls. Modern studies of coral reef growth suggest that existing Kaneohe Bay reefs are no more than thirty to fifty feet thick and developed in the last 6,000 to 8,000 years.

Beneath a splendor of blue-green mountains, the bay held a variety of littoral habitats and sustained a wealth of aquatic life quite different from that of the shorelines and reefs of the outer coast. The lower streams were estuaries, grading from fresh water to marine as they reached the bay. Low-lying shore areas near the mouths of major streams were wetlands, some covering hundreds of acres. Such marshes were probably wide and open (since there were no native mangrove trees) and raucous with vanished Hawaiian birds and flocks of seasonal migrants. On the steep hills flanking parts of the bay, native Hawaiian forests composed of trees and other plants now utterly erased from this region (and nearly everywhere else in the Hawaiian lowlands) helped to retard runoff and slow erosion. Along miles of bay shore, a fringing reef developed, a qualitatively different reef than occurs along the open coast. At its surface and edge, the bay's fringing reef has a smoother and trimmer appearance than its oceanfront counterpart. Bay reefs also lack the large surge channels and so-called buttressed architecture that develop in reefs that stand against the open sea. Framework structures and the corals themselves are more fragile. One species of finger coral, *Porites compressa,* overwhelmingly dominates the bay's reefs; the even more delicate lace coral, *Pocillopora damicornis,* which is nearly impossible to find on shallow oceanfront reefs, is commonly seen by snorkelers in the bay. Instead of pounding breakers, the main coral-destroying forces here are fresh water and smothering silt. Both have been in the ascendancy since humans began to rend the local ecological fabric, which featured important woven connections between the bay and the land. Especially critical was mass human wastage of the lowland marshes and forests that once soaked up the fierce windward rains like massive green sponges.

◆◆◆◆

A THOUSAND LEAGUES OF BLUE

When the first Hawaiians arrived, these clear waters and quiet shores must have been a maritime Eden. During the Hawaiian era, environmental change, especially the clearing of lowland forests, had major impacts on the coastal zone, and probably degraded or destroyed a number of land ecosystems around Kaneohe Bay. However, it is clear that much of the bay itself remained essentially pristine and highly productive. Perhaps having lost some ground, the bay settled into a new ecological equilibrium that accommodated Hawaiian activities. Much later, just after Captain Cook but before the tragic epidemics of white people's diseases, conservative estimates of the Hawaiian population around Kaneohe Bay ranged between ten and twenty thousand people, making this region a major population center on Oahu. Primary settlements were situated in several major watersheds between Kaneohe proper and Kualoa Point at the bay's northern end. The people subsisted on a few agricultural staples dominated by taro. Their protein came largely from Kaneohe Bay.

The treasured fish of the region was the mullet (*Mugil cephalus*), called *ama-ama* or *anae* in Hawaiian. These plump, densely schooling, blunt-headed fish reach about eighteen to twenty inches in length. Their young, small silvery fry, are found in shallow pools on rocky shores, where they can be netted by the hundreds. Observing such concentrated young mullet with their vacuum-cleaner style of feeding (they eat algae and bits of organic detritus strained from the water and bottom sediments) probably gave the Hawaiians the idea of artificially cultivating them in stone-walled fish ponds. By the time of European contact, Kaneohe Bay had perhaps the greatest concentration of such aquaculture in the islands. Along the fringing reefs of the bay, at least thirty fish ponds still existed in the midnineteenth century. Remains of only twelve can be identified today. Some of them were nearly a mile wide; reportedly their operation

◆━◆━◆━◆━◆

278

was sophisticated. For example, excessive evaporation and rising salinity in the shallow ponds was countered by opening sluice gates that connected to an adjoining freshwater stream. Besides mullet, the Hawaiians stocked juveniles of other species, especially milkfish, or *awa* (*Chanos chanos*) in the ponds.

Although pond construction and operation as well as intensive gleaning by thousands of Hawaiians must have caused considerable environmental change on the fringing reefs of Kaneohe Bay, the essentially organic Hawaiian culture probably did not greatly impair the productive marine ecosystem of the bay at large. Even peak populations in the region probably did not exceed the bay's capacity to support them. Intensive mullet and milkfish cultivation, although it reduced diversity along the coastal flats, actually may have lessened fishery impacts elsewhere in the bay. Because these two species are nearly exclusively herbivorous, their flesh is produced with the lowest possible expenditure of energy available in the bay for the growth of fish. Thus, the Hawaiians were fostering an ecologically efficient protein resource; in modern jargon, they were eating low on the ocean's food chain.

Hawaiian lore as well as early historical records indicate that bay reef lands and basins were rich in species that indicated diverse food chains. Besides mullet and milkfish, the fish called *nehu, Stolephorus purpureus* (an anchovy); *aholehole, Kuhlia sandvicensis* (an endemic sea perch that ranges into freshwater streams); and *ulua* (large jacks, family Carangidae) receive special mention along with octopus as traditionally abundant seafood items in Kaneohe Bay.

Today, these fisheries are sadly depleted. Of *nehu,* only small, scattered remnants of reportedly once immense living shoals remain. These little fishes have long been the preferred chum and baitfish for the local fresh tuna industry. Kaneohe Bay and Pearl Harbor are the only locations on Oahu (and the best in the state) for large populations of *nehu*. In both places its numbers have declined so greatly that efforts are being made to find substitute baits. However, none seems to attract tuna quite as well, and *nehu* are still avidly sought by fishermen. The problem is that the very tight schooling behavior of this surface-dwelling species makes it fairly easy to locate and a cinch to catch, even when its overall population is very low. Hence, commercial extinction will come perilously close to the real thing.

The stream-running sea perch called *aholehole*, a small, silvery predator reaching about a foot in length, is a common reef dweller as an adult; juveniles prefer brackish to fresh water. One of the major watershed valleys, Waiahole, near the north end of the bay, was named in prehistoric times for this fish.

At least one species of large jack, known to the Hawaiians as *ulua*, was formerly abundant in the bay. Some of these swift, powerful predators attain a length of five feet and weigh more than 100 pounds. Typically fishes of clear ocean waters along the outer reefs, certain jacks occasionally congregate inshore, even in the mouths of tropical estuaries. Here they flirt with the tides, perhaps seeking aggregations of prey—*nehu* or *aholehole*. In the late nineteenth century, big jacks, probably either *Caranx ignobilis* or *Gnathodon speciosus*, could still be found in the Waikalua River at Kaneohe. They came far enough into this estuary at the south end of the bay to enter drainage channels of the rice fields that covered the area at that time, and in that improbable habitat field hands caught the big fish. Today, while juvenile jacks, known as *papio*, occur sporadically in the bay, adult *ulua* have become scarce nearly everywhere around Oahu.

Octopus, called *hee*, were once found in great abundance on the reefs of Kaneohe Bay. Nevertheless, Hawaiian chiefs declared lengthy annual *kapu* restrictions on the octopus fishery, a sign that this resource was carefully managed. Often the eccentric mollusks

◆—◆—◆—◆—◆

were forbidden game for four to six months. As the end of the ban approached, specially appointed scouts would tour the reef flats of a district to assess the prospects for the coming octopus harvest. They focused in particular on areas, such as around Kapapa Island and Kualoa in Kaneohe Bay, that were renowned for concentrated populations of octopus. In those places, the bottom was covered with these animals' burrows in such density that it was likened to ground rooted up by pigs. Everywhere in the clear shallows, the animals' bulky heads were visible, looking like clumps of dark earth.

Despite the Hawaiians' exploitation of the bay and their ecological remaking of its shores and watersheds, this picture of the bay as a marine Eden in productive equilibrium with its harvesters persisted into the historic period. Then, beginning around the midnineteenth century, came a renewed onslaught on the bay and its supporting environs that continues today. No new equilibrium is in sight.

First there was a new round of wholesale land clearing around the bay—the beginning of agribusiness Hawaiian style. From the 1850s to the 1920s, a succession of intensive cattle ranching, sugar cane cultivation, and pineapple planting spread far and wide over the lands bordering the bay. From 1880 to the 1920s, commercial rice production was intensively pursued in the well-watered valley bottoms of the region. This latter enterprise all but submerged the pitiful remnants of taro farming here that formerly sustained whole valleys of Hawaiians. The new waves of deforestation, grazing, and ploughing brought unprecedented erosion—gross tonnages of silt injected directly from bald hillsides into the bay.

Then came the water withdrawals. Beginning in 1916, a series of irrigation tunnels was bored into and through the Koolau mountain wall to the arid slopes overlooking central Oahu. These water projects were as ambitious as the one fictionalized in Michener's novel

Hawaii; one of the tunnels was four miles long. The water from rainy windward valleys, among them major watersheds feeding Kaneohe Bay, triggered an immense burst of agriculture on the lee side of the Koolau Range, but the diversions drastically curtailed the normal freshwater flow to the bay, especially in its northern reaches. Because the irrigation systems were built to overflow into the valley at high water, however, they did nothing to relieve the inundations of mud from torrential rains.

Nevertheless, early twentieth century was a time when some parts of the bay were still clear and clean, with healthy coral reefs and a host of colorful fishes still apparent. And for the first time, the bay's environmental wonders were publicly acknowledged. The southern region near Kaneohe became known for its "coral gardens." Around 1911, the Coral Gardens Hotel was built here on the shore of the bay. This resort's featured attraction was a glassbottom-boat tour of the nearby reefs. A brochure printed in 1919 described the underwater scenery:

> Only those who have seen the Gardens can appreciate the marvelous beauty of their marine growth and the variety of undersea life they hold. Looking through the glass bottom boat, one sees a natural aquarium of vast extent, set in an undersea forest of strange trees and crags, valleys and hills.

These enthusiastic remarks were written by then territorial governor C. J. McCarthy. They may constitute the first promotion of an underwater tourist attraction in Hawaii.

The original Coral Gardens resort and its tours persisted until shortly before World War II. Then, more than a decade of massive dredging and removal of whole reefs for primarily military purposes obliterated the coral gardens in the calm, sheltered southern bay. Much of the dredged reef mass here, at least 15 million cubic yards,

◆◆◆◆◆

went into landfill and runway construction at the base now known as Kaneohe Marine Corps Air Station on Mokapu Peninsula. Many of the south bay's pedestal reefs, which had loomed pale and lovely just below the water's surface, were blasted apart to clear landing zones for seaplanes.

Dredging kills marine life over a much wider area than the actual wholesale removal of reef mass itself and in a variety of ways. Fine-grained sediments by the ton are churned up and spread along the paths of tidal currents in smothering clouds. This is especially true during the removal of soft sediments to deepen ship channels. Dredging for that purpose has occurred all over the bay, most intensively during the 1940s and 1950s. Aerial photographs of Kaneohe Bay during dredging episodes in the 1940s show milky, silt-laden water covering several square miles at a time. Dredging also releases noxious and toxic chemicals, such as spilled petroleum products, that have been buried in the sediments, and it raises and stirs into the water fertilizing nutrients for marine plant growth. The result is widespread poisoning of many organisms and the rapid growth of a few hardy kinds of phytoplankton and bottom algae, which can be just as smothering to delicate coral tissues as silt. In addition, increased turbidity in the water drastically dims the light needed for normal growth by the reef builders. Since the 1950s, continued dredging and a host of other activities associated with urban development and military operations have largely prevented regrowth and reestablishment of the ruined reefs in the south bay, and degradation has crept northward.

Another debilitating environmental disease in the bay resulted from the buildup of sewage effluent through the mid-1970s. Piped from the sprawling military complex on the Mokapu Peninsula and from the largest civilian centers in windward Oahu, this immense load of plant nutrients and toxins was rapidly turning the southern

◆—◆—◆—◆—◆

bay into a cesspool. The exchange of these waters with cleaner waters to the north and seaward was slow. Marine scientists measure such exchange of water in a semi-isolated basin as a *flushing rate*, an especially apt phrase in the case of southern Kaneohe Bay. Stimulation of algal growth was one of the worst effects of the sewage pollution in the bay. Plankton blooms clouded the water nearly continuously, and on the bottom a proliferation of *Dictyospheria cavernosa*, the so-called green bubble algae, reached alarming dimensions. Its growth form, a quilted, rubbery green mat, spread over nearly every kind of exposed hard surface, including living corals, which promptly died. By the 1970s any surviving remnants of the old coral gardens in southern Kaneohe Bay were merely limestone banks beneath carpets of *Dictyospheria* often inches thick. To find healthy, living reefs, one had to go well into the northern half of the bay, and even there the green bubble algae was spreading.

Removal of the sewage outfall in 1977 and its relocation to the open ocean beyond the fringing reef off Kailua helped to stabilize the bay's environmental health, but at this writing the bay's condition can only be listed as guarded, and continued intensive care is needed merely to treat the symptoms of further decline in its vital ecosystems. A full recovery is highly unlikely.

Using medical metaphors for the bay's condition requires some clarification. The bay is not about to die in the sense that an organism does. Life can be found in places that are far more polluted than Kaneohe Bay; a few kinds of the hardiest life forms thrive in the filthiest of the world's harbors. Nevertheless, the kinds of living organisms present are greatly diminished in such places.

At present the bay can be said to be aging rapidly and unnaturally. Sediment buildup is a measure of age in a coastal basin such as Kaneohe Bay. Given a static sea level, all such bodies of water eventually fill, becoming mud flats and finally marshes. But human

◆—◆—◆—◆—◆

erosion-promoting activities can accelerate this process tremendously. By any reasonable estimate, Kaneohe Bay has aged more in the last century than perhaps in the previous thousand years, roughly the tenure of the Hawaiians in the area.

During World War II, national need in wartime prevailed over any expressed concern for environmental conservation in Kaneohe Bay. Today, however, despite volumes of paper protection for the bay's environment, a vast and expanding carelessness manifests itself in numerous ways—as a petroleum sheen that can sometimes be traced all across the southern bay to the Marine Corps Air Station and, to a lesser extent, to private marinas and yacht anchorages; as inadequately controlled siltation from construction on the bay's hilly shores; as agricultural and domestic pesticide runoff dangerously uncontrolled by the state of Hawaii. These environmental impacts and insults continue to sap the bay's vitality and diminish the dappled vistas that once delighted visitors to the Coral Gardens.

Perhaps one human influence in the bay with a positive effect was the introduction of mangrove trees, but this seems to have happened by accident. Mangroves, those tropical saltwater shoreline trees whose seeds float and sprout as they drift, are not native to Hawaii. The first import seems to have been the Florida species *Rhizophora mangle,* which was planted on the South Molokai shoreline about 1902. By the 1920s, young specimens were found growing in several places around Kaneohe Bay, and the speculation of the time was that the green, pencil-like floating seeds (or seedlings) had drifted some sixty minutes downwind from Molokai, where the only mature trees then existed. Other species of mangroves were later introduced from the Philippines, and one of them, *Bruguiera sexangula,* is also now established in Kaneohe Bay. These trees sprout tangles of buttressing prop roots that trap silt and stabilize muddy shores. They also contribute greatly to certain near-shore food

◆━◆━◆━◆━◆

chains. But that contribution is in the form of masses of decomposing leaves, and mangroves can grow like woody weeds over shallow reef flats. The presumed beneficial role of mangroves in Kaneohe Bay has not yet been proven.

Many other plants and animals have been introduced in and around the bay. Underwater, one of the most conspicuous plants is the large, fleshy red algae, *Eucheuma,* several species of which were introduced from the Philippines in the mid-1970s. As escapees from experimental cultivation at the University of Hawaii's Institute of Marine Biology at Coconut Island, *Eucheuma* can now be found all over the bay. They are especially abundant in the southern portion, where these alien plants festoon the reefs around Coconut Island.

Animal invaders of Kaneohe Bay include a variety of invertebrates and fishes. The earliest of them to be purposefully introduced was probably the Chesapeake oyster, *Crassostrea virginica.* It was initially seeded into Pearl Harbor in 1866 and was flourishing in Kaneohe Bay by 1890. To what extent such foreign organisms have changed the bay's ecology is simply not known. Adjustments in biotic communities after species invasions often take decades or longer, and in the shallow marine environment changes due to interactions between aliens and natives may be masked by effects of dredging, pollution, and the like.

There are still a few places in the bay, well to the north, away from the worst of the chronic oil spills, urbanization, and epicenters of species invasions, where one can glimpse fragments of former underwater splendors—stretches of reef crowded with finger corals, lacelike forms, and tiered clusters of stony plates up to several feet in diameter. The landscape is alive with color; coral hues range from soft beige and brown to bright yellow and electric blue. A kaleidoscopic display of life swims, crawls, glides, and hops about the living

◆◆◆◆◆

rockery. Striking invertebrates such as tropical lobsters and octopus are not yet uncommon in a few scattered retreats. Tribes of painted fishes—butterflies, wrasses, parrots, tangs, the silvery *aholehole*, clownish Moorish idols, and elegant lyre-tailed *kala*—revel over these last aboriginal reefs in Oahu's lagoon.

Once again there is a glassbottom-boat tour in the bay. Now it embarks from Heeia, well north of Kaneohe proper, and it seeks the remaining beauty spots. But sometimes weather or scheduling delays prevent the long trip to the best remaining reefs, and tourists have to settle for the average underwater attractions of the bay. The view is obscured by drifting detritus and plankton blooms. Amid dimly seen yellow and brown coral heads with a *Dictyospheria* fringe, a few fishes—species labeled mudfish and poopfish by bay area residents—turn and weave, their colors dulled by the cloudy water. The populations of some of these hardy types such as the sergeant major are high, but this merely indicates that a polluted bay is an analog of a garbage dump, where rats and mice, seagulls and starlings, may abound but from which other wildlife has retreated.

In a more environmentally sensitive time and society than plantation-era Oahu, Kaneohe Bay might have become a national park. Many other countries in the world would probably have accorded it such status. The uniqueness and spectacle of its topography and life forms would have argued well for its protection. Today, the bay's fate should prompt the citizens of Hawaii and the United States to safeguard what remains of the bay's natural heritage and warn against further avoidable destruction of the remaining unique habitats in the Hawaiian Islands.

18

SYMBOLS

IN THE ROCK

FRANK STEWART

Kilauea and Mauna Loa, and the area surrounding these two
nearly adjoining volcanoes, comprise the most active volcanic region in the world. Mauna Loa, on the island of Hawaii, is the
planet's largest mountain, nearly thirty-four thousand feet high
when measured from the sea floor to the summit and immensely
broad. Just to the southwest, leaning against Mauna Loa, the caldera of Kilauea presses so closely that geologists have wondered
whether they share the same volcanic venting system. From this
lower summit, Kilauea's massive southern flank descends gradually
toward the sea, but breaks abruptly along a jagged array of high volcanic cliffs, or fault scarps, several miles before it reaches the Pacific.
Below the cliffs is a broad plain of lava, a smooth expanse nearly
twenty miles long and over five miles wide.

An immense geologic downthrust has torn this unstable plain
away from the relatively stationary volcano that looms above it. The

sparsely vegetated plain that fans out far below the cliffs is all black—shining in even blacker bands where the most recent and therefore less weathered lava flows have crossed it—and tilts toward the sea. On its far southern edge, where it encounters the ocean, the plain breaks abruptly again, this time along sea cliffs that overhang some of the deepest blue waters in the Pacific.

The large-scale slumping of Keahou Lava Plain (as it is called) along this major rift zone of Kilauea is constantly vulnerable to rattling earthquakes generated by the volcanoes. Frequently the quakes arrive with devastating force. As recently as November 1975, in the hours before dawn on Thanksgiving weekend, a pair of earthquakes struck suddenly along this fault system. The first, at 3:36 in the morning, set off rumbling landslides and a volcanic eruption at the Kilauea summit ten miles away. When the second, much more violent quake struck an hour later, the entire plain dropped as much as fifteen feet and shifted farther seaward. Within minutes the downthrust along the fault set off a series of local tsunami, tidal waves that swept across a small beach below an oasis of palms at the southwest edge of the plain. The point of land, called Halape, was thrust some ten feet below the water as the tsunami washed violently across the quickly disappearing ocean front, and in the churning waves nineteen young campers and fishermen were swept out to sea in the darkness. Some clung to trees and rocks to save themselves; two of them died.

Traveling toward this plain by car, down from Kilauea's summit, you're looking southeast across a horizon of deep, intensely blue water. The steep cliffs you descend on the narrow road of switchbacks are called Holei Pali, and for centuries lava has poured down them from the summit, creating jumbled patterns of light and dark rock. The road to the coast has been covered over by lava and rebuilt many times in recent years by National Park work crews. The lower part of the road, however, has kept generally the same route. After reaching the foot of the cliffs, but before reaching the sea, the road winds past the head of a narrow foot trail. Travelers in passing cars note this trail only as a wide shoulder on the road marked with a wooden sign. Not many stop; most of the rented Pontiac Sunbirds flash on toward the sea without even pausing.

The travelers who do pull over need to look hard to see the faint trail leading off into the lava field. If they decide not to take the trail, perhaps it's because there's too much above and below the stark plain to tempt them out onto the dry, black rock. The air is hot, and the trail is inhospitable compared to the blue ocean only a few miles farther on, and unpromising compared to the dramatic, streaming calderas that can be visited in the landscape high above.

Even at the end of this relatively short trail, no more than a mile, a traveler may wonder what he or she has reached. The trail-head sign and the maps say it's a field of Hawaiian petroglyphs, images and signs carved into a low volcanic mound called Pu'u Loa. Still, it would be easy for a traveler to miss the mound and the petroglyphs, were it not for a circle of wooden walkways constructed by the Park Service at the trail's end. The walkways were built to discourage hikers from stepping on the fragile carvings in the rock. The wind blows hard across the lava field; the walkways are weathered and the carvings, along with the land, are eroding. In the glare of the nearly constant sunlight, the grasses in the creases of the lava are scorched. The thirteen-hundred-foot cliffs of Holei Pali are too distant to shade them, and the white-capped sea is too distant to cool the air. Wind and sun have relentlessly worked on these eroding symbols for a long time.

Once you reach the end of the trail to Pu'u Loa, you may be tempted to wander away from the wooden planks built to contain the curiosity and tramplings of the casual traveler. The walkway, in fact,

◆━◆━◆━◆

is a decoy. Step beyond it and behind the mound, which you might at first have mistaken for Pu'u Loa itself, and suddenly you find yourself gazing down at not a dozen petroglyphs, but at thousands—stone drawings so closely bunched they overlay each other in a tangle of human and animal forms, enigmatic lines, and symbols. The field of petroglyphs at Pu'u Loa is in fact the most extensive in all of Polynesia.

When a traveler first comes across these remote stone etchings, several physical reactions sometimes occur. The scalp tightens just above the forehead, ears draw back, and the throat may begin to constrict. The tightening is centered at the base of the skull; the small hairs are bristling, and the skin at the nape is registering fluctuations in temperature. The sensations are brought on by the heightened attentiveness this place evokes. Other physical changes may occur, including a more rapid heart rate and the release of hormones, particularly adrenaline and glucocorticoids. But the self-conscious mind, oddly enough, may be paying little attention to itself and to these physical changes. Instead, it becomes preoccupied with resolving the unsettling qualities of the landscape entering the eyes, the ears, and along the skin—a fusion of bright colors, the hot and cool gusts from the east, the dry metallic smell of lava, sea salt in the wind mixed with fine droplets of hydrochloric acid from the white volcanic plume venting on the horizon. The undulating ground appears both solid and fluid, and the uncertain perspective caused by the vast horizon, with its high clouds rushing toward the plain, supplies few references for scale. All of this is happening while at your feet is a tangled array of symbols and human forms, clearly part of the lava rock for hundreds of years. For a few moments, disjointed perceptions crowd into the mind. The sensation may feel strikingly like experiences described by artists or visionaries, scientists in the moments before discovery, or by hunters in the silence of coming

◆—◆—◆—◆—◆

upon their quarry. Still, it doesn't last long. The mind in a reflexive wince soon blinks against this heightened concentration and quickly returns to the normal ways of looking and sorting: shifting from one perception to the next, reassuring the consciousness at each point that there is nothing so unusual here, nothing really to feel unsettled about.

I have these sensations of wonder—what Descartes called "the first of all the passions" and Spinoza regarded as a distinct form of cognition—no matter how often I go to Pu'u Loa. While the sensations may feel irrational and disconcerting, somehow I find them also able to clarify thoughts that may have preoccupied me for months living in the city; a sort of distillation takes place, the unclear becoming lucid and the vague becoming grounded. As much as anything, the large-scale violence in volcanic landscapes compels respect and caution, focusing your attention and making you alert. I remember once, while standing on the lava plain, finding a note on Cézanne that I had folded into my fieldbook and forgotten. I had been struck months earlier by this same odd sensation of alertness or wonder while looking at one of his landscapes painted at L'Estaque. At the same time I had found this quote, written it down, and put it into the fieldbook. An artist had said of the older painter, "When he is before a tree he looks attentively at what he has before his eyes; he looks at it fixedly, like a hunter lining up the animal he wants to kill. If he has a leaf, he doesn't let go. Having the leaf, he has the branch. And the tree won't escape him. . . . One must give it all one's attention. . . . Ah, if only everyone were capable of it!" In moments here, it occurred to me, anyone might suddenly, briefly, have such eyes and such an experience of looking.

The mound named Pu'u Loa is slightly broader and higher than those surrounding it, but otherwise it's unremarkable in an immense field of similar fractured lava mounds, called *tumuli*. When the first petroglyphs were made here, as much as twelve hundred years ago, the land may have been even starker, with no vegetation, or dotted with small, cultivated patches—we can't know for sure. Something powerful must have occurred at this spot, though, on this pressure ridge in the middle of the isolated lava plain, for the Native Hawaiians to have chosen it for its special purposes. Certain geological events may have been associated with the mound; or perhaps some human event occurred here to mark it as a sacred place, a very precise place. The incised drawings and pecked-out holes are limited to this specific, relatively small site, and don't spill over to the low tumuli scattered all around, though the other mounds appear in most ways to be identical. There may be more than fifteen thousand densely packed figures carved here. Pu'u Loa: in the Hawaiian language, it is the enduring hill, the hill of longevity, the place of life and long life.

The lava here is ancient, crumbling pahoehoe, a type of lava whose low viscosity and high temperature when it flows results, when cool, in a relatively smooth-skinned surface. Some of the lava formations create what geologists call "entrails" pahoehoe, because of the shape of the long folds, like the spilled and fossilized intestines of some giant. Erosion and age have further rounded it; the hardened rivulets and ropy formations are cracked and flaking. There are ants in the small patches of dirt, and their activity erodes the lava even faster, working with the wind and rain to soften it and break it down. In the thin soil you also find many small, glassy beads, called Pele's tears (named after the goddess of the volcano), black droplets ejected from lava fountains nearby or from the summit above. There are also tufts of reticulite, a gold-colored, sponge-like mass of stone froth, more material ejected during eruptions. Out of the cracks and larger fissures grow a few stunted 'ōhi'a trees, multi-colored lantana, scrubby yellow guava, reddish a'ali'i, sword ferns, dwarf san-

◆ ◆ ◆ ◆ ◆

dalwood, and deep-green mimosa. All cling low to the earth, out of the wind.

On one visit not long ago, to escape the heat I crawled into a shallow cave covered on its outside with petroglyphs. The cave could have been used for shelter often over the hundreds of years people were coming here, but nothing I could see inside indicated use. In fact, across this plain only the petroglyphs themselves suggest to the untrained eye a human presence—unless it's the occasional noni (*Morinda citrifolia*), a species of fruiting tree brought purposefully to the islands and planted by the earliest Hawaiian voyagers. Noni trees produce an ovoid, yellowish-white fruit, slimy and bitter to eat but dependable in times of famine. The tree also produces yellow and red dyes for tapa, and a medicine against tuberculosis and other ailments. Frequently planted in communities near the shore, noni is often a mark of ancient habitation. The few noni on this plain, though, could have germinated from seed dispersal from the coastal settlements. Like the guava, the tree could have been brought here by birds or, like the grasses, by the wind.

Except for the wind, Pu'u Loa is silent. High clouds gather over the cliffs, whitecaps froth on the surface of the abysmal ocean. But the impression is one of stillness. It's possible to disappear utterly. Many times I've been reminded while here—or in the city while thinking of this place—of the attention and loss of self described by Simone Weil in the notebooks she left with her friend Gustav Thibon, a farmer for whom she worked in the south of France in 1942. "Attention alone—that attention which is so full that the 'I' disappears—is required of me," she wrote. "I have to deprive all that I call 'I' of the light of my attention and turn it on to that which cannot be conceived." If non-Hawaiians are ever to comprehend even remotely what it was like for the native people who once lived in this place—*an inconceivable thought*—surely the understanding could

◆ ◆ ◆ ◆

come about only through the kind of attention that Simone Weil (a person dedicated to understanding others, and who died in the attempt) described as "absolutely unmixed attention."

Among the marks and figures carved on the rocks, some are clearly human forms—some appear to be dancing, some posed in a muscular, protective stance; others are joined in what seem to be scenes of birth or family groupings. Some drawings suggest sailing canoes or implements of farming and fishing; many carvings are too cryptic to speculate about at all. But the great majority of marks, perhaps seven thousand, consist of simple holes, usually about two inches wide and one inch deep. Sometimes a hole will be within an incised circle; sometimes there are clusters of holes within larger circles; and in some instances the circles are joined by lines. Probably no one knows for sure the specific meaning of these holes and lines anymore, but all agree they are associated with births and birthing. One common suggestion is that each hole was made for the umbilical stump of a child. The cord or stump was placed in the hole and covered with a stone; a prayer was said and other rites may have been performed. If the umbilicus remained overnight without being disturbed by animals, a long life was presaged, or uprightness, or some other fate for the child. There are many other speculations. One suggests that the cord's disappearance overnight meant the child would be a thief or exhibit other bad behavior; in fact, there may be many true explanations. For the early native people, according to Hawaiian scholar Mary Kawena Pukui, the umbilicus was the physical manifestation of each individual's link with his or her mother and father, and therefore the link with kin and forebears all the way back to the gods of creation. The umbilicus having made each individual's birth possible, it was also the link to his or her descendants, even ones yet to be born. The natal cord strung together

◆—◆—◆—◆—◆

the generations like beads, connecting them through the mother to the mythical past and to the future.

It is intensely moving to stand amid these thousands of relics and symbols of births, so many of which must have been carved with great happiness and expectancy: a field of newborns, of children and their parents, where for tens of generations each self of the community was written on the black stone of the lava plain between the volcano's fire and the sea. And if, as Simone Weil says, there is a sacred link between writing (in its fullest sense of creating figurative representation of concepts and lived perceptions) and giving birth, then these figures present an engraved experience that transmutes the physical and symbolic past, even now, into something luminous and present to be "read": writing (and reading), like birth, she says, requires of us "the supreme effort," nothing less. That supreme effort—by which is created the symbolic and the physical joined intimately and immediately—is one of the things that have happened at Pu'u Loa. There is perhaps no need, much less prerogative, to inquire after other sacred knowledge in this place: there is more than enough of the sacred and transforming to be had in knowing just this much, then drawing back before the writing effected on this site. "We do nothing if we have not first drawn back," Weil says.

I first came to Pu'u Loa in 1981. Though I had lived in the Hawaiian Islands for nearly fifteen years, I seldom had spent time on this coast or on this island. That year, a Hawaiian educational research center hired me to help write a documentary film about the children of a Native Hawaiian family in Kalapana, a coastal village famous for the Kaimu black sand beach nearby, just east of Pu'u Loa. Late morning on the day our film crew arrived on the island, the film's director, Alika Myers, a Hawaiian in his early thirties, drove with me out of Kalapana toward Halape. I was one of several non-Hawaiians on the crew, and since Alika and I had become friends working together in Honolulu, he wanted to show me a part of the islands I had never seen.

The coast was wild and steep, and the road ran closely adjacent to it much of the way. Screeching noddies, their voices muted by the crash of waves, hovered and swerved toward their nesting sites in the cliffs just above the spray. Because these waves struck the coast through deep water, not slowed by reef or continental shelf, they shouldered into the rugged land with a relentless battering, throwing spume high into the air. After about three miles we stopped at a pool of cold, slightly saline water set into the rocks near the sea, shaded by large mango trees and overhung with broad ferns, hala, and moist vegetation. We got out, stripped, and lowered ourselves into the cold, glassy, bright water. The pool was called Queen's Bath on the maps, possibly after Queen Emma, widow of Kamehameha IV, who visited the area in 1883 and died two years later. Several miles farther we reached Waha'ula heiau, a Hawaiian temple complex built of stone walls and terraces in perhaps the thirteenth century, said to emanate considerable religious power. The temple had been the scene of human sacrifices and in historic times was dedicated to the war god Kuka'ilimoku; the temple's name means Red Mouth. Hala, coconut palms, noni, and breadfruit grew abundantly throughout the ruins of the temple overlooking the coast. Like all the ancient temples in Hawaii, Waha'ula was abandoned by royal decree early in the nineteenth century. The National Park Service, though, had restored what remained of the rock walls and kept up a system of trails that wound through the temple complex down to the sea cliffs.

From Waha'ula, we drove across the lava plain toward the Holei Pali until we came upon the trail to Pu'u Loa. After we had hiked

◆━◆━◆━◆━◆

across the lava to the site of the petroglyphs, we stopped, broke out the water and food we carried, and sat for a long time in the buffeting wind. We talked about the color of the sunlight and how it would affect the filming that would begin the next day. We explored the petroglyphs, speculating on some of the more puzzling figures, their function in an ancient culture without a written language.

Brought up on the island of Oahu, Alika was making a career of cinematography; he had a flawless sense of composition through a camera, of light, color, and line. He also owned a German-made car and lived in a middle-class suburb east of Honolulu with his wife, also Hawaiian, and three young children, who attended a private school. He had no sentimentality about returning to "the old ways" and expressed dismay over young, middle-class Hawaiians with university educations who advocated that all native people should embrace subsistence farming and fishing, and should break with everything Western in order to save their vanishing culture. At the same time, he knew as well as anyone the tragic conditions of most Native Hawaiians, displaced from their land and, since the end of the nineteenth century, physically and culturally decimated as a result of foreign contact. Recovery of the culture is slowly being done, but repossession of the land, most people believe, will be difficult to achieve. What Alika himself possessed of Hawaiian culture, he said, did not require him to be poor and semiliterate. Nevertheless, the injustice, along with dreams of Hawaiian sovereignty, weighed on him as it does on most people who know the history of the islands.

We began filming the next day. The family we had come to document lived in an open, rambling structure near the Kaimu black sand beach adjacent to Kalapana. In addition to the husband and wife, there were ten children of various ages—seven boys and three girls. During the week that followed, the family opened their doors to us early each morning when we arrived (we stayed in a hotel thirty miles away, left it at dawn, and often returned after sunset). They fed us, led us around, answered our polite but intrusive questions, and with great patience let us film them in all their domestic activities. Often an older child was paired with a younger one, and all had significant chores to do. There was no discord and none of the children seemed to need adult urging or supervision. We filmed the little children feeding the pigs and chickens in the early morning and the slightly bigger children tending the vegetable garden. We followed them with our cameras out to the school bus, filmed them in class and on the playground, and stayed with them when they got home again. The whole family spoke Hawaiian as well as English—something rare except in very rural places—and worked hard all day.

At the end of the week, we were ready to shoot one of the final interviews with the mother and father. According to the film's outline, they were to talk about their personal values, one of the most important of which, we knew, was education for the children; after all, that was the point of the film. It would be used to encourage changes in school reading programs for young Hawaiians. But, having gotten as close to them as was possible in a week, having heard their stories and songs and shared their food, I was also hoping they would talk specifically about their cultural values as Native Hawaiians.

"Yes," the mother said, as we reached that part of the interview, "our culture is very important; our family has lived in this district a long time." She paused and looked all around, glancing up the slope toward the volcano. "We love it here." She paused again, as if looking for the words. "And we want our children to read. Not like us, always running away from school. We're especially proud when they read to us about the rosary, and about the Our Father, the Glorious Mysteries, the Joyful Mysteries, and—what is the other one?—the Sorrowful Mysteries."

◆—◆—◆—◆—◆

Though I had seen pictures of flaming hearts and reposing lambs around the house during the week, the reference to the family's Catholic devotion suddenly took me aback. Many of those pictures, we were told, had been drawn and colored by the children for their Sunday studies. The parents brought them out and showed them to us proudly. The father described how the family supported and helped maintain the little church nearby, called Star of the Sea. Built about 1928, the one-room wooden structure was covered ceiling to floor with brightly colored pictures of saints, and behind the altar was a naïvely painted *trompe l'oeil* passageway into the infinite. Most of the heartfelt, bright oils, rendered directly onto the walls, had been executed by the church's founding priest, a self-taught artist. Other painted scenes had been added over the years, along with small but stunning stained-glass windows. Some books say that in even older times, two hundred years before Captain Cook first "discovered" Hawaii, a priest from Spain had landed near Kalapana to found a church. The famous Belgian priest Father Damien had also worshipped in a small church just down the road; he later died of leprosy contracted from his congregation of outcasts on the island of Moloka'i.

I shouldn't have been surprised to find Catholic intensity among the oldest Hawaiian families here. My surprise seems to me now to have been a failure of my imagination and attentiveness to the people. I also hadn't understood how decidedly questions about culture are in essence about spiritual ties, especially concerning family. I had brought to the moment my own expectation of an idealized simplicity, a nostalgia, perhaps, for something I thought of as "purely Hawaiian" and separate, but which was merely an invention of my own mind, not what "culture" truly is, regardless of its forms.

The next day we all said goodbye and most of the crew headed back to Honolulu. In all the years since, though, I've never been able to shake the impression the region and the people made on me then. I began to return to this part of Hawaii whenever I could, at first once a year or so, but in recent years much more frequently. Just this past summer I again went back to Kilauea and drove from the summit down the switchbacks of Holei Pali, across the plain to the edge of the sea. I left the car and hiked along the ocean cliffs across an immense plateau of new black lava, created by a series of eruptions that began in 1983 on the flank of Kilauea. The eruptions have been continuous for eight years, making them the longest-lived series in Hawaiian records. By 1986, the lava began to destroy homes downslope from Kilauea crater; Queen's Bath was enveloped and completely obliterated in March of 1987. An average of 650,000 cubic yards of molten lava was surging daily into a system of tubes at the summit, some lava overflowing down the cliffs and some going underground until emptying through vents into the sea. In 1989, the Waha'ula heiau was approached by a wall of molten lava; the searing rock mass incinerated and engulfed the wooden visitors' center, paused as if about to turn away from the temple itself, then overran all but the highest stone walls on the temple grounds. A year later, the new flow had advanced into the village of Kalapana, burying the roads and houses, covering Kaimu black sand beach and driving out everyone who had once lived there, including the family I had met; the Star of the Sea church was laboriously lifted from its foundations by members of the congregation and trucked away, out of the path of the lava. The site of Father Damien's old church is gone, too. The road along the sea cliffs is gone, as are the cliffs themselves. They've been replaced by a mountainous, rolling plateau of twisted new lava over twenty feet deep, which has extended a shelf of land out into the ocean, ending in altogether new cliffs, buttressed with huge

◆ ◆ ◆ ◆ ◆

Gothic-looking columns and jagged spires, and collapsing into crevices, each with its own small, unstable beach of black sand.

Returning to my car, I drove to the Pu'u Loa trailhead, well up-slope from the new lava, and hiked to the site of the petroglyphs. I tried to write in my fieldbook what it was like to watch the booming hydrochloric billows of steam caused by molten lava hitting the sea, the expansive bands of rich blues above and beyond the coastline in the glaring summer light. But my thoughts kept returning to the surface of the rocks that held the old petroglyphs. This landscape of old and new rock, populated and depopulated in long cycles, is not to admire or adore, I saw, not to sentimentalize or to hold as pictur-esque. It is resistant, in more than one sense, to writing and to being written about. At least in human terms, the volcanic land seemed to compel an enormous kind of remembering and binding, some transformation of the past into the present, into the future and back again. That continues to be its glory, and part of what was written out in the petroglyphs. I recalled how many of the coastal villages around this spot had been depopulated by the great earthquake of April 1868. With a magnitude of 8.0, the quake had been centered just a few miles from here and generated a local tsunami estimated to have been fifty feet high. Reportedly, every building in the district collapsed or was destroyed. When the people in the area deserted their villages after that, only small numbers may have returned here to carve petroglyphs and perform ceremonies with the umbilicals of their children. In any case, they may have used the site less and less after 1819, when the formal Hawaiian religious system was decreed to be dead by the monarchy, under the influence of American mis-sionaries. There is no way to know either the oldest or the youngest of the births etched here, or to know much about the people who wrote into the rock their linkage to time, to the land, and to each other. Now, with Kalapana destroyed, there would be even fewer people nearby with kinship to the figures at Puʻu Loa.

It started to rain. I put the fieldbook away and watched the rain falling from a cloudless blue sky, spattering on the warm lava; it made the stuttering sound of long syllables, like the wind.

◆◆◆◆◆

19

SACRED DARKNESS

PAM FRIERSON

Pele is my goddess,
a chiefess of sacred darkness
and of light.
> fragment of chant recited at dawn and dusk
> by Mary Kawena Pukui's grandmother

Enter not prayerless the house of Pele.
> from chant translated by Emerson in *Pele and Hiiaka*

At its highest point, the scarp of the Hilina Pali plummets 1,200 feet to a broad lava plain. To the east, the plain declines gently and then sweeps up again, like a nearly cresting wave, to the back of Puʻu Kapukapu. Puʻu Kapukapu is what geologists call a *horst*—a piece of land left high and dry as fault systems all around it allowed its surrounding terrain to sink downward. To either side of Kapukapu, the land slopes more gently to the coast. Out of sight, in the shadow of the horst's seaward cliffs, is Halapē, the once-idyllic

◆◆◆◆◆◆◆◆◆◆◆◆◆◆◆◆◆◆◆◆

cove and stand of coconut trees, much of the land now submerged, the broken remnants of trees immersed in water at high tide. But the beach there is slowly filling in again, and small new palms have sprouted, hiding the scars of the land shattered by the 1975 earthquake under their green fronds.

From here at the top of the Pali, one can see more than forty miles of coast. To the southeast, basalt seacliffs emerge again beyond the shadow of Puʻu Kapukapu, and curve into points and shallow bays until they vanish in a volcanic haze. To the southwest, the land bends outward and disappears into the horizon at the distant point of Ka Lae. The rain clouds that have shrouded Kīlauea for the last two weeks are breaking up just to the northwest, and a rainbow arches from them, falling over the edge of the Pali. Thunder and rain season, the inseminating rain of Lono.

There are four of us here at the top of Hilina Pali, eyeing the first steep switchback of the trail down. Archeologist Laura Carter. Fay-Lyn Jardine, a tall, graceful backcountry park ranger of Hawaiian-Portuguese blood. And Tamar Elias, an athlete and jill-of-all-trades, currently employed changing the recording papers on the seismographs at the observatory.

We are headed into the midst of the lava plain below us to find two lava tube caves containing petroglyphs and cultural remains. The caves were discovered in the 1970s. No archeologist has visited them since, and Laura wants to see how they are faring, and to leave a sign in one of them reminding hikers that might stumble on the site to leave the remains undisturbed.

The trail down the Pali makes a dozen turns down the rocky face, over stretches of rubbly aʻā. Halfway down, Fay-Lyn points out the place where a Park Service packhorse named Battle Star got off the trail and tumbled "ass-over-teakettle" fifty feet down to the next

◄━◆━◆━◆━◆►

switchback, emerging, miraculously, with just a few scrapes, but a strong aversion to packing.

At the bottom of the Pali, we take an altimeter reading, then fan out across the rough country to look for the caves. Waist-high grass masks jagged flows of *a'ā*, in between billowy mounds of *pāhoehoe;* the land dips and sways like a choppy sea. The "cave" opening is actually the fallen roof of a lava tube, so its entry will be from a depression in the ground; in this country, one could walk within ten yards of it and not see it.

But I come across it just as I think we may have walked too far. The collapsed roof of the lava tube has created a pit thirty feet or so wide, and a low opening yawns at the north end. It is like a thousand such "caves" in the layered lava of this country, but the pile of stones at the entrance is arranged into a low wall. I climb down to the wall, and find that its top is laid with water-worn stones, here, three to four miles inland. In front of the wall, an area of the rocky pit has been leveled and thin, flat stones upended in a square to form a hearth.

The petroglyphs cluster so thickly at the entrance that at first I don't perceive them. Then my eyes register the darker, incised rock on the mottled, vitreous surface of the cave's inner walls, and human figures startle me, crowding forward from the darkness.

The shapes are cut or pecked into the thin, glazed coating left by the molten river that once flowed through the lava tube. Perhaps because this surface is easier to work, these petroglyphs are richer in detail than others I have seen: many of the human figures have fingers and toes; some have spiky hair or headdresses. There is a hawk-headed man with bird feet and an arrow-shaped penis. Turtles, dogs, and chickens. And three life-sized incised feet, the broad shovel-shape of Hawaiian feet, good for walking on lava.

The archeologists who explored the cave a decade ago uncovered more petroglyphs under rubble and midden. Charcoal in the midden furnished a date of plus or minus 300 years. No historic artifacts (such as nails) were found in this cave, and none of the petroglyphs are of European motifs (horses, for instance), suggesting that use of this site ceased before Western settlement. These caves may have provided seasonal water and shelter, as a large number of water gourds found in a nearby cave would seem to indicate; crops may have been grown nearby at times in the year, and water carried down to fishing villages on the coast. But these figures spilling from the darkness hint at other uses than water and shelter, at other powers felt or honored here.

Perhaps the hawk-headed figures are a key to the *mana* of this particular place, for, though not unknown elsewhere, such petroglyphs are rare, and there are several here. But what secrets the cave holds it does not readily reveal. The figures thin out and then stop some twenty feet into the cave. Forty feet farther, the cave narrows down to a space one could crawl through, painfully, with some padded clothes. My flashlight is not strong enough to penetrate the night beyond.

We return to the caved-in pit and open sky to eat our lunches, next to the heart with its surrounding midden of *'opihi* (limpet) shells, evidence of meals eaten here long ago. Then we explore the south entrance to the lava tube, crawling over the fallen rocks that narrow the opening. A few petroglyphs cluster at the entrance, but the glazed walls farther in are empty of figures. The lava tube appears to continue on into a pitch blackness. Laura and Fay-Lyn and Tamar turn back to the entrance, determining to go search for the other cave mentioned in the archeological report, the one that contained fragments of many water gourds.

I linger behind, deciding on impulse to do something I've never done alone before, to follow that dark passage.

◆—◆—◆—◆—◆

Left to myself, I reconsider. Beyond the reach of my light, the tube opening is a dense, black maw. I have one flashlight, no spare batteries. But if I watch carefully to make sure the tube does not branch anywhere, I could feel my way back out if I had to. I have long since lost all but a reflex anxiety, in this country, about predatory animals or snakes. The only large animals that frequent the lava tubes are feral goats, who shelter in them, and in sickness or old age may crawl into their recesses to die.

Indeed, fifty feet in, at the furthest reach of the light from the entrance, a goat skull and bones are scattered across the floor, white remnants of a natural death, but I can't stifle an inner shiver that makes me read them as sentinel or warning to the dark passage beyond. Some deep-seated reflex in me links darkness with death, but it has come to seem less like a primal response and more like a cultural legacy. I am reminded once more of H. Rider Haggard's nightmare journey, in his novel *She,* into the caverns of earth somewhere in darkest Africa. There his hero found a savage tribe inhabiting vast catacombs, ruled by a strangely immortal female given over to a cult of death. A fantastical story, but compelling, as it must have been to Haggard himself, who wrote it, it is said, in six weeks, as though it poured in some great stream from the unconscious.

Haggard's images are crude, as dreamscapes often are, but disturbingly familiar, as though they tap a deep vein in the Western mind where the shadow side of the natural world has been replaced by an inner darkness. The darkness, loosed from its moorings in the natural cycles of birth and death, no longer something we can reach or touch, or make our peace with, terrifies us from within, elicits rage and fear toward all that is alien or wild or "other," all that reminds us of the tenuousness of human control.

Armed only, as in Haggard's dreamscape, with a sense of the darkness as unholy, one would find in this landscape only a mirror of

◆—◆—◆—◆

inner terrors. But other visions rise from the land, and are given voice in Hawaiian myth: images, prolific in this volcanic world, of the deep-rooted, creative powers of darkness:

An incandescent river pours through a black labyrinth, streams briefly into the light at the edge of a seacliff, cools to steaming black at the edge of an ocean wave, shatters from the pressure of its still-molten heart, and is flung back on shore as tiny grains of glistening jet. "Born was the island, it grew, it spouted, it flourished, lengthened, rooted deeply, budded." From the black maws of the lava of last year, tiny ferns sprout like lambent green flames. As the legends of the land tell, the mouths of darkness, like the wombs of women, are the channels through which flows *pō nui ho 'olakolako,* "the great night that supplies."

I walk into the black tunnel of the lava tube. The walls curve gently to the right, ridged horizontally like striations of muscles, marking the levels of the molten lava as it diminished and narrowed. The tube must once have been filled to the brim with a fiery river; as it drained, it cascaded and pooled, creating intricate, molded patterns on the floor. When the molten rock subsided, the residue on the ceiling hardened into smooth, conical drips, teat-shaped, like some vast statuary of a many-breasted mother goddess.

For a few hundred paces, the smooth musculature of the cave makes walking easy, but then the ceiling narrows to a crawlspace. I shut off the light and lean against the laminated wall.

Absolute night surrounds me, warm, moist, palpable—the pressure of amniotic fluid, or of the eyelid on the eye. It is a nonhuman presence so overwhelming that it threatens to dissolve the fragile boundaries of self. Nothing in it seems benign or disposed toward humans. Nor indisposed. Simply there, a vast mystery behind every element of this landscape. I switch the flashlight back on quickly. *"Enter not prayerless the house of Pele."* Some great current seems to flow from the inner recesses, propelling me back toward the entrance.

And into an astoundingly noisy outer world, where the darkness fractures into a million forms. The wind is hissing through grass, and for the first time I hear in its lower register the base note of waves pounding the coast. I glance at the crowd of human figures at the north mouth of the lava tube. Midway between the light and the darkness, arms akimbo, some pointing up, some pointing down, guarding the passage, or pointing the way.

20

HAWAII

RICK BASS

had expected fully to hate Hawaii. I had expected that I would be homesick for Montana and the good crisp weather of mid-December the whole time. I imagined it as a place seething with traffic, sun and glimmer. I imagined it as America's ultimate hype: not only a rip-off, but one for which you had to travel interminably in order to be ripped off. I imagined a sort of pig pen, where nothing was sincere, everything a parody of itself, and everything for sale.

I was also afraid that the islands would be overrun with game-show winners, and the terrible vacuous smiles of newlyweds. But I thought if I headed into Hawaii's high mountains (some of the peaks almost fourteen thousand feet tall), and into the upland rain forests and out across the tortured, barren lava fields, then maybe I could stay out of sight of the lemming hordes of beach tourists. And with the exception of the megafleet of turbo-helicopters that followed me everywhere, my theory was correct, and I found solace and rest, and had a lovely time.

Look out! Here comes the geologist! Run!

The Hawaiian Islands consist of seven separate islands. The islands were formed one at a time, assembly-line fashion, as the Earth's tectonic plate slid slowly over an undersea rift, a "hot spot" in the Earth's crust. The lava, the energy of the earth, blasts up through the tectonic plate, mounding up millions of square acres as the cone of the underwater lava mountain growing, reaching for the shining lights above.

The lava reaches the ocean's surface then (after a mile or more of mountain-building), but still it keeps welling up, spreading, until it is a giant cone-shaped mountain. (As in the case of the youngest and easternmost island, the Big Island of Hawaii, such a mountain can be 14,000 feet above the sea.)

The Hawaiian Islands' hot spot tends to give birth to slow-building, cone-shaped volcanoes—"gentle" volcanoes. Other hot spots around the world are more sporadic in their mountain-building. They don't have the regular pressure-release flows and rifts that the Hawaiian Islands have, and instead build up terrible pressures beneath their caps until finally, one day, the whole top of the mountain blows. (Krakatoa.)

So the tectonic plate drifts—is pushed—westward, at the rate of about four inches a year. The first island to be formed in the chain of Hawaii was, of course, the westernmost, about 1500 miles west of the hot spot (which now lies beneath the newest island, the Big Island). At four inches a year, this makes the westernmost and oldest island 70 million years old.

Seventy million years may sound old, but even that is young—*infantile*—compared to the rest of the world. Most geologists believe that the "mainland" of the seven continents—which were once one huge continent called Pangea—is about four-and-a-half billion years old.

◆ ◆ ◆ ◆ ◆

The Big Island is only 500,000 years old. Someday it will drift west, too—it's drifting west even now, at that four inches a year—and some day there will be an eighth island. (Perhaps just as the westernmost island disintegrates and disappears . . . The chain of islands, the skyline, moving up and down in this fashion like the pistons of the earth, the pistons of life . . .)

Look out! Here comes the geologist!

Although this story is about my visit to the uplands of the two youngest islands, I think it's important for the reader to understand what lies ahead for each island—the process of its death wedded immutably to the process of its birth. There is no word for it other than fate.

Each island that rises from the sea will heat up each day in the near-equatorial sun. Each mountain will also block the cooler trade winds, which blow from east to west. This creates thunderstorms on the windward (east) side of the mountain, which creates life—lush rain forests (there are places in the Hawaiian mountains that get an estimated 600 inches of rain per year)—but these rains, in addition to producing a quick explosion of varied life forms, also guarantee quick death. The island literally washes away to the sea, cut and carved by the rains. Nutrients are also swept out to sea.

Coral reefs form around the island, nourished by the high-nutrient runoff. These reefs make a protective ring around the island, slowing the island's destruction by the surf, while the island's forests blossom.

But in the meantime, the rain is cutting the mountain down—the rain that the mountain itself creates—until it crumbles to nothing, and becomes like the hole in a donut, with the circular coral reef—the atoll—the only evidence that all that glorious life ever blossomed. There are atolls like this all over the Pacific—ancient ghosts of what were once islands.

◆━◆━◆━◆

I came into this story determined not to view Hawaii as "paradise," to never, ever use that word, for it is a stereotype, and when a writer resorts to stereotypes, he or she—and the story—are sunk, like one of those old, westernmost islands.

And for a while I saw the islands as a terrible, beautiful, floating prison—each island destined for an extremely short life, drifting to oblivion—but then immediately after that I saw, while indeed that was true, there was also no other word—it *was* a paradise. A short one, like the one day of life given to the mayfly in midsummer, but paradise, nonetheless.

You go to Hawaii, and if your eyes are open, you come away marveling not so much at how tropical and lovely Hawaii is (though you do that, too), but more amazed, really, at how special and lucky your own life is, back on the mainland. Deadlines and the distractions of your doomed municipal financial inconveniences may be forming lava mounds in your brain, but you look at the long odds the islands have of ever making it, and the larger odds of any life forms arising from or on those islands—they're 2000 miles from any mainland—and you suddenly realize how peachy we've got it, to be upright and walking around on two legs, on firm ground, and *in the world*.

You don't think of magma (it's only called lava when it escapes to the Earth's surface)—of the molten rock at the center of the Earth—as being the source of life. But the way it rises and blocks those trade winds and secures water and creates life (carbon and hydrogen), you realize that it *is* the source. You realize that the earth *desires* life—that rocks desire life—that it is all a partnership, and that it starts with the fury and passion of magma.

I went to the Big Island first—the youngest one, the only one that still has active lava flows. (The next-youngest island, Maui, which

◆—◆—◆—◆—◆

lies just west of the Big Island, had its last eruption in the 1700s; it's since drifted far enough west to no longer be affected by the hot spot that gave it its birth.)

I don't know if I can describe how glorious, how *serene* it felt, to be standing in the high rain forest on that incredibly young, incredibly healthy, raw, hopeful mountain, in the village of Volcano, just outside Volcanoes National Park. I'm used to walking around in mountains that are almost a billion years old. But to be on a mountain that is only 300,000 years old—and to be standing on hardened lava, basalt, that is only ten or twelve years old? You must believe me when I say that I could feel the difference, and that it was immense.

The village of Volcano is green, with every leaf shape so new and different that the effect is like going back in time to childhood, when the woods were new and unnamed then, too.

Elizabeth, my wife, passed up coming with me on the trip I had to make to northern Wisconsin earlier in the month, but has decided to join me on this one. We've got our nine-month-old daughter, Mary Katherine, with us, and she heightens the sense of newness. Things will be as new to me as they are to her.

While traveling through two immense national parks—Volcanoes National Park, on the Big Island, and the even larger Haleakala National Park, on the island of Maui—I would realize how much we rely, for better or worse, on our memories, rather than a willingness to look at a thing—anything—anew. At times I would catch a glimpse of landscape—a certain tree, or a meadow, or even an angle of light—and find in my notes my disturbing, confusing, almost nonsensical attempts to make order—that is, to make comparison— of what I was seeing, and what it was like.

Texas. Arizona. Vermont. Montana. California. Costa Rica. Arkansas. No, Mississippi. No . . .

Elizabeth and Mary Katherine stayed at the lodge the first evening, while I went up into the park and walked around in the dusk. Steam rose from the trees—little rifts in the earth that had worked up to the surface—and it was windy and cold. Water dripped from the green bushes along the hiking trails. It's all or nothing at Volcanoes: beautiful, twisted, folded sheets of hardened lava spread for great distances, as if on the moon, or—if you're in a place spared by the lava flows—then it's lush, dripping with greenery and bird song.

The name for such jungle islands around which the lava flowed and then hardened is *kipakus,* and they are of tremendous ecological significance. Life—and the rapid evolution characteristic of Hawaii, or of any new landform—proceeds at a startlingly brisk, sometimes explosive pace. I really want to leap ahead in the story and begin talking about the bugs, the birds, the seething *life,* but know I can't match the island's accelerated pace. Scientists chasing flora and fauna on the island can't keep up with the furious changes their quarry is making, either—mutations and adaptations—and the last thing one wants to do in Hawaii is get in a hurry anyway.

You just want to rest, and watch. You just want to look. Ninety-five percent of the species in the Hawaiian Islands are endemic—found nowhere else in the world. For them, Hawaii is their sacred home.

Every time I blink, 95 percent of what comes into my field of vision is new. Of course I must go slow, and must stick with the story of the rocks: I must learn that, first.

I head up toward the great Southwest Rift, a beautiful prairie of twisted, rough *aá* (pronounced ah-ah) lava. Bubbles of gas in the cooling lava have given it a vesicular structure, almost like coral: a boulder the size of an ice chest might weigh only a few pounds. (All through Hawaii there are gorgeous stone walls built from lava rock, iridescent black and iron-blood-red, rock fences being swarmed

◆◆◆◆◆

under with greenery, and I'm jealous, wishing to have such rocks available for my stone wall in Montana, which suddenly seems as ponderous and sledge-footed—as *freighted*—as a dinosaur.) After a while, metaphor can become reality, and everywhere I look I see the lightness of the things, the easiness of existence: the youth of the island. It is like looking at a scrapbook of one's parents when they were children. You think, *So this is what it was like.*

The jungle—the *kipakus* and other jungles—are impenetrable in most places, and because the rough lava fields are so treacherous, the national parks in Hawaii have a wonderful system of hiking trails. Back on the mainland, and especially in the West, I abhor trails, which are often just a conduit for passing horse turds up and down the mountain, and ultimately lead to violent erosion. But in this unfamiliar place, they're welcome, and because most everyone else is down on the beaches, here at about 9000 feet, I have them to myself. The crunch of the crushed volcanic rock underfoot reminds me of the cinder running tracks in high school, and I realize that's exactly what it is: ground-up cinders. There's no soil for me to disturb or erode on these trails; it hasn't even formed yet.

I walk out across the Southwest Rift, into the most unusual, coppery sunset I've ever seen—it's 6:00 P.M., almost right on the equator—and then I head back to the park entrance, to the Volcano Bar, to watch a bit of "Monday Night Football." My beloved Houston Oilers and the aging, heroic Warren Moon are playing. The game is already over back in Houston, but it's on a time delay here; it hasn't even started.

I'm the only customer in the bar or restaurant. This is the only public television in the village of Volcano. A few tourists in shorts walk around in the parking lot, hunch-shouldered against the chill winds, plotting no doubt to amend their itinerary and head back to the beaches a few days early.

◆—◆—◆—◆—◆

A full moon rises beyond the scenic windows of the restaurant, casting an eerie silver-blue glow on the guts of Kilauea crater, which only years ago was a pool of roiling lava; it erupts every seven or eight years. It could happen again at any time—is due, in fact, at any time. A hundred years ago, Mark Twain came here to live for a while and to watch Kilauea erupt, the boiling pit sending plumes of lava 2000 feet into the air. The magma beneath Kilauea is only two miles below, boiling, searching for a rift or fissure—straining to make one, to launch still more lava into the air, to bring more life into the world.

Two miles down is not very far, for such a force of the world. Any day now.

That night, lying in bed a short distance from the park, I remember reading how the last eruption gave hikers out on the trails only about a three-hour warning.

It could go off while I sleep! It could explode, flow down the road, turn left at the Kilauea Lodge, and turn cottage number six into a *kipaku*. Or worse!

Volcanoes, earthquakes, and other forces of nature—it's delicious, in this unthinking age of arrogance, to rediscover humility. It's silly, but I get up out of bed and look out at the night garden—at all the night-blooming flowers—and I gaze upon their beauty as if it could be my last night on earth. Silly, but delicious. *We are not in control*. Delicious.

The next day, we walk. There are a few other tourists about, but mostly they seem to be restricting their walking to the Visitors' Center parking lot. We walk the Bird Park Trail through a beautiful, dense forest, a *kipaku*, that was surrounded by a lava flow. We move through that strange forest, listening to the chirps of honeycreepers. It's a lovely walk for about half an hour—Mary Katherine looking at the canopy above in wonder, with stripes of green light camouflaging us—but then when we hear the helicopter, something in the woods changes. Certainly it's not as peaceful, and it no longer seems so new or special. It's like being in church and having a crop duster soar past, flying level with the stained-glass windows. I would have to say, in the language of the government officials who try to decide what's right and what's wrong (not understanding that their hearts can tell them this better than any visitor questionnaire), that yes, the helicopter overflights did indeed "significantly reduce the quality of our experience," the experience for which we traveled so far and so long.

But I can say it in fewer words. It's sick. It sucks.

We strike out on another walk, this time across the Kilauea Rim, all lava wasteland and all glorious, both, when you think of it for what it is—hundreds of square miles of just-cooled lava—and for what it will soon become—a seedbed for Hawaii's diversity, Hawaii's writhing, lovely forests.

We say the words out loud—*pahoehoe* (pronounced pa-hoyee-hoyee), lava that is smooth, ropy, almost intestinal, and *aá*, the chunky, savage, bomblike pieces. We look for the wispy strands known as Pele's hair (Pele, the fire goddess, the power and meaning beneath the Pacific Plate) and for Pele's tears, the drop-shaped pieces formed when lava is sprayed a long way from a volcano, flying through the air and cooling into teardrop shapes that harden even before they land.

Most dramatic to me are the incredible, ghostly lava trees, where the lava crept up on a standing tree and covered it, but then drained away, rejoining the rest of the lava flow. The retreating lava leaves only a hardened crust around the now-dead tree, with the tree's branches still intact (but cloaked in that crusty lava), the branches still lifted to the sky.

What happens when the lava flows up and over a tree, but does *not*

◆—◆—◆—◆—◆

recede, is just as startling. Called a tree mold, the lava engulfs the tree, but the sap and moisture inside the tree keep the tree from burning up completely. The lava eventually hardens, and the fried tree trunk left standing in the middle of that lava field smolders, dries, rots, and disappears, leaving a perfect hole in the lava—looking for all the world as if someone has drilled wells out in the lava field. Big and little holes, all perfectly round, are the only clue that there was once a green forest.

To look at the lava we're walking across, and to look back into the mysterious recent past, and to understand—to see the clues, the story—is not unlike following the tracks of animals in the snow back in Montana.

The smooth *pahoehoe* lava is hotter and glows brighter than does the rough *aá*, because rather than bubbling its gas out like the *aá* (which is what makes the *aá* so broken, vesicular, and rough), the *pahoehoe* instead retains its gas, which keeps the lava hotter, producing the smoother, more liquid flow.

I tell you, I love this stuff.

We're having a great time—just walking, carrying the baby, loving the feel of good, hard, *new* rock under our feet, walking across the wasteland, reveling in how new it is. The first humans to live on the Hawaiian Islands arrived here only 1500 years ago; the previous 298,350 years (give or take) belonged to lonely Pele, and to the flowers, and the forests. The first non-Hawaiian did not look upon a Kilauea eruption until 1823.

Where I live, I'm used to finding 10,000-year-old relics, such as spear points and arrowheads, left by Paleolithic settlers. I knew that the world—even "our" world, the human world—was old, but I had no idea that it was also so young.

Walking across the crunchy, twisted lava, around the edge of the napping Kilauea, I'm incredibly refreshed, and incredibly humbled.

◆–◆–◆–◆

We could do it again if we had to, I think—survive, I mean. Mile-wide meteorites ripping past the Earth every few years, sometimes hitting it, other times missing it by a few thousand miles . . . A dropped gene here or there . . . I know that the odds are long against our survival, that we're the product of either divine luck or divine grace—that we're damn lucky to be here at all. But walking across the lava fields, I find myself exuberant, thinking *yes, we could do it again.*

Looking out at a new world of nothing but rock, with nothing but sunlight above and empty sky (though already, lichens are beginning to form on some of the older lava, and photosynthesis is releasing oxygen into the air, an atom at a time)—looking out at the rubble of lava, at nothing but lava—is like gazing at the pattern, the blueprint, for the possibility of life, for the possibility of everything.

It's a lovely, spiritual moment, or at least it is until the helicopter comes bopping up over the rim of the crater, defiling the sound of the wind and the sight of that open sky.

The helicopter hovers, banks, casts a commercial eye down into the crater, then whirls away, departs like a motorized pterodactyl, and somehow, where before I felt awe, I now feel only slightly foolish, and it is not a good trade, that of awe for foolishness.

Not yet knowing the myths—no, the *truths*—of the island, what Hawaiians refer to as the *kapu* of their island—the do's and don'ts—I pick up a rugged, fist-size piece of *aá* to take home to a friend's son, noting that the rock is the same age as the boy. It is only by chance, however, later in the day, that I hear one of the park rangers telling another visitor about the file the Park Service keeps on people who take lava back to the mainland. It's a drawer full of letters from people who've had bad luck descend suddenly upon them, bad luck in spades, after taking Hawaiian rocks back to the mainland. Broken legs, back injuries, financial catastrophes, car wrecks—all manner

◆━◆━◆━◆

of heavy-handed stuff from the goddess Pele, says the ranger; she's rarely subtle. And it's not a psychosomatic manifestation of guilt— the accidents befall the rock-snatchers whether they're aware of the curse or not. It's real; no placebo.

I'm just overhearing this conversation, mind you. No one's got me made. The rock's still in the back of the car, hidden, just riding around with me. I haven't tried to take it away from its home—yet. I'll just think on it a bit, and try to rationalize. Madame Pele, it's for a little *boy*, etc.

The thought stays in my mind, however—the overheard warning—and puts its roots into my brain and slowly strengthens its hold there, expanding ever so slightly all the while, like water freezing in a wedge between two rocks.

And it acts like a filter, changing still further the way I look at the island.

There are stories for everything on Hawaii. I've lost the statistics, but I remember reading that Hawaii's native culture has more stories, more oral mythologies, than any other culture in the world—not just one or two extra tales, but *three times* the "usual" number. And that makes sense, for if you've got such an extraordinary diversity of life, and if everyone gets a story, from turtles to crickets, then of course there'll be more stories. It is a way of honoring life, of honoring the force and power of things.

If it sounds like I am edging toward a defense of native myths, well, maybe I am. I am fully aware of the cynical eye Western culture places on most myths and miracles (save a select few). I'm aware, too, that our earnest desire to explain away the mystery is sometimes as bad as our cynicism—to find, in our oh-so-clever way, scientific reasons for the various myths and miracles.

Our native, myth-based cultures are always right, it seems. I am learning to respect that more and more. Sometimes the myths and miracles are metaphors that have been so carefully crafted (which is what a story does) to match a reality that not even scientists can separate (not even with their electron-splitting microscopes) the metaphor—the myth—from the reality.

And other times, when scientists *can* split the story and explain away the mystery, the two halves of the whole that they hand back to us are so identical, so parallel, that one wonders why there was ever any bother.

And still other times, the myth is more than truth: sometimes, certainly, it is fact as well as truth, and the scientist's microscopes melt, and the ends of their fingers get burned, as they look too closely at a thing that lies behind science.

But it's just one rock—and such a small one!

In Martha Beckwith's massive oral-history collection, *Hawaiian Mythology,* she alludes to the at-times rather insignificant distinctions between fact and fiction, as long as the metaphor is true:

> Hawaiians use the term *kaao* for a fictional story or one in which fancy plays an important part, [and] *moolelo* for a narrative about a historical figure, one which is supposed to follow historical events . . . Nor can the distinction between *kaao* . . . and *moolelo* . . . be pressed too closely. It is rather in the intention than in the fact. Many a so-called *moolelo* which a foreigner would reject as fantastic nevertheless corresponds with the Hawaiian view of the relation between nature and man.

The Pele myth encompasses geological reality—and who knows?—perhaps once (whether 1500 years ago or 10,000) a young woman from a large family (seven brothers and five other sisters) did set out to sea in a canoe, and did settle on the islands, in the manner of drifting plant seeds' and insects' colonization.

◆━◆━◆━◆

Beckwith reports that "Pele is very beautiful with a back straight as a cliff and breasts rounded like the moon. She longs to travel and, tucking her little sister, born in the shape of an egg, under her armpit, hence called Hi'iaka-i-ka-poli-o-Pele (in the armpit of Pele), she seeks her brother Ka-moho-ali'i," who gives her his canoe with the forces of his brothers Whirlwind, Tide, and Current for paddlers.

I said I wasn't going to do that meaningless scientist's stuff, but I'm a white man, European stock, and I can't resist it any more than an otter can resist biting into a fish head.

Consider Pele's sister's strange (metaphorical or factual) characteristic—"born in the shape of an egg." This is, of course, how scientists believe the islands were colonized by almost all the various life forms—the arrival of a pregnant female, or, to use their language (admittedly less lyrical than "in the armpit of Pele"), long-distance colonizers arriving with oceanic and atmospheric transmissions via *whirlwinds, tides,* and *currents.*

The Pele myth is long and involved—she goes here and there, does this and that, finds a love interest (the sensuality of Hawaii is so specific as to be a certain kind of thickness in the air, a green, growing, lushy kind of emotion; everywhere there is the spirit and feeling of "breasts rounded like the moon" and other things)—and Pele ultimately drifts southeasterly, having had an affair (in spirit form) with a handsome young chief. Jealousy's involved, and some forms of the myth say that her little sister chases Pele to the southeast. It's a complex, beautiful story, and finally Pele settles on the most southeasterly island, the Big Island of Hawaii, where "she attempts to dig a home in which she can receive her lover . . . and there is successful in digging deep without striking water, and in an element inimical to her fiery nature."

The question for me isn't Was there really such a woman? but

◆◆◆◆◆

rather Is or was there such a spirit, such a force, in the world? And the answer to that, as any geologist can tell you is, well, sure, hell yes. The Pacific Plate slides northwesterly; the youngest, hottest, most active island is therefore the most southeasterly island, the Big Island. The nest, the force of that hot spot, is real. Spirit, by any definition, must be a kind of force. Do things that exhibit force have a tangible presence in the world—a tide, a current, a wind, a beautiful young woman? Of course they do. So perhaps if spirit exists, then surely we can say that some reality exists even if we can't see it.

Look out! Here comes the constipated theologian! Run! Hide! Let's get on with the fun places to eat, the good things to see and do. But if you come to Hawaii, you need to understand at least a little of the story of Pele, and have a certain respect for it, and for the place— that is to say, the nature and the spirit of it—a place still very early in the stages of its creation, and where anything can happen.

Late that afternoon, Elizabeth and Mary Katherine and I drive down to the sea, roughly 6000 miles from our home in what's labeled the Pacific Northwest. It's the same ocean, but it feels like a different planet. There aren't any calderas brimming with open pools of lava, such as when Kilauea blows, but there is a nice creeping *aá* flow on the east end of the park, running from a rift in the highlands across the down-faulted flats next to the ocean. It is here that lava is running out into the ocean.

And that's where the tourists are—a couple hundred of them driving the twenty-plus miles down to the beautiful shining sea and the black lava sand beach, to hike a mile across a still-smoldering crust of new lava and stand beachside, fumaroles all around, and watch from a cordoned-off distance as this *aá* flow makes its way to the sea.

Even from a distance, we can see a column of steam stretching across the ocean, winding its way to the horizon and beyond, steam from where the 2000-degree lava is entering the eighty-degree water.

Like pilgrims, old and young, the well and the infirm alike, we make our way through the brush down an ancient trail (there used to be a village here, at about the time Columbus was striking west toward the big forests of North America). We pass a still-standing rock wall. A couple of tour bus battalions, all elderly retirees, push on gamely down the trail: *See the lava before you die. See the force that seethes beneath us, which has always seethed beneath us.* There is a wild grimness in their eyes, and a quickness to their steps.

Elizabeth and Mary Katherine and I approach from the upwind side. The steam's all blowing out to sea, but we protect ourselves against a wind change nonetheless. The sulfur in the lava mixes with water when it hits the ocean and forms dense clouds of sulfuric acid, which in great enough concentrations can irritate your eyes and lungs. That same morbid fellow, the park ranger who was so gleefully detailing the various revenges of Madame Pele upon rock-snatchers, has also been telling a tale (*not* a myth) about a recent group of tourists who went past the roped-off viewing area, desiring to get right up to the lava flow. The wind suddenly shifted, surrounding them completely with a great mass of sulfur fog, so that even if their eyes hadn't been burning, they wouldn't have been able to see their hands in front of their faces.

They had to fall to the ground like supplicants, and huddled there for more than eight hours until rescuers went in and found them. It was a good thing they didn't try and outrun the fog, too, said the ranger, because all around them was an oh-so-thin crust, which if they had punched through would have dumped them ankle- or waist- or even neck-deep into gleaming red lava.

◆◆◆◆◆

So I'm nervous, even behind the single strand of yellow nylon "safety rope." The crusty, hardened lava on which we're standing is still streaked and swirled with iridescent orange hues, and little pockets of rainwater are trapped in its folds and depressions. The rainwater is still steaming and sometimes bubbling.

We can't really see the lava flow, about seventy yards down the coast, but we can hear the steady, crashing hiss as it continues to pour into the ocean—a sound not unlike a sticking a hot skillet under cold running water, only magnified a million times; a sound that has no cessation, no cooling relief.

At any given time there are only a dozen or so pilgrims standing on the beach, peering north, craning their heads in a futile effort to see the lure of what lies around the bend: the lava flow. The rest of the hundred or so visitors are straggled out all through the brush, some still coming, and some leaving, perhaps disappointed. Occasionally a great backlash of cool, red *aá* will explode into the sky, rising up and out of the steam for us to see. A collective gasp will go up, as if our hearts have been torn out, or as if we have *touched* the lava—and then that brief sight will vanish back into the steam.

It's the worst thing we do in nature, perhaps—well, one of the worst—preferring the immense and the immediate to the subtle. Perhaps it is some gene that is in us; perhaps predators *need* to think big, to have an eye for the spectacle of boom-and-bust. Or perhaps it's simply further ruination of our lives by the satanic qualities of television. Nonetheless, I'm disappointed at not having seen the Time-Life or National Geographic version of the process, and I suddenly remember, with pride, that my parents were told they were the only visitors in the history of Yellowstone National Park who booed Old Faithful.

◆━◆━◆━◆━◆

We head back, walking south along the black sand beach. It's dusk. Once again there's the feeling that this is the only world there is, the new world, and that we are its settlers: the colonists.

All that is needed is here: water, shelter, food. Myths. The blue waters of the Pacific. Normally I get a bit queasy when I think about eating fish, understanding that all the world's various heavy metals can accumulate in their tissues as if the fish were nothing more than sponges. All I like to eat now is wild game—deer that live their lives high in the mountains, far out of that kind of harm's way.

But these blue waters—they make me desire fish. That seafood phobia, that *repression,* is lifted, so that I find myself wanting to run crazily into the ocean and capture a luscious fish with my hands, if need be, and feast on the sweet, clean flesh right then and there.

It is the cleanest, bluest water I have ever seen. It seems to be speaking to me in a language and on a level that I am not familiar with, a kind of communication from childhood, or the womb, or even before, perhaps: *Eat me; come eat my fish.*

We walk down the glistening black beach in silence, save for the crashing of the surf: a family, our first December. The sand gives way to a new lava that has not yet been broken up into beautiful black sand (Hawaii's white beaches are from washed-ashore coral fragments). In some of these rough passages across the new lava, dramatic stone arches stand right at the water's edge—sea caves and blowholes where the ocean rushes up under the land, racing through an underground tunnel, the ocean spout then emerging square in the middle of the lava flat, farther inland. It's like a journey through the imagination—a child's imagination.

These tunnels—called lava tubes—are formed during a certain kind of lava flow in which the surface of the lava cools as it creeps across the land. This cooling, hardened exterior of the creeping flow (like the scuzz on top of cream left out too long, is how I think of it) insulates the fluid lava beneath it, allowing that lava to stay molten longer (rather than cooling and hardening it). The lava beneath this cooling outer skin continues to flow until it has all gone on its way, leaving behind only the empty, hardened outer shell, that crusty exterior skin, which becomes roof, the ceiling, of the tunnel below. Like veins and arteries, these hollow lava tubes wander all over the island, and sometimes out to sea.

Does anyone besides geologists give a damn about all this? Myself, I find it difficult to understand how such a diverse and different place can exist in the world. There is the old Pangea—all of the seven continents before they split off from one another—like Pele's seven brothers, perhaps—and then there are the Hawaiian Islands, which seem immune to the homogeneity, the at-times barely discernible but always present air of malaise that exists on the continents, sometimes hovering just in the tops of the trees, but almost always somewhere nearby.

But this place—these islands—like only the wildest mountaintops, or the most sere deserts, has a kind of a grace, a wild grace so tangible that it startles me.

We drive up out of the lava flats, up from the down-faulted block of the island that's not so much a thousand-foot fault as a slump from where the island grew too fast. We drive through lush forests and through wasteland, back up to the Southwest Rift, and around the edge of Kilauea, whose steam clouds glow green in the odd wet light of the setting sun.

The giant moon rises behind us, heightening the feeling that we are on another planet. Never have I seen such lushness, and never have I seen such splendid desolation, and never have I seen anything like this, the two of them side by side, in harmony.

◆—◆—◆—◆

At the Visitors' Center on the way out, while buying a few post-cards, I overhear a middle-aged woman from Chicago buying some kind of island amulet—a string of shells, a tinkling necklace.

"Maybe this will make my daughter fertile," the woman tells her companion, and I have the sudden and certain feeling, I don't know where from, that indeed that woman's daughter *is* going to finally conceive, and it seems as natural and uncomplicated a thought as looking at a purple sky to the north and thinking that yes, rain is coming.

As the place where lushness and devastation collide and then prosper, science and religion also have their harmony up here. The Thomas A. Jagger Museum, right at the edge of Kilauea, has been devoting itself to research on and study of volcanoes for years now. (They're *not* the silly-assed people who sent that poor robot over a volcano's rim and down into the magma, a $2-million-dollar boon-doggle, cold-hearted premeditated robocide—that was NASA, in Antarctica.)

The Jagger Museum employs real people, dressed in huge silver asbestos suits, looking like knights of old, to take measurements from the volcanoes, and they use lasers, too, to try and measure the infinitesimal swellings and stretchings of the Earth's surface (so goes the theory, anyway) that occur just hours before an explosion.

This is good. This is *great*. It's wonderful to learn something new—something new every day, if you can, as my ninety-five-year-old Grandma Robson tells me. But the trouble our species, or our culture, seems to have with knowledge is that it seems to bring arrogance, and seems to diminish rather than nurture respect. You'd think the more you understood something, the more you'd respect it, too, but that's just not always the case.

The lasers and all are wonderful—sweller than swell—and I get

◆◆◆◆◆

the impression from the vulcanologists that they have that respect, an acknowledgment of the power and workings of mystery, which certain other scientists and cultures are not always comfortable with—a force that is sometimes ignored or dismissed as myth.

One reason for the vulcanologists' respect could be that it's right before their eyes—that mixture of long-ago myths fitting the truth long before their microscopes ever arrived on the scene, and the knowledge that those myths will continue to fit the truth long after the microscopes are gone.

About twenty miles offshore from the Big Island's east coast—toward the direction we were watching the vaporous spirits of the lava flow drift, floating just above the waters to the horizon—scientists have discovered that a new "sister" island is forming—that Pele is continuing, in both spirit and the physical world, her southeasterly trick of old, trying to find a new place in which to receive her lover, which I think we can safely say is life itself.

Called Loihi Seamount by scientists, the top of the new coming island is still about 3000 feet below the ocean's surface. If Loihi continues to grow at the rate that the Big Island grew (and is growing), it'll be about 60,000 years before Loihi rises from beneath the sea.

Likely as not, an asteroid will have smacked the Earth again during that time, making another ice age: a fine exclamation mark to the greenhouse warming we're currently aiding and abetting. Likely as not, we'll be gone, and the survivors—bacteria, ferns, and perhaps a few multicelled ocean organisms—will have to start all over again.

The planet desires life; even at its very molten core, there is a seething, a *desire*, for life.

Perhaps Loihi will be up and about, by then. Likely as not, this is what that new world will look like, then. Lichens. *Kipakus.*

◆—◆—◆—◆—◆

It is impossible to be arrogant.

In the morning, before leaving, I drive up the tiny winding road to the 9000-foot trailhead that leads to Red Hill, toward the summit of Mauna Loa. I return the lava rock I had stashed in my car to the base of Mauna Loa—back to its source—and know, in a way that I rarely get to feel anymore, that I have done something correct and right.

◆◆◆◆◆

21

POEMS

OFFERINGS

Waha'ula Lava Flow, the Big Island

Past twisted girders of the eaten building
    past black stone bunting slung
over squared-off cliffs, past
ropy footholds, vast satin folds, jagged
'a'ā brittle and raw

we wander, breathing sulfur, kneeling
to hold a hand for a moment over
molten earth flowing not far
below. For years, the lava opened
around the chosen

stones of the heiau. But now,
the place of sacrifice

A THOUSAND LEAGUES OF BLUE

lives submerged,
its only marker
a hip-deep stone corral,

still harboring
offerings—a morsel wrapped in ti leaves,
a glinting flask of gin. Behind us,
islands of rainforest rise from the lava,
spared for no reason.

The earth has taken back the black
sand beach, the smooth terrace, the birds'
mountainside. Huge
spumes of acid and steam blast
out of the hissing ocean.

Forces so great leave behind
strands of glass too fine to hold,
leave golden pools of glass
wafers thin as wings
of dragonflies watching.

◆◆◆◆

PASSING THROUGH, PASSING ON

Waipoʻo Falls, Kauaʻi

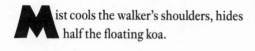ist cools the walker's shoulders, hides
half the floating koa.

The red dragonfly drinks
from the still place.

Not afraid to fall, not afraid
of flight, water

repaints air,
earth, light.

Lizard-smooth bottom stones
cradle the swimmer's arch.

Deep water, very cold,
disguises itself with clarity.

Far down Waimea Canyon, the river
stirs red dirt.

Honeycreepers, guardians of canoe makers, call
ʻelepaio, ʻākepa, ʻiʻiwi, ʻapapane.

These breaths—red tufts of ʻōhiʻa,
whistles of the shama thrush.

◆◆◆◆◆

A THOUSAND LEAGUES OF BLUE

A child, grown and unsure, listens.
For so many years

she has not heard.
The mother who suffers in this life

speaks from the next
in this place, the last.

Feral pigs hook their tusks
under native roots. Ti falls easily.

At the last moment, the very last
cliff dwellers tuck in their wings.

◆◆◆◆◆

22

LEGEND OF IWA

TRADITIONAL HAWAIIAN FOLK STORY,
RECOUNTED BY HENRY FORNANDER

The scene of this legend is laid in Keaau, Puna, in which part of the country there once lived a man by the name of Keaau, who owned two *leho** shells (cowries) called Kalokuna. Whenever the possessor of these shells went out squid fishing all that was necessary to do was to take and expose them and the squids would come up and enter the canoe. This was Keaau's regular occupation every day. The existence of these extraordinary shells was in time carried to Umi, who was then living in Kona. Whereupon he ordered his messengers to go to the home of Keaau and obtain possession of them, and at their demand† the shells were given up and the messengers returned with them to the king.

After the shells were secured by Umi, a deep yearning sprang up

---

* The cowrie shells of greatest value to Hawaiians in squid fishing were those of dark reddish hue, containing the attractive fire, as they called it, necessary for baiting the octopus.

†Old-time Hawaiians had nothing they could hold as their own; everything they possessed was liable to seizure by one or another of rank above them.

◆◆◆◆◆◆◆◆◆◆◆◆◆◆◆◆◆◆◆◆◆◆

in the breast of Keaau for them. After studying for a time for means of recovering the shells, he one day prepared his canoe for sea, procured a pig, some awa and ouholowai* and eleuli, kapas of Olaa. The kapas he put into a calabash and then the pig, the awa and the calabash were placed into the canoe, which he then boarded and set out on a journey around Hawaii in search of someone who could steal back his shells from Umi.

All through the district of Puna he found no smart thief.† He next traveled through the district of Kau, without success; then through Kona, still unable to find his man. He next touched at Kohala, and on through that district and the district of Hamakua and Hilo, meeting with the same failure; he found no one smart enough. Keaau then left Hawaii for Maui and traveled around that island; still he met the same disappointment. He found men good in the art of stealing, but none smart enough to recover his shells. He next set out for Lanai and traveled around that island, but he met the same fate. He then set out for Molokai and journeyed around it till, off the point of Kalaeokalaau, he met a man of that island who was out fishing. The man upon seeing him called out, saying: "Where is your canoe sailing for?" Keaau replied: "I am in search of a person who can steal back my leho shells from Umi. I have here with me in my canoe several valuable things which I shall give as presents to the thief who could return my shells to me." The man replied: "You have found him. You sail on until you come to Makapuu and after you have passed that place steer your canoe for a point between the bird islands and Mokapu. When you reach that point look for the cliff

---

* The frequent mention in tradition of these kapas of Olaa indicate them as treasurable products of high value. The *Ouholowai* kapa was made from the bark of the *mamaki* (*Pipturus albidus*), dyed differently on its two sides. The *eleuli* is described as a perfumed kapa, rarely met with.

†Even in ancient Hawaii the principle of setting a thief to catch a thief was understood and observed.

◆◆◆◆◆

which resembles the roof of a house, above, and directly below the cliff you will see a grove of Kukui trees; there you will find Iwa, the thieving son of Kukui."

(Iwa was a small boy at this time, but while he was yet in his mother's womb he used to go out stealing. He was the greatest thief in his day.)

"When you come to land, look for a small boy who goes about along the beach without a loin cloth; that is Iwa. Take out your pig and the other articles of value and lay them before him. Don't forget this, else all your things will be stolen from you by Iwa."

After receiving these instructions, Keaau set out, and after he had sailed past the different points he came to the landing below the home of Iwa. Upon touching land he looked about him and saw a small boy without his loin cloth running along the beach. Keaau then called out to him: "Is your name Iwa?" The boy replied: "No, Iwa is at the house."* When Keaau arrived at the house he found Kukui, the father of Iwa. Keaau then asked him: "Where is Iwa?" Kukui replied: "Did you not meet a small boy on the beach running about without his loin cloth?" "Yes, there was such a small boy." "Go back and present him your pig." When Keaau heard this, he returned and said to Iwa: "There, you are Iwa after all; you misdirected me." Keaau then took the pig and presented it to Iwa saying: "Here, I present this to Iwa, the thieving son of Kukui, together with the articles of value in my canoe and the canoe itself." Iwa then said to Keaau: "Let us return to the house." When they arrived at the house, the pig was killed and put into the oven, and the awa was prepared. After the meal was over, Iwa turned and asked of Keaau: "What is the object of your journey that has brought you here?" Keaau replied: "I had two shells which were taken away from me by

---

* Lying evidently came easy to this noted thief.

orders from the king, Umi, and he has them in his possession now. I value these shells so much that I am distracted, and that is the reason of my being present here." "We must await until tomorrow morning," said Iwa.

They retired for the night, and on daylight the next day they boarded the canoe and set out to sea. Iwa took the stern of the canoe with his paddle called Kapahi, while Keaau took the seat at the bow. After they were seated in the canoe, Iwa called out: "Kapahi, take Iwa out to sea," at the same time he dipped his paddle into the sea. (This meant that one stroke of the paddle was all that was needed.) With this one stroke, they passed between Niihau and Kauai. Iwa then asked: "Have we arrived?" "This is not Hawaii, these islands are Kauai and Niihau." Iwa then turned the stern of the canoe around and again called out to his paddle, Kapahi: "Kapahi, take Iwa out to sea." When Iwa drew his paddle out of the sea they were passing outside of Kawaihoa. He then asked of Keaau: "Have we arrived at Hawaii?" "No," said Keaau. Again Iwa took up his paddle and gave one stroke and they left Molokai and Lanai to their rear and they went floating between the island of Molokini and Pohakueaea, a point of land looking toward Hawaii. Iwa then asked: "Have we arrived?" "Yes," replied Keaau, "but it is at that point of land where the cloud hangs over the mountain that we want to go; it is to the west of that point that Umi is now living." Iwa then took up his paddle, Kapahi, and gave one stroke and they arrived outside of Kalaea-keahole, a point of land looking towards Kailua, where Umi had his residence. When they looked about them, they saw Umi just below them, in his canoe. Iwa then said to Keaau: "There is Umi in his canoe with the shells. Let us get our canoe to the rear and out of sight of Umi." When they were some distance from Umi, Iwa said: "Say, Keaau, you must float right at this spot until I return with your

◆—◆—◆—◆—◆

shells." Keaau therefore kept his canoe floating on the same spot while Iwa dove down and swam until he had reached the bottom of the ocean, then walked under water to the place where the canoe of Umi was floating, then swam up until he was almost up to the surface; and as the shells were being let down on the side of the canoe, Iwa grabbed them and took them down with him to a large coral, there he fastened the fish-line, then he took the shells and swam under water until he reached their canoe and got into it. The two then returned and landed at Leleiwi, in Hilo, where they made their home. Upon the recovery of his shells Keaau again took up his favorite occupation, that of squid fishing, taking along his shells, Kalokuna. The squids at sight of the shells climbed and entered the canoe until it was loaded down when they returned to shore.

(We will here leave Keaau and let us return to Umi.)

After the shells were taken by Iwa and the line fastened to a coral, Umi after a time pulled up on his line, but to his surprise it would not yield and thinking that the line was entangled to the coral he did not wish to pull very strong, thinking the line would break and he would lose the shells. Fearing he would lose them he remained in his canoe all day, and that night he slept out at sea with his men, and for some days he lived there, while his men dove down to untangle the fish-line and thus recover the much valued shells. Men noted for being able to stay under water a long time were sent for, and these men were told to go down, but the best they could do was to go down three times forty fathoms, seven hundred and twenty feet,* not deep enough to reach the bottom where the line was tangled. This was kept up for a week. Umi then sent out his runners to make a circuit of Hawaii to look for a man who could stay under water long enough

* This is considerably over twice the record depth by expert divers of the present day.

to recover the shells. In this trip around the island of Hawaii, Iwa was found at Leleiwi, the point of land adjoining Kumukahi, between Puna and Hilo. When Iwa heard the king's wish through his runner, Iwa said to him: "There are no shells at the end of the line. The line only is fastened to some coral in the bottom of the ocean. The shells have been recovered by Keaau." When the runner heard this he returned to Umi taking Iwa with him and told Umi of what he had heard from Iwa. Umi then asked Iwa regarding the shells and Iwa told Umi just what the runner had told him. At the close of the report Umi asked Iwa: "Can you get these shells for me if you should go for them?" Iwa replied: "Yes."* Iwa then journeyed back to the home of Keaau in Leleiwi.

It was Keaau's custom to hide these shells on the end of the house, up next to the curve of the rafters; and the other shells, the ones that he did not care so much for, he kept them in the house hung up on a cord.

About dusk Iwa made his appearance near the house and knowing where the shells were secreted he went up and removed them from the place they were hidden and he then returned to Kona, and handed them over to Umi. When Umi saw the shells he was made very happy and he then said to Iwa: "You are a smart thief, but I am not going to praise you just yet, not until you can produce my axe, which is being kept in Waipio in the temple of Pakaalana. The name of the axe is Waipu." Iwa then made reply: "I don't know whether I will be able to steal it or not, but I shall try."

(We will here speak a few words relating to the axe and how it was kept by its guards.)

This axe, Waipu, was kept by two old women. It was fastened to the middle of a piece of rope and the ends of the rope were fastened

---

* The alleged "honor among thieves" was not a governing principle in this boy's character.

◆◆◆◆◆

around the necks of the two old women allowing the axe to dangle between the two.*

There was a very strict kaput placed on this axe; no person was allowed to pass near the place, and during the period of time when the kapu was in force, the pigs were not allowed to run about, the dogs were not allowed to bark, and even the roosters were kept from crowing. The kapu was extended from Waipio to Puuepa, a hill between Waimea and Kawaihae. At dusk, just before it gets real dark in the evening, the crier‡ would run from Puuepa to the cliff of Puaahuku overlooking Waipio, carrying oloa kapa in his right hand, held between the palm of the hand and the wrist as a flag and would cry out: "Sleep ye, sleep ye because of the axe of Umi. Persons are kapued from walking about, the dogs are kapued from barking, the roosters are kapued from crowing, the pigs are kapued from running about. Sleep ye." The crier was required to make five trips back and forth before daylight.

After Umi had told Iwa what he wanted, the sun was past the meridian. Iwa did not, however, wait for further directions but started out on his way to Waipio. Just before dusk he arrived at Puuepa and immediately started running and crying out like the king's crier with a flag in his hand. He continued running until he reached the cliff of Puaahuku, looking down into Waipio. In calling out the way he did, the crier, whose duty it was to make the cry, was forced to go to sleep like the rest of the people, for to get up and go about meant death. Because of this Iwa was the only one about, all the people believed it

---

* An ingenious way of guarding a sacred article, one safeguarding the other and both insuring protection.

†The reason of this strict kapu upon the axe of Umi is not shown, and is difficult to understand in connection with its limitations, whether as a weapon or a utensil.

‡The crier of old time was called *kuhaua;* another term was kukala, which, by the former custom of auctions being announced by aid of a red flag and hand bell became identified therewith.

◆—◆—◆—◆—◆

was the usual crier and the crier himself believed that the king had appointed some one else to take his place. Furthermore the people could not recognize any difference; the build was the same, the flag looked the same, the voice sounded the same and the speed in running was the same.

Iwa continued running from the top of the cliff down to the temple of Pakaalana* and then he called out: "Are you two still asleep?" The old women replied: "No, we are not asleep, we are still awake." Iwa then asked quietly: "Where is the axe? Let me feel of it." "Here it is," answered the old women. "You must come nearer so that I can touch it with my hand. I just want to feel of it." When the old women drew nearer to Iwa, he reached out and pulled at the axe, getting it away from them. The old women then called out: "Here is a thief! The king's axe is gone! We are killed! We had thought this was a good man!" When the people heard this, they all got up and gave chase. When the old women made the first outcry, Iwa had reached the top of Puaahuku with the axe in hand. When the pursuers reached there he had reached Mahiki. This chase was kept up until Iwa reached Puuepa. When those in pursuit reached this place, he was at Puako. They therefore gave up the chase as the country beyond that place was outside of the kapued area, while Iwa continued on until he arrived in Kona. He then slept until daylight the next day. When it was about time for Umi to have his morning meal, Iwa went up to him. When Umi saw Iwa he asked jokingly: "I don't think you have been able to get my axe." Iwa then replied: "Perhaps not, but I want you to look at this axe and see if it is not yours." When Umi saw it, he said: "How strange! I thought you never would be able to get it; but here you have gotten it. You are smart." After his Umi said to Iwa:

* *Pakaalana* was one of the temples made famous in island history as a place of refuge for windward Hawaii. It was built before the time of Umi's grandfather, Kiha, and was destroyed by Kaeokulani, king of Kauai, in 1791.

◆◆◆◆◆

"Here is my thought regarding you. I want you to try with my six best thieves. There are two houses to be filled in one night, one for you and one for them. If you will not be able to fill yours first, you will be killed; so shall it be with the others." Iwa then replied: "Yes, no doubt the others will fill theirs first for there are six of them. Mine will not be filled because I am alone."

There are six districts in the island of Hawaii and Umi had six expert thieves.* While it was still daylight the six thieves went out to see what things they could steal; and when it became dark they began to steal and to carry everything they could lay their hands on into their house. This was kept up until the first cock crow, when there was very little room left in the house. At about this same time Iwa woke up and as soon as the six men went to sleep he proceeded to steal the things stolen by them of Umi's men, men, women, children, canoes, animals and various other things. Before he could remove all the things into his house there was no space left, so he had to leave some of them. When it was daylight the next day they found that the house belonging to the six men was almost empty, while Iwa's house was filled with the different things. The six men were therefore declared beaten and were killed† in the place of Iwa.

---

* When it was a recognized right of the king to take whatever he desired of his subjects' possessions, there would seem to be little need for expert thieves in his service, yet even Kamehameha, with all his good qualities, is said to have had one Kaikioewa as superintendent of this particular work, at the formation of his government.
†Rough treatment for napping after a successful raid.

23

JAPAN'S

WILD NATURE

DAVID RAINS WALLACE

This clear bright pond
Ruffled in the wind;
Pines that nod from their crags in greeting;
Rocks shining from the river bottom beneath drifting
watery mirrors;
Scattered clouds that cloak the summits in shadows;
The half-risen moon which lights the vales,
When from tree to tree dart crying birds:
To these will I abandon, will I entrust my life.
    Isonolcami no Yalcatsugu (729–81); translated by Burton Watson

Japan has perhaps come closer than any other nation to making nature the center of its aesthetic. There's something exceptional about a culture that has arts of moon and firefly watching and insect listening as well as landscape painting and poetry. I had mixed feelings about this when I had an opportunity to go to Japan for a couple of weeks. On the one hand, I looked forward to seeing the landscapes of the paintings and poems. On the other, I was afraid the Japanese had made such an art out of their land that it would contain nothing I could relate to directly—that the whole place would be a kind of giant landscape scroll, woodblock album, or Zen garden. Much as I like landscape scrolls, woodblock albums, and Zen gardens, a whole country of them somehow doesn't appeal. Art is a nice place to visit, but I wouldn't want to live there.

There was nothing in the least "Japanese" about the landscape over which our Thai Airlines jet flew on its way to Tokyo, though. It was a tangle of steep, forested ridges that might have been in North Carolina. The only odd note was that some of the ridges had golf courses on their tops, which is not what one would find on a North Carolina ridgetop. But only a fifth of Japan is flat, and almost all of that is used for buildings or growing food, so golf courses—which are very popular in Japan—have to go somewhere. The forests that shared the ridgetops with the golf courses didn't look particularly natural—even-aged stands of cedar evidently planted for reforestation—but they didn't look like landscape scrolls. Japan was a real place. Tokyo certainly didn't look very "Japanese." Except for its newness, tidiness, and "icanji"-lettered billboards, it might have been Baltimore, especially seen through its midsummer petrochemical haze. Fragments of the natural world in Tokyo were about the same as one would find in any modern city. Robust, heavy-beaked crows sat on telephone poles, oblivious to the rapids of Datsuns and Toyotas that roared beneath them. Brown jays and wood pigeons squawked and cooed respectively in parks (but there was a complete absence of squirrels in city parks or elsewhere, so far as I could see during my short visit). Sidewalks were frequented by the usual sparrows, starlings (brown and tan instead of black like ours),

◆ ◆ ◆ ◆ ◆

and blue city pigeons. I suppose there must be a point at which human congestion crowds out even sparrows and starlings, but that point hasn't been reached yet even in Tokyo.

Japan and nature reasserted themselves when we went to a little town called Yumigahama on the Izu Peninsula, seventy miles from Tokyo. The roads on the way were so narrow and winding that mirrors had been set up at every curve to let drivers know if another car was coming. It seemed likely that the Japanese mountains have kept Tokyo at bay to some extent. Neither the nature nor the Japan at Yumigahama were quite what I'd expected, though.

I'd always thought of Japan as a cool-temperate place, but Yumigahama was a lively, disheveled subtropical resort town that reminded me of Puerto Vallarta: little, winding streets piled with crates of fish, mocking children, thousands of scuttling, bright-red land crabs that blanched yellow and pinched fiercely if picked up. Brown hawks called kites joined the crows on telephone poles, the birds evidently performing the same garbage removal function of "zopilotes" in Mexican towns.

The crescent-shaped beach was the dirtiest I've ever seen, a dense mosaic of Styrofoam, tar, old campfires, cans, and bottles that came as a surprise after Tokyo's cleanliness. There'd been a typhoon the day before, which partly explained the mess, but all that crap had to come from somewhere. The Japanese seem to have an opposite approach to throwaway culture than we do. We litter city streets, but tend to keep beaches and other out-of-the-way places clean. I suppose the Japanese approach is more rational—one generally spends more time on city streets than on beaches—but it's still a little uncomfortable to set up your beach blanket, radio, suntan oil, and other accessories in the remains of last night's Japanese equivalent of a wienie roast.

Outside the high rise-dotted resort area, things were more as I'd

◆—◆—◆—◆—◆

expected. The small river valley that ran into the hills was still an exquisite network of stone-diked rice paddies full of crabs, red crayfish, and frogs, brooded over by dark herons. A shrine on a hillside hinted at a very ancient integration of land and culture. A recently restored wooden temple at the base of the hill gave way to a long flight of mossy steps heavily overshadowed by huge cedars and hardwoods, which led up to a strange little cedar-board box of a building, decayed and rat-holed, but somehow full of presence. A tiny brown frog hopped across the moss like a character from a folktale. Off to one side was a wild, marshy meadow, evidently left to itself for religious reasons, and probably representing an economic sacrifice in flatland-poor Japan. It seemed a very quiet, secret place; and although it was neglected compared with the temples and gardens of Nara or Kyoto, it struck me as a truer harmony of wildness and artifice. It was only a few yards from a tile-roofed hamlet full of television aerials and Honda bikes, but the two didn't really seem at odds.

The hills and ocean headlands above Yumigahama were buzzing with life, literally. Slender green cicadas made the biggest racket I've ever heard from insects, a deafening whir that swept over the slopes in waves, so that we would be standing in perfect silence at one moment, then be engulfed by a rush of noise that left our ears ringing (Yukio Mishima gives cicadas a lot of space in one of his novels, *Spring Snow*, I believe.) The Izu hills also supported the showiest butterflies I've seen. I spent most of an afternoon on a rocky knoll, watching them flutter over the dwarf woodland of chestnut, live oak, ailanthus, rhododendron, and wild hydrangea that covered the headlands. There were huge black and white swallowtails with a bright red blush on their lower wings, and a jet black species with spots of iridescent turquoise. In the weeds beside the path, a pair of red, green, yellow, and black mottled snakes was copulating. Their brilliant red was the same as that of the crabs and crayfish—I think

◆◆◆◆◆

it's called Chinese red, the same color one sees on lacquered objects. I wondered if some element in the soil caused so many creatures to be that color.

The Izu coastline was pure Japanese blockprint—little islands with fantastic rocks and silhouetted pines; a pale, greenish-blue sea; distant ships; graceful lines of seabirds and dolphins (as yet unliquidated by fisheries authorities). But the quaintness was complicated when we followed the beach around a rocky point and came to a cove that must have been a World War II military installation—huge concrete abutments rising from the water, now covered with chitons, anemones, and other tidepool creatures, but obviously not built to enhance the scenery. The cove reminded me of one of those paintings one sees from the People's Republic of China that depicts mountain scenes in perfect Sung Dynasty style but also happens to contain hydroelectric dams and ranks of high-tension cables. Imagine a Hokusai print with a submarine installation in it and you have that cove.

Monkeys live on the Izu Peninsula, and we stopped at a Japanese national park service designated "monkey habitat" on the way back to Tokyo. It wasn't where I'd have expected to see monkeys. In fact, it was a lot like Golden Gate National Recreation Area, with brushy cliffs dropping steeply to the ocean. The monkeys lived on the cliffs, although it wasn't exactly a wilderness life. They drank from the water faucets provided for visitors, hung around the food concession and eagerly tried to intimidate us tourists into handing over edibles, the presence of which they could discern from a person's bearing, and which they would go after whether in hands, purses, or pockets. They made the Yosemite black bears seem downright reclusive. I got the feeling they would just as soon have gotten in the car with us and gone to Tokyo to take on the restaurants and markets.

A couple of hundred miles inland from Tokyo is Shiga Heights, a

◆—◆—◆—◆—◆

segment of the massif that cuts across most of central Honshu. We spent two nights there at an enormous high-rise ski and hot springs resort built on top of a gorge. The parking lot was the only flat place for miles. It was as subalpine as the Izu Peninsula had been subtropical, and the slopes around the resort were covered with lush hemlock, fir, beech, and birch forest. The wildflowers reminded me of California backpacking—fireweed, bunchberry, tiger lily, gentian. We saw large black and white birds quite similar to the Clark's crows of the High Sierra, and the woods were full of little chickadee- and nuthatch-like songbirds. The only distinctly oriental note I could see was a thick underbrush of bamboo that grew almost everywhere.

Shiga Heights is part of Josin-Etsu Highlands National Park, but the Japanese have a somewhat different concept of the national park than we Americans. There was a dammed reservoir and evidence of large-scale mining within an hour's walk of the resort, which itself wasn't what Americans would expect in a park unless they start building high rises in Yosemite. I can't read Japanese, but there didn't seem to be any clear park boundaries—no ubiquitous wooden signs or Smokey-hatted rangers. Hiking trails were not maintained although they were so heavily used they'd been beaten into avenues of mud and puddles. Switchbacks apparently were unheard of. The trail downhill from a ridgetop we'd climbed was a dizzying mudslide whereon the presence of other hikers was belied by their thumps, grunts, and curses as they slipped and slid on the slick clay. A peak visible from the ridgetop had an unbroken line of colorfully clad climbers—probably a tour group—from its base to its summit.

There did seem to be some wilderness at Shiga Heights, though we didn't have time to get into it. Beyond the ridge we hiked was a steep, faraway gorge with no sign of human occupancy, just unbroken forest and dragons of mist crawling up the ravines. Wild boars and small bears supposedly live in the area, though we saw no signs

◆—◆—◆—◆—◆

of them. We did catch a glimpse of a pine marten, a creature I'd be excited to see in any wildland. Maybe there are plans to build a resort in that gorge too, but for the present it seems that even a country as densely settled—both physically and culturally—as Japan has yet to exhaust completely its wild nature. Which means, among other things, that the nature-centered tradition of Japanese art still has some room to grow.

24

HUNTING

THE BIG BEAR

CHARLES SHELDON

May 7.—During the night the thermometer registered 32°, and it was drizzling in the morning, but nevertheless we packed the bidarka, or rather the natives did, as only they understand how to do it. It could hold only a limited supply besides our blankets. At 7.45 in the morning we started. I occupied the middle port-hole of the three-hole bidarka, which was so shallow and small that I could neither get in nor out without assistance; once inside, I was completely wedged in, and the thought of capsizing was not a pleasant one. The bidarkas of Nuchek are very small compared with those of the Aleut natives. Misha was ahead and carried, inserted under a thong on the outside of the bow, his rifle and spear, which latter is used to fasten to and hold up a seal if one is killed.

Swiftly we glided along, the paddles plying the water first on one side and then on the other, for these natives never paddle in any other way. The calm bay was full of the fantastic, beautiful harlequin ducks, geese were returning from their feeding-grounds near the shore, numerous horned puffins dotted the surface, and on the land itself, varied thrushes and sparrows were singing in the trees. We passed out of the bay and along the rocky east coast, which is full of continuous reefs extending from one to five hundred yards out from shore and, as the swell broke over them, the whole coast as far as I could see was dotted with white foam and spray, up to the irregular white line of breakers on the beach. We dodged among the reefs, slipped through great quantities of sea-weed, everywhere abundant, until noon, when we reached the first barrábara, ten miles down the coast, from which point I was to make my first hunt for bears.

It had cleared, and the day was beautiful and sunny. Immediately after taking a bite to eat, I started with my usual equipment, rifle, field-glasses, and kodak. Most unfortunately, not being familiar with the character of the country I was to traverse, I wore leather moccasins. I started up the creek to reach the basin at its head. Avoiding the devil's-club and salmon-berry bush, climbing up and down the steep hills and ridges, I came to a point where the creek emerges from a deep gorge, above which two streams join, dashing down in beautiful cascades over cliffs several hundred feet high. Beyond was the basin surrounded by mountains, all glistening in the sun. At once I started to climb the south mountain slope at the entrance to the basin, trying to force my way through the thick salmon-berry growth, and for the first time learning the difficulty of such an undertaking. After a vexatious experience, I reached the clear slope, which was very steep, and soon realized that on the slippery, icy ground my moccasins were totally unfit for walking and indeed very dangerous. Slowly I kept ascending diagonally, perhaps for a thousand feet, until I reached the snow line, and paused to enjoy the scenery. Again, at last, I was in an amphitheatre of rugged moun-

◆━◆━◆━◆━◆

tains, extending in a well-defined circle, enclosing the rolling pastures of the basin below, which reached down to the green hills and uneven ridges of the valley. Beyond was the broad ocean, now rocking and sleeping, a vast expanse, with its white border of breakers distinctly sounding on the beach. A bald eagle was soaring above me in evident curiosity, rock ptarmigan were flying about the rocks higher up, and below the sparrows were responding in song to the spring sun.

I had to press on and took a course downward toward the basin, finding it extremely difficult to descend over the steep ground, made very slippery by the melting of much snow on the slopes, and my moccasins affording no foothold whatever. Lying on my side I worked slowly along until I came to a long strip of snow stretching downward in such a way that in order to reach the basin I was obliged to cross it. It extended down a thousand feet, to precipices rising from the stream which there left the foot of the basin. I had crept out over the snow only a few feet when suddenly it gave way, carrying me with it about five feet, before I succeeded in stopping myself, but I was in a position where it seemed doubtful if I could move either up or down, and the danger was extreme. Obliged to act, I jammed the butt of my rifle into the ground and took a step or two, then the snow again gave way, and I went with it. Quickly dropping the rifle, turning on my stomach, and stretching out my arms to try to cling to the ground, I went on constantly slipping with increasing momentum and feeling that I was going to eternity. I began to revolve and to descend diagonally, when suddenly, at a depression in the slope, I stopped myself with feet and hands at the edge of the snow bank. The rifle, having followed me downward, slipped under me as I stopped. The entire surface of my hands was badly torn and bleeding, the front sight of the rifle was broken off, and the barrel was filled with snow. Taking off the slippery moccasins, I found it much easier to proceed. Then I cleaned the rifle with the string cleaner always carried in the butt, and slowly descended to a point not so steep, where, after putting on my moccasins, I sat on a rock to look over the basin.

Suddenly, to my intense surprise and satisfaction, I saw a large bear just emerging from the woods across the entrance to the foot of the basin. It at once began to feed on the grass growing on a little knoll. It would pick out the grass, and every few moments throw up its head and toss it about, sniffing. Not once did it look about, but seemed to depend wholly on its power of scent to detect the approach of danger. I was a quarter of a mile from the bear, well above it, and the wind was exactly right for an approach in a straight line. I soon began to move down the incline, watching carefully as I did so; stooping low as the bear faced me, and advancing whenever its head turned in any other direction. Not once did it look or listen, and I was safe from its scenting me. I had studied the ground; and having reached the steep hillside traversing the foot of the basin I worked across it to within two hundred yards of the bear, which was still feeding about the little knoll. I had reached a point where the slope was so steep that I could not advance with safety, yet the salmonberry bush and alders which covered the knoll made it difficult to get a shot here. Seating myself, however, I watched my chance to fire. Though I tried to aim behind the foreshoulder, on account of the broken sight it was somewhat a matter of guesswork, but I heard the bullet strike and saw the bear jump; it ran a few feet upward and stopped a moment in bewilderment. When I fired again and evidently missed, it quickly turned with a spring and came running at full speed directly toward me. I was surprised to see how rapidly it covered the ground on a steep slope.

My footing was not secure, and in a sitting position I could not seem to cover the running bear with the rifle; hence as it came to within a hundred yards of me, I half rose; then it saw me and turned, rushing down hill. Had I been that hundred yards nearer and without experience, I could, conscientiously perhaps, have written a fine story about a vicious, charging bear. It crossed the stream with a splash, and stopped for a moment *to look up at the spot where it had been feeding.* This seems to show that, even after seeing me, the bear thought the shot had come from the opposite direction. Somewhat similar to this, I believe, are most of the reported cases of the "charging" of bears; some true, but misunderstood. As it paused, I fired, and when the bullet struck it the bear gave a great spring upward and ran for the timber. As I fired again it almost turned a somersault, but kept on and soon entered the woods as my fifth shot missed. Though an indifferent shot, I could certainly have killed this bear before it reached the woods had not my rifle-sight been broken off.

Crossing the stream, I found a very bloody trail, which indicated that one of the bullets at least had touched a lung. I followed rapidly through the woods on the trail which led down a steep hill to another creek. The bear had descended with long jumps, and wherever its forefeet had touched the ground, there was a quantity of blood, evidently thrown from its mouth and nose. Just before reaching the creek, it had leaped down a ledge ten feet high. The trail led up another steep hill, and down again to another creek, and then upward until it reached ground covered with snow. It was now six o'clock. Higher and higher it went, up to the deep snow, where each step had sunk in a foot or more. Now I was near timber line. The snow was so soft and deep, the slope so steep, that I could scarcely follow the trail, but kept on as it began to wind up the mountain-side. Finally, rounding an elevation on the slope higher up above timber, I saw the well-defined bloody trail leading up the mountain-side in the distance, and just under the crest of the range, the bear itself, slowly struggling, step by step, upward. I thought at first it would not reach the top, that it would fall and roll at any moment, and from time to time it did stop, apparently staggering, but only again to toil on.

In my moccasins it was impossible to follow up the steep slope at that late hour, and suicidal to be caught in the dark on top of that rough, bleak, snowy mountain; reluctantly, therefore, I sat and watched the bear through my field-glasses. It would lie down a moment, then rise staggering, take a few steps, and rest again, until it finally reached the crest, along which it began to walk slowly, its form clearly visible on the sky-line, where it still kept looking about for danger. It was a magnificent sight, that bear displaying its huge dark bulk on the sky-line of that mountain-girdled valley, while it walked along the crest to the top of the highest, roughest peak, slowly pacing back and forth, looking for a place to lie down. As the twilight deepened, it descended a few feet to the side of the peak facing the basin and lay down on the verge of a precipice falling into what appeared to be a great pit surrounded by perpendicular cliffs. The bear kept changing its position, apparently in distress, and every few moments would struggle to its feet and look about, as if an enemy were approaching. Finally it stretched out on its side and moved a little, as if it were panting. I knew it would die, and as darkness began to come on, had to leave, smarting under keen disappointment. I was sure that it would fall into the great pit, which looked inaccessible. I descended, and started through the dark forest toward camp, thinking how all this demonstrated the wild, cautious nature of the bear, and what inaccessible, rough places it seeks when frightened and wounded. On Montague Island bears had never been systematically pursued or hunted, and every experience I have had with them, there and elsewhere, leads me to doubt most of the stories of their aggressive boldness in times past.

With some difficulty I progressed slowly through the darkness,

◆◆◆◆◆

feeling my way with a staff, occasionally listening to hear the echoes of the owl's hooting or feel the charm of the single notes of the varied thrushes, sweetly sounding in the stillness of the woods. My hands were in bad condition, and I had been severely punished by the devil's-club, when I reached camp at 11 P.M., to find that my men had put provisions for only one day in the bidarka—an example of the usual lack of foresight in the native. But I slept soundly in the wretched little barrábara, my hope still high of getting that bear the next day.

May 8.—I breakfasted before daylight and put a new front sight on my rifle as the dawn ushered in a perfect day, calm, sunny, and mild. Sending my natives back to the bay for provisions, I started for the basin. Reaching the foot and climbing to timber line, I looked through my glasses. I could not see the bear where it had been the evening before, but the bloody slide over the snow below indicated plainly what had happened. I was now wearing hobnail shoes, and at once began the ascent. There was some danger from the numerous snow-slides occurring at intervals, and the last two hundred feet were doubtful, but finally climbing to the crest and walking along it, I reached the point, looked over with eagerness, and this is what I beheld: a great circular pit about three hundred feet across, completely surrounded by perpendicular cliffs and precipices, falling two hundred or three hundred feet to the bottom. There, partly stretched on its side, was my bear lying dead, while two male bald eagles were tearing out and eating its entrails. Through my glasses it appeared about six feet long, whitish on the back and sides. Its legs were dark, and a narrow blackish tinge extended from its head along the spine to the tail. I circled the pit, but could find no possible path of descent. Only the impressive beauty of snow, mountains, green woods, and vast expanse of sea softened my deep disappointment when I was forced to leave and retrace my steps down the mountain-

◆━◆━◆━◆

side to a point where I could look well over the basin and the bare slopes about.

At exactly 2 P.M., high up near the mountain crest, near the head of the basin, a mile distant, I saw through my glasses a bear descending over the snow, the trail behind showing that it had just come over the mountain-top, probably having left its winter cave shortly before. Soon I saw a cub running about with it.

It was not possible to attempt a stalk high up in the snow, on the steep slopes. Quickly descending, I reached the snow field at the head of the basin and climbed to a point where I could watch her. The old bear did not descend, but was pottering about, digging in the snow to reach grass or mice, while she fed over a few bare rocky spaces that were exposed. At short intervals she kept throwing up her head, swinging it back and forth to sniff the air, but not once did she *look* about for danger. She continued to feed over a small area for some time without descending, and then started circling the mountain-side, high up, just under the cliffs and precipices of the crest. I noticed that she travelled ahead, while the cub followed, lagging somewhat behind, but always stepping in the mother's tracks, so that the trail, except when the cub occasionally deviated for a short distance in shallow snow, appeared as one continuous track. I noticed also that the cub was limping. At first the old bear travelled only short distances, still digging and feeding while the cub played about, now lying down, now running, now watching its mother dig.

I yielded to the fascinating pastime of watching them through my glasses, until the old bear began to travel without stopping, descending slightly; then I thought that by crossing the basin and reaching a clump of spruces fairly high on the slope, I might anticipate them and get a shot. Descending, I crossed the narrow gorge, choked with ice and snow and full of deep cracks through which I could hear the creek rushing twenty or thirty feet below; I reached

◆ ◆ ◆ ◆ ◆

the spruces, and had a favorable wind for their approach. I soon caught a glimpse of them, now higher up, travelling ahead, but they quickly disappeared around a swell in the ridge and did not come in sight for some time. When they did, they were just under the crest and moving fast. My hopes sank as I saw them continue to go forward and completely circle the basin without descending below the snow. At last they reached some jutting cliffs and stopped to feed about the rocks, climbing over and among them like mountain sheep. I would never have believed that any large animal, except a sheep or a goat, could appear so much at home in such a place. High on the cliffs was a depression extending into a space where some stunted spruces grew, and in this wild, lofty spot, at 8 P.M., the old bear laid herself down to sleep, and the cub soon joined her. I was greatly puzzled to find this bear so cautious and timid, as her every action indicated, and could not understand why she had not descended to the grassy pastures of the mountain slopes below the snow. But as twilight was deepening I had to restrain my eagerness for a closer acquaintance, and started back, intending soon to visit this basin again. As I walked, a beautiful white rock ptarmigan strutted before me on the snow, erecting its red combs, and allowing me to approach within ten feet before it flew and alighted only a few yards below.

When I entered the woods it was clear above and absolutely still, yet not quite dark enough to obscure the ground. The air was soft and balmy, and as I passed gorges, water-falls, and spots of strange beauty, the towering white mountains were indistinctly visible through the trees. Many a time, as I crossed the open glades, when I could enjoy a more unobstructed view of the encircling mountain crests, I paused to listen to the sweet, single, drawn-out notes of the varied thrushes, then sounding from the tree tops, beginning low, swelling to full vibrant tones, and at last melting away in the myste-

◆◆◆◆◆

rious darkness of the forest—a mystic cradle song, lulling the dim woods to sleep. It was long after dark when I reached camp, to find the natives returned with the provisions and the report that they had seen two bears feeding high on a spur near the coast, about two miles below camp. Old Mark and two native boys, having left the schooner at the north end of the island, had also come to visit us.

May 9.—They passed the night in the little barrábara, while I slept, eagerly waiting for the next day's hunt. The stars were twinkling in a clear sky when I breakfasted, but there was a light breeze from the northeast—a bad sign. Old Mark and the boys were leaving, so as to get back to Nuchek before the wind increased. I started up the beach with Misha, who was to show me the mountain where he had seen the bears feeding. We had gone only a short distance when a shout was heard, and we knew at once that Mark was calling us and was in sight of bears. Quickly we returned, the bidarka was launched, and soon we were gliding toward Mark's bidarka, which was well out from the shore, nearly a mile up the coast. When we reached it he explained that he had seen two bears, which had just disappeared in a hollow below the crest of the spur. I was quickly put ashore, and having selected, from the boat, a line of ascent and approach, returned half a mile to circle upward on the spur and get the wind in my favor. The bears were seen on a high ridge, grassy on and near the top, where clear spaces alternated with patches of snow. The ridge extended parallel with the coast, connecting with a mountain, higher and more massive, just beyond. As I entered the woods to cross over and ascend the lower end of the ridge, clouds began to gather. At last I reached the top, to find it at this end covered with stunted spruce, alders, and dense salmon-berry brush, through which I had to force my way, and as I circled to the other side and began to move in the direction of the bears, progress was slow.

It soon became like a typical stalk for mountain sheep, except that

I was uncertain just where the bears were. The view of the basin on the left, as I caught glimpses of it between the mists continually drifting by in the wind, was particularly beautiful. It was very narrow, the surface was broken and rugged, and the slopes of the mountains seemed to wall it in, so that it appeared very deep. A dense fog soon settled down, the wind freshened, and I kept on in great uncertainty, but coming nearer to the spot where the bears had been seen, which had been indicated as a hundred yards below the top. The fog kept lifting and falling, a circumstance which only added to my caution. As I approached what I thought was the spot, I found the crest clear, its rolling, grassy surface covered with bear tracks, and all about were fresh diggings where the animals had been pawing the earth for mice. Now I was keenly alert, knowing that in the fog I might at any moment come close upon the bears. I was well back on the crest, the wind was entirely in my favor, and the ground was so soft that my shoes made no noise.

It was with strange sensations that I advanced through that mysterious fog, with eyes and ears strained to detect any sign of the bears which at any moment might appear before me. Finally, crossing the top, I looked over, believing that I was nearly opposite the point where the bears had been last seen. The fog had suddenly cleared, the blue sky appeared with a shining sun. I was not quite far enough; and again dropping back behind the crest, I kept on for three hundred yards and cautiously advanced to look over. There I saw, a hundred yards below, the bulky body of a whitish bear stretched out sound asleep, its head curled under its chest, its back toward me. It was lying on the edge of a dense patch of alders in a hollow depression of the slope, which just beyond was very steep and thickly covered with salmon-berry and alders—a well-chosen spot for concealment and rest. The natives had told me that when two bears were together the dark one was always a male, the light one a female,

◆ ◆ ◆ ◆ ◆

and both Mark and Misha had reported that one of these bears was dark. I could see only the light one, but knew that the other was lying near, in the alders.

With rifle cocked and ready, slowly and noiselessly I began moving down the slope, my eyes fastened on the sleeping bear. Imagine the fascination of such moments—high up on that mountain-side, facing the sea below boiling with white-caps and sounding with the distant roar of the breakers! Step by step I approached. Soon I stooped low and crept to within almost a hundred feet, when I caught sight of a blackish object in the alders, a few feet to the right of the sleeping bear, and knew it to be the other lying concealed. What wild, shy, timid animals! Little by little I crept on, coming nearer and nearer, until there were only seventy-five feet between us, when suddenly I saw the head of the dark bear in the alders rise. Almost simultaneously I sat down, with rifle pointed. Its head was toward me, and, having seen me as it half rose in surprise, I fired at its heart. Up it came with a great spring, and I fired again at the same spot. It began to run, and with a few jumps disappeared over the slope as I fired a third shot at its hind-quarters.

At the first shot the other bear had sprung to its feet, and was jumping a few feet in one direction, a few feet in another, in great excitement and alarm, thoroughly perplexed, and completely uncertain as to what was happening until, when the dark bear ran, it began to follow. As it ran, I fired at the side toward me; it swerved to the right, and again I fired as it disappeared down the slope. Quickly putting in a fresh clip of cartridges and running forward, I saw the dark bear lying dead, twenty feet below in the thick brush. Without stopping, I turned to the right, and found a bloody trail leading to a thicket of low, dense spruces fifty feet down the slope in the thick salmon-berry brush. There I heard the light bear thrashing about, but could not see it. Cocking my rifle and forcing my way into the spruces, I came to within ten feet of it—thoroughly excited by such close proximity to a wounded bear in dense brush—before I heard it run out on the other side and descend. Following as fast as I could down the steep salmon-berry slopes, I soon saw it indistinctly through the brush fifty yards below. I fired twice, but it kept on. I forced my way downward on the bloody trail, knowing the bear was hard hit. Coming to a landslide, I found the bear had jumped onto it and had run or slid a hundred yards to the thick brush below. The landslide was too steep for me to keep my footing, and crossing above, I descended parallel with it over ground so steep that I was obliged to let myself slowly down by holding on to the alders. Having descended two hundred yards, I noticed the salmon-berry bushes shaking, and going a little farther, saw the bear, badly wounded, a hundred yards below. Finally, succeeding in finding a clear space between myself and the bear, I fired at the centre of its body. It dropped and remained motionless. I reached it quickly and found it lying on its stomach, caught in the alders, one hind foot completely wedged in. It did not stir, though it was breathing heavily. It died without a struggle, and proved to be a male. The first shot had been fired at eleven-thirty, and it was now twelve.

The clouds and mists had again gathered, and since it was then too dark to photograph, without touching it I started for camp, reaching there at two-thirty. It was impossible to convince the natives that the two bears were dead, but after taking a bite of bread and a cup of tea I started back with them, trying to rouse them from their reluctance and indifference. Their doubts, however, were replaced by great excitement when we reached the light bear, and this became enthusiasm when, after passing on, we arrived at the spot where the other lay.

After cutting away the brush, I had tried to photograph the light bear, but the sky was heavily overcast and a slight rain was falling.

◆◆◆◆◆

The dark bear also proved to be a male. It was in fair pelage up to the neck, where the hair had begun to wear off. After photographing it as it fell, we pulled it up to a more level place at the edge of the depression, where I photographed it again, and carefully measured it, after which we skinned it. While we were thus occupied, two ravens, evidently greatly excited, kept darting down at us again and again. Taking the skin and skull, we descended to the other bear, and after taking off its skin, also cut off a quantity of meat, which I put in my rücksack together with the two skulls. Each man took a skin, and we reached camp at 10 P.M. The dark bear had received two bullets through the heart, both of which passed entirely out on the other side, and one in the hind-quarters, which broke one leg and penetrated well into the interior of the body. Its length was five feet six and one-half inches, height at foreshoulder four feet. All five bullets had entered the second bear. The first struck the neck, severing the jugular, the second broke a foreleg, two struck the hind-quarters, while the last hit the centre of the body. The slope was so steep and the brush so thick that even with the assistance of two men I found it impossible to measure it accurately. Neither bear had much fat, and the pelage on both was about the same. They were young bears, evidently twins, and had not separated since leaving the mother four or five years before. The stomachs of both contained nothing but grass and *Microtus* mice; the first contained five, the second four. The heads of all the mice were crushed, but the bodies were unmutilated.

Between the time of going up the beach and returning later we saw two places where land-otters had passed to the water to feed. These are exceedingly abundant on the island, as shown by their numerous tracks on the beach and slides on the benches of the creeks. Oyster-catchers were common on the shore, and a great number of crows were feeding about the kelp at low tide, while cormorants were

◆◆◆◆◆

perched in picturesque attitudes on nearly every high rock and reef. Up to that day, since I had only seen the bald eagles sitting on the trees near the shore, or flying low, I had begun to feel a little ashamed of our national emblem; but my pride was partially restored when, after the fog cleared, I saw them sailing against the sun, re-splendent with white head and tail, soaring high over the mountain tops, circling about the snowy crests, and floating across the valleys.

There I was, sitting by the fire with two fine bear-skins and skulls before me! On the two previous days I had killed one bear and seen another with a cub. Complete was my exultation and bright were my hopes for the days to come. Before sleeping I prepared some shrews and mice that had been taken in the traps.

25

HOW VARIOUS LARGE

AND SMALL PIECES

OF CALIFORNIA

MOVE AROUND FROM

ONE PLACE TO

ANOTHER

JAMES D. HOUSTON

Gary Griggs is a geologist here in Santa Cruz County. In his view, any account of where people live, and why and how, should properly begin with the earth itself, with the rocks and the riverbeds and the soils beneath our feet. Why? These things were here first. They have seniority.

It may seem obvious to point this out. But in California it is not obvious.

A while back, Gary drove me up the coast a few miles to look at a pile of sand by the side of a very famous road. As he saw it, this humble pile of grimy sand was a perfect metaphor for something about the way life is lived out west. It was half an hour north of town, up Highway 1, not far from where the sign says NEXT GAS TWENTY-THREE MILES. Row crops, brussels sprouts and artichokes, spread back on one side of us. Toward the ocean, it was sand dunes sprinkled with sparse tufts of grass. The dune grass used to be thicker, but the four-wheel drivers and the Honda three-wheelers with the big balloon tires had been coming in there chasing each other up and down the dunes and across the tide flats near the surf line and in and out of the sandy hillocks, and this played hell with the dunes.

"It takes a long time for this stuff to root," Gary said. "Once it's rooted, the sand and the grass and the wind have a nice system going. The sand stays put, and the dunes hold their shape for years and years. But now you have these huge patches of open dune where the grass has been torn away or mutilated, and you have this onshore wind which picks up the loose sand and pushes it out toward the highway. When it gets too far out into the road, it is a traffic hazard. Since this is supposed to be one of the state's great scenic drives, the road crews have to come in with their sand movers and dump trucks, load it up and carry it down the road a ways and dump it. So, in addition to the ecological fact that the dunes are being systematically destroyed, there is a direct correlation between the damage done by one set of vehicles and what it costs the state to bring in another set of vehicles, at probably a hundred-and-eighty-five dollars an hour, to clean up the mess."

"They ought to be keeping those four-wheelers out of there," I said.

"They try," said Gary. "It's county beach. The county has passed an ordinance. But they don't really have the personnel to enforce it.

◆◆◆◆◆

And the four-wheel drivers don't always see the connection between the fun they are having on the beach and the sand drifting toward the traffic a hundred yards away. 'Put up some barriers,' they say. 'Turn off the wind. Who's responsible for the goddam wind anyway?' they say."

The earth has seniority, yet we who live here overlook this all the time. Who can blame us, living where the land and the dream have this inverted relationship that goes back so many years. The earth has seniority, and yet the dream came first.

Like America itself, California was dreamed about long before anyone knew it was really here. The name first appeared in a sixteenth-century novel called *The Adventures of Esplandian*, by Garci Ordoñez de Montalvo, wherein the author invented a fantastical island "very close to the side of the Terrestrial Paradise." It was published in Madrid twenty-five years before Cortez named the lower peninsula, thirty-two years before the Cabrillo expedition first sailed up this coast. "Their island," Montalvo wrote, "was the strongest in all the world, with its steep cliffs and rocky shores. Their arms were all of gold, and so was the harness of the wild beasts which they tamed and rode. For, in the whole island, there was no metal but gold."

It was a concoction that actually influenced the hopes of the earliest adventurers. And this sequence—the dream running well in advance of the reality—has shaped the life of the state from the outset. Nowadays the dream shifts and turns and trembles, while the earth itself refuses to stand still. These two coexist, in a zany and tumultuous kind of marriage, a tug-of-war. They are never going to separate. They are going to tough it out to the bitter end. You can see the evidence everywhere, along the beaches, in the mountains, in the deserts and in the delta marshes, and in certain subdivisions built across a fault line, in the broken pads of concrete there, where sports cars were meant to park.

My nearest vantage point happens to be my own front porch. For almost twenty years I have lived in the same house, watching Monterey Bay, observing the change of seasons register in the colors and rufflings of the bay, in the surge of tides and the angle of the waves approaching shore. In the summer, waves roll up from the south, stirred to life by storms below the equator, moving straight across the bay to meet these beaches head-on. Sometime during the fall the approach angle shifts, as the storm centers shift to the north Pacific. By November or December the waves are rolling down from Alaska. They swing around the headland west of here, which protects our inshore waters from the colder, harsher currents of the open sea, and they approach the beach with a northeasterly turn, usually with great force. This delights the surfers and alarms the yachtsmen and the fishing fleet, since these fall and winter swells not only send breaking waves into the harbor mouth, they can haul sand in too.

The sand fills the channel between the jetties, and then the great, gloomy, non-pastoral, non-resort town dredge is put to work sucking sand and sludge from the channel so the sloops and launches can continue to glide in and out. A twelve-inch pipe is strung along the beach for a few hundred yards, to carry the sludge back into the tide, and you can hear the gravel and scraps of clam shell rattling along inside the pipe and smell the stink of buried boat oil and refuse that spreads across the beach in a murky fan. A good onshore wind will send the fumes back into the neighborhoods. On those days you hold your nose and watch the sunset backlighting the spectacular winter surf that humps outside Seal Rock, at the headland of this historic bay, and you are fully in touch with both the glory and the undoing of the California Dream.

◆—◆—◆—◆—◆

In the dream, pleasure holds a high priority. And this harbor exists primarily for pleasure craft—yachts, ketches, Boston whalers, catamarans. People from all over northern California berth them here or haul them in on trailers to be launched down the concrete ramp into the inviting waters of the sunny and irresistible bay. The sailing is so good, so exhilarating, and the mooring so benign, there have never been enough berths to go around. It is like Yale or Princeton in the old days: you put your newborn child on the waiting list. Then, when the fall and winter swells arrive you watch with dread as the pleasure principle collides with the stubborn will of the coastal sands.

Carried by wave-generated currents, the sand moves down the coast from northwest to southeast. Thousands of tons are swept up and swirled along by wave action. Whole beaches are transported from one district to another. The Army Corps of Engineers designed these jetties to fend off heavy swells, but they underestimated the flow of sand. The westward jetty has trapped acres and acres of it, creating a vast beach that did not exist before 1965. This now forces sand around the jetty and into the harbor mouth until sometimes nothing wider or deeper than a kayak can move in and out. During a minus tide in December, even the kayak is stuck.

Griggs the geologist, who has studied this coastline for most of his life, says the habits of the sand are not likely to change. The sand, he says, has been carrying on this way for thousands of years. To solve the problem, the harbor must be redesigned. But the county doesn't have that kind of money at the moment, and the Corps is reluctant to accept any blame. So every winter there is panic and consternation, followed by a gloomy reaching into the public pocketbook, while the dredge is called in to pump out the sand and the accumulated sludge, which in turn befouls the beach and fills the neighborhoods with noxious fumes and a day-long, night-long in-

◆━◆━◆━◆━◆

dustrial rumbling like the sound of a tugboat pulling us all toward deeper water.

The dredging only lasts a few weeks, of course. Then the bulldozers roll in and push over the mounds of debris that have piled up around the mouth of the overflow pipe. A couple of high tides later the beach is restored, and all of us who use these sands, tides, offshore waters and stirring vistas are content—the boaters and fishermen, the surfers and surf casters in their hip boots waiting for perch, the joggers, skimboarders and scampering dogs, the Frisbee masters with dogs trained for startling mid-air catches, the scuba divers and volleyball players and young meditators in the lotus, the ponchoed smoker who wants a hassle-free toke while the tawny sun goes down, and the retirement couple right behind him in their straw hats, who hike the sand most evenings.

According to Griggs, this annual skirmish between the harbor users and the restless sand is another typical California event. Whenever I talk to him, I am reminded again how delicately balanced is this seemingly solid surface we walk and drive around on. I am reminded of the many fluid tendencies our human plans keep running counter to. In this ongoing contest, Gary is a kind of attorney for the earth and its habits, filing briefs on its behalf. He often finds himself explaining or defending these habits to people who see the earth as an adversary or who don't seem to see it at all.

He also happens to be a born-in-Pasadena Californian, and an unrepentant native son. For most of his life he has lived within hiking or biking distance of a coastal beach. His father taught school in San Fernando Valley, and Gary remembers many summer trips into redwood country and the northern mountains. There is no denying that this influenced his chosen line of work. He is endlessly fascinated with the land and landscape of his home region, the way it behaves. Right now he lives on a wooded slope, at the top of a four-mile

◆◆◆◆◆

uphill road, with a view of the Pacific, in a house he designed and built himself. The house is made of fir and redwood. His office at the University of California's Santa Cruz campus, where I was meeting him for another lesson in the geology of recreation, is made of concrete: floors, ceilings, and the walls which are covered with slope maps, satellite photos, tiers of books.

His field is called Earth Sciences. He made full professor not long ago, at thirty-five. This is like making brigadier general when you're thirty-five, or senior vice-president at Humble Oil, where he was once offered a job. He looks and dresses younger. In his office he wears jeans, a buff-colored leather shirt, and hiking boots. He would make an excellent frontier scout, lean and hardy and intently pleased to be doing what he does. He is away from campus much of the time, looking at where people hope to locate buildings or moor their boats or maneuver their off-road vehicles. This work has taken him to New Zealand, to Greece, and to all parts of California. The day I called on him was a typical day. He had invited me to join him on a little trip to a place called Hungry Valley, below Bakersfield, where he had been measuring the impact of dirt-bikes and four-by-fours, the ways they reshape the surface of the world.

The State Department of Parks and Recreation had hired him for this project. Before we left the office, he showed me some of the material he had gathered, beginning with a photo of a hilly region taken from five miles up. It resembled a cross-section of human flesh, with the capillaries and nerves exposed. The capillary lines were dirt-bike trails in the high desert. He showed me close-ups of gullies etched into one of those same hillsides. One was four feet wide, eight feet deep. Gary stood inside the gulley with a measuring rod. It was an impressive sight, the way serious damage is always impressive, and awesome—a crumpled front-end, a wind-torn tree across the road. The damage, he told me, was even more impressive than it

◆◆◆◆

looked: tons of soil torn loose by that kind of gullying was displacing valuable water storage space in Pyramid Lake, part of Los Angeles County's intricate reservoir system.

"Off-road vehicles have been in there for six or seven years now," Gary said. "And we are talking about thousands of vehicles. Part of the valley is National Forest, part of it is private property. As usual, the state gets involved after the damage is done. Now they are thinking about buying up some parcels and turning a big area into an ORV park. You can't keep them out, so you look for ways to legalize the activity and contain it."

When he describes these dilemmas Gary has a way of laughing, not *at* anyone in particular, but *with* the way the world goes. He has compassion for the state officials who inherit these headaches. He understands the will of the riders who want to scale those hills. But his deeper sympathies lie with the will of the rainfall to flow where it has to flow, with the will of the sand to migrate through these coastal waters like schools of whales.

We were out of town right after lunch, cutting cross-country toward the San Joaquin, where we would pick up the high-speed north-south trunk route. Heading past Watsonville, we followed the Pajaro River east along Highway 124. On its way to Monterey Bay, the river has carved a trough through this fold in the Coast Range. The trough is called Chittenden Pass, and it happens to be a place where the river crosses the San Andreas Fault. I would not say that Gary is obsessed with the San Andreas, but the substructure of this state is on his mind most of the time. As we were leaving his office, with its layers of maps, charts, graphs and high-altitude photos, I had asked him if he could describe in twenty-five words or less a line of work that included a blocked harbor mouth, the price of real estate, earthquake prediction and four-wheel drive.

◆—◆—◆—◆—◆

His eyes opened wide, as if he had never thought of it quite that way before. Then he laughed his way-the-world-goes laugh.

"I guess you could say that I spend a lot of time thinking about how various large and small pieces of California move around from one place to another."

Of all this state's innumerable moving parts, the rift zone is the one that interests him most. He never wearies of discussing it, speculating, pondering. When he pulled to a sudden stop, halfway through Chittenden Pass, we were two pilgrims paying homage to the visible signs of certain planetary forces greater than our puny human selves.

The fault line marks the zone where two pieces of the earth's crust meet and grind together, the Pacific Plate and the North American Plate. Thanks to deep cuts through this pass made by highway crews in the 1930s, we could stand on the road that follows the river and see the meeting ground of these two vast slabs, spread before us like an open-faced sandwich. On the western side there was a chunky wall of granite, overgrown with brush and, higher up, with eucalyptus. To the east, a brighter wall of buff-colored shale, stratified at about a forty-five-degree angle, pointed up and west, as if the granite side were steadily nosing in under the shale. Above this layering there was a low dip in the ridge, the kind of dip that makes the trace line visible from airplanes.

In 1906 the concrete pillars holding up the railroad bridge at Chittenden cracked and almost toppled. The tracks were thrown so far out of alignment that a train moving through just after the main tremor hit was rolled on its side like a toy. It is said that in the old train depot at Chittenden a thousand-pound safe was overturned. Nowadays there is a granite quarry working full-time, right across the river. We stood and contemplated the million years of silent grinding made visible there, and listened to the distant clank of con-

◆━◆━◆━◆━◆

veyor belts at the quarry, the heavy trucks hauling out gravel, and the various creaking and clanking machines of men chipping away, chipping away, at the surface of the earth.

We had stopped there once before, back in 1973, when Gary first introduced me to the mysteries of the fault line. We had followed it that day for about fifty miles, examining the surface effects on the land and in the towns. We saw sag ponds, little avalanches, displaced creek beds. Outside San Juan Bautista we had stopped at a fence that happens to straddle the fault, where students of his had driven markers to measure the creep. As we passed it again, Gary glanced at the same markers, and told me the fence line had moved a bit less than an inch this year.

In Hollister, we took five minutes to swing a few blocks off the highway. Gary turned down a side street notable for an asphalt warp he likes to check from time to time. On both sides of the street stand immaculately kept Victorian cottages and farm-town homes. Sighting down the center of this street, we could observe the tar line, which is offset about eight inches. Hollister sits right in the rift zone, as does the former Almaden winery a few miles south, on La Cienega Road. The winery is being gradually torn in two. For students of ground flow, the winery is a historic site—it is where the fault line's pattern of steady creep was first identified, back in 1956. A government plaque stands by the side of the road, outside the tasting room.

> This site possesses exceptional value in illustrating the natural history of the United States. (U.S. Dept. of Interior, National Park Service, 1965.)

That is exactly the role it played for me, driving down there with Gary in 1973. Until that day I had not given much thought to the look or the behavior of this fault line. Dimly I had imagined a long

◆◆◆◆◆

gash or trench that stretched like a zipper from somewhere in the north to somewhere in the south. I had lived most of my life within a few miles of this region's most influential natural feature, and knew it not at all. I began talking to other Californians about this and discovered that most of us were in the same boat. For a couple of months after a major quake, you will hear a swell of conversation, a run of gallows humor. Meetings will be called and legislation passed. But interest soon wanes. If a tremor measures less than 4.4 on the Richter, few people care to read past the headline. They seldom give it a passing thought.

A passing dream, however? That was another matter. I ran into a number of people who confessed to vivid and recurring dreams such as this one:

> The ground opens up. We are running in a panic, screaming and yelling, and then this tidal wave is moving toward shore. I am riding the wave, kind of body-surfing, when it turns to ice. It freezes before it breaks, and I am hanging there, frozen too, inside the wave.

Lurking underground the fault line lives its hidden life, while on the surface the busy rush prevails, with a disregard that sometimes seems calculated, some kind of testing, or challenging, like the bullfighter who turns his back on the bull.

As we dropped through Pacheco Pass, with the broad valley before us, Gary said, "Back there in Hollister, not far from the winery, there is an ORV park called Hollister Hills, which happens to be bisected by the fault line. Where the bikers ride, you can see two kinds of damage, depending on which side you look at: sedimentary rock on one side, granite on the other. For some strange reason, the San Andreas also skirts the northern edge of the Hungry Valley site. Isn't that bizarre? I mean, when you think about all the things in this state that occur right on top of the San Andreas—high schools, dams and reservoirs, housing projects, parking lots, Pacific Gas and Electric substations, a winery, one of the original Spanish missions, and now these off-road vehicle playgrounds."

"Don't forget the late James Dean," I told him.

"What does he have to do with it?"

"Star of *East of Eden,* set right over the ridge there, in Salinas. Star of *Rebel Without a Cause,* sad saga of southern Cal teenagers cast adrift in the fifties. It is a little-known fact that in 1955, when Dean's Porsche piled into a station wagon at a hundred and ten miles per hour, killing him instantly, he was crossing the San Andreas Fault."

"I don't believe it."

"He was driving west on Highway Forty-six out of Wasco, on his way to Paso Robles. He crashed at Cholame. That is a historical fact, and you know yourself that Cholame is right there in the rift zone."

Gary grinned. He wanted to believe it. He muttered, "I'll be damned," then, after a moment, "but what does it mean?"

"Cars," I said. "Vehicles. Traffic and geology. It is the whole story of California."

"That's right! Traffic and geology," exclaimed Griggs the geologist, stomping his accelerator, pushing his van to seventy miles per hour as we swung through the intersection and out among the semis and diesel rigs barreling south on Interstate 5.

Like so many of the world's fertile regions, the central valley was once under water, a flat-bottomed sea, contained on one side by the Sierra Nevada, on the other by the Coast Range, and at its southern rim by the Tehachapi Mountains which, a couple of hours later, were looming in front of us, mountains with a character all their own, bringing to mind the sharp-edged tropical peaks at the center of Tahiti and Kauai. Geologists call this the Transverse Range, for the

◆ ◆ ◆ ◆ ◆

way it cuts across the grain of the state. According to the theory of Continental Drift, the Pacific Plate, of which the coastal edge is an exposed lip, pushes north and west against the North American Plate. In eons past, as this movement confronted the southern end of the deeply rooted Sierra Nevada, the mountains of the Transverse Range occurred. Some say this bend in the landscape and in the fault line blocks the steady creep. Thus, they say, accumulating stress makes it the most likely region for the next "big event."

The San Fernando quake of 1971 was centered in these mountains, as well as the legendary Tejon quake of 1857, the first to draw wide attention to this feature of California life, since it was the first to hit after major settlement began. That quake, an estimated eight on the Richter, was centered at Fort Tejon, a small outpost built by the army to control a narrow pass which is still the main pass connecting the central valley with the L.A. basin. The pass itself happens to be a feature of the rift zone, and once again we crossed the San Andreas, at four thousand feet, surrounded by the produce trucks and highballing Peterbilts that grind through there all day and night, back and forth between the world's richest agricultural valley and the world's most improbable collection of appetites.

We left the Interstate at Gorman, a cluster of filling stations just over the brow of the pass and just inside the L.A. County line. A mile out of Gorman we turned onto Hungry Valley Road, where a sign said ENTERING LOS PADRES NATIONAL FOREST. Past the sign there was a dusty clearing, rimmed with trees, a camping site that had become the staging area for what lay beyond. Vans and campers were scattered around, with dirt-bike trailers attached. There were high-wheeled pickups with dirt-bikes braced upright behind quadruple spotlights. Young kids in helmets and masks whipped Hondas and Yamahas around the clearing, warming up. The sound was like a heavy-duty chainsaw, that same high sputtering whine. Half-

◆━◆━◆━◆

a-dozen were revving up near the campsite, careening through the blinding dust, making the sound of half-a-dozen chainsaws.

In the middle of the clearing, like a totem for the circling riders, stood a Forest Service bulletin board, where signs and pamphlets were stapled. One was large enough to read from the road:

Save Our Vegetation. Stay On The Roadway.

Beyond the bulletin board, beyond the line of trees, we could see the first hillside, perhaps sixty feet high, totally denuded, striped with wheel tracks, lined with ruts and parallel gullies, as if the fingers of some enormous hands had been dragged through what used to be the topsoil of this slope.

One of the kids who had been kicking up dust swung out onto the road, made a wide turn, gathering speed, and roared up the far side of the hill, his thin arms tense, his body rising over the handlebars. From his build I figured him to be about thirteen. We watched him make the climb and level out at the top, with a couple of triumphant revs from the whining engine. He was motoring across the ridge against a gorgeous blue sky.

I said, "It looks like fun."

"It is. That's the whole trouble. It is a hell of a lot of fun."

Past the campsite the road followed a low rise and the valley opened before us, high desert country, the flat zones rugged enough to challenge the riders, the slopes and ridges rising on both sides, some denuded, others sprinkled with scrub juniper, low oaks here and there, all striped with trails, gouges, ruts, deltas where several tracks intersected at the top of a climb.

Kids on bikes roared toward us down the road, more vans, more campers, more pickups. Across the valley we could see them parked—a van next to a clump of juniper where a fellow squatted adjusting his wheel. Halfway up a slope, two camper rigs awaited the re-

◆◆◆◆◆

turn of their owners, who had taken off across country. A VW bug with an exposed engine rumbled up a barren incline, swerving with the effort, in the loosened dirt, to join two other VWs up on top. A young girl came toward us popping a wheelie, lifting off the ground in exuberant greeting. Behind her a father and son were riding together along the narrow asphalt road, the father's bike a size larger. The son looked to be about eleven. They wore matching Yamaha T-shirts.

It was late afternoon. As the sun dropped, the light spread, catching sharp edges, throwing the convoluted dips and arroyos into shadow, brightening the juniper's dusty green. We parked below a high straight ridge that blocked the sun. Its top emanated a buttery glow, an aura, and a young rider whined along up there, raising a plume. From that altitude his view must have been even more spectacular than ours on the valley floor. I envied him. He had climbed high to make his own connection with this glorious landscape. He whirled and motored back the other way, and I thought of other pastimes that put you *into* nature. I thought of surfing, and skiing. You want to take the rising wave, or the snowy slope, make your mark upon it and, for that brief run, possess it. The difference is, after you have drawn your line across the wave's sheer wall, it breaks. It turns to water and the line is gone. The snow melts, and the skier's tracks melt with it. The tracks of the dirt-bike do not go away. Just below that lone biker, there was a bare hillside streaked with tracks, a steep slope that had been climbed so many times no one climbed it any longer. There were too many ruts, sunk too deeply into the soil, gullies too dangerous for the churning wheels.

We locked the van and hiked a hundred yards to the foot of this slope, then climbed to the lower end of the deepest gully and followed it until we were in up to our waists. It was about three feet across, three-and-a-half feet down, a ragged channel cut into the slope and littered with large cobbles, tumbleweeds.

◆◆◆◆◆

"When you're a biker," Gary said, "the steepest hill is the biggest thrill. It is also where you can do the worst damage to the soil."

He leaned against the embankment, picking at the sand and gravel and talking about the fragile systems that hold the thin layer of topsoil together in these semi-arid regions. When the vehicles arrive, the vegetation goes first, and with it the root networks that help control the natural erosion rate. Over time the wheels and the weight compact the soil, which makes it less receptive to water, thus more difficult for vegetation to recover, if any topsoil remains to grab onto. Here on the western edge of the desert, it seldom rains. But for a day or two it can fall in torrents. Then, instead of flowing evenly down a slope, the water will pick out a wheel track and turn it into a channel, deepen it into a rut, and the gullying begins. Soil and sediment pour down onto the flat basin below the gulley we were standing in. Gary noted how the runoff had deltaed out. It would have been grazing land, he said. Now it was covered with coarse-grain sand and gravel. Nothing would be growing there again for many years. Multiply that by dozens of hillsides and thousands of wheel tracks, and eventually the drainage system of an entire area is thrown out of balance.

"The sediment heads toward Piru Creek, just south of here," said Gary. "And since Piru Creek empties into Pyramid Lake, a lot of sediment ripped loose by ORV activity in Hungry Valley ends up displacing water in what is supposed to be a reservoir for the city and county where most of these bikers come from. Isn't that a twist?"

The previous winter, he had been there during a storm and had the chance to measure sediment displacement in three parts of the drainage basin: one where there had been *no* ORV use, the second where there had been *limited* use, the third in an area of *heavy* use. The differences were appalling. Sediment yield from this desert in its natural state was about fourteen tons per square mile per day. In the area of limited vehicle use it was fifty-one tons, while in the area

◆◆◆◆◆

of high use it was seven hundred and twenty-one tons per square mile per day—topsoil, sand, and gravel torn loose and swept along in the hundreds of gullies twisting down barren slopes, across the vales and deltas.

According to studies made in 1968, before Piru Creek was dammed, and before the ORVs arrived, normal erosion would fill six percent of the proposed lake in fifty years. Gary's figures suggested that wheel damage in Hungry Valley could double this rate. The evidence was all under water, of course, and he was only guessing. The effects on L.A.'s water system interested him as yet another result of the ongoing battle between human and earthly habits. But the precise numbers were outside the range of his assignment, which was to consider the feasibility of turning some thirty square miles of this region into a permanent park for off-road vehicles. He was here to measure rainfall, soil composition and erosion rate, and to think about ways to arrest or slow down the flow of so many thousands of tons of the state of California from one place to another.

As we hiked back to the van, he talked about reseeding the soil. He talked about hydro-mulching and erecting sediment traps to contain the runoff. I asked him about the deep gullies. "What can you do, on a hill that steep?"

"Not a whole hell of a lot," he said. "You can't use equipment. The slope is too critical. It's hand work, and that gets expensive—laying jute netting, in-filling with rocks. They figure anywhere from two to six thousand dollars an acre to start, to restore land like this. Then, it is only effective if you can keep the riders out. So you can close this area for a while and work on the hillsides and let them ride over on the next ridge, or the next one. But eventually this area gets opened again, and the whole process starts over."

"So what's the solution?"

"You are looking at the solution. The theory is, you sort of give

◆━◆━◆━◆

them Hungry Valley, which they have already taken, plus a little more surrounding space for expanding into, because what has usually happened, you close off one area entirely, they go out and find another area. They move on to some other spot that has the rolling hills and the bumps and the climbs, and they start working that place over. They use a hillside like this one until it isn't good for anything, not even ORVs, then they move on. So you sacrifice Hungry Valley, and you hope to save a few other places from this type of invasion."

Gary wasn't laughing his zen laugh now. He was trying not to let his feelings boil over.

"That heats your blood, doesn't it?" I said.

"To be perfectly honest," he said, "sometimes it's hard to maintain the professional distance. A lot of this land is supposed to be National Forest, for Christ's sake! It's supposed to be dedicated to preservation, not destruction: Back there on that bulletin board one of the pamphlets says, 'Off-road Vehicles Are Welcome in Los Padres National Forest,' followed by a list of rules. They are supposed to stay on the marked roads. Some of them do. A lot of them don't. The state has never had the personnel to enforce the rules. And they might *never* have the personnel, because that requires heavy backing in Sacramento and Washington, D.C., and the American Motorcycle Association has a lobby that makes as much noise as the bikes do."

Back in the van we followed the road a few more miles, and I was prepared to see a regiment of Hell's Angels come over the rise with afterburners blazing. Grizzled gangs would not have surprised me, wielding chains and buck knives to terrorize the rangers and hold sway over their desert domain. They did not appear. What we saw were more kids wearing Yamaha jerseys, more loners, more young guys in cowboy hats roaring along in the pickups, more folks from the cities looking for a way to let off steam. Families. Husband-and-wife teams. Fathers and sons, the father a carpenter, or an auto parts salesman. They live in Altadena or in Fresno. They get up early on Saturday morning and pack a lunch, fill the thermos, grab some beer, hop into the truck or the van and head for open country. They want to be cowboys for a day or two. Who can blame them? We all want to be cowboys for a day or two. In the movies you usually see one or two cowboys at a time, galloping through the canyon. Butch Cassidy and the Sundance Kid. But what would that canyon be like if a thousand cowboys all decided to gallop through at once? Or a hundred thousand? On a fall weekend you might have a hundred thousand cowboys, or more, out there tearing up the dirt in places like Hungry Valley. There are nearly as many motorcycles registered in the state of California (about a million) as there are human beings in the states of Wyoming and Montana combined. This is what makes it interesting, and also ominous and alarming. More dirt-bikes, more four-by-fours, more leisure time, more money to spend on it, more sunny days, more people, more undersupervised public land to ride around on, and generally more support for pursuits that draw people toward this region in the first place: outdoor living, self-expression, personal fulfillment.

That young dirt-biker at the top of the ridge, backlit against the faultless desert sky, was the perfect photo for an article on what people will do in their searches for fulfillment, especially here, where vehicles are more sacred than the soil, sometimes more sacred than life itself. And that waist-deep gully we stood in was the perfect photo for an article about what the earth will do when it is ignored or underestimated. It is a pairing Gary sees everywhere he goes, in one form or another. It is both commonplace and shocking. An attorney for the earth, he marvels at the forces conspiring against it.

◆◆◆◆

In the case of off-road vehicles he sees a clear example of ego gratification taking top priority over whatever is being done to the land.
With a great deal of property development, it is ego gratification
mingling with profit. People continually put money into properties
poorly located, he says. They build on the fault line, in a tide zone, or
on some slope where the erosion is going to cut them to pieces and
send their deck sliding into the ravine. But the investment is so
great, the property becomes so valuable, they won't abandon the location, so they pour money into it, trying to counteract the sands or
the tides or the gullying or the slippage.

Such costs add up to a kind of interest, or holding fee, exacted by
the earth for overlaying this precarious geology with one of the
world's heaviest concentrations of capital and investment. The town
of Santa Cruz now wrestles with the problem of how to contain the
San Lorenzo River, because a century ago someone decided to locate the commercial district in the middle of a flood plain. To counteract a river's will to flood and silt's will to gather, the city may spend
millions. It is now costing the public half-a-million every winter to
pump the restless sand out of the harbor mouth. It cost the state over
sixteen million dollars to buy up the private parcels in and around
Hungry Valley, in order to contain that particular form of damage.
The purchase was completed soon after Gary submitted his final
report to Parks and Recreation. During the first full year under
Parks and Rec., another $200,000 went into soil protection and ero-
sion control. And bills such as these are nothing, Gary says, compared with the bill that will come due if the San Andreas ever
releases the stress some experts say has been accumulating under
our feet since 1906.

We had wound our way back to Gorman. We stopped for a six pack
of Rainier ale, then eased out onto the Interstate, heading north to-

◆ ◆ ◆ ◆ ◆

ward Bakersfield, where we would listen to some country music and spend the night. Tomorrow we'd be back for a day of photos and measurings.

After the first sip I said, "I don't think the Santa Cruz city leaders would appreciate being put in the same bag with the bikers."

"It's just one point of view," he said. "When I am being totally objective, these are the two forces pushing back and forth all over the state. The people have this will to build where they are going to build, or ride where they are going to ride. The sand and the silt and the surface of the earth has this will to go where it is going to go. Can you stop either one of them? I tell people what I see happening, and then usually I stand there and watch the process work itself out. Just look at this!" he exclaimed. "This highway! Six lanes wide, all these cars racing from Bakersfield down to L.A., all these trucks hauling stuff through Tejon Pass, right here where the Interstate crosses the rift zone!"

At that very moment his van was thrown sideways, the road beneath us seemed to swerve. I gripped the seat, while the windows rattled. I blinked away the ale's first rush, staring out at a sky that was suddenly darker. I saw that the shadow was cast by a high wall of moving metal. The windows vibrated again in the wake of air, as a passing diesel rig doing eighty registered 4.7 on the Richter Scale for rolling stock.

With a nervous laugh Gary straightened out the wheel. A mile later, we were coasting down the Grapevine grade, and the valley's lights were twinkling in the distance.

◆◆◆◆

26

THE PACIFIC COAST OF CALIFORNIA

JOHN A. MURRAY

*The 5. day of June, being in 43. degrees towards the pole Arctike,
we found the ayre so colde, that our men being grievously pinched
with the same, complained of the extremitie thereof, and the further
we went, the more the colde increased upon us. Whereupon we
thought it best for that time to seek the land, and did so, finding it
not mountainous, but low plaine land, till wee came within 38.
degrees towards the line. In which height it pleased God to send us
into a faire and good Baye, with a good winde to enter the same. In
this Baye wee anchored, and the people of the Countrey having their
houses close by the waters side, shewed themselves unto us, and sent
a present to our Generall.*
    from *The Voyage of Sir Francis Drake into the South Sea,
    Begun in the Yeere of Our Lord, 1577*

I first saw the Pacific in late August of my twenty-fourth year.
There it was, shining bright and blue as a polished stone at the
end of Wilshire Boulevard in Santa Monica, California. Seagulls

overhead. Tall green palm trees. Fragrant-smelling sidewalk cafés. Georgia O'Keeffe and Fritz Scholder art galleries. Newly arrived millionaires in red Corvettes. Former heroin addicts pushing grocery carts on the way to the methadone clinic. Proud young mothers pushing baby carriages. Streetwalkers arguing the Koran with Muslim missionaries. We got off the city bus at the intersection with Highway 1 and walked west over a sidewalk spray-painted with peace signs, initialed hearts, and Pompeiian graffiti. A trace of coconut oil guided us past the wooden pier and down the blood-stained concrete steps to the beach, which was about as hot as the inside of a Monterey pottery kiln. Mercifully, a breeze rolled inland from the breakers, bringing with it the memory of saltwater fish and the promise of cool water beyond. As they have been every Saturday since before I was born, the sun-worshippers were packed as thickly as elephant seals on a haul-out. They avoided eye contact—the territorial imperative—as my friend Ken led the way. Another pair of Marines back to the world from their noisy base among the Joshua trees and scorpions of the Mojave Desert.

One glance told me the Santa Monica littoral was an ecological disaster area. The fertile salt marshes and grassy dune fields that Sir Francis Drake would have seen in 1579 were long gone, not to mention the floating rafts of California sea otters (*Enhydra lutris nereis*) that were plentiful until the Russians built Fort Ross on the Mendocino coast in 1812. The gentle Indians, of course, were all buried back in the madrone canyons with their beautiful sea shells. The giant California condor (*Gymnogyps californianus*) might as well have been in the Rancho La Brea tar pits by then (1970s) and the last Los Angeles County grizzly bear (*Ursus arctos horribilis*) died in a hail of gunfire at the head of Tujunga Canyon in the San Gabriel Mountains on May 16, 1894. His crime? Being alive, I guess. Of the wolves (*Canis lupus linnaeus*) not much has come down, except that they have not been reported in California since about the same time the first domestic sheep were driven up from Old Mexico. Numerous other vanished plants and animals are now consigned to the insolence of museum drawers, barely known even to the curators. The whales—alas, the poor whales. And each time it rains for three or four days, the sewers overflow and the wastewater treatment plants break down and all sorts of unspeakable filth pours, like something out of Charles Baudelaire's *Les Fleurs du Mal,* into the Pacific.

After centuries of aimless wandering, we finally dumped our seabags on an unclaimed spot, rented a psychedelic-colored umbrella, and settled back to cold pizza and warm beer. We were ostensibly celebrating my promotion to corporal, but the mood was bittersweet; seven men in our unit had just been killed in a helicopter crash. From the parking lot above the tidal wave zone, Janis Joplin belted out "Piece of my Heart" from a fairly good set of car speakers. About a dozen volleyball games were in progress just below the seawall. Everywhere, the radiant sun darkened taut, oiled bodies that could have been legitimately displayed in a living gallery at the Louvre. (Oncologists must be kept busy with melanoma cases in L.A.) What few elders were about seemed, outwardly, to be in equally fine shape. I suppose it is axiomatic that when you walk around all day in a bathing suit you tend to look after your physical appearance more carefully than when you are dressed in a down parka. In a crowd numbering in the thousands, the only people working that day were the lifeguards. Sitting on top of sturdy wooden towers with oversized binoculars, they vigilantly scanned the surf for, among other things, five-ton, twenty-five-foot great white sharks (*Carcharaodon carcharias*). Each year, a number of people are attacked and seriously injured or killed by sharks in the Pacific, although most incidents occur in the turbid seas of the Land Down Under, where the shark is referred to as "White Death." As

◆-◆-◆-◆-◆

A THOUSAND LEAGUES OF BLUE

Ken and I looked over our shoulders at the Santa Monica Mountains it was easy to imagine, with the steep, dry hills fading from olive to gray in the morning haze, that we were on the French coast near Saint-Tropez, or somewhere up the road from Naples in southern Italy, just across the Straits of Sicily from Africa. Trace Santa Monica back far enough, historically, and you arrive on the rat-infested docks of Europe. The vast Mediterranean where Ulysses roamed for ten years is, as a point of information, about one sixty-fifth the size of the Pacific.

In those days I carried the Everyman's Library edition of *The Voyage of the Beagle* with me at all times, as a kind of scripture and also as an antidote to the deracination of military life. Through Darwin's narratives—those panoramic Victorian word pictures before landscape photography began to supplant descriptive prose—I voyaged like Emily Dickinson far out on the world: to the Galápagos, and New Zealand, and Tahiti (some of the best writing in the book), and Botany Bay in Australia. Darwin's Pacific was not unlike the body of water before me: ancient, enormous, silent, long-abused, uncaring. A nature that was both the source and repudiation of civilization. My friend and I spent the day on the front lines, fighting the sand fleas, quietly reading our books, talking to our new neighbors about their unemployed alcoholic boyfriends and the winter mud slides and the autumn forest fires and the inscrutable San Andreas Fault, body-surfing (the water is colder and the drop-off more sudden and the swells more powerful than the Atlantic), and finally watching the sun set beyond the offshore oil rigs and incoming freighters and jumbo jets outbound for Seoul and Shanghai and Sydney. After dark we walked an hour to find a hotel with a vacancy.

Northern California was quite a different experience, many years later. It was the mid-1980s. I was in graduate school then, toiling like a monk at Anglo-Saxon and *Finnegans Wake* in my tiny, book-crammed apartment three blocks from the University of Denver. My parents moved to San Francisco from the nation's capital after my father was attacked by a gang in the parking lot outside EPA headquarters, where he worked. Each time I visited S.F., Dad and I drove north over the Golden Gate Bridge to explore Marin County. (Long, tall bridges always make me uncomfortable, especially the devilish, twenty-nine-mile causeway over Lake Pontchartrain in Louisiana, which I discovered by accident, nearly passing out at the wheel from vertigo, while exploring Cajun Country in December 1989.) First stop was the Marin headlands, on the far side of the bridge. Hour after hour, we sat among the sagebrush and wild sunflowers, watching the great tides sweep in and out, the sea fogs build and dissipate, the tremendous flocks of ocean-dwelling birds go about their daily affairs. Once a huge aircraft carrier steamed back in from patrol, bristling with antennae and phalanx guns and surface-to-surface missiles, the broad decks covered with all species of deadly aircraft, a thing of terrible beauty. What would Drake have thought if he had seen that ship looming out of the fog? The sea lions and harbor seals at the bottom of the cliffs were oblivious to the nuclear leviathan, more concerned with roving packs of killer whales.

San Francisco is lovely from that perspective—the gleaming steel and glass towers of downtown finance, the solemn eucalyptus groves of the military cemetery at the Presidio, the mossy ramparts of Fort Point, the rhythmic rise and fall of the bridge—but why does that city, or any city, have to keep forever expanding? More than 7 million people now inhabit the Bay Area. Studio apartment rents on the San Francisco Peninsula are equal to house payments elsewhere. Parking can be impossible. Quality of life dwindles with each passing year. A eucalyptus tree (native Australian) grows until it reaches maturity and then maintains a stable size. Theoretically, it could live

◆━◆━◆━◆━◆

forever. Gravity, terrain, soil, exposure, the seasons, the root mass, the liquid nutrient transport system—all act as fixed but gentle limiting factors. Human cities, especially those around the Pacific Rim, become ever larger, until people are forced to live as they now do in Tokyo, with entire extended families confined to 600-square-foot cubicles. This is no way for human beings to live. We are not bacteria, not termites, not ground-dwelling rodents. People evolved on the plains and steppes of Africa and Asia with plenty of space around them, and require space to fulfill all that is human within them. We have voyaged beyond the atmosphere, walked on the moon, landed our first scouting probes on Mars. We have seen our destiny in the stars, in all the distant worlds of the galaxy. We deserve better here on Earth. Unfortunately, given present trends, an increasingly crowded twenty-first century faces our grandchildren in San Diego, Los Angeles, San Francisco, Seattle, and Vancouver. Wouldn't it be nice (title of a Brian Wilson song) if we modeled our societies on the eucalyptus tree, living in restraint and harmony with its environment, and not the carcinoma cell, greedily and suicidally destroying the body that sustains it?

A few miles up the coast from the Marin headlands is Muir Woods, an isolated 500-acre stand of redwoods at the base of Mount Tamalpais. Before the Golden Gate Bridge was built (or even imagined) people took a ferry across the narrows and then rented a horse-drawn surrey to reach the forest and the coast past Inverness around Point Reyes. In the sheltered valley the 250-foot-tall coastal redwoods (*Sequoia sempervirens*) loom like the pillars of heaven over a lush understory of dogwood, bigleaf maple, tanbark oak, rhododendron, laurels, and wild azalea. Black-tailed deer (*Odocoileus heionus columbanus*) tiptoe through the moss and gray squirrels scamper up and down trees ten feet in diameter. Ferns abound: woodfern, sword fern, bracken fern, deer fern, licorice fern, West-

◆◆◆◆◆

ern five-finger fern, and one not found in any guidebook I simply call the Murphy fern. Each winter, when heavy rains fill Redwood Creek in Muir Woods, mature salmon and steelhead fight their way upstream to spawning beds. (Across the northern Pacific, clear-cutting and hydroelectric dam projects have seriously depleted salmon access to their breeding locations.) Once flying reptiles nested in redwood groves, and miniature dinosaurs, the ancestors of the human race, ran through the branches, gaining dexterity and agility. Redwoods, in many ways vitally linked with our evolution, have been on Earth for 130 million years. Sadly, of the 2 million acres of old growth present in California in 1840, only 60,000 acres remain in parkland today.

It is a special place, Muir Woods, its trails offering a walk back in time to when redwoods were found abundantly across North America. There is a sense of timelessness in the groves, of trees that were seedlings when Julius Caesar took his ill-fated walk to the Forum, of a ground sanctified through age and beauty. It is always twilight under the thick canopy, always April cool, with the morning freshness of the biblical Garden. It is also always crowded. The last time I was there I overheard a man joke that, once in the forest, his shoes left the ground and the mob carried him up and down the trail to Cathedral Grove twice before his feet finally touched Earth again. Anyone who has been to Muir Woods, or, a day's ride to the east, among the sequoias of Yosemite, knows that California needs more and bigger parks. Muir Woods is the most—I hesitate to use so sentimental a word—magical place I have ever seen. One almost expects Ansel Adams to step out from a shadowy green wall of ferns with his priceless Hasselblad camera in hand, "Dead? Me? Why, goodness no. I've been here taking pictures in the forest all the while. Wait a moment. I'll be right back. John Muir and Ed Abbey are calling for me."

On our third and final trip to Point Reyes, which is about an hour

◆ ◆ ◆ ◆ ◆

beyond Muir Woods, my father and I took a long walk on North Beach. This is as wild a beach as you'll find anywhere in the world. Even Alaska, where I recently lived for six years, has nothing to surpass it. Row after row, the white, churning combers charge like Tennyson's cavalry, beating relentlessly against the land, never retreating. One day, according to the geologists, the Pacific will win the assault, and the whole beach—in fact, the first fifty miles of California coastline—will be submerged beneath the sea. The North American Plate, it seems, is steadily slipping beneath the Pacific Plate, which is much larger and stronger. But on the day of our hike the edge of North America was, thankfully, still holding its own.

Here Sir Francis Drake came in June of 1579, after having plundered Spanish forts and ships from Chile to Peru. (Shakespeare was fifteen that summer, yet uncorrupted by Anne Hathaway, still discovering the marvels of Plutarch and Ovid.) Drake's cargo bay fairly bulged with captured gold and silver, and he knew a return to Plymouth, his home port, by way of South America was not feasible. The entire Spanish Pacific fleet was waiting, with a vengeance, somewhere between the *Golden Hinde* and Cape Horn. The Captain's only hope was to sail west around the backside of the planet, following Magellan's pioneering 1522 route past Indonesia and around the Cape of Good Hope. After an abortive probe up north to Oregon, searching for a northerly wind, the royal pirates wound up in California, at thirty-six degrees north latitude, where they put in for rest and repairs. As a result of that historic visit, we now have Drake's Bay just down the coast, Sir Francis Drake Boulevard over in Inverness, Drake's Seaside Curio Shop, Drake's Bait and Tackle, and Sir Francis Drake Bed and Breakfast. I'm certain Drake would appreciate the humor, for the Elizabethans—one of the endearing qualities of their age—loved nothing more than to laugh at themselves.

◆◆◆◆◆

(With that humor, they conquered the world, for where there is humor there is balance and awareness. Beware of the face that does not smile, for there you will likely find intolerance, which is the root of much evil in this world.)

The country around Point Reyes is similar to England—rolling green pastureland, clear running streams, bird-filled oak woodlands nestled in ravines—and, perhaps as a consequence, the crew of the *Golden Hinde* felt at home and stayed awhile. Exactly how long we don't know. Perhaps two weeks. Drake was reminded most of Dover, in the south of England, with the white chalk cliffs, and so he named California "Nova Albion" and claimed it for Elizabeth, the petite, red-haired monarch who proved women can lead nations 400 years before the issue came up for discussion in the former colonies. There were in Nova Albion, according to Drake's scribe, "hordes of Deere by 1000 in a company, being large and fat of body." Black-tailed deer are still abundant today and seen by the dozens along with tule elk, but most prevalent are cattle and sheep, which are present in the thousands. Also noted by the British were "a strange kind of Coney" with "the taile of a Rat being of great length" and "a bag" on either side of the chin in which the animal "gathereth (their) meate." The Indians made "great account" of the fine skins of this animal and fashioned the coat of their king from them entirely. These were beaver, which are still industriously building trout and duck ponds in the broad upland valleys. Drake did not mention grizzlies, but they were certainly about. Spanish explorer Sebastián Vizcaíno wrote in 1602 that he had seen a number of grizzlies at Monterey feeding on whale carcasses. Today the bears are found only on the California state flag. (Hopefully one day to be returned to the Sierra.)

The coastal Indians were friendly and each day brought gifts down to the beach where Drake and his men had pitched their tents. The men wore the skins of deer and beaver, and the women wore cloth skirts fashioned from "a sort of hempe." Eventually, Drake and a squad of marines followed the natives inland and visited several of their villages, noting that the houses were dug into the earth, with wooden roofs overhead. On one of these occasions they assembled for a sort of party, singing songs and making speeches to one another. Neither side understood a word the other was speaking. I would give the state of Ohio to be able to travel back in time and observe that spectacle—a seasoned band of Elizabethans, educated in Latin, Greek, French, Italian, and English, fully aware of the movements of the planets around the sun and of the moon around the Earth, practiced in the compass and the astrolabe and the sea chart, meeting for hours with a nation of souls whose cosmos was so radically different, whose faces were painted in some cases black and in others white, who could not imagine how the ships sailed, or where they came from, or what the metal cannons and muskets were for. Not one non-European native was killed, injured, or enslaved on Drake's voyage, which must be some kind of record for the age, a time in which Sir John Hawkins was already transporting the first West Africans to the Caribbean to trade for rum he then sold in England.

We walked for miles down the beach that winter day, watching the storm (waves oblique and from the northwest, driving from the Arctic), looking for beautiful shells, stopping to examine a washed-up redwood tree, and following deer trails around the dunes. In the sheltered hollows behind the foredunes we found bayberry and beach plum, sea grape and prickly pear cactus, and on the larger hills farther back the pygmy forests of bishop pine and dwarf oak and maple. Here the deer lived in plentiful numbers. At one point I came

◆◆◆◆◆

across the sun-bleached skeleton of a young deer curled up in the wild raspberries, and we marveled at the smooth perfection of the bones, and left them there, undisturbed, for the beach mice to gnaw upon. The oldest dunes, a quarter-mile back from the sea, had soil mixed in with the sand, and canopied forests, and there were fresh-water ponds behind them with many of the birds—tundra swans and loons and white-fronted geese—I saw in the Alaska Range every summer for half a dozen years.

Back on the beach, the long-legged sandpipers cruised the edge of the waves, stopping to pluck morsels from the seaweed and drift-wood. Gulls scavenged the wave troughs, swooping down to pick up small fish and crabs, and then fought over them in the air, sometimes dropping their catch back into the sea. About every quarter-mile along the beach a prominent sign warned hikers not to go near the water. Great white sharks were about, it seemed, and there was a fierce undertow and a sudden drop-off that made for "sleeper waves." Apparently, the sea would appear normal, a steady seven- or eight-foot surf, and then suddenly a prodigious wave of fifteen or more feet would rise up out of nowhere like Poseidon and overwhelm a person. According to the sign, several people had been full-fathom-fived by these rogue waves, and a couple of others had been returned to the food chain by the killer sharks. So my father and I kept a respectful distance. We would have anyway, though, because the storm was coming in fast on the high tide. We had heard about it on the car radio driving up the coast, the "storm of the century" as they are always called. Thick clouds the color of a gun muzzle were building to the west, pushing in front of them a pale, pearl-colored fog bank. The sea was being driven wild by the winds, and it was something to behold. Though walking side by side, my father and I had to shout to be heard over the surf. It was the sort of storm you

◆—◆—◆—◆—◆

might see if you could peer into the imagination of Beethoven as he sat at the piano pondering his next creation, about to pound the clashing, violent major and minor chords of his titanic anguish.

After a while we retired to a bunker of sand just out of the wind, watching the unruly sea and the otherworldly fog, not saying much. What is there to say when you have known each other, in all moods foul and fair, for more than thirty years? Love is all that is left, and love is best expressed in the things we do, the time we take together. So we sat there buried in our winter coats, staring out at that gray and white expanse, me thinking of the empty quarters ranging beyond, of the far-off coast of Japan and all the secret worlds of Asia (that amazing grove of giant redwoods, for example, that was not discovered until 1944 in the Szechuan Province of China), and Dad no doubt meditating on the trip down the coast past Stinson Beach and over the bridge (which we both disliked but pretended not to mind) to my mother's bright, warm kitchen. The waves were not so much crashing now as exploding. In the middle of a thought Dad abruptly said he was cold, stood up and turned back, and left me there to be alone with the sea.

Why do we need churches, synagogues, temples, I thought, when we have this? What more proof could a skeptical mind require? What better place to pay our respects? Bring those proud atheists John Stuart Mill and Bertrand Russell to Point Reyes and let them walk around for a month or two breathing the fresh air and looking at the wildflowers. Let the architects come here, too, and build places of worship elsewhere that truly do justice to the beauty and grace and originality of creation. The complete instructions on how to live, how to govern, even how to die—everything is around us in nature, in the tides, in the storm, in the way the sea grass, moved back and forth by the wind, etches a curve in the sand. A child understands the language and looks at us with pity that we do not. We spend our

◆◆◆◆◆

lives trying to learn what we knew before we were taught how to read and write.

I started to make a list of all the amazing facts I'd ever heard about the Pacific. I decided the most amazing was that the heart of a blue whale weighs a thousand pounds, and after that the fact that in 1820, off the western coast of South America, an enraged sperm whale repeatedly struck and sank the 238-ton Nantucket whaler *Essex*. But then I thought a bit longer and concluded that the most amazing thing is that we know so little about the Pacific. All the books ever written on the subject could be placed in one large wooden crate and dropped into the waves and have just that much effect on the universe. An insignificant splash. Can we create a storm, even a small one? Can any person ever born or ever to be born follow a sperm whale to the basement of the Pacific, where it feeds at 8000 feet on bottom-dwelling sharks? Can we translate the language of the porpoise, even a single phrase? How does a golden plover navigate, year after year, from Antarctica to Alaska? Thoreau was right. We need to know there are forces, like the Krakatoa volcano or the El Niño effect, that are greater than history, lovely undersea gardens with strange sea horses we will never see, typhoons and tidal waves that could swallow an aircraft carrier whole, and not leave one floating cork, and animals gentle and wise, like the blue whales, that have lived as we have seen them for millions of years. Their hearts are formidable, but think of their brains. Consider a brain that has not 150,000 years of evolution behind it, but 2 million years. What marvels do those frontal lobes contain? What do the humpback whales sing about, in those half-hour symphonies off the coast of Hawaii each winter? I listened to the waves for a long time, hearing many things, reassured that there is so much we will never know, realizing that only in such humility will we as a species, like the long-persisting whales, ever endure.

◆—◆—◆—◆

Sometime after that the cold rain hit my face and I turned to look for my father, but he was gone, lost in the fog, and so I followed his tracks over the wet sand, putting one foot after the other in each of his steps, knowing I would catch up farther on, even after his tracks disappeared in the rain that was coming hard now from the north and west, from a place I would never know.

◆◆◆◆◆

If only I could have just another ten years . . .
just another five years—
then I could become a real artist.

Japanese artist Hokusai on his deathbed,
in 1849, at the age of ninety

ABOUT THE

CONTRIBUTORS

EDWARD ABBEY (1927–1989) authored more than two dozen works of fiction and nonfiction and thoroughly dominated the American environmental literature scene for two decades. His second novel, *The Brave Cowboy* (1956), was made into the critically acclaimed film *Lonely Are the Brave* (1962). In the early 1970s, National Geographic commissioned Abbey to visit and write an article about Australia; "The Reef" was one of several essays resulting from that adventure and later appeared in *Abbey's Road* (1974).

RICK BASS (1957–   ) has, in just a few short years, established himself as one of America's major new prose writers. With books such as *The Deer Pasture* (1985), *Wild to the Heart* (1987), *The Watch* (1989), *Oil Notes* (1989), *Winter* (1991), and *Ninemile Wolves* (1992), he has dazzled readers with his craft, spirit, and vitality. Bass makes his home in northwestern Montana with his wife, Elizabeth, and daughter, Mary Katherine. His first novel, *Where the Sea Used to Be*, will be published soon.

KENNETH BROWER (1945–) Son of conservationist David Brower, who helped shape the Sierra Club in the formative 1960s, Kenneth Brower has carved out his own niche as one of the finest nature writers of our time. His early format books—*Earth and the Great Weather* (1970) and *Micronesia* (1973)—are now considered classics of the genre. Brower lives in San Francisco with his wife and young son and travels widely around the world, writing and speaking out on conservation issues.

DAVID CAMPBELL spent three summers at the Brazilian Antarctic Research Station on Admiralty Bay in Antarctica. He is Henry Luce Professor of Nations and the Global Environment at Grinnell College in Iowa. His book *The Crystal Desert: Summers in Antarctica*, which was a Houghton Mifflin Literary Fellowship book in 1992, examines the "other Antarctica," the relatively fertile Antarctic Peninsula. Campbell focuses particularly on the sea, which "is like no other on Earth."

R. H. CODDINGTON (South Pacific Folklore). First gathered in *The Melanesians, Study in Their Anthropology and Folk-Lore* (1891), these folktales present Western readers with a radically different view of nature and humanity than their own. Professor R. H. Coddington, a fellow of Wadham College, Oxford University, painstakingly gathered these stories, knowing that the culture of the native islanders was imperiled by non-native visitors. Above all Coddington understood the following: "When a European has been living for two or three years among savages he is sure to be fully convinced that he knows all about them; when he has been ten years or so amongst them, if he be an observant man, he finds that he knows very little about them, and so begins to learn." He also acknowledged that his was a book "written by a missionary, with his full share of the preju-

◆—◆—◆—◆—◆

dices and predilections belonging to missionaries." Coddington's honesty and diligence have made his work a classic in early ethnographic literature.

JAMES COOK (1728–1779) was the son of a farm laborer and worked his way up through the ranks from common seaman to ship's captain. Historian William Goetzmann has written of Cook that his two "Pacific voyages were . . . models of rigorous, exact exploration as he rediscovered, in the name of science, the oceanic world." They represented, in Goetzmann's words, "the epitome of Baconian or Lockean empiral observations conducted over a huge portion of the world." In February 1779 Cook was killed by angry natives in the Hawaiian Islands following a dispute over stolen goods.

JOHN L. CULLINEY (1942–) is a professor of marine biology at Hawaii Loa College on Oahu. His critically acclaimed book *Islands in a Far Sea: Nature and Man in Hawaii* (1988) is a six-part study of the complex and beleaguered ecosystems of the Hawaiian Archipelago. It is a sobering account of how human civilization has devastated nature on these fragile islands and in these easily disrupted marine environments.

CHARLES DARWIN (1809–1882) will forever be associated with the theory of natural evolution put forward in *The Origin of Species* (1859). A geologist by training, Darwin relied upon his world travels on the HMS *Beagle* (1831–1836) and his encyclopedic knowledge of fossils to propose an explanation that accounted for the development of life on this planet. Few travelers to the Pacific have written so freshly and beautifully of the region as Darwin; more than a century and a half after its publication, his *The Voyage of the Beagle* (1839) still transports readers immediately to the exotic locales of Darwin's youthful journey.

ANNIE DILLARD (1943–   ) was born in Pittsburgh, Pennsylvania, and graduated from the creative writing program at Hollins College in Virginia. She has been one of America's most distinguished authors for nearly two decades. Her first book of prose, *Pilgrim at Tinker Creek* (1974), was awarded the Pulitzer Prize for general nonfiction. Later works have included poetry, literary criticism, personal essays, a memoir, and, most recently, a novel (*The Living*, 1992).

PAM FRIERSON is a graduate of the creative writing program at San Francisco State University, worked as a reporter and editor for the *Hawai'i Observer* for several years, and has written regularly about conservation issues on the Hawaiian Islands. Her book *The Burning Islands: A Journey Through Myth and History in Volcano Country, Hawai'i* (1991) rigorously examines the natural and human history of the area in and around Hawaii Volcanoes National Park on the island of Hawaii.

JAMES D. HOUSTON (1946–   ) is a visiting professor of literature at the University of California at Santa Cruz and is well known for his novels, which include *Continental Drift* (1978) and *Love Life* (1985), and his works of nonfiction, such as *Three Songs for My Father* (1974) and *The Men in My Life* (1987). He and his wife, Jeanne Wakatsuki Houston, with whom he co-wrote *Farewell to Manzanar* (1973), received an Emmy Award nomination and the Humanitas Prize for the television script based on *Farewell to Manzanar.*

JACK LONDON (1876–1916) was born in San Francisco and spent time as a hobo, drifter, waterfront loafer, and Klondike prospector. Despite his lack of formal education, London began to write and publish stories as early as 1898 and 1899 in the *Overland Monthly* and the *Atlantic Monthly*. Response to his first book, *The Son of the Wolf* (1900), was so positive that he wrote a sequel, *The Call of the Wild* (1903), that ignited his career as one of the major authors of his time. London wrote a total of fifty books, several of which, including *The Cruise of the Snark* (1911), were devoted to his beloved Pacific.

BARRY LOPEZ (1944–   ) was raised in both southern California and New York, educated at Notre Dame, and, since the late 1960s, has made his home in the Cascade Mountains of Oregon. His works include *Of Wolves and Men* (1975) and *Arctic Dreams* (1986); the latter was awarded the American Book Award in the year it was published. Few writers in recent memory have so committed their energy and their craft to the conservation of nature as has Lopez.

PETER MATTHIESSEN (1938–   ), one of the founders of the influential *Paris Review* in the 1950s, has also distinguished himself as one of the most versatile writers of his time. Matthiessen's works include *The Cloud Forest* (1961), *The Tree Where Man Was Born* (1972), *The Snow Leopard* (1978), and, most recently, *African Silences* (1991). In 1992 a film version of his novel *At Play in the Fields of the Lord* (1965) was released. Research for his work *Under the Mountain Wall* (1962) took Matthiessen to New Guinea, where he lived among and studied indigenous peoples with the late David Rockefeller.

HERMAN MELVILLE (1819–1891), sailed, as a young man, on the Pacific whaler *Acushnet* (1841–1842), deserted the vessel in the Marquesas Islands, and finally returned to America as a seaman aboard the frigate *United States* (1843–1844). These adventures served as the basis for his works *Typee* (1846), *Omoo* (1847), *Moby*

◆━◆━◆━◆

Dick (1851), and the posthumous novel *Billy Budd* (1924). Although any of these works would have probably secured Melville's name in literary history, he is best known at this time for *Moby Dick*, an enormously complex work of fiction that appeals to the sensibilities of the current age. *Typee* is commonly regarded as both a work of fiction and nonfiction and provides insights into the culture and geography of the Marquesas.

ANDREW MITCHELL is a British naturalist and television producer who has written seven books, among them *The Fragile South Pacific: An Ecological Odyssey* (1990). The book is a brilliant study of the region, beginning at Palau in Micronesia, moving through Melanesia and the Solomon Islands, and finishing with Polynesia at Hawaii and Tahiti.

JOHN MURRAY (1841–1914), a pioneering marine biologist and oceanographer, was educated at the University of Edinburgh and subsequently served as chief naturalist on the historic three-and-a-half-year voyage of the HMS *Challenger* (1873–1876). Murray was the editor of the monumental *Report on the Scientific Results of the Voyage of the H.M.S. Challenger* (1880–1895), which ultimately filled fifty royal quarto volumes. His biological paper *A Monograph of Christmas Island* (1900) helped lay the groundwork for the modern science of island ecology. He was made a Fellow of the Royal Society in 1876 and was knighted in 1893.

CHARLES SHELDON (1867–1929) made a fortune in a Mexican mining venture, then spent the rest of his life exploring, hunting, writing, and working for the conservation of nature. Sheldon is credited with being the father of Mount McKinley (now Denali)

◆ ◆ ◆ ◆

National Park in Alaska. His many books include *The Wilderness of the North Pacific* (1909), *The Wilderness of the Upper Yukon* (1911), and *The Wilderness of Denali* (1930).

PEGGY SHUMAKER (1949–   ) is currently president of Associated Writing Programs, the governing body of the more than 220 creative writing programs in the United States, and has distinguished herself as one of the most gifted young poets in the country. Her work has appeared widely in literary quarterlies and periodicals, and she has published two volumes of poetry, *Esperanza's Hair* (1987) and *The Circle of Totems* (1989). She has also been awarded a grant from the National Endowment for the Arts. Shumaker has taught at Arizona State University, the University of Alaska, and the University of Arizona. She lives in a log home in the mountain community of Ester, Alaska.

FRANK STEWART (1946–   ) is an English professor in the creative writing program at the University of Hawaii at Manoa. He has authored several books of poetry and won a Whiting Award. As editor of the anthology *A World Between the Waves* (1992), Stewart gathered together fourteen writings on Hawaii by such authors as W. S. Merwin, Maxine Hong Kingston, and John McPhee. Stewart also serves as editor of *Manoa, A Pacific Journal of International Writing,* which is published by the University of Hawaii Press.

MARK TWAIN (1835–1910), born Samuel Langhorne Clemens, became the consummate American writer of his century. His books include *The Innocents Abroad* (1869), *Roughing It* (1872), *The Gilded Age* (1873), *The Adventures of Tom Sawyer* (1876), *The Prince and the Pauper* (1882), *Life on the Mississippi* (1883), and *The Adventures of Huckleberry Finn* (1884). In the final chapters of *Roughing It,* Twain took readers with him on a sea voyage to the Hawaiian Islands. His vivid portrayal of the beauty of Polynesia inspired hundreds of thousands of American tourists to visit the islands, where they fell in love with the legendary land and people.

ALFRED RUSSEL WALLACE (1823–1913), after visiting the Malay Archipelago (1854–1862), sent Darwin an account of natural selection that Wallace had arrived at independently of the more famous biologist. The English naturalist is best known today for discovering the Wallace Line, a boundary between Asian and Australian species in the Malay Archipelago. Wallace wrote extensively and left such works as *Travels on the Amazon and Rio Negro* (1853), *The Malay Archipelago* (1869, a book dedicated to Darwin), and *The Wonderful Century* (1869).

DAVID RAINS WALLACE (1949–   ), who makes his home in San Francisco with his artist wife, Betsy, is the author of more than a dozen works of natural history and fiction, including *The Dark Range: A Naturalist's Notebook* (1978), *The Klamath Knot: Explorations of Myth and Evolution* (1983), *The Untamed Garden and Other Personal Essays* (1986), *Bulow Hammock: Mind in a Forest* (1989), *The Vermilion Parrot* (1991), and *The Quetzal and the Macaw: The Story of Costa Rica's National Parks* (1992). Wallace was awarded the John Burroughs Medal for *The Klamath Knot* and has been called a "modern Thoreau" by the *Chicago Sun-Times*.

EDWARD O. WILSON (1929–   ) is Baird Professor of Science at Harvard University. His books include *Sociobiology* (1975), *On Hu-*

◆◆◆◆◆

man Nature (1979), *Biophilia* (1984), *The Ants* (1990), and *The Diversity of Life* (1992). Wilson is, simply put, one of the most outspoken defenders of biodiversity around and has carved out a niche that puts him among the giants in his field: Mendel, Darwin, and Watson.

FURTHER READING

Aston, William George, *Shinto, the Ancient Religion of Japan*.
   London, 1907.
Bacon, Alice Mable, *In the Land of the Gods: Some Stories of Japan*.
   Boston, 1907.
Beaglehole, J. C., *The Exploration of the Pacific*. Palo Alto: Stanford
   University Press, 1966.
Beehler, B. M., et al. *Birds of New Guinea*. Princeton: Princeton
   University Press, 1966.
Bellwood, P., *Man's Conquest of the Pacific*. Oxford: Oxford
   University Press, 1979.
Brown, G., *Melanesians and Polynesians*. London, 1910.
Carlquist, S. J., *Hawaii: A Natural History*. Honolulu: Pacific
   Tropical Garden, 1980.
Celhay, J., *Plants and Flowers of Tahiti*. Papeete: Editions du Pacific,
   1974.
Christian, F. W., *Eastern Pacific Islands: Tahiti and the Marquesas
   Islands*. London, 1910.
Cole, Mabel Cook, *Philippine Folk Tales*. Chicago, 1916.
Danielsson, B., *Gaugin in the South Seas*. New York: Doubleday,
   1966.

Ellis, William, *Polynesian Researches,* 4 volumes. New York, 1833.

Emerson, Nathaniel B., *Unwritten Literature of Hawaii.* Washington, 1909.

Fielding, A., *Hawaii Reefs and Tidepools.* Honolulu: Oriental Publishing Company, 1980.

Fison, Lorimer, *Tales from Old Fiji.* London, 1904.

Fornander, Abraham, *An Account of the Polynesian Race,* 3 volumes. London, 1878.

Freeman, O. W. (ed.), *Geography of the Pacific.* New York: J. Wiley, 1951.

Frierson, Pamela, *The Burning Island.* San Francisco: Sierra Club Books, 1991.

Gill, William, *Myths and Songs from the South Pacific.* London, 1876.

Grace, A., *Folk-Tales of the Maori.* Wellington, 1907.

Guppy, H. B., *Observations of a Naturalist in the Pacific Between 1896–1899.* London, 1906.

Hadden, D., *Birds of the North Solomons.* Papua, New Guinea: Wau Ecology Institute Handbook No. 8, 1981.

Haley, D., *Seabirds of the Eastern North Pacific and Arctic Waters.* Seattle: Pacific Search Press, 1984.

Hargreaves, D. and B., *Tropical Trees of the Pacific.* Kauilua, Hawaii: Hargreaves Co., Inc., 1970.

Hobson, E. S., *Hawaiian Reef Animals.* Honolulu: University of Hawaii Press, 1972.

Im, Bang, *Korean Folk Tales,* trans. James S. Gale. London, 1913.

Journal of Polynesian Society, The. Wellington, New Zealand.

Kay, A., *Little Worlds of the Pacific.* Honolulu: Bishop Museum, 1980.

Ker, Annie, *Papuan Fairy Tales.* London, 1910.

◆◆◆◆◆

Knappert, Jan, *Pacific Mythology*. New York: HarperCollins, 1992.

Loveridge, A., *Reptiles of the Pacific World*. London: Macmillan, 1946.

Magruder, W. H., *Seaweeds of Hawaii*. Honolulu: Oriental Publishing Company, 1979.

Mayer, J. F., *Birds of the Southwest Pacific*. New York: Macmillan, 1945.

Metraux, Alfred, *Easter Island*. Andre Deutsch, 1957.

Mitchell, Andrew, *The Fragile South Pacific: An Ecological Odyssey*. Austin: University of Texas Press, 1990.

Murray, John, *A Pattern of Islands*. London: Penguin, 1981.

Oceania. [Quarterly.] New South Wales, Australia: University of Sydney.

Oliver, Douglas L., *The Pacific Islands*. Cambridge: Harvard University Press, 1961.

Randall, J. E., *Guide to Hawaiian Reef Fishes*. Newton Square, Pennsylvania: Harrowwood, 1985.

Rice, W. H., *Hawaiian Legends*. Bishop Museum, Honolulu, 1896.

Robin, B., *Living Corals*. Papeete, Editions du Pacifique, 1980.

Roth, H. Ling, *The Natives of Sarawak and British North Borneo*. London, 1896.

Ryan, P., *Fiji's Natural Heritage*. Auckland, New Zealand: Southwestern Publishing Company Ltd., 1988.

Stanley, D., *Micronesia Handbook*. Chico: Moon Publishing, 1985.

Stewart, Frank, *A World Between Waves*. Washington, D.C.: Island Press, 1992.

Thomson, Basil, *The Fijians*. London, 1908.

Tomich, P. Q., *Mammals in Hawaii*. Honolulu: Bishop Museum Press, 1986.

Watling, D., *Mai Veikau: Tales of Fijian Wildlife.* Suva: Shell Fiji, Ltd., 1986.

Whistler, W. A., *Coastal Flowers of the Pacific.* Honolulu: Oriental Publishing Co., 1980.

PERMISSIONS